ISLAM
and the
STATE
in
INDONESIA

This series of publications on Africa, Latin America, Southeast Asia, and Global and Comparative Studies is designed to present significant research, translation, and opinion to area specialists and to a wide community of persons interested in world affairs. The editor seeks manuscripts of quality on any subject and can usually make a decision regarding publication within three months of receipt of the original work. Production methods generally permit a work to appear within one year of acceptance. The editor works closely with authors to produce a high quality book. The series appears in a paperback format and is distributed world-wide. For more information, contact the executive editor at Ohio University Press, Scott Quadrangle, University Terrace, Athens, Ohio 45701.

Executive editor: Gillian Berchowitz
AREA CONSULTANTS
Africa: Diane M. Ciekawy
Latin America: Thomas Walker
Southeast Asia: William H. Frederick
Global and Comparative Studies: Ann R. Tickamyer

The Ohio University Research in International Studies series is published for the Center for International Studies by Ohio University Press. The views expressed in individual volumes are those of the authors and should not be considered to represent the policies or beliefs of the Center for International Studies, Ohio University Press, or Ohio University.

The **Institute of Southeast Asian Studies (ISEAS)** was established as an autonomous organization in 1968. It is a regional research centre for scholars and other specialists concerned with modern Southeast Asia, particularly the many-faceted problems of stability and security, economic development, and political and social change.

The Institute's research programmes are the Regional Economic Studies (RES, including ASEAN and APEC), Regional Strategic and Political Studies (RSPS), and Regional Social and Cultural Studies (RSCS).

ISEAS has published over 1,000 books and scholarly journals, all pertaining to Southeast Asia.

ISLAM
and the
STATE
in
INDONESIA

Bahtiar Effendy

Ohio University
Research in International Studies
Southeast Asia Series No. 109
Ohio University Press
Athens

Institute of Southeast Asian Studies
Singapore

First published in ISEAS Series on Islam, Singapore in 2003 by
Institute of Southeast Asian Studies
30 Heng Mui Keng Terrace
Pasir Panjang
Singapore 119614
E-mail: publish@iseas.edu.sg
Website: <http://bookshop.iseas.edu.sg>

This edition is co-published by
Ohio University Press
Scott Quadrangle
Athens, Ohio 45701
USA
for exclusive distribution in North and South America.
Ohio University Press edition: ISBN 0-89680-238-8

*The responsibility for facts and opinions in this publication rests exclusively with
the author and his interpretations do not necessarily reflect the views or the policy
of the publisher or its supporters.*

ISEAS Library Cataloguing-in-Publication Data

Effendy, Bahtiar.
    Islam and the state in Indonesia / by Bahtiar Effendy.
    1. Islam and state—Indonesia.
    2. Islam and politics—Indonesia.
    3. Indonesia—Politics and government—1966–1998.
    4. Indonesia—Politics and government—1998–
    I. Title.
BP63 I5E271   2003   sls2003004726

ISBN 981-230-082-1 (soft cover)
ISBN 981-230-083-X (hard cover)

Typeset by Stallion Press (S) Pte Ltd
Printed in Singapore by Photoplates Pte Ltd

Dedicated to

Muchlis Ramli in Jakarta

Contents

Abbreviations

Bappenas	–	Badan Perencanaan Pembangunan Nasional
Bazis	–	Badan Amil Zakat, Infak dan Sadaqah
BMI	–	Bank Muamalat Indonesia
BPHN	–	Badan Pembinaan Hukum Nasional
BPPT	–	Badan Pengkajian dan Penerapan Teknologi
BPR	–	Bank Perkreditan Rakyat
BPUPKI	–	Badan Penyelidik Usaha-Usaha Persiapan Kemerdekaan Indonesia
DPR	–	Dewan Perwakilan Rakyat
DPRGR	–	Dewan Perwakilan Rakyat Gotong Royong
FKASWJ	–	Forum Komunikasi Ahlus Sunnah Wal Jamaah
FKPI	–	Forum Komunikasi Pembangunan Indonesia
FOSKO	–	Forum Studi dan Komunikasi
FPI	–	Front Pembela Islam
GBHN	–	Garis-Garis Besar Haluan Negara
GKBI	–	Gabungan Koperasi Batik Indonesia
Golkar	–	Golongan Karya
GPII	–	Gerakan Pemuda Islam Indonesia
GUPPI	–	Gabungan Usaha Perbaikan Pendidikan Islam
HMI	–	Himpunan Mahasiswa Islam
IAIN	–	Institut Agama Islam Negeri
ICMI	–	Ikatan Cendekiawan Muslim Se-Indonesia
ISDV	–	Indische Sociaal Democratische Vereeniging
ITB	–	Institut Teknologi Bandung
KHI	–	Kompilasi Hukum Islam
Kisdi	–	Komite Indonesia untuk Solidaritas Dunia Islam
KNPI	–	Komite Nasional Pemuda Indonesia
Kopkamtib	–	Komando Pemulihan Keamanan dan Ketertiban
KPSI	–	Komite Pelaksana Syariat Islam
KSOB	–	Kupon Sumbangan Olah Raga Berhadiah
LP3ES	–	Lembaga Penelitian, Pendidikan dan Penerangan Ekonomi dan Sosial
LSAF	–	Lembaga Studi Agama dan Filsafat
LSM	–	Lembaga Swadaya Masyarakat
LSP	–	Lembaga Studi Pembangunan

Masyumi	–	Majlis Syura Muslimin Indonesia
MDI	–	Majelis Dakwah Islamiyah
MI	–	Muslimin Indonesia
MMI	–	Majelis Mujahidin Indonesia
MPR	–	Majelis Permusyawaratan Rakyat
MPRS	–	Majelis Permusyawaratan Rakyat Sementara
MUI	–	Majelis Ulama Indonesia
NII	–	Negara Islam Indonesia
NIP	–	Nationale Indische Partij
NU	–	Nahdlatul Ulama
P3M	–	Perhimpunan Pengembangan Pesantren dan Masyarakat
PAN	–	Partai Amanat Nasional
Parmusi	–	Partai Muslimin Indonesia
PBB	–	Partai Bulan Bintang
PDI	–	Partai Demokrasi Indonesia
PDI-P	–	Partai Demokrasi Indonesia - Perjuangan
PDU	–	Perserikatan Daulatul Ummah
Permesta	–	Perjuangan Semesta Alam
Permi	–	Persatuan Muslimin Indonesia
Persami	–	Persatuan Sarjana Muslim Indonesia
Persis	–	Persatuan Islam
Perti	–	Persatuan Tarbiah Islam
PII	–	Pelajar Islam Indonesia
PIR	–	Partai Indonesia Raya
PK	–	Partai Keadilan
PKB	–	Partai Kebangkitan Bangsa
PKI	–	Partij der Kommunisten in Indie
PKU	–	Partai Kebangkitan Umat
PMII	–	Pergerakan Mahasiswa Islam Indonesia
PNI	–	Partai Nasional Indonesia
PNU	–	Partai Nahdlatul Ummah
PP	–	Partai Persatuan
PPA	–	Pusat Pengembangan Agribisnis
PPII	–	Partai Persatuan Islam Indonesia
PPKI	–	Panitia Persiapan Kemerdekaan Indonesia
PPP	–	Partai Persatuan Pembangunan
PPPB	–	Persatuan Pegawai Pegadaian Bumiputera
PPSK	–	Pusat Pengkajian Strategi dan Kebijakan
PPSW	–	Pusat Pengembangan Sumberdaya Wanita
PRRI	–	Pemerintah Revolusioner Republik Indonesia

PSI	– Partai Sosialis Indonesia
PSII	– Partai Sarekat Islam Indonesia
PTDI	– Pendidikan Tinggi Dakwah Islam
SDI	– Sarekat Dagang Islam
SDSB	– Sumbangan Dermawan Sosial Berhadiah
TII	– Tentara Islam Indonesia
TNI	– Tentara Nasional Indonesia
TSSB	– Tanda Sumbangan Sosial Berhadiah
UII	– Universitas Islam Indonesia
UUPA	– Undang-Undang Peradilan Agama
UUPN	– Undang-Undang Pendidikan Nasional
YLKB	– Yayasan Lembaga Kesadaran Berkonstitusi

Acknowledgements

This book grew out of my dissertation which I submitted to the Department of Political Science at the Ohio State University. Obviously, I am indebted to many individuals and institutions in finishing my study at the Ohio State University. First of all I would like to extend my gratitude to Professor R. William Liddle who not only convinced me to study political science, but also secured me a fellowship from Midwest Universities Consortium for International Activities (MUCIA) during my first year at Ohio State. My sincere thanks are also due to the Asia Foundation which had been so generous in offering me the grant (1989-94) which made my doctorate study at Ohio State possible. In this regard, several individuals deserve mentioning: John O. Sutter, Gordon Hein, Nancy Yuan, Marylin Grimstad, and Jon Summers.

The work of this dissertation, I must admit, was possible mostly because of the encouragement I received from my dissertation committee members: Professors R. William Liddle, Anthony Mughan, Stephen Dale, and Donald McCloud. They not only supervised the writing of the dissertation from the beginning, but also inspired my approach to the subject. But more importantly, in times of great agony and ordeal throughout the process of writing, they often became sources of support, intellectually as well as psychologically. To these individuals my appreciation is due. I would also like to thank Donald K. Emmerson, John O. Sutter, and Howard Federspiel, who commented on the proposal of the dissertation at the earlier stage.

My field research in Indonesia (July-September 1991) and the long process of writing would not have been possible without the help of many institutions and individuals. For this, I would like to take the opportunity to extend my gratitude to the Asia Foundation, MUCIA, Yayasan Amanah Umat, and the Department of Religion for their financial support which enabled me to conduct interviews with a number of intellectuals in Jakarta, Bandung, Surabaya, Yogyakarta, and Montreal as well as to finish the writing of this dissertation. More especially, I would like to express my appreciation to Nancy Yuan, William Flinn, Donald McCloud, Lukman Harun, Zarkowi Soejoeti, and Tarmizi Taher.

In Indonesia many individuals extended a helping hand to me. First, I would like to thank my principal sources who spared some time for me to

xii ISLAM AND THE STATE

discuss the development of Indonesia's Islamic political intellectualism and activism. They included Abdurrahman Wahid, Nurcholish Madjid, M. Dawam Rahardjo, Adi Sasono, Munawir Syadzali, Hartono Mardjono, Ridwan Saidi, Sulastomo, M. Imaduddin Abdurrahim, Aswab Mahasin, Djohan Effendi, Deliar Noer, Lukman Harun, Endang Saifuddin Anshari, Yusuf Amir Feisal, Jalaluddin Rakhmat, Ichlasul Amal, M. Amien Rais, Kuntowijoyo, Yahya Muhaimin, A. Watik Pratiknya, Fuad Amsyari, Victor Tanja, Hajriyanto Y. Thohari, B.J. Habibie, and Aswar Hassan.

A number of friends have made my field research more convenient. Several of them deserve mentioning: Din Syamsuddin, Komaruddin Hidayat, Suud Achyar, Edy Soewono, Syafiq Mughny, Afan Gaffar, Mohtar Mas'oed, Bambang Cipto, M. Toha Hamim, A. Zaenuri, and Nurul Fajri.

For the completion of the dissertation, I would like to express my sincere gratitude to MUCIA who offered me a research associateship, a convenient office to work in, and technical support. For this, I would like to thank William Flinn, Donald McCloud, Mark Simpson, Patty Inman, and Andy Shulman. The last two individuals have been so kind to help me with the computing processes.

I would also like to express my gratitude to friends and colleagues who made our stay in Columbus for a little over six years more joyful. More particularly, I would like to thank the families of Liddle, Sonhaji, Budi Rahardjo, Hermawan Dipoyono, Machfudz, Mulya Siregar, Triono, Rosyiadi, Budi Yuwono, Takeshi Kohno, Rizal, and Blair.

In transforming this work into a publishable manuscript, the Asia Foundation, MUCIA, and the Liddles time and again, have been very helpful. Separately, they provided me a grant, space to work, and place to stay. All of this support enabled me to go to Columbus in 1999 to do the revision.

It is to my wife Fardiah and my three daughters, Nurul, Arina, and Atia, that my utmost appreciation is due. Their love, patience, and understanding have made my intellectual journeys possible.

I alone, however, shall bear the responsibility for any errors and imperfections in this study.

1

Introduction
The Problem of Political Relationship between Islam and the State

> To say that Islam deals with the spiritual life, with no interference in society and the state, may be as far from reality as saying that Islam provides a comprehensive and detailed social, economic and political system. The law of Islam, shari'a, in its two divine sources — the Qur'an and the Sunnah, the verbal and practical traditions of the Prophet — is permanent, but its direct legal rules are limited; at the same time, the intellectual derivatives (as represented in the voluminous jurisprudential works) and the accumulated practical behavior of Muslim societies during successive centuries in different places (as represented in historical records) are changeable and extensive. Both parts are sometimes mixed and confused, not only in the view of some non-Muslim observers and scholars, but also in the view of some enthusiastic Islamic propagators.
>
> Fathi Osman[1]

Since the unravelling of Western colonialism in the mid-twentieth century, Muslim countries (for example, Turkey, Egypt, Sudan, Morocco, Pakistan, Malaysia, and Algeria) have experienced difficulties in attempting to establish a viable synthesis between Islamic political movements and ideas and the state in their respective localities. In these countries the political relationship between Islam and the state has been characterized by severe tensions, if not hostilities. Given the preponderant position of Islam in these regions, that is, being the religion of the majority of their inhabitants, this is indeed a puzzling reality. As such it has attracted many students of political Islam to raise the question as to whether or not Islam is actually compatible with a modern political system, in which the idea of the nation state serves as a major ingredient.[2]

In Indonesia Islam has long been at an impasse in terms of its political relationship with the state. The regimes of both Presidents Soekarno and Soeharto regarded political parties based on Islam as potential power contenders capable of undermining the nationalist basis of the state. Primarily because of this, both the regimes worked to contain and "domesticate" the Islamic parties. As a result, not only did the leaders and activists of political Islam fail to make Islam the state ideology and religion in 1945 (on the eve of Indonesia's independence) and again in the late 1950s (during the Constituent Assembly debates over Indonesia's constitutional future), but they also found themselves repeatedly labelled "minorities" or "outsiders".[3] In short, as some have suggested, political Islam has been constitutionally, physically, electorally, bureaucratically, and symbolically defeated.[4] Most distressing, political Islam has frequently been a target of distrust, suspected of being opposed to the state ideology Pancasila.[5]

For their part, politically active Muslims have looked with suspicion on the state. In spite of the willingness of the state to recognize and assist Muslims in the practice of their religious rituals, they consider the state as manoeuvring to dethrone the political significance of Islam and embrace the idea of a secular polity. In fact, this situation has often been treated as an indication that the state is applying a dual policy on Islam. That is, while allowing the ritual dimension of Islam to flourish, it provides neither chances nor opportunities for political Islam to develop.[6] In this respect, suffice it to say that a mutual suspicion between Islam and the state occurs in a country in which the majority of its people (87per cent) are Muslims.[7]

Why is this the case? What factors account for such hostility? Is there a way out of it, that is, a way to transform the political relationship between Islam and the state from animosity into amicability?

In attempting to deal with this puzzle, many observers of political Islam tend to see it as "monolithic".[8] Adhering to a paradigmatic statement that the relationship between Islam and politics is by nature organic,[9] they see Islam as inherently a political religion.[10] Because of this, they view the problem of Islam–state relationship in the light of a clash between orthodoxy and syncretism, between *santri* (devout Muslims) and *abangan* (less devout Muslims), between religious group and nationalist group, rather than as a conflict of vision among the state elites (the majority of whom are Muslims) concerning what constitutes an ideal Indonesia.

The major pitfall of this approach is that it does not take into account the fact that Islam is a polyinterpretable religion. Even though at the most general level there is only one Islam, its form and expression vary from one Muslim individual to another. Thus, understandably, the above theoretical model fails to explain the fact that there are *santri* who not only align themselves with non-Islamic political groupings (and ideologies for that matter), but also reject the political agendas of their fellow Muslims associated with Islamic parties.

Because of this, I intend to address the problem of Islam–state relationship in the light of the polyinterpretability of Islam. My focus is to examine the emergence of a new wave of Islamic intellectualism in the 1980s, the nucleus of which had developed a decade earlier. My interest is in the potential of this movement to overcome the traditional hostility that has tainted the political relationship between Islam and the state. Though differences exist in styles and substance, in tactics and strategy, the general spectrum of this new intellectualism has pointed in the direction of creating a "different" type of Islam, which is less ideological, but more intellectually and practically relevant to the needs of Indonesian Muslims.[11]

SOME REMARKS ON ISLAMIC POLITICAL THEORIZING

One way to put the subject into comparative historical perspective is by understanding the nature of Islamic political thinking. The problem of the political relationship between Islam and the state is often derived from certain perceptions conceptualized in such a way that the former is confrontatively juxtaposed with the latter. It seems as though some sort of complementary relationship cannot be established between the two. Thus, at least at the very beginning, ideological content and constitutional arrangement become very important factors in determining the character of an Islamic state. If this is the case, a general overview of Islamic political theorizing may provide a basis to better understanding of the nature of the problem.[12]

Religion, as some have argued, may be seen as a divine instrument to understand the world.[13] Islam — in comparison with other religions — is conceivably the one with the least difficulty in accepting such a premise. An obvious reason lies in one of Islam's most conspicuous characteristics: its "omnipresence". This is a notion which recognizes that "everywhere" the presence of Islam should provide "the right moral attitude for human action".[14]

This notion has led many adherents to believe that Islam is a total way of life. The embodiment of this is expressed in the *shari'a* (Islamic law). A sizeable group of Muslims even push it further, asserting that "Islam is an integrated totality that offers a solution to all problems of life". Undoubtedly, they

> believe in the complete and holistic nature of revealed Islam so that, according to them, it encompasses the three famous 'Ds' (*din*, religion; *dunya*, life; and *dawla*, State). ... [Thus] Islam is an integrated totality that offers a solution to all problems of life. It has to be accepted in its entirety, and to be applied to the family, to the economy and to politics. [For this group of Muslims] the realisation of an Islamic society is predicated on the establishment of an Islamic State, that is, an 'ideological State' based on the comprehensive precepts of Islam.[15]

In its present context it is not surprising, though it is sometimes alarming, that the contemporary world of Islam witnesses many Muslims who want to base their socio-economic, cultural, and political life exclusively on Islamic teachings, without realizing their limitations and constraints. Their expressions are found in popularly symbolic terms such as Islamic revivalism, Islamic resurgence, Islamic revolution, Islamic reassertion, and Islamic fundamentalism.[16] While such expressions are well motivated, they are not well thought out and in fact are rather apologetic in nature.[17] Their central ideas, as Mohammed Arkoun has put it, "remain prisoners of the image of a provincial, ethnographic Islam, locked in its classical formulations inadequately and poorly formulated in contemporary ideological slogans". Furthermore, "[their] presentation [is] still dominated by the ideological need to legitimate the present regimes in Muslim societies".[18]

The holistic view of Islam as described above has its own implications. One of these is that it has excessively encouraged a tendency to understand Islam in its literal sense, emphasizing merely its exterior dimension. And this has been carried out so far at the expense of the contextual and interior dimensions of Islamic principles. Thus, what might lie beyond its textual appearances is almost completely neglected, if not avoided. In the extreme case this tendency has hindered many Muslims from understanding the message of the Qur'an as a divine instrument which provides the right moral and ethical values for human action. On the question of the holistic nature of Islam, Qamaruddin Khan noticed that

> There is a prevailing misconception in the minds of many Muslims that the Qur'an contains exposition of all things. This misunderstanding has been created by the following verse of the Qur'an: 'And We have sent down on thee the Book making clear everything and as a guidance and a mercy, and as good tiding to those who surrender'(16:89). The verse is intended to explain that the Qur'an contains information about every aspect of moral guidance, and not that it provides knowledge about every object in creation. The Qur'an is not an inventory of general knowledge.[19]

Recognizing the Islamic *shari'a* as a total way of life is one thing. Understanding it properly is quite another. In fact the crux of the problem is to be found in the context of "how is the *shari'a* to be known", as noted by Fazlur Rahman. [20] There are a number of factors which can influence and shape the outcome of Muslims' understanding of the *shari'a*. Sociological, cultural, and intellectual circumstances, or what Arkoun describes as the "aesthetics of reception", are significant in determining the forms and substances of interpretation.[21] Different intellectual inclinations — whether the motive is to recover the true meaning of the doctrine as literally expressed in the text, or to find out the general principles of the doctrine beyond its literal or textual expression[22] — in the effort to understand the *shari'a* may lead to different interpretations of a particular doctrine. Thus while accepting the general principles of the *shari'a*, Muslims do not adhere to a single interpretation of it.

The emergence of a number of different schools of thought in Islamic jurisprudence or various theological and philosophical streams, for instance, shows that Islamic teachings are polyinterpretable.[23] The interpretive nature of Islam has functioned as the basis of Islamic flexibility in history. In addition, it also confirms the necessity of pluralism in Islamic tradition. Therefore, as many have argued, Islam could not and should not be perceived as monolithic.[24]

This means that empirical or actually-existing Islam — because of "the divergence in the social, economic and political context" — has meant different things to different people. And quite equally, "it is both understood differently and utilized differently".[25] To put this in the context of contemporary Islamic politics, the struggle to form an Islamic state — even though its theological/religious necessity remains a controversial

issue — may denote different meanings to other Muslims. As a consequence, to cite the most controversial and extreme position on this issue,
what is perceived as an Islamic state by Iranian Muslims has been seen
rather differently by their brothers in faith in Saudi Arabia. In fact, as
widely understood, both have been campaigning for the repudiation of
each other's claim for being Islamic.[26]

Islamic politics cannot escape this history of polyinterpretability. On
the other hand, many have generally admitted the important role of
Islamic principles in politics. At the same time, because of Islam's potential for differing interpretation, there has been no single unified notion of
how Islam and politics should be properly related. In fact, as far as can be
deduced from both the intellectual and historical discourses of Islamic
political ideas and practices, there has been a wide range of different —
some even contradictory — opinions regarding the proper relationship
between Islam and politics.[27]

By and large, there are two different intellectual currents in contemporary Islamic political thinking. While both recognize the importance of
Islamic principles in all spheres of life, they differ greatly in their interpretation, their congeniality to the modern situation — thus, for some
there may be a further need for reinterpretation beyond their textual
meaning — and their applicability in the real world.

At one end of the spectrum, there are those who argue that Islam should
be the basis of the state; that *shari'a* ought to be adopted as the state
constitution; that political sovereignty rests in the hands of the Divine;
that the idea of the modern nation state is contradictory to the concept of
umma (Islamic community) which recognizes no political boundary; and
while recognizing the principle of *shura* (consultation), its realization is
different from the contemporary notion of democracy. Put differently,
within such a perspective, the modern (Western) political system — upon
which many of the newly independent Muslim states are based — is
placed in a contradictory position to Islamic teachings.[28]

At the other end of the spectrum, there are those who believe the notion
that Islam does not "lay down any clear cut and dried pattern of state
theory [or political theory] to be followed by the *umma*".[29] In the words
of Muhammad 'Imara, an Egyptian Muslim thinker,

> Islam as a religion has not specified a particular system of
> government for Muslims, for the logic of this religion's suit-
> ability for all times and places requires that matters which will
> always be changing by the force of evolution should be left to

the rational human mind, to be shaped according to the public interest and within the framework of the general precepts that this religion has dictated.[30]

According to this theoretical stream, even the term "state" (*dawla*) cannot be found in the Qur'an. Although "there are numerous expressions in the Qur'an which refer or seem to refer to political power and authority, [t]hese expressions are, however, incidental remarks and have no bearing on political theory". Indeed, they argue, "the Qur'an is not a treatise on political science".[31] Nonetheless, it is important to note that this position recognizes the fact that the Qur'an does contain "ethical values and injunctions ... on human socio-political activities". These include the principles of "justice, equality, brotherhood, and freedom".[32] For them, therefore, as long as the state adheres to such principles, it conforms to Islamic teachings.

Based on this line of argument, the establishment of an Islamic state in its formal ideological terms is not very significant. What is important is that the state — recognizing the state as instrumental in the realization of religious teachings — guarantees the existence of those basic values. As long as this is the case, there is no theological/religious reason to reject the idea of popular sovereignty, the nation state as the legitimate territorial modern political unit, and other general principles of modern political theory. In other words, there is no legitimate basis to put Islam in a contradictory position to the modern political system.[33]

The first Islamic theoretical model reflects the tendency to emphasize the legal and formal aspect of Islamic political idealism. This is typically signified by the direct application of *shari'a* as the constitutional basis of the state. In contemporary nation states such as Turkey, Egypt, Sudan, Morocco, Pakistan, Malaysia, Algeria, and Indonesia, this formalist model has the potential to come into conflict with the modern political systems.

Conversely, the second model stresses substance rather than the formal and legal aspect of the state. Given its substantialist character (emphasizing values such as justice, equality, consultation, and participation which do not contradict Islamic principles), it has the potential to serve as a viable approach to relate Islam with modern politics in which the nation state is its major component.

At this point it seems fair to conclude that the tradition of Islamic political thinking is actually rich, diverse, and flexible. Given this perspective, in his "Islam and Political Development", Michael Hudson argues that "[t]he question to be asked is not the crude, falsely dichotomous 'Is Islam compatible with political development?' but rather 'How much and what kinds of Islam are compatible with (or necessary for) political development in the Muslim world?'".[34] Placed in the Indonesian context, in the effort to address the principal issues of this study as stated before, the question would appropriately be: what kinds of Islam (in the interpretative sense), or what kinds of Islamic political ideas and practices, are capable of building a better relationship with the nation state in Indonesia?

Having said this, several basic assumptions govern the responses to these questions. First, the problem of the political relationship between Islam and the state developed out of different visions among the country's founding fathers concerning what constitutes an ideal Indonesia. It is a historically grounded problem. Second, the uncomfortable political relationship between Islam and the nation state does not stem from the doctrines of Islam *per se*. Rather, it derives from the way Islam is articulated socio-culturally, economically, and politically in Indonesia. The legalistic or formalistic conception of Islam, because of its exclusive tendency, is likely to breed tensions in a socio-religiously and culturally heterogeneous society. On the other hand, what might be called a substantialist conception — that is, one that favours justice, equality, participation, and consultation — of Islam can lay the necessary groundwork for establishing a viable synthesis between Islam and the state to reshape the terms of their political relationship.

CHAPTERS IN THIS VOLUME

Following this introductory overview, chapter 2 discusses the difficulty experienced by Indonesian Muslims in establishing a harmonious political relationship with the state. It describes chronologically the hostile relationship between Islam and the state during the pre-independence, Liberal Democracy, Guided Democracy, and New Order periods. Given the nature of the study, the emphasis is placed on scrutinizing the idealism and activism of the earlier generations of political Muslims and the extent to which their own views and actions contributed to the increasing animosity. In addition, it will also address the consequences of this unhappy marriage for the leaders and activists of political Islam in particular, and their constituents in general.

Chapters 3, 4, and 5 analyse the endeavours of a new generation of Muslim political thinkers and activists to overcome the political hostility between Islam and the state. It describes the content of the new Islamic intellectualism and examines its implications for articulation of new Islamic political ideas and practices.

Chapter 6 addresses the responses of the state towards Islam in the attempt to establish the fact that the traditional hostility between Islam and the state has decreased substantially, if not entirely disappeared. To do so, it examines the evidence, form, and nature of the state's recent accommodative moves towards political Islam. In addition, it also assesses the political significance of accommodation (that is, whether substantial or symbolic) in creating an amicable political relationship between Islam and the state.

The conclusions of the study are presented in chapter 7. Other than summarizing the themes developed in the preceding chapters, this chapter is intended to show that the puzzles raised in this study are satisfactorily explained. More importantly, it is hoped that it will shed light on the nature of the problem as well as the way out of it.

Had nothing changed, the contents of this book would be sufficient to explain the relationship between Islam and the state and/or politics in contemporary Indonesia. But on 21 May 1998 President Soeharto stepped down from the presidency in a situation which he obviously did not desire. His departure from office brought tremendous and far-reaching impacts on Indonesia's political landscape. At least 181 new political parties came into being, a sizeable portion of which use Islam as their symbol and ideological basis. Mainly because of this, a postscript on post-Soeharto Indonesian political Islam is needed.

Notes

1. Fathi Osman, "Parameters of the Islamic State", *Arabia: The Islamic World Review*, no. 17 (January 1983), p. 10.

2. References on this issue are many. Important works include: Leonard Binder, *Religion and Politics in Pakistan* (Berkeley and Los Angeles: University of California Press, 1963); Mohammed Ayoob, ed., *The Politics of Islamic Reassertion* (London: Croom Helm, 1981); Edward Mortimer, *Faith and Power: The Politics of Islam* (London: Faber and Faber, 1982); James P. Piscatori, ed., *Islam in the Political Process* (Cambridge: Cambridge University Press, 1983); John L. Esposito, *Islam and Politics* (Syracuse: Syracuse University Press, 1984); Fred Halliday and Hamzah Alavi, eds., *State and Ideology in the Middle East and Pakistan* (New York: Monthly Review Press, 1988); R. Hrair Dekmejian, *Islam in Revolution: Fundamentalism in the Arab World* (Syracuse: Syracuse University Press, 1985); Nazih Ayubi, *Political Islam: Religion and Politics in the Arab World* (London and New York: Routledge, 1991).

3. See Ruth McVey, "Faith as the Outsider: Islam in Indonesian Politics", in *Islam in the Political Process*, edited by James P. Piscatori (Cambridge: Cambridge

University Press, 1983), pp. 199–225; W.F. Wertheim, "Indonesian Moslems under Sukarno and Suharto: Majority with Minority Mentality", in *Studies on Indonesian Islam* (Townsville: Occasional Paper no. 19, Centre for Southeast Asian Studies, James Cook University of North Queensland, 1986).

4. For a concise account on the defeat of political Islam, see Donald K. Emmerson, "Islam and Regime in Indonesia: Who's Coopting Whom?" (Paper delivered at the annual meeting of the American Political Science Association, Atlanta, Georgia, USA, 31 August 1989).

5. Introduced by Soekarno on 1 June 1945, Pancasila comprises five basic principles: (1) Belief in One God; (2) Just and civilized humanity; (3) Unity of Indonesia; (4) Democracy which is guided by the inner wisdom in unanimity arising out of deliberation amongst representatives; and (5) Social justice for all the people of Indonesia.

6. This approach is widely perceived as the legacy of the Dutch colonial policy on Islam, formulated by its chief architect Snouck Hurgronje. For a fuller account, see Harry J. Benda, *The Crescent and the Rising Sun: Indonesian Islam under the Japanese Occupation 1942–1945* (The Hague and Bandung: W. van Hoeve Ltd., 1958), pp. 9–31.

7. See, for instance, Robert Jay, *Religion and Politics in Rural Central Java* (New Haven: Southeast Asia Studies, Yale University, 1963); Deliar Noer, *The Modernist Muslim Movement in Indonesia 1900–1942* (Oxford, New York, and Jakarta: Oxford University Press, 1978); B.J. Boland, *The Struggle of Islam in Modern Indonesia* (The Hague: Martinus Nijhoff, 1971); Allan Samson, "Islam and Politics in Indonesia" (Ph.D. dissertation, University of California Berkeley, 1972).

8. The term is borrowed from Mohammed Ayoob. See his "Myth of the Monolith", in *The Politics of Islamic Reassertion,* edited by Mohammed Ayoob (London: Croom Helm, 1983), p. 3. A similar view is also suggested by John L. Esposito in his "Secular Bias and Islamic Revivalism", *The Chronicle of Higher Education*, 26 May 1993, p. A 44.

9. This paradigm is developed, among others, by Donald Eugene Smith. See Donald Eugene Smith, ed., *Religion, Politics, and Social Change in the Third World* (New York: Free Press, 1971). See also his *Religion and Political Modernization* (New Haven and London: Yale University Press, 1974).

10. This view is represented, among others, by Bernard Lewis. See Bernard Lewis, *The Political Language of Islam* (Chicago: University of Chicago Press, 1988).

11. See, for instance, M. Rusli Karim, *Dinamika Islam di Indonesia: Suatu Tinjauan Sosial Politik* (Yogyakarta: PT Hanindita, 1985); Fachry Ali and Bahtiar Effendy, *Merambah Jalan Baru Islam: Rekonstruksi Pemikiran Islam Indonesia Masa Order Baru* (Bandung: Mizan, 1986); Howard M. Federspiel, *Muslim Intellectuals and National Development in Indonesia* (New York: Nova Science Publishers Inc., 1992).

12. The problem of the uneasy synthesis between Islam and the state in terms of their political relationship is discussed, among others, in Leonard Binder, *The Ideological Revolution in the Middle East* (New York: Robert E. Krieger Publishing Company, 1979).

13. This argument is advocated rather strongly by Robert N. Bellah. See his "Islamic Tradition and the Problems of Modernization", in *Beyond Belief: Essays on Religion*

in a Post-Traditionalist World, edited by Robert N. Bellah (Berkeley and Los Angeles: University of California Press, 1991), p. 146. See also Leonard Binder, *Islamic Liberalism: A Critique of Development Ideologies* (Chicago and London: University of Chicago Press, 1988), p. 4.

14. Fazlur Rahman, *Islam* (New York, Chicago, and San Francisco: Holt, Rinehart, and Winston, 1966), p. 241.

15. Nazih Ayubi, *Political Islam: Religion and Politics in the Arab World* (London and New York: Routledge, 1991), pp. 63–64.

16. In this movement, Mohammed Arkoun identifies two different groups of supporters: "Those who enjoy all economic and social privileges are ready to share conformist and very conservative views on Islam, because they do not have access to intellectual modernity! We also know that many students in technical sciences adhere to the fundamentalist movements: they have no notion of critical views developed in human and social sciences, especially history." See his "The Concept of Authority in Islamic Thought", in *Islam: State and Society*, edited by Klauss Ferdinand and Mehdi Mozaffari (London: Curzon Press, 1988), pp. 70–71.

17. A general criticism of such a tendency is also discussed in Fazlur Rahman, *Islam and Modernity: Transformation of an Intellectual Tradition* (Chicago and London: University of Chicago Press, 1982). See also his "Roots of Islamic Neo-Fundamentalism", in *Change and the Muslim World*, edited by Philip H. Stoddard, David C. Cuthell, and Margaret W. Sullivan (Syracuse: Syracuse University Press, 1981), pp. 23–35.

18. Arkoun, op.cit., pp. 53, 72–73.

19. Qamaruddin Khan, *Political Concepts in the Qur'an* (Lahore: Islamic Book Foundation, 1982), pp. 75–76.

20. Rahman, *Islam*, p. 101.

21. In his critiques Arkoun says that much attention has been given to treat "the texts [Qur'anic verses] as material documents to be used by historians". In so doing Muslims have generally overlooked the *aesthetics of reception*, that is, "how a discourse — oral or written — is received by listeners or readers". This issue "refers to the conditions of perception of each culture, or, more precisely, each level of culture corresponding to each social group in every phase of historical development". See Arkoun, op.cit., p. 58.

22. A comparable theory is also developed by many social theorists. An excellent introductory comment on this issue is made by Michael T. Gibbons in his *Interpreting Politics* (New York: New York University Press, 1987), pp. 1–31.

23. A lengthy socio-historical discussion on this issue is found in, among others, Marshall G.S. Hodgson, *The Venture of Islam: Conscience and History in a World Civilization*, vols. 1–3 (Chicago: University of Chicago Press, 1974).

24. On the tendency to perceive Islam in a monolithic way, see Mohammed Ayoob's introductory remarks in The *Politics of Islamic Reassertion*, pp. 1–6.

25. Ayubi, op.cit., pp. 60–61.

26. See *Al-Jazirah*, Riyadh, 22 August 1987; *Al-Nadwah*, Mecca, 22 August 1987; and *Kayhan al-Arabi*, Teheran, 25 May 1991. Cited from Nurcholish Madjid, "Agama dan Negara dalam Islam: Sebuah Telaah atas Fiqh Siyasi Sunni" (Paper delivered at Paramadina Religious Study Club, Jakarta, 1991), pp. 6–9.

27. For a wide range of discussions on the relationship between Islam and politics (classical, medieval, and contemporary period), see W. Montgomery Watt, *Islamic Political Thought* (Edinburgh: Edinburgh University Press, 1960); Erwin I.J. Rosenthal, *Political Thought in Medieval Islam: An Introductory Outline* (Cambridge: Cambridge University Press, 1958); Munawir Syadzali, *Islam dan Tatanegara: Ajaran, Sejarah dan Pemikiran* (Jakarta: UI Press, 1990); Qamaruddin Khan, *The Political Thought of Ibn Taymiyah* (Lahore: Islamic Book Foundation, 1983); Qamaruddin Khan, *Political Concepts in the Qur'an* (Lahore: Islamic Book Foundation, 1982); Muhammad Asad, *The Principles of State and Government in Islam* (Berkeley and Los Angeles: University of California Press, 1961); Darlene R. May, "Al-Mawardi's Al-Ahkam as-Sultaniyyah: A Partial Translation with Introduction and Annotations" (Ph.D. dissertation, Indiana University, 1981); Erwin I.J. Rosenthal, *Islam in the Modern National State* (Cambridge: Cambridge University Press, 1965); James P. Piscatori, *Islam in a World of Nation States* (Cambridge: Cambridge University Press, 1986); P.J. Vatikiotis, *Islam and the State* (London, New York, and Sydney: Croom Helm, 1987); John L. Esposito, ed., *Voices of Resurgent Islam* (New York and Oxford: Oxford University Press, 1983).

28. Among those who fall into this theoretical current are Egyptians Rashid Ridha and Sayyid Qutb; and Pakistanis Abu A'la al-Maududi and Ali al-Nadvi. Comparative accounts on this issue are discussed in Piscatori, *Islam in a World of Nation States*; and Rosenthal, *Islam in the Modern National State*.

29. Ahmad Syafii Maarif, "Islam as the Basis of State: A Study of the Islamic Political Ideas as Reflected in the Constituent Assembly Debates in Indonesia" (Ph.D. dissertation, University of Chicago, 1983), p. 23.

30. Muhammad 'Imara, *Al-Islam wa al-Sultah al-Diniyah* (Cairo: Dar al-Thaqafa al-Jadida, 1979), pp. 76–77. Cited from Ayubi, op.cit., p. 64.

31. Quotations are from Khan, *Political Concepts in the Qur'an*, p. 3.

32. Maarif, "Islam as the Basis of State", p. 23. Upon a closer look at the earliest political document in the history of Islam, those principles are also mentioned in the Constitution of Medina (*al-Mitsaq al-Madinah*). It contains, among other things, the principles of equality, participation, and justice. On the Constitution of Medina, see Muhammad Husayn Haykal, *The Life of Muhammad*, translated by Isma'il Ragi al-Faruqi (North American Publications, 1976), pp. 180–83; Ibn Hisham, *The Life of Muhammad*, a translation of Ishaq's Sirat al-Rasul Allah, with introduction and notes by A. Guillaume (Lahore, Karachi, and Dacca: Oxford University Press, 1970), pp. 231–33; W. Montgomery Watt, *Muhammad at Medina* (Oxford: Clarendon Press, 1956), pp. 221–28.

33. Advocates of this view include Egyptian Muhammad Husayn Haykal; and Pakistanis Fazlur Rahman and Qamaruddin Khan.

34. Michael C. Hudson, "Islam and Political Development", in *Islam and Development*, edited by John L. Esposito (Syracuse: Syracuse University Press, 1980), pp. 1–24.

2

Explaining the Uneasy Relationship
Political Antagonism between Islam and the State in Indonesia

The crux of the political problem is simply this: The resurgence of Qur'anic Islam in the last century has contributed greatly to the emergence of the collective consciousness of the Muslim peoples, to what Karl Deutsch would call their "social mobilization." The limitations inherent in this process do not derive chiefly from the problem of converting Muslim consciousness into national loyalty, or from unrealistic attempts to implement detailed prescriptions of the Shari'a. The limitation comes, rather, from the veto power that Islamic consciousness continues to exercise over the whole realms of political ideology and action. Of course this may not be entirely a bad thing. It perhaps exercises restraint over totalitarian tendencies. But it is also related to the tendency in many Muslim lands to rely on what Soedjatmoko calls "virtual images," rhetorical devices as a substitute for any serious and thorough program of political reform.

Robert N. Bellah[1]

The political relationship between Islam and the state in Indonesia has been largely a story of mutual antagonism and distrust. This adversarial relationship has been due primarily, but not wholly, to the conflicting ideas among the nation's founding fathers, the majority of whom were Muslims, on what constituted an ideal Indonesian independent state. Crucial in the debate was whether the state should be "Islamic" or "nationalist" in character. The former necessitated that Islam, given its holistic nature and the fact that it is professed by the majority, be adopted as the ideological basis of the state. On the ground that Indonesia is socio-religiously heterogeneous, for the sake of the country's unity, the latter required that the state be based on a "deconfessionalized"[2] ideology — Pancasila.

The fact that such ideological discourse instigated conflict was not so much because of the different degree of religious devotion among the Muslims — a notion which underpins the famous *santri–abangan* and Islamic–secular (or religiously neutral) nationalist concepts.[3] Rather, it was due largely to the inability of the nation's political elite to negotiate and reconcile those differences, as if Islam and nationalism are mutually exclusive entities.

This chapter is intended to (1) sketch in some detail the earlier discourse of political Islam as ventured by its thinkers and activists; (2) assess the implications of such a political discourse; and (3) explain why such a particular discourse generated an uneasy political relationship between Islam and the state.

THE DISCOURSE OF POLITICAL ISLAM IN MODERN INDONESIA: AN OVERVIEW

Muslims (and non-Muslims alike) generally believe in the holistic nature of Islam. As a divine instrument to understand the world, it is often conceived as more than a religion. Many have suggested that it can also be perceived as "a civil society",[4] "a complete civilization",[5] and in fact both "religion and the state".[6] What lies behind these formulations is actually a widely held notion that Islam constitutes more than theological and/or ritual systems. Moreover, Islam does not recognize the wall of separation of the spiritual and temporal; rather it governs all aspects of life.

While such perceptions remain largely unanimous, articulating them — not necessarily because of the different degree of devotion among Muslims, but primarily because of the general character of the vast major-ity of Islamic doctrines, which allows polyinterpretation, depending on the circumstances — is quite problematical. As previously implied, there are those who are inclined to understand the holistic nature of Islam in an organic way. This is in the sense that the relationship between Islam and all aspects of life should be established in a legal/formal manner. Others prefer to interpret the holistic feature of Islam in a more substantive fashion, in which essence rather than form serves as core orientation in their societal life. Failure to reconcile these conflicting views, as experienced by a large number of Muslim countries, has resulted in the development of an uneasy synthesis between Islam and the state in terms of their political relationships. As such it has been generally followed by the latter's deliberate attempts to contain the former's political idealism and activism perceived as threatening to national unity.

Modern Indonesia's Islamic political discourse has not escaped from such a predicament. Its genesis can be traced back to the early years of the country's nationalist movement, when the political elite engaged in the debates concerning the role of Islam in an independent Indonesian state. This search for a viable political relationship between Islam and the state continued well into the independence and post-revolutionary period. To no avail, this ideological discourse, in turn, led to the development of a greater political animosity between Islam and the state, especially during the first twenty years of the New Order period.

THE PRE-INDEPENDENCE PERIOD:
A CALL FOR THE UNION BETWEEN ISLAM AND THE STATE

With the dawn of the country's nationalism in the first decades of the twentieth century, indigenous-organized movements began to emerge, struggling to confront Dutch colonialism and demanding independence for Indonesia. In this nationalistic venture, there was no doubt that Islam played a very pivotal role. As noted by students of Indonesian nationalism, Islam served as a link which tied together the sentiment of national unity against the Dutch colonialism. "The Mohammedan religion," wrote George Mc.T. Kahin in his classical work, *Nationalism and Revolution in Indonesia*, "was not just a common bond; it was, indeed, a sort of in-group symbol against an alien intruder and oppressor of a different religion."[7] Or, as put forward by Fred R. von der Mehden in his "Islam and the Rise of Nationalism in Indonesia":

> Islam was the most obvious means of both establishing national unity and disassociating the Indonesians from the Dutch ruling elite. The Islands which composed the Netherlands East Indies had never existed as a linguistic, cultural or historical entity. The last areas to fall under the Dutch control did not succumb until the beginning of the twentieth century. Thus, consisting of

various historical traditions, languages, cultures, and geographic forms, the only universal which prevailed, outside of colonial rule, was Islam.[8]

Early in this nationalist saga, the sole political embodiment of Islam was Sarekat Islam (Islamic Association). Developed from a commercial organization, Sarekat Dagang Islam (SDI, Islamic Trading Association), founded by H. Samanhoedi in Solo in 1911, it was "the first politically based Indonesian nationalist organization" to evolve.[9] Under the leadership of H.O.S. Tjokroaminoto, Agus Salim, and Abdoel Moeis, it was a pioneering organization which "embarked upon a political program calling for self-government" and "complete independence".[10]

The fact that Sarekat Islam was the first nationalist political organization to emerge was not only because of its nationalist agenda: preaching for an independent Indonesia. To a large extent, it was also due to its ability to attract mass support and a following which transcended the country's social cleavages.[11] As elucidated by Benda, "[a]ddressing itself to an exclusively Indonesian audience, it found followers among all classes, urban as well as rural. Muslim traders, workers in cities, *kyai* and *ulama* [religious leaders], even some *priyayi* [indigenous aristocrats], but above all peasants, were drawn into this first — and last — political mass movement in colonial Indonesia".[12] In short, with regard to the place of Sarekat Islam in the archipelago's nationalist movement, suffice it to say that "Sarekat Islam formed the center of the Indonesian national awakening".[13]

It was rather unfortunate, however, that Sarekat Islam's towering position could not be maintained. Its crucial role as the catalyst of Indonesia's nationalist movement began to unravel in the late 1920s. In spite of later endeavours by its leaders and activists to recapture the nationalist leadership, Sarekat Islam failed to sustain its all-encompassing leadership in the drive towards independence. Instead, in the ensuing years, its political idealism and activism were largely overshadowed by other socio-political groups, which did not formally endorse Islam as their ideological bases.[14]

Several factors contributed to the decline of Sarekat Islam. The most important was the inability of its leaders and activists to resolve their differences, especially with regard to the political course of Sarekat Islam, after Marxism was introduced to the organization.[15]

Interest in Marxist ideas originally developed outside the indigenous nationalist movements. In the archipelago it was initially associated with the minority membership of Nationale Indische Partij (NIP, National Indies Party) — a Eurasian–Indonesian political organization, established in 1912, which advocated the idea of "racial equality, socio-economic justice, and independence, based upon Eurasian–Indonesian cooperation".[16] Suppressed by the colonial government, its minority group aligned with the leftist Indische Sociaal Democratische Vereeniging (ISDV, Indies Social Democratic Association), founded by Hendrik Sneevliet in 1914. Sneevliet himself was a former activist of the Social Democratic Labour Party in the Netherlands who came to the archipelago in 1913.[17]

Soon it became obvious that the European outlook of ISDV was the main stumbling block to attracting indigenous support. "As long as the movement [ISDV]," wrote Bernard Vlekke, "remained restricted to the European and Indo-European section of the population, it had little chance of success, or even of gaining great importance."[18] In other words, "its European leadership would be able to acquire little Indonesian and, therefore, little mass support".[19] It was in the context of trying to acquire support from the indigenous masses that Sarekat Islam, because of its mass-based appeal, became a logical choice for the ISDV leadership to infiltrate. As Kahin has noted:

> There was nothing casual in the infiltration of the Sarekat Islam branches by Sneevliet's organization, which, it should be noted, became increasingly influenced by events in Russia. Sneevliet recognized that the rapidly growing mass-based Sarekat Islam was the ideal medium for his group to work through in order to establish contact with and capture support of the Indonesian masses.[20]

By 1917 the Marxist ideological thinking began to be felt in Sarekat Islam. Semaun and Darsono of the Semarang branch became its primary articulators. And when ISDV was transformed into a full-fledged communist political party in 1920, Partij der Kommunisten in Indie (PKI, Indies Communist Party), both these individuals — while maintaining their membership with Sarekat Islam — stood at the apex of the party leadership.[21]

The introduction of Marxism in Sarekat Islam generated conflicts, creating schisms within the leadership of the organization. This was especially the case with regard to the attempts by both factions (that is, the Islamic and Marxist factions) to exert control and influence in defining the movement's socialistic and revolutionary agenda. To secure unity, the central leadership of Sarekat Islam was compelled to emphasize the socialistic and revolutionary outlook of the association. As Vlekke has described:

> Urged on by the socialist competition for the support of the masses, feeling that the Marxist slogans were extremely useful in capturing the masses for their party, and, finally, strongly encouraged by the course of events in Europe, the Sarekat Islam shifted from political, non-violent opposition to open hostility toward the [colonial] government. It demanded immediate provisions for the masses of the laborers, supported the strikes that broke out time and again in the larger cities of Java, and refused further cooperation with the government in parliamentary work.[22]

Furthermore, Tjokroaminoto also issued a statement, suggesting that "if the [colonial] government did not speedily undertake wide social reforms Sarekat Islam would do so by itself".[23] In spite of this, the Marxist faction was still far from satisfied. It severely criticized the central leadership of Sarekat Islam as less revolutionary, willing only to fight "sinful capitalism".[24]

Adding fuel to the conflict was the differing theological-ideological underpinning of each faction. The triumvirate of Tjokroaminoto, Agus Salim, and Abdoel Moeis were determined to stress Islam as the party's ideology, and move along the line of the Middle East's Pan Islamism. On the other hand, Semaun and Darsono "favored the elimination of religion from practical politics", orienting themselves and the course of their actions to follow Marxist principles.[25]

Failure to reconcile these differences, especially with regard to Sarekat Islam's socialistic and revolutionary character, led to the association's disintegration. Losing the battle, at the sixth congress of Sarekat Islam, held in Surabaya in 1921, the Marxist faction was expelled from the organization on the grounds that they violated party discipline by maintaining their membership with the communist party (PKI).[26] For the Islamic faction, the victory was a Pyrrhic one, in the sense that the success in purging the organization of the Marxist element came at a heavy cost: "the virtual destruction of Sarekat Islam as a mass movement".[27] As von der Mehden has noted:

> The Surabaya Congress of 1921 resulted in more than the severance of the radical socialists from the movement. It also signaled the end of an era for Sarekat Islam and the demise of

the organization as a mass movement. The years to follow were to see the evolvement of a much smaller party with strongly Islamic character.[28]

In the following years Sarekat Islam suffered from further internal struggles and fragmentation. Disputes over policy and personal issues led to the withdrawal and/or dismissal of a number of important party leaders and activists. Abdoel Moeis receded from the leadership following his disagreement with Tjokroaminoto in handling matters related to the pawnshop employees union (Persatuan Pegawai Pegadaian Bumiputera, PPPB), of which the former had been the acting chairman.[29] Similar disputes of an ethical nature led to the dismissals of Sukiman and Surjopranoto from Sarekat Islam.[30] Furthermore, the growing friction between Sarekat Islam and Muhammadiyah (a modernist Muslim socio-religious organization) encouraged the former to take disciplinary measures against the latter, ending with the expulsion of all Muhammadiyah members from the party.[31]

Finally, with the death of Tjokroaminoto in 1934, conflict over the *hijrah* policy (that is, a disassociation policy with the colonial government, formulated in 1922) resurfaced. Abikusno Tjokrosujoso, who chaired the executive body of Sarekat Islam, was determined to continue the organization's policy of non-co-operation. On the ground that the colonial government had begun to apply stricter regulations towards non-co-operation movements, Agus Salim suggested that the *hijrah* policy be reviewed. Unable to resolve the differences on this matter, the latter created a faction called Barisan Penyadar (Consciousness-Raising Front) in 1936. One of its major goals was to reverse the *hijrah* policy in favour of limited co-operation with the colonial government. To no avail, in 1937 the Penyadar group was dismissed from Sarekat Islam.[32] This move only made the party smaller and less effective.[33]

This disintegrating situation in Sarekat Islam, which began in the mid-1920s, made the organization less attractive to many Western-educated younger intellectuals. Among them was Soekarno, Tjokroaminoto's very own protégé, who chose to form his own political organization in 1927 — Partai Nasional Indonesia (PNI, Indonesian National Party) — and developed a different ideological-political world view. Like many other nationalist organizations, PNI's aim was "complete independence for Indonesia, economic as well as political, with a government elected by and responsible to the whole Indonesian people".[34] Preoccupied with the idea of unity of all Indonesians in the effort to achieve independence, this party based its nationalist venture on the ideological notion of *kebangsaan* (nationalism). Himself a Muslim, "Soekarno frequently stressed that the party could not have an Islamic basis". For him, this was so "for independence was as much the objective of Indonesian Christians as of Mohammedans".[35]

From the 1930s onwards, this group — along with other Western-educated intellectual-activists returning from the Netherlands (especially Sjahrir and Mohammad Hatta) — formed the nucleus of the nationalist movement. With the notion of *kebangsaan* as their rallying point, they dominated and directed the course of Indonesia's nationalist movement towards independence. And as it turned out, this nationalist movement, more than the earlier encounter with Marxism, set the stage for the ideological confrontation between the leaders and activists of political Islam and their nationalist counterparts, especially with regard to the relationship between religion (that is, Islam) and the state in an independent Indonesia. It was in this historical context that two differing groups emerged in Indonesia's political discourse: (1) *golongan Islam* (Islamic group) and (2) *golongan kebangsaan* (nationalist group).[36]

Initially, the clash between these two groups revolved around the nature of nationalism. In the attempt to find a common denominator in the struggle for Indonesia's independence, Soekarno broadly defined nationalism as "love of fatherland, [the] sincere preparedness to serve and devote oneself to Mother Indonesia, [the] willingness to set aside narrow party interests".[37] Elsewhere, he wrote that "nationalism is the conviction, the consciousness of a people, that they are united in one group, one nation".[38]

For a leader and activist of political Islam like Agus Salim, this perception elevated nationalism to the rank of religion. Should this be allowed, it "enslaves man to the fatherland-idol". The ramifications of this could be far-reaching. Conceivably, it might "water down the idea of *tawhid* [Islamic monotheism] and reduce one's devotion to God". For this reason, Agus Salim argued strongly that nationalism should be placed in the framework of our "service to Allah". Accordingly, its principle should be Islam.[39]

Ahmad Hassan, a leader of the reformist organization Persatuan Islam (Persis, Islamic Union),[40] criticized Soekarno's nationalism as chauvinistic in nature. It was a nationalistic stance comparable to the Arabs' world view of tribal partisanship before the coming of Islam (*'ashabiyah*). This is forbidden in Islam, as it created a wall of separation among Muslims (that is, between Indonesian Muslims and Muslims of the rest of the world). In addition, he also perceived that the *kebangsaan* group "would naturally not carry out Islamic laws since the party needs to be neutral in religion; it will not take a certain religion as the basis of its organization or its government in the future".[41]

It was not until Mohammad Natsir, a disciple of Ahmad Hassan who had significant Western educational background,[42] joined in the polemics that the religious-ideological contention between these two groups became so intense and deliberate. They not only engaged in religious-ideological debates concerning the nature of Indonesia's nationalism, but extended the polemics to a much broader theme: what constitutes an ideal modern, independent Indonesian state?

Natsir shared his mentor's apprehension about Soekarno's idea of nationalism becoming a new form of 'ashabiyah. It may entail "… fanaticism … which breaks up the bond of brotherhood of all Muslims of various nationalities".[43] For Natsir, there should be some kind of theological underpinning to the idea of nationalism. In other words, nationalism should be based on a divine, beyond material, intention (niat). Thus, like Agus Salim, he argued that the struggle for Indonesia's independence should be oriented or intended as part of our devotion to Allah. In one of his essays in Pembela Islam (Defender of Islam), a socio-religious journal published by Persatuan Islam, he wrote:

> … let us be frank and blunt to each other. For our aim and purpose are not similar. You seek independence for Indonesia on account of the Indonesian nation, on account of Mother Indonesia. We struggle for independence because of Allah, for the well-being of all the inhabitants of the Indonesian archipelago.[44]

Natsir also believed that Indonesia's nationalism should be Islamic in nature. For this, he introduced the notion of kebangsaan Muslim (Muslim nationalism). He based his conviction on the historical fact that it was Islam which initially defined the country's nationalism. Elucidating the historical origins of the country's nationalism, he wrote:

> It was the Islamic movement [that is, Sarekat Islam] which first paved the way in this country for political actions aiming at independence, which first planted the seed of Indonesian unity, which removed the isolated looks of the various islands as well as any provincial features, which first planted the seed of brotherhood with those of the same faith outside the boundaries of Indonesia … .[45]

On another occasion, he even claimed that "without Islam, there was no Indonesian nationalism since Islam had 'first planted the seed of Indonesian unity, (and had) removed the attitudes of isolation of various islands'".[46]

Given this nationalist perception, Natsir maintained that independence was not the ultimate goal of the Islamic nationalist movement. Instead, it should be perceived simply as a medium to seek the transcendental consent of Allah (ridha). This should be done by way of making Islam the law of the land. Accordingly, he indicated that "the Muslims would not stop at that [that is, independence] and would continue their struggle 'as long as [the country is] not based and not administered according to the laws and regulation of Islam'".[47]

It is difficult to gauge the overall nature of Soekarno's concept of nationalism. But certainly, he did not appreciate criticism. Refuting his critics, he maintained that his was not a chauvinistic, jingoistic nationalism. It was a tolerant, Eastern, and not an aggressive European nationalism.[48] It was a nationalism which made Indonesians an "instrument of God", and which led them to a "life of the spirit".[49] If his controversial view in *Nationalism, Islam and Marxism* is any indication, it was an obsession to unite what he (and many others) saw as three ideological streams which led him to conceive nationalism in such a broad and encompassing fashion. A definition which was (as he liked to describe it) "broad as the air" would enable each current to form a viable alliance in the pursuit of independence. For this, he frequently suggested that "there is nothing to prevent Nationalists from working together with Muslims and Marxists".[50]

An intermediary measure taken by the less influential Persatuan Muslimin Indonesia (Permi, Indonesian Muslim Union) failed to resolve the differences. Advocating the idea of a complementary relationship between Islam and *kebangsaan* in the struggle for independence,[51] Permi's attempt was rejected by other Muslim reformists, such as Haji Rasul, A.R. Sutan Mansur, and Hamka. In this regard, they argued that "Islam 'is already complete, sufficient in itself and does not need any additional attributes' like *kebangsaan*". In the view of Natsir, "there was no need to plant in someone the seed of love of his community. [This is] inherent in man's nature ... ".[52]

In the early 1940s the polemics developed beyond the question of nationalism. It touched upon a much more crucial issue: the political relationship between Islam and the state. In this period it was no exaggeration to say that there were no other figures who were more fervently involved in the debates than Soekarno and Natsir.

From his early writings on Islam, published by a Medan-based journal *Pandji Islam* (the Banner of Islam) in 1940, we know that basically Soekarno was in favour of the separation of Islam from the state.[53] He was not, however, suggesting that there should be no relationship of any kind between these two religious-political realms. Obviously, he was against the idea of a formal-legal relationship between Islam and the state, especially in a country where its inhabitants are not uniformly adherents of Islam. For him, such a mode would only create a sense of discrimination, particularly in the view of its non-Muslim communities. In his "Saya Kurang Dinamis" he wrote:

> Thus reality shows us that the principle of the unity of state and religion for a country which its inhabitant is not 100% Muslim could not be in line with [the principle of] democracy. In such a country, there are only two alternatives; there are only two choices: the unity of state-religion, but without democracy, or democracy, but the state is separated from religion![54]

Nevertheless, as a Muslim he subscribed to the notion of a substantialistic or ethical relationship between Islam and the state. This is in the sense that through democratic representation, Muslims — because of their majority status — would be able to set and determine the state agenda, resulting ultimately in the formulation of policy decisions which would be imbued with Islamic values. Thus for Soekarno, the authenticity of an "Islamic state" was found not so much in the formal and/or legal adoption of Islam as the ideological and constitutional basis of the state, but more on the personal and mass manifestation of the "flame" and "spirit" of Islam in the state policies. For this, he argued:

> Would it not be better, would it not be more manly [courageous], if we say: "Alright, we accept the state to be separated from religion, but we will inflame all people with the flame of Islam, so that all members of the [state] representative agency are Islamic delegates, and all decisions of the representative agency are of Islamic in spirit and soul!"[55]

In another passage, he stated:

> Inflame the spirit of Islam among your people, so that every nose [that is, individual] becomes Islamic nose, every brain becomes Islamic brain, from Abdul the sweeper to the rich who cruises the city with his car — and the representative

agency will be overflowed with delegates whose politics are Islamic, their hearts are Islamic, their blood is Islamic, and all of their body-hairs are Islamic! Thus, with such overabundance [of Islamic representation] all aspirations of Islamic shari'a would automatically materialize in every decision of the representative agency ... . So the state by itself becomes Islamic in character, without an article in its constitution that it is a theocratic state, without mentioning that it is a theocratic state.[56]

It is clear for Soekarno that as long as Muslims (of any religious school and orientation) participated in the political process, there should be no policies which are not Islamic in character. For this he elucidated:

As long as the majority of the members of parliament adhere to religious politics, all decisions of parliament would be religious in character. As long as the majority of parliament adhere to Islamic politics, no single proposal would come into effect unless it is Islamic in nature. ... If people are inflamed with Islamic spirit, parliament would certainly overflow with the spirit of Islam; and all decisions of parliament would be Islamic in character.[57]

He restated many of his arguments five years later (1945) in the committee for the preparation of independence (BPUPKI) meeting, where he (and other members of the *golongan kebangsaan)* engaged in a formal discussion with his Islamic counterparts in an effort to find a viable compromise with regard to the ideological formulation and constitutional arrangement of Indonesia as an independent state.

To understand this religious-political stance, one should go beyond the textual appearances of Soekarno's rhetorical discourse on the relationship between Islam and the state and look at the contextual circumstances that influenced the development of such a religious-political position.

As reflected in his *Surat-Surat Islam dari Endeh* (Islamic Letters from Endeh),[58] Soekarno believed that "ideal Islam" (that is, Islam as presented in the Qur'an and Sunnah) was by nature flexible, rational, and progressive. But the "historical or empirical Islam" which he saw and read, especially during the period of its decline, was shackled by backwardness, heresy, superstition, and anti-rationalism. He regarded Islam of that time as paralysed and unable to cope with modernity. In his judgment, as implied in his eighth letter to Ahmad Hassan, "Not for a hundred years, but for a thousand years Islam has stayed behind the times."[59]

Influenced by the writings of a number of Muslim thinkers, especially Syed Ameer Ali,[60] Soekarno was quick to suggest that Muslims should rejuvenate their understanding of Islam. For him, the permanent and universal nature of Islam required its adherents to understand Islamic doctrines (especially those which concern issues of societal nature) beyond their textual appearances. It is only through such an endeavour that Muslims could grasp the "flame" or "spirit" of Islam in their encounters with modernity and the changing world.[61]

Dwelling on the religious-ideological ventures of Turkey's political elite (that is, Kamal Ataturk, Halide Edib Hanoum, and Mahmud Essad Bey) in their attempt to establish a modern state, Soekarno found part of the answer to Islam's decline. Sharing their conviction, he was very much convinced that the unity of Islam with the state contributed to the stagnancy of Islam.

In the view of these political elite, involvement in the processes of state politics posed tremendous obstacles for Islam. Being part of state politics, Islam is prone to become an instrument for worldly reward and punishment. In the hands of a dictator, it could well serve as a means for political oppression. Because of this, it would be in the best interest of Islam to be separated from the state and left solely in the hands of its adherents. In this context the separation of Islam from the state in Turkey, as perceived by its elite, was meant to liberate Islam from the institutional tutelage of the state.[62]

With these perceptions in mind and coupled with a theological understanding that Islam has no definite political preference (with respect to its political relationship with the state), a viewpoint which he took indirectly from Abd al-Raziq's controversial *al-Islam wa Ushul al-Hukm* published in the mid-1920s,[63] Soekarno became the main advocate of the notion of separation between state and religion. "Islam in Indonesia," he said, "should not become the affair of the state."[64]

It was this notion of separation of Islam from the state and not the non-formal/legal relationship between Islam and the state which provoked criticism from a number of leaders and activists of political Islam, especially Mohammad Natsir. Contradicting Soekarno's ideas, Natsir championed the idea of unity between religion and the state.[65] Like many other Muslims, Natsir believed in the holistic nature of Islam. He was very much in agreement with H.A.R. Gibb's celebrated assessment that "Islam is indeed much more than a system of theology, it is a complete civilization".[66] For him, Islam does not constitute only ritual but also comprises general principles relevant for regulating the relationships between the individual and society.[67]

Nonetheless, Natsir was very much aware that the Qur'an and Muhammad traditions do not have "hands and legs" to make the individuals faithful to the rules of Islam. "Like many other books of law," he wrote, "the Qur'an could not do anything by itself; and its regulations could not function by themselves … ."[68] As an illustration, he said that "Islam obliges Muslims to pay *zakat* (religious alms) appropriately. How could such a 'societal' regulation come into effect properly, if there is no government to oversee its implementation."[69]

Thus, in his view there is no doubt that Islam needs a viable instrument to make its injunctions operative. It was in this particular context that he saw the state as a viable instrument to make Islamic injunctions and laws operative. As he himself noted, "to make those [Islamic] regulations and directives operative and functional in a manner they are supposed to be, there should and must be a power in a living relationship [known] as the state … ".[70]

Given this perspective, Natsir was strongly of the opinion that Islam and the state are integrated religious-political entities. "For us," he said, "a state is not a goal, it is a tool. In principle, the affairs of the state are an integral part *(intergreerend deel)* of Islam."[71] For him, this was the primary distinction between Muslims and non-Muslims as far as their political outlooks are concerned.[72]

In spite of this, it is important to note that Natsir also recognized that in this venture, Islam provides only general guidelines. A detailed prescription on how a state should be organized or structured rests in the ability of its leaders to conduct their own *ijtihad* (independent judgment) in order to meet the challenges of modernity, provided such a task is carried out in a democratic manner. With this statement, he thus rejected the perception that Islam runs counter to the idea of progress.[73]

The polemics of Soekarno and Natsir were basically explorative in character. From the beginning, they were intended neither to formulate workable conceptions of state–religion relationships, nor to seek a common ground. Instead, they were designed to display each other's ideological-political positions. Consequently, the debates simply highlighted the seemingly unbridgeable differences between these two different political groups. Representing the *kebangsaan* group, Soekarno fell short in providing meaningful religious substance to his "deconfessionalized" Islam–state relationship. Because of this (even though his idea implied the notion of a non-formal or ethical relationship between Islam and the state), in the view of many activists of political Islam, his concept was basically overshadowed by Ataturk's "secularistic" zeal, expressed infamously as the separation of Islam from the state.

On the other hand, Natsir's responses were not well thought out. His answers to Soekarno's challenges failed to meaningfully articulate the nature and construct of the political relationship between Islam and the state. Instead, he stopped at the normative and general statement of Islam which may shape the mode of the relationship between these religious-political domains. Or as suggested by Deliar Noer, "[b]eing on the defensive, Natsir's writings were mostly apologetic in character".[74]

Soekarno's and Natsir's polemics ceased temporarily with the coming of the Japanese military forces to the archipelago in 1942. But the political competition between these two groups remained prevalent nonetheless.

The Japanese occupation lasted only for a little over three years, from March 1942 until August 1945. "In spite of its brevity," as noted by Harry J. Benda, "the Japanese interregnum was a traumatic episode that profoundly affected many aspects of Indonesian life."[75] For the Islamic group it provided far better chances for the enhancement of its socio-political stature. In fact, as described by Daniel S. Lev, "Islamic leaders saw a chance in the occupation to regain what had been lost during the 1920s and 1930s, perhaps more, and pressed the Japanese military administration to restore the rights of the Islamic *ummah*".[76] It is important to note, however, that this was not without the challenge from the *kebangsaan* group which evidently "parried this pressure at nearly every turn".[77]

Yet the Islamic group did make gains. Unlike the Dutch colonial government, the Japanese administration allied itself with the Islamic leadership for the purpose of winning the war effort. Moreover, they seemed "more ready to make concessions to Islamic, rather than to nationalist, let alone *priyayi* [aristocrat] demands".[78] These included (1) the establishment of Shumubu (Office of Religious Affairs); (2) the founding of Majlis Syura Muslimin Indonesia (Masyumi, Indonesian Muslim Consultative Council); and (3) the creation of Hizbullah, a military organization for the Muslim youths.[79]

To some extent, Shumubu resembled in function the Dutch Office for Native Affairs. The primary difference lay in the fact that Shumubu was entrusted in the hands of Muslims. Given the circumstances, it appeared that this leadership position played a major role, especially in "wield[ing] greater influence [of Islamic leaders] in matters Islamic on Java".[80]

Taken together, it seems fair to argue that the Japanese interregnum had actually strengthened the position of the Islamic group. At the more tangible level, it provided more institutional experiences for Islamic leaders with regard to the administration of Islamic religious affairs. Comparing the situation of Islam in the two different periods of colonialism, Abikusno Tjokrosujoso observed that "Dutch policy rendered Islam weak. Islam had no well-trained religious officials in the mosques or Islamic courts. Andalso Islamic leadership was not of top quality. The Dutch took a policy of undercutting and weakening Islam. When the Japanese came, they realized that Islam was a force in Indonesia that could be used."[81]

More importantly, the Japanese administration ended (albeit limited in scope) the Dutch's policy of separating Islam from politics. For this, M.A. Aziz said that with the occupation "[t]he separation between church and state came practically to an end. Islam obtained a privileged position in the political system in which, next to the secular administration, a religious apparatus had been created. The Japanese thus brought about fundamental change in the traditional method of governing, by the increase of power for Islam."[82]

But in the end, as the strategic efforts of the Japanese to win the war deteriorated (thus making independence more feasible), the Japanese changed policy directions. They became increasingly and decisively more supportive of *kebangsaan* leaders. In this case, it is safe to say that basically the Japanese administration entrusted the *kebangsaan* group with the leadership of Indonesia's future independent state. Accordingly, important state agencies and committees pertinent for the preparation of independence were assigned mostly to the *kebangsaan* leaders. These included the Sanyo Kaigi (Advisers Council)[83] and the Dokuritsu Zyunbi Tyoosakai (also known as Badan Penyelidik Usaha-Usaha Persiapan Kemerdekaan Indonesia [BPUPKI, Investigatory Committee for the Efforts for the Preparation of Indonesian Independence]).[84]

It was in the Sanyo Kaigi and especially BPUPKI that the Islamic and *kebangsaan* groups renewed their ideological-political disputes. As far as their perceptions of the nature of the political relationship between Islam and the state are concerned, they seemed to follow the same mode of reasoning as articulated a decade earlier. The Islamic group, at this time led by Ki Bagus Hadikusumo, Abdul Kahar Muzakkir, Abikusno Tjokrosujoso, and A. Wachid Hasjim, basically argued that, given the preponderant position of Islam in Indonesia, the state should be based on Islam. On the other hand, the *kebangsaan* group, led by Soekarno, Hatta, and Supomo, maintained that for the sake of unity the state should be "deconfessionalized" (though by no means irreligious) in character.

But unlike the earlier debates, which were concerned basically with the general themes regarding the ideological and political relationship between Islam and the state, at both Sanyo Kaigi and BPUPKI the discussion covered detailed areas perceived as relevant to the construction of either an Islamic state or a "deconfessionalized" unitary nation state. This included the debates on the ideological and constitutional bases of the state; whether or not the president should be a Muslim; whether or not Islam ought to be the state religion; the necessity of having the state apparatus and agencies relevant for the implementation of Islamic law; and on the possibility of Friday becoming a national holiday. There was nothing peculiar with this development other than the fact that the political elites, whether Islamic or nationalist, began to feel that at this stage the prospect for independence became highly probable.[85]

In the Sanyo Kaigi, led by Abikusno Tjokrosujoso and A. Wachid Hasjim from February until April 1945, the Islamic group renewed its religious-political ventures by striving to strengthen the position of the Islamic courts (*peradilan agama*). Following the earlier mode of reasoning, the *kebangsaan* group rejected the idea of establishing Islamic courts in the future independent Indonesian state. For Sartono, there was no need to have religious courts as the affairs of the state would be separated from the affairs of religion. In his view, "[i]t is sufficient for all cases to be tried by an ordinary court, which can ask the advice of a religious expert".[86] Hatta, a devout Muslim from West Sumatra, took the matter further by arguing that the Qur'an could not serve as a pure basis for national law. For him,

> The Qur'an is especially the basis of religion, not book of law. The various legal needs of today find no regulations in the Qur'an. ... Of course the Qur'an establishes a basis for justice and welfare, which must be followed by Muslims. But this basis ... is only a guiding goal. ... The people of the state themselves must establish orderly law by their mutual deliberations. Of course every person will express his conceptions based on his religious convictions. But the resulting law will be state law, not religious law. Possibly it will be state law much influenced by religious law or its spirit may be infused with religious spirit. ... We will not establish a state with a separation of religion and state, but a separation of religious

affairs and state affairs. If religious affairs are also handled by the state, then the religion will become state equipment and ... its eternal character will disappear. State affairs belong to all of us. The affairs of Islam are exclusively the affairs of the Islamic *ummah* and Islamic society.[87]

It was in the BPUPKI (which later became the PPKI [Panitia Persiapan Kemerdekaan Indonesia, Preparatory Committee for Indonesian Independence]), which convened from late May to mid-August 1945, that a full-fledged ideological confrontation between the Islamic and *kebangsaan* groups took place. Reiterating the previous line of theological and sociological reasoning, the former argued that Indonesia should become an Islamic state, or that Islam should become the ideological basis of the state.

The latter, as expressed by Hatta and Supomo, proposed the creation of a national unitary state in which the affairs of the state would be separated from the affairs of religion. Other than basing their argument on the fact that Islam had no definite, unified conception of the state–religion relationship, these *kebangsaan* leaders reminded their Islamic counterparts that Indonesia was not religiously homogeneous.[88]

In Supomo's view "[i]f an Islamic [s]tate is created in Indonesia, then certainly the problem of minorities will arise, the problem of small religious groups, of Christians and others".[89] He believed that an Islamic state "will safeguard the interests of other groups as well as possible". Nevertheless, he was equally convinced that in such a state "[those] smaller religious groups will certainly not be able to feel involved in the state".[90]

In spite of the strong preference to establish a national unitary state, the *kebangsaan* group maintained that such a state would not be an irreligious one. For this, complementing Soekarno's and Hatta's earlier views, Supomo stated:

> ... in the state of Indonesia, citizens must be stimulated to love their fatherland, to devote themselves to and sacrifice themselves for the sake of the country, to gladly serve the fatherland, to love and serve their leaders and the state, to bow down to God, to think of God every moment. All this must constantly be promoted and used as a *moral basis* for this national unitary state. And I am convinced that Islam will strengthen *these principles* ... .[91]

To solidify the idea of a "deconfessionalized" state, Soekarno proposed that five basic principles, later known as Pancasila, be adopted as the *philosophische grondslag* (philosophical basis) of the state. As conceived by Soekarno, this ideological *weltanschauung* (world view) comprised principles such as (in its initial order): *kebangsaan* (nationalism); *internasionalisme* or *peri-kemanusiaan* (internationalism or humanism); *mufakat* or *demokrasi* (deliberation or democracy); *kesejahteraan sosial* (social welfare); and *Ketuhanan* (Belief in God).[92]

To bridge the differences between the Islamic and *kebangsaan* groups, a small committee was set up. Consisting of Soekarno, Hatta, Achmad Subardjo, Muhammad Yamin, Abikusno Tjokrosujoso, A. Kahar Muzakkir, Agus Salim, A. Wachid Hasjim, and A.A. Maramis,[93] this committee drafted a "gentlemen's agreement", known as the Jakarta Charter. Basically, this charter endorsed Pancasila as the ideological basis of the state with the addition that its theological principle read as "Belief in God *with the obligation to carry out Islamic shari'a for its adherents*".[94]

It appeared that this ideological *modus vivendi* was far more difficult to sell than formulate. The Islamic group maintained that it was not strong enough to "place the state unequivocally behind Islam".[95] For this reason, Wahid Hasjim stipulated that "only Muslims could be elected as President or Vice-President of the Republic". Furthermore, he also suggested that Islam be adopted as the state religion.[96] Pushing further towards the direction of Islamic statehood, Ki Bagus Hadikusumo demanded that the theological principle be stated as "Belief in God with the obligation to carry out Islamic *shari'a*", without the condition that it was only applicable to Muslims.[97]

For the opposite reasons, the *kebangsaan* group, particularly those members with non-Islamic origins, objected to this compromise. Fearful of possible discrimination against other religions (Latuharhary) and the growth of religious fanaticism (Djajadiningrat and Wongsonegoro), they demanded that the state must be unequivocally "deconfessionalized".[98]

It was only after Soekarno's appeal to both sides to make great sacrifices that the debates came to a halt. The Investigatory Committee "agreed" that the future independent state would be based on the principle of "Belief in God with the obligation to carry out Islamic *shari'a* for its adherents". It also "accepted" Islam as the state religion, and that the President of the Republic must be a Muslim.[99]

Soon it became obvious that the compromise was basically founded on unstable ground. On 18 August 1945, one day after the declaration of independence, the Jakarta Charter was nullified. Reportedly, a Japanese navy officer came to Hatta informing him that Christians (the majority of whom resided in the archipelago's eastern regions) would not join the Republic unless several elements of the Jakarta Charter (that is, the obligation to carry out Islamic *shari'a* for its adherents, Islam as the state religion, and the requirement for an Islamic president) be deleted. They realized that the implementation of the Jakarta Charter would not pose any threats towards their socio-religious and political activities. Nevertheless, in their view such a constitutional arrangement implied discriminatory measures.[100]

Thus, like Sisyphus, Indonesia's founding fathers were forced to undertake a laborious endeavour to modify the ideological and constitutional basis of the state. In this venture Hatta suggested that certain modifications be made to ensure the unity of Indonesia's national state. Moved by Hatta's insistence, the Islamic group (represented by Ki Bagus Hadikusumo, Wachid Hasjim, Kasman Singodimedjo, and Teuku Mohammad Hassan), agreed to eliminate the legalistic/formalistic elements of Islam, primarily including the removal of "articles on Islam as the official religion of the state, the condition that the President must be a Muslim and the 'obligation for adherents of Islam to practice Islamic law' … ".[101]

In return, a monotheistic theological element was inserted in the first principle of Pancasila, thereby making the formulation of the first principle of Pancasila as "Belief in *One* God" (*Ketuhanan Yang Maha Esa*).

There was speculation as to why the leaders of the Islamic group so quickly accepted the nullification of the Jakarta Charter — a constitutional *modus vivendi* which they had fought for relentlessly in the PPKI. First, the inclusion of "Oneness" (*Yang Maha Esa*) could have been seen as a symbolic gesture to denote the presence of Islamic monotheistic element in the state ideology. In this regard Wachid Hasjim was especially convinced that the addition of this monotheistic ingredient in Pancasila was a reflection of (or at least in tune with) the principle of Islamic *tawhid*.[102] For a Muslim like Hatta, it provided "an escape route … for any obligations, as an orthodox Muslim and the son of an *ulama*, to support the Islamic state".[103]

Second, the circumstances following independence required the country's founding fathers to stand united in facing other problems. Most notable was the anticipated attempt by the Dutch to reoccupy the archipelago. Engulfed by a sense of electoral optimism, they believed that through a general election, to be held in the not-too-distant future, they would have another chance to constitutionally make the state unequivocally Islamic. For this reason, Ki Bagus Hadikusumo (at the encouragement of Kasman Singodimedjo) reluctantly agreed to accept Hatta's proposals.[104]

Other Islamic leaders were not so willing. Isa Anshary simply perceived the event as "a deceit perpetrated upon the Moslems". "This conspicuous happening," he said more than a decade later, "has been felt by the Islamic community to be a 'magic trick', still wrapped up in a mysterious fog ... a political embezzlement against the Moslem stance."[105]

In any case, it is fair to conclude that such an event marked the first defeat of the Islamic group in its attempt to bring the idea of a formal and legal union between Islam and the state into reality. This defeat, as it was unfolding in the years to follow, was accepted only temporarily, "until an elected Constituent Assembly began the work of fashioning a new constitution".[106]

THE POST-REVOLUTIONARY PERIOD:
A QUEST FOR ISLAM AS THE IDEOLOGICAL BASIS OF THE STATE

For nearly five years after the declaration of independence (1945–50), Indonesia was in revolution. Following the defeat of the Japanese by the allied forces, the Dutch managed to reoccupy the archipelago. During this period nothing significant hampered the political relationship between the mainstream leaders and activists of political Islam and the *kebangsaan* group. Debates on the nature of the relationship between Islam and the state appeared to have been put to rest. At least temporarily, the leaders were prepared to put their ideological differences behind them. Obviously, at that time there was a sense of urgency among the nation's founding fathers to exert all energies and strengths for the defence of the Republic and to prevent the Dutch from recolonizing the country.

Though not without conflicts, both of these groups were able to develop a relatively harmonious political relationship. The *kebangsaan* group remained at the centre of the leadership. In the meantime, especially following the transfer of authority from the Dutch to the Republic in December 1949, the Islamic group gradually emerged as a significant force in the national political discourse. With Masyumi, formed in November 1945, as its sole political representation, this group was able to attract a substantial number of followers.[107] As early as 1946 Sjahrir (leader of the Socialist Party and three times premier of the revolutionary Cabinets) had predicted that "if free elections were to be held [around that year], the Masyumi group — at the time combining modernists [for example, Muhammadiyah with a huge urban membership] and orthodox [for example, Nahdlatul Ulama with a massive rural following] — would obtain 80 per cent of the vote".[108]

This was not a baseless prediction. The electoral strength of Masyumi between 1946 and 1951 was real. Herbert Feith observes that "[i]n regional elections held in a number of parts of Java in 1946 and in the closely watched election in the Special Territory of [Y]ogyakarta in 1951, the Masyumi had gained absolute majorities of the vote or at least many more votes than any other contender". Because of this, "the Masyumi was generally expected to emerge as the strongest single party in national elections".[109]

To further illustrate the increasingly significant political position of the Islamic group in the Republic's post-revolutionary period, several historical records are relevant. First, by August 1950 the activity of Indonesian political parties had been rejuvenating and "had recovered from its lull of 1949". In the newly established parliament of 236 members, Masyumi emerged as the largest party with forty-nine seats. Yet, because of the existence of many parties, organizations, and associations represented in the parliament (no fewer than twenty-two), together with Partai Sarekat Islam Indonesia (PSII), the Islamic group took only fifty-four seats (23 per cent). Second, on several occasions Masyumi was asked to form and lead Cabinets. Out of the seven Cabinets which operated under the constitutional democratic system (1950–57), three were entrusted to Masyumi (that is, the Natsir Cabinet from 1950–51; Sukiman Cabinet from 1951–52; and Burhanuddin Harahap Cabinet from 1955–56). Other than that, when Partai Nasional Indonesia (PNI, Indonesian National Party) was given mandates to form the government, either Masyumi or Nahdlatul Ulama (NU) (the latter departed from Masyumi and converted itself into a political organization in 1952) served as the primary coalition partner. Finally, as the result of the first general elections held in September 1955, the Islamic group (this time comprising Masyumi, NU, PSII, and Perti) controlled 114 out of 257 seats (43.5 per cent of the votes) in the parliament. Though the election result was obviously far below Sjahrir's prediction, it nonetheless doubled the representation of the Islamic group in the parliament.[110]

This fact, coupled with the absence of open ideological controversies, may have contributed to the development of a relatively easy political relationship between these two religious-political leviathans during the early years of Indonesia's post-revolutionary politics (1950–53). Overt criticism of Pancasila by leaders and activists of political Islam was a rarity.[111] In fact, Mohammad Natsir even argued that — because of the adoption of the Belief in One God principle in Pancasila — Indonesia has not excluded religion from statehood.[112]

In spite of this, it is important to note that as a unified political entity Indonesia (at that time) was conspicuously weak.[113] From the state theory perspective, it unequivocally fell "on the lower end of the spectrum in [its] ability to achieve social control and effective appropriation of resources".[114] The inability of the state to "penetrate" society, to "regulate" its relationships with some socio-political groupings, and to "extract" and "appropriate" both human and natural resources in more or less determined ways contributed to the outbreak of a number of insurgencies which posed tremendous challenges to the national leadership.[115] Notable instances included the Darul Islam, Pemerintah Revolusioner Republik Indonesia (PRRI, Revolutionary Government of the Republic of Indonesia), and Perjuangan Semesta Alam (Permesta, Inclusive Struggle) rebellions.[116]

To a large extent, all of these insurgencies were direct results of the inability of the central government to extract strong loyalties from certain regional political elites ("strongmen"). It was only the Darul Islam movement, however, which was waged "under the banner of Islam". As such, though with different modes and reasoning, and without the acquiescence of the mainstream leaders and activists of political Islam, it rekindled the formalistic/legalistic ideological-political discourse on Islam and the state.

In West Java the Darul Islam movement was more a product of Kartosuwirjo's disagreement with the leaders of the Republic than his theological-political consciousness. It was true that he first proclaimed an Islamic state on 14 August 1945. But following Indonesia's declaration of independence on 17 August 1945, he relinquished his aspiration for an Islamic statehood by siding with the Republic. His political idealism and activism were then channelled through Masyumi. In this party he was appointed to its executive body and subsequently became a commissioner for West Java.[117]

Soon it became obvious that Kartosuwirjo was very much disenchanted with the way the central leadership pursued its strategy to prevent the Dutch from recolonizing the archipelago. Because of this, he withdrew from the country's mainstream political activities. Rejecting the post of second vice-minister of defence under the premiership of Amir Syarifuddin, he concentrated instead "on building up the Hizbullah units under his control and successfully resisted incorporation of these fighting units into the Indonesian army".[118]

When control over the Indonesian territory deteriorated, as the result of the first Dutch Police Action (1947), Kartosuwirjo called for *jihad* (holy war) against the Dutch. He rejected the Renville Agreement (1948), ratified by the Republic and the Netherlands, under which "West Java was abandoned, and approximately thirty thousand Republican troops withdrew to the truncated Republican territory in Central Java".[119] Instead, he retreated to the mountainous areas of West Java, calling for the continuation of *jihad* against the Dutch. As a response to the creation of the puppet state of Pasundan, formed in a Dutch-controlled area of West Java (1948), he proclaimed the foundation of the Negara Islam Indonesia (NII, Indonesian Islamic State).[120]

With the launching of the second Dutch Police Action (1948), Indonesia was at the brink of territorial and political disaster. Yogyakarta (then the capital of the Republic) was seized, and Soekarno and Hatta (President and Vice-President) and most Cabinet members were captured. Encountering this situation, Kartosuwirjo not only renewed his call for *jihad* but was also determined to once again proclaim the establishment of an Islamic state (1949), embracing the whole of Indonesia.[121] At this time, as noted by Boland, his proclamation was intended "as the alternative to the Republic of Indonesia [Yogyakarta] ".[122]

The institutionalization of the fighting units at the disposal of Kartosuwirjo (later known as Tentara Islam Indonesia [TII, Indonesian Islamic Army]) as a separate entity generated conflict with the Tentara Nasional Indonesia (TNI, Indonesian National Army). Based on the circumstances described above, TII considered West Java as *de facto* its territory. When the TNI returned to its territorial origins (following the breakdown of the Renville Agreement), the arrival of the Siliwangi division in West Java was "perceived as a flagrant infringement of the authority of an existing sovereign state".[123]

This perception grew stronger when Indonesia's sovereignty was recognized by the Dutch in December 1949. Like the return of the Siliwangi division to West Java, the attempts to reincorporate West Java into the fold of the Republic were perceived as overt territorial encroachment of Kartosuwirjo's Indonesian Islamic State. Armed conflicts were therefore unavoidable. During the entire course of the conflict (1949–62), as noted by Karl D. Jackson, "approximately 25,000 civilians and members of the Indonesian armed forces lost their lives, 120,000 homes were burned, and property losses totaled 650 million rupiahs".[124]

The initial spurt of rebellion in South Sulawesi had nothing to do with the theological-political consciousness of its leaders and supporters. Rather, it originated from a military policy unacceptable to ex-guerilla forces in the region. These ex-guerilla units demanded to be incorporated *en bloc* into the national army, and they wanted to remain a separate military unit. Kawilarang, who was then the military commander for East Indonesia, rejected the idea. Discharging the vast majority of this ex-guerilla fighters, he wanted only a selected few of them in the TNI. Kahar Muzakkar (who was then in Java, and himself was a charismatic ex-guerilla leader) was brought in to mediate the conflict. To no avail, he joined and led the guerilla struggle instead.[125]

With the passage of time, this military resentment transformed itself into full-blown political disenchantment with the very concept of the unitary state as defined by the central government. It was only at this stage of the struggle that Kahar Muzakkar contacted Kartosuwirjo and accepted his appointment as "Sulawesi commander of Kartosuwirjo's Islamic Army of Indonesia", and became "a part of Kartosuwirjo's Islamic State of Indonesia in West Java".[126]

The Acehnese rebellion perhaps provides more vivid evidence with regard to the weak nature of Indonesia's revolutionary state. The inability of the state to penetrate the society of this region, especially in the circumstances of 1945–49, made the central government vulnerable to Acehnese demands. In this regard, of particular importance was the demand for greater regional autonomy in social, economic, and political affairs.[127] In 1949, as observed by Boland, the West Sumatra-based Republican emergency government "accepted Aceh's demand to become, *de jure*, an autonomous province of the Republic, with Daud Beureueh as governor".[128]

In the 1950s attempts were made by the central government to reverse the autonomous status of Aceh. The increasing power of the central leadership, especially following the Netherlands' recognition of the Republic's sovereignty, encouraged the state to launch "a campaign against Aceh as a separate province".[129] This immediately "ended the good relationship that had ensued between the Central Government and the Acehnese leaders" and eventually "drove the Acehnese towards rebellion".[130] In other words, it was only when the existence of regional autonomy was threatened that the problem of political relationship between the centre (Jakarta) and periphery (Aceh) began to develop.[131]

In 1953 Daud Beureueh led the Darul Islam movement in Aceh — a regional saga which marked the attempted separation of this area at the northern tip of Sumatra from the Republic. After several years of armed encounters, Jakarta realized that a military solution was unlikely to bring the Acehnese rebellion to a halt. A negotiated settlement was pursued to end the conflict. In the late 1950s Aceh was "recognized as *daerah istimewa* (a special administrative district) with autonomy particularly in religious affairs, in questions of *adat* [customary law] and in matters of education, on the understanding that this autonomy should not come into conflict with the Constitution".[132]

Aside from these regional rebellions waged under the Islamic flag, the political relationship between Islam and the state remained basically cordial. The adoption of Pancasila as the state ideology was not perceived as the embodiment of a wall which separates religion (that is, Islam) from the state. In fact, because of the inclusion of the monotheistic statement in the state's *philosophische grondslag*, Indonesia was perceived as an Islamic country. In this respect, there was no better illustration than Mohammad Natsir's address at the Pakistan Institute of World Affairs in 1952:

> Pakistan is decidedly an Islamic country by population and by choice as it has declared Islam as the state religion. So is Indonesia an Islamic country by the fact that Islam is recognised as the religion of the Indonesian people, though no express mention is made in our constitution to make it the state's religion. But neither has Indonesia excluded religion from the statehood. In fact it has put the monotheistic belief in the one and only God, at the head of the Pantjasila — The Five Principles adopted as the spiritual, moral and ethical foundation of the state and the nation.[133]

But this political congeniality between Islam and the state did not last long. The ideological consensus achieved one day after the declaration of independence was clearly built on permeable ground. For this reason, once again the state political elites were drawn into an ideological-political debate concerning the construct of the state and its constitutional arrangements. At this time the triggering factor revolved around the question of electioneering, with the Constituent Assembly serving as its primary setting.

One of the most important agenda items for Indonesia's post-independent Cabinets was to hold general elections for parliament and Constituent Assembly. The Sjahrir Cabinet promised to schedule the first general elections as early as January 1946. Unfortunately, the country's revolutionary situation (1945–49) did not allow these elections to take place. In the period following the transfer of authority from the Dutch, as noted by Feith, "every cabinet made elections for a Constituent Assembly an important part of its program".[134] In spite of this, it was not until the Burhanuddin Harahap Cabinet that the first general elections were held (1955).[135]

A number of factors caused the delay in holding the general elections. Most significant was the fear among the state and party elites, especially those from the *kebangsaan* group, that these political festivities might pose a threat to the existing "deconfessionalized" political relationship between religion (that is, Islam) and the state. They believed that political events such as general elections could be used by their Islamic counterparts to marshal public support for the realization of Islamic statehood. Realizing their potential to win the majority of the votes, electoral success of the Islamic group could well pave the way for Islam to become the basis of state in the Constituent Assembly.[136]

This is where the politics of fear came into play. Concern over the possibility that the Islamic group might win the elections led many leaders and activists of the *kebangsaan* group to refashion their strategy with regard to the holding of elections. In this case one of the most viable options was simply to delay the elections. As stated by A.R. Djokoprawiro of Partai Indonesia Raya (PIR, Greater Indonesian Party), his party's strategy was "to work for the postponement of elections until the position of the supporters of Pantja Sila was stronger".[137] Other leaders like Soekarno, who was then the head of state, managed to influence the country's political discourse in the direction of a "deconfessionalized" politics. On 27 January 1953 at Amuntai (a stronghold of the Muslim community in the southern part of Kalimantan), he reminded his listeners of the necessity to maintain Indonesia as a national unitary state. "The state we want," he said, "is a national state consisting of all Indonesia. If we establish a state based on Islam, many areas whose population is not Islamic, such as the Moluccas, Bali, Flores, Timor, the Kai Islands, and Sulawesi, will secede. And West Irian, which has not yet become part of the territory of Indonesia, will not want to be part of the Republic."[138]

The Islamic group was especially irritated with Soekarno's address. They considered the President's move undemocratic and unconstitutional. In their view Soekarno "had exceeded his constitutional limitations, that his speech had sown seeds of separatism, and that it represented a taking of sides by the head of state with groups opposed to the ideology of Islam".[139] In other words, "... President Soekarno, as a vigorous defender of the Pantja Sila ... came to be seen as a spokesman for one side in the struggle, instead of a non-partisan head of state".[140]

Defending the President, the PNI supported Soekarno's action, saying it was based on "the special prerogatives of President Soekarno as a man who was a revolutionary leader and inspirer of his people as well as a constitutional head of state".[141] In their view the speech should have been seen as his endeavour to preserve the unity of Indonesia, to prevent any attempts which might result in the development of a political oppression by the majority, and to articulate fears of the minority groups with regard to their place in the Republic, should Indonesia be based on the religion of the majority (that is, Islam).[142]

In spite of the attempts by several important Masyumi leaders such as Natsir and Sukiman to cool down the controversy, these ideological-political exchanges continued. Unintentionally, such exchanges severely damaged the previous consensus, especially with respect to the adoption of Pancasila as the nation's common ideological-political platform. In this regard Josef A. Mestenhauser has observed that the state ideology (Pancasila) "was no longer the umbrella under which political competition took place, but instead became part of the political competition and struggle itself".[143] Put differently, Pancasila, which was previously perceived by leaders and activists of political Islam as "a symbol to which they could give at least tentative assent, now became anti-Moslem property".[144]

In any event this development rekindled the old ideological-political conflict between the Islamic and *kebangsaan* groups concerning the nature of the political relationship between Islam and the state. Because of this, the question of Islam as the ideological basis of the state resurfaced during the campaign period for the 1955 general elections. Led by Masyumi, the Islamic group reintroduced the notion of Islam as the ideological basis of the state as a major campaign theme.[145] As noted by many, this agenda was then fought vigorously in the Constituent Assembly (1956–59).[146]

The fact that the Islamic group controlled only 43.5 per cent of the seats made it difficult to assess their determination in pushing ahead the idea of Islam as the ideological basis of the state. In spite of this, some speculation can be made along religious and political lines. Religiously, as one of their leaders indicated, they were driven by a transcendental obligation to bring the holistic nature of Islam into reality. Politically, the fact that their electoral strength had not brought about ideological success demonstrated that they were, nevertheless, politicians faithful to their campaign promise. At best, it was intended, while accepting Pancasila as the state ideology, to serve as a bargaining chip for lesser goals (for example, the reinstatement of the Jakarta Charter, Islam as the state religion).[147]

From 1950 to about 1959, a decade which was known as the period of constitutional democracy, Indonesia operated under the 1950 Constitution. In spite of the fact that the country had experienced several different constitutional arrangements, the 1950 Constitution was still considered provisional.[148] Accordingly, it could be concluded that the principal task of the Constituent Assembly was indeed to fashion a permanent constitutional arrangement.

It was within this legal-constitutional framework that members of the Assembly engaged in the heated ideological-political debate. Though not without difficulties, this Assembly was able to complete most of its tasks. During its two and a half years of existence (November 1956–June 1959), the Assembly finished 90 per cent of its duties,[149] including decisions on human rights, the policy principles of the state, and the form of government.[150] All these subjects were considered substantive elements of the constitution.

Unfortunately, the debate on the basis of the state did not go as well as the deliberations of these other issues. In fact, it contributed greatly to the impasse of the Constituent Assembly. The uncompromising and hostile nature of the debate appeared to have been responsible for driving the parties further apart. As assessed by Adnan Buyung Nasution, "[t]he debate was ideological, absolutist, and antagonistic, so that the parties [especially the Islamic and *kebangsaan* groups] did not come close to each other but on the contrary were driven farther apart".[151] Three ideological streams evolved during the debates on the ideological basis of the state: Islam, Pancasila, and socio-economy. But, considering the history of the country's ideological debates, the real contest occurred only between proponents of the first two ideological currents.[152]

In this discourse the Islamic group basically restated their pre-independent ideological-political aspirations to establish a state which was unequivocally behind Islam. Basing their arguments on (1) the holistic nature of Islam, (2) the superiority of Islam over other worldly ideologies, and (3) the fact that Islam was adhered to by the majority of the country's population, they proposed that Islam be adopted as the state ideology.[153] Led by Mohammad Natsir, Kasman Singodimedjo, Zaenal Abidin

Ahmad, Isa Anshari, and K.H. Masjkur, they took a strong stance with regard to the holistic nature of Islam. They believed that Islam regulated every aspect of life. Accordingly, in their view, a state which was basically an organization comprising the whole society and all its institutions, which had the authority to make and implement the binding rules, could make no exception but to base itself on the divine principles.

Based on these theological-ideological perceptions, they considered Pancasila as essentially a secular (*ladiniyah*) ideology with no definite religious source. Though its first principle recognized the importance of the belief in one God, its conceptualization was actually based on a sociological necessity rather than religious divinity. In other words, it was a man-made conception of God which could change any time, depending on circumstances. In short, in their view, Pancasila was neutral and colourless, and its five principles had no relationship with interdependence.[154] Thus, they rejected the notion of Pancasila as the basis of state. Voicing his objection, Mohammad Natsir declared:

> Pantja Sila as a state philosophy is for us obscure and has nothing to say to the soul of [the] Muslim community which already possesses a definite, clear, and complete ideology, one which burns in the hearts of the Indonesian people as a living inspiration and source of strength, namely Islam. To exchange the Islamic ideology for Pantja Sila is, for Muslims, like leaping from the solid earth into empty space, into a vacuum.[155]

The response of the proponents of Pancasila was no less antagonistic. In line with their earlier reasoning, individuals like Roeslan Abdulgani, who himself is a Muslim with a *kebangsaan* ideological and political orientation, refused to accept the idea that Pancasila was a purely neutral concept, let alone a secular ideology. The facts that Pancasila contained a principle such as belief in one God and that the state had an agency which regulated issues related to religious matters (that is, the Department of Religious Affairs) were clear indications that Indonesia was not based on a secular ideology. More importantly, he believed that Pancasila contained Islamic (though not only Islamic) elements.[156]

In the context of Pancasila as the state ideology, many *kebangsaan* figures saw Pancasila as, given the heterogeneity of Indonesia's religious community, a common platform. For PNI politicians and Christian activists such as Arnold Mononutu, Pancasila was a viable ideological synthesis for those with different religious faiths. Should Islam become the basis of state, they were especially concerned about the place of other religious groups in the archipelago. In any case this would entail an image of constitutional discrimination.[157]

Some based their objections to Islam as the basis of state on its workability. Considering the socio-religious heterogeneity of the country's population, they doubted that Islam could serve as an ideological-political world view for all the people. In the meantime Pancasila, regardless of its imperfectness, had proved itself to be a viable common ideological ground for all Indonesians.[158] Others rejected Islam for fear that its law might be imposed on all Indonesians.[159] For these reasons, in response to Mohammad Natsir's statement regarding the position of Muslims *vis-à-vis* Pancasila, Arnold Mononutu stated:

> From the Pancasila ideology to an Indonesian state based on Islam, for Christians is like leaping from the earth, which is calm and peaceful for implementing their religion as *volwaardig* Indonesians, into empty space, *vacuum*, with no air.[160]

With these absolutist stances, a compromise would certainly have been difficult to establish. Even after the Islamic group backed down from its original proposal for Islam as the basis of state and was prepared to settle for the reinstatement of the Jakarta Charter, the conflict had already created a stalemate within the Constituent Assembly. Given their electoral strength, neither group had the necessary votes (two-thirds majority) to pass its ideological preference.[161] Likewise, the government proposal to return to the 1945 Constitution did not receive the required support.[162] All of these circumstances led President Soekarno, with the support of the army, to issue a decree for the return to the 1945 Constitution. This manoeuvre, a strategy which he apparently had aspired to for a long time, provided him with a strong executive power to control the state.[163]

Once again, the Islamic group was symbolically defeated. Beyond this symbolic subjugation, during Soekarno's period of Guided Democracy the legalistic/formalistic articulations of Islamic political ideas and practices, especially with regard to the idea of Islam as the ideological basis of the state, began to exhibit their more negative ramifications. With the exception of NU, which quickly redirected its political orientation[164] and accepted Soekarno's Manipol Usdek,[165] the political strength of Islam was drastically reduced. Masyumi leaders in particular, who since the beginning of Indonesia's ideological discourse were considered ardent proponents of an Islamic state, were detained in prison because of their continued opposition to the regime. And finally, on the grounds that several of its prominent leaders (for example,, Mohammad Natsir and Sjafruddin Prawiranegara) participated in the PRRI rebellion, Soekarno dissolved Masyumi in 1960.[166]

THE NEW ORDER PERIOD:
THE CONTAINMENT OF ISLAMIC POLITICAL IDEALISM
AND ACTIVISM

With the ascension of the New Order regime following the PKI's abortive coup in 1965, hopes ran high for many leaders and activists of political Islam. This was especially the case with respect to many former Masyumi leaders and their constituents who had been politically persecuted during the Guided Democracy period. Being an important part of the coalition forces (for example, the military, functional groups, student organizations, socio-religious associations), which had brought down the Communist Party and Soekarno's regime, they anticipated the return of Islam in the discourse of national politics. The New Order regime's move to release former Masyumi figures, including Mohammad Natsir, Sjafruddin Prawiranegara, Mohammad Roem, Kasman Singodimedjo, Prawoto Mangkusasmito, and Hamka, detained by Soekarno further raised their expectations of the imminent rehabilitation of Masyumi. For this, a committee known as Badan Kordinasi Amal Muslimin, or Co-ordinating Body of Muslim Activities, was set up to pursue this particular cause.[167]

But soon it became obvious that the New Order regime was not about to grant rehabilitation for Masyumi. Reportedly, in an attempt to solidify its role as the defender of Pancasila and the 1945 Constitution, in December 1966 the military stated that it

> would take firm steps against anyone, whichever side, what-
> ever group which will deviate from *Pantja Sila* and the 1945
> constitution as which has already been done by the Communist
> Party Revolt in Madiun, *Gestapu*, Darul Islam/Islamic Army
> of Indonesia [a fanatical Islamic movement — most powerful
> in the 1950s and deriving its base of support in West Java —
> which attempted to create an Islamic state by force of arms]
> and Masyumi — Socialist Party of Indonesia … .[168]

In fact, in early 1967 Soeharto himself had made it clear that "the army would not countenance the revival of the party [Masyumi]".[169]

With those statements, many felt that the prospects of Masyumi for being rehabilitated were closed. Obviously, the military remained suspicious towards political Islam. Armed encounters with several elements of political Islam in the past seemed to have played a decisive role in this regard. This was, as noted by Harold Crouch, especially true among "officers who had fought against the Darul Islam and other Muslim-inspired regional revolts". Likewise, those who had "participated in the central government's campaign against PRRI were extremely bitter about the Masyumi's 'treachery' in sympathising with, or at least not condemning, a revolt which cost the lives of 2,500 soldiers".[170]

These unexpected responses made many former Masyumi leaders and activists realize that the rehabilitation of their party was virtually impossible. Given the firm stance of the military leadership on this issue, many came to the realization that only by the willingness of Masyumi leaders to redefine their political agenda in more acceptable terms could their political representation in the New Order be ensured. In this regard the establishment of a new political organization (with the hope that this new party could reproduce Masyumi's political character and spirit) seemed to be their only choice. For this, in mid-1967 a Committee of Seven was formed to negotiate with the New Order government about the possibility of establishing a new party. This new political receptacle (*wadah*) was intended to "unite all Islamic strength and organizations which exist and which are not grouped in a party".[171]

With regard to this particular agenda, the New Order regime did not seem to stand in the way of these former Masyumi leaders. In spite of their firm rejection of Masyumi's rehabilitation, the New Order leadership was actually concerned about the future representation of the Islamic political constituents. They were especially worried that the lack of a political mechanism to articulate and aggregate their interests would create a deeper sense of frustration, which, in turn, would encourage them to resort to political extremism. Mainly because of this, the New Order government shared their goal for a new political organization. After a series of hard-fought battles, permission to form a new political party was eventually granted to former Masyumi constituents.

It is important to note, however, that the government's consent to the founding of a new party was not without limitations. Throughout the process, it was clear that the New Order regime wanted to curb the political activities of former Masyumi members, especially those of its leaders. Because of this, the new political organization was approved on condition that former senior Masyumi leaders not occupy leadership positions. Thus, on 20 February 1968 Partai Muslimin Indonesia (Parmusi, Indonesian Muslim Party) was founded under the leadership of Djarnawi Hadikusumo and Lukman Harun. Both were Muhammadiyah activists.[172]

The manner in which Parmusi was created, and the conditions imposed upon it, did not please many former Masyumi activists. They were dissatisfied with the "dearth of genuine leadership", especially with the lack of "men of great personal authority". For this reason, a plan was made to bring some former senior Masyumi figures into the party leadership. Therefore, it was not a coincidence that Mohammad Roem, a former Foreign Minister, Deputy Prime Minister, and top-ranking Masyumi leader, was elected as Parmusi's general chairman in the party's first congress, held in Malang in November 1968.[173]

To their dismay, this leadership choice was unacceptable to the New Order regime. But rather than running the risk of being dissolved, the party backed down, accepting the pre-congress leadership structure. In spite of this, the influence of former senior Masyumi leaders within the party remained strong. Parmusi's younger leaders continued to respect the former senior Masyumi leaders, as described by Harold Crouch:

> Especially after the passage of the electoral laws at the end of 1969, they turned increasingly to former Masyumi figures, both in Jakarta and in the regions, to mobilize support for the Parmusi. A General Elections Committee was established, headed by Roem, former Masyumi figures were appointed to leadership position in the regions, and preparations were made to include senior Masyumi leaders in the party's list of candidates for the election. At the same time, Parmusi spokesmen in the regions adopted an increasingly critical line toward the government.[174]

Reportedly, because of these factors (that is, the growing influence of former senior Masyumi figures in Parmusi as well as the party's critical stance towards the government) John (Jaelani) Naro, one of the party chairmen, "who was considered close to President Suharto's right-hand man, Major General Ali Murtopo", launched a coup in 1970. More than anything else, this internal upheaval paved the way for the government's deeper penetration of the party's leadership. It resulted in the replacement of Djarnawi Hadikusumo by M.S. Mintaredja — one of President Soeharto's Cabinet members with a strong Islamic background.[175]

The formation of Parmusi did not seem to indicate any change with regard to the relationship between the leaders and activists of political Islam and the New Order's governing elites. The circumstances surrounding the emergence of this party suggested that the New Order government was, at best, as wary as its predecessor with regard to the ideological and political articulations of the Islamic group. This became increasingly obvious when the New Order regime rejected (1) the demands of the Islamic group for the legalization of the Jakarta Charter during the Majelis Permusyawaratan Rakyat Sementara (MPRS, Provisional People's Consultative Assembly) session in 1968; and (2) the holding of an Indonesian Muslim Congress (Kongres Umat Islam Indonesia) in that year.[176]

The implications of these early developments were far-reaching. In the first place, the hopes of the Islamic group for a greater role in the New Order regime evaporated. More distressingly, they planted even deeper seeds of mutual distrust and hostility between the leaders and activists of political Islam and the New Order's governing elites. In this regard suffice it to say that while the former perceived the latter as gradually moving towards secularization and sympathy to Christian interests,[177] the latter considered the former's support for Pancasila as expedient and suspect.[178]

The strength of political Islam was further seriously eroded by the result of the 1971 general election, in part because through an orchestrated manoeuvre, the New Order regime was able to create "conditions that were very unfavourable for the political parties".[179] In this general election the government used the Sekretariat Bersama Golongan Karya (Sekber Golkar, Joint Secretariat of Functional Group) as their electoral machine. They reinvigorated and expanded this former coalition force to counterbalance PKI's influence in the government to become a viable political contender. But the obsession to win a landslide victory in this election led the New Order's military-dominated regime to undertake a combination of coercive and co-optative measures to influence the outcome.

Both the armed forces and the bureaucracy became the backbones of Golkar. Through his infamous decision, Amir Machmud, then the Minister of Home Affairs, issued a ministerial regulation (Permen 12/1969) "which was directed towards 'purification' of Golkar representation in provincial and local legislatures". This decision stipulated that "all members of the functional groups designation in provincial and local bodies would be replaced if they were in fact affiliated with political parties [PNI, NU, Parmusi, PSII, Perti, etc.]".[180] In addition, he issued a governmental regulation (PP 6/1970) which had enormous consequences on the election, because it specified that

> certain categories of civil servants were forbidden membership of political parties: ABRI members, all civilian employees of the Defence Ministry, judges and public prosecutors, a small number of specified officials including the governor and deputy governor of the Bank of Indonesia, and other important office-holders to be stipulated by the president.[181]

These government regulations were used to create *monoloyalitas* (monoloyalty). The regulations stipulated that civil servants were prohibited from carrying out party activities or becoming members of certain political parties. Instead, they were pressed to remain loyal to the government which employed them or face failed promotion, if not dismissal. These moves, of course, guaranteed exclusive support for Golkar.[182]

In the meantime the military intimidated both party leaders and voters, especially at the local level. Those who voiced strong criticism of the government, particularly on issues related to the holding of the election, were arrested or questioned by the military authorities. In this regard some have observed that former PKI supporters were the most susceptible to intimidation. They were often "called into subdistrict military headquarters and instructed to vote for Golkar".[183]

With all of these measures, coupled with the restricted campaign issues (for example, parties were forbidden to use Soekarno's name [PNI] and Islamic sentiment which might stir controversy with regard to Pancasila as the state ideology [NU, Parmusi, PSII, Perti] as the campaign themes) as well as the procedure for candidate selection and screening imposed by the government,[184] Golkar was able to score a resounding victory, gaining 62.8 per cent of the votes. Because it was relatively free from outside intervention, NU was able to gain 18.67 per cent — slightly better than its 1955 performance (18.4 per cent). But Parmusi, the often perceived Masyumi successor, was severely inhibited, registering only 5.36 per cent (in 1955 Masyumi obtained 20.9 per cent). Two other small Islamic parties (PSII and Perti) also lost support. While obtaining 2.9 per cent and 1.3 per cent respectively in 1955, they won only 2.39 per cent and 0.7 per cent in 1971.[185]

Post-1971 election developments only exacerbated the sense of frustration within the Islamic political community. The electoral defeat did not manifest itself only in the reduction of Islamic representation in the parliament. It was also evident in the new Cabinet composition, where the involvement of Islamic political figures was substantially curtailed. One of the most notable cases in point was the removal of the NU from the leadership of the Department of Religious Affairs. This long-time political and bureaucratic base of NU was entrusted to Mukti Ali, a modernist Muslim and professor at Yogyakarta's State Institute for Islamic Studies (IAIN) who had no affiliation with the existing political parties.

Finally, the old construct of Islamic parties, especially in terms of body politics (that is, Islamic political party), diminished when the New Order government restructured the party system in January 1973. With the exception of Golkar, the government pressured the nine existing parties to merge into two new political parties. In this framework all four Islamic parties became Partai Persatuan Pembangunan (PPP, Development Unity Party). The other five, which basically comprised nationalist and Christian parties, were grouped into Partai Demokrasi Indonesia (PDI, Indonesia Democracy Party). Due to the presence of Islam as a common religion of its leaders and constituents, PPP was relatively more cohesive than PDI. In spite of this, however, PPP was plagued with internal disputes (an indication of the lack of an integrated fusion), which in turn affected its political performance.[186]

In spite of the New Order's continued process of depoliticization (following the 1971 election it was strengthened by the concept of the floating mass, in which party activities at the village and subdistrict levels were virtually banned), coupled with the regime's adoption of basically a non-competitive political system, PPP managed to secure more votes in the 1977 election (29.29 per cent compared with 27.12 per cent in 1971). But the continued friction within PPP, especially during John Naro's leadership (in addition to the government's intensified co-optative strategy to many prominent Muslim figures and intellectuals)[187] inhibited the electoral strength of PPP. Thus, in 1982 and 1987 PPP obtained only 27.78 per cent and 15.97 per cent respectively.[188]

The hostility of the Muslim community towards the state was also strengthened by a number of the New Order's policies perceived as offensive to their religious beliefs. In the early years of the New Order regime, Muslim leaders were particularly discontented with Ali Sadikin's (then the flamboyant governor of Jakarta) legalization of gambling.[189]

But what seemed to have aroused the ire of the larger segment of the Muslim community was the government's introduction of a marriage law in 1973, which was perceived by many as contradictory to Islamic teachings. Not surprisingly, the proposal provoked massive Muslim reactions; members of the parliament walked out and Muslim youths temporarily occupied the floor of the parliament. But a compromise was finally reached with the removal and/or modification of articles considered most disagreeable with Islamic principles.[190]

In 1978 the Muslim community was once again theologically offended. They resented the attempt of the regime during the Majelis Permusyawaratan Rakyat (MPR) session to elevate *aliran kepercayaan* (Javanese mysticism) to the position of a religion such as Islam and Christianity. Strong reactions by Muslim leaders and activists, including those in the parliament (especially from the PPP), led the regime to abort the idea.[191] Unwilling to challenge both the ritual and theological aspects of Islam, President Soeharto, himself a Muslim, refused to recognize *aliran kepercayaan* as a religion. In 1979 this mysticism stream was officially recognized as an element of Indonesian culture. Its supervision was therefore entrusted to the Department of Education and Culture instead of the Department of Religious Affairs.[192]

The final blow to the old construct of political Islam, especially in terms of its ideological symbolism, came in 1983. In spite of the New Order's massive campaigns to socialize Pancasila,[193] the government believed that certain socio-religious and political forces remained suspect with regard to their commitment to the state ideology. In the president's view, they were still "not trusting Pancasila one hundred percent".[194] In fact, Soeharto was also alarmed that "there were groups seeking to change Pancasila".[195] This viewpoint, coupled with a perception that religiously based ideological sentiments were partly responsible for the brutality of the 1982 election campaign (as exemplified in the Lapangan Banteng Affair),[196] led the government to enforce the idea of Pancasila as the sole basis (*asas tunggal*) of all existing political organizations (that is, Golkar, PPP, and PDI). In his annual address to the Dewan Perwakilan Rakyat (DPR, People's Representative Assembly), on 16 August 1982, President Soeharto proposed that "[a]ll social and political forces have to assert that their sole ideological basis is Pancasila".[197]

Succumbing to this ideological pressure, both PPP and PDI had no choice but to endorse Pancasila as their ideological bases. In the party congress held in August 1984, PPP replaced Islam with Pancasila as its ideological basis. Prior to the holding of the 1987 general election, the party also changed its symbol, from the Ka'bah (denoting the holy shrine in Mecca, where Muslims orient their faces during their five daily prayers) to the Bintang (Star, one of the five Pancasila symbols).[198]

Having secured compliance from the existing political organizations with regard to the idea of Pancasila as *asas tunggal*, the New Order regime pressured all socio-religious and student organizations to follow suit. When the new law on social organizations (Undang-Undang Keormasan) came into being in 1985, Islamic socio-religious and student organizations such as NU, Muhammadiyah, Majelis Ulama Indonesia (MUI, Indonesian Council of Ulama), Himpunan Mahasiswa Islam (HMI, Islamic University Student Association), Pergerakan Mahasiswa Islam Indonesia (PMII, Indonesian Islamic Student Movement), to name only some of them, had to adopt Pancasila as their organizational basis.[199]

These developments generated severe discontent among the larger part of Indonesia's Muslim community. They felt that not only had their leaders been left out of the mainstream national politics, but, to some extent, the country's political discourse did not reflect the fact that the majority of the archipelago's population was Muslim. For this, as bitter as it was, they felt that the New Order's military-dominated government had treated Muslim political leaders and activists, especially of Masyumi origin, "as *kutjing kurap* (cats with ring-worm)".[200] Understandably, many of them viewed the politics of *asas tunggal* as a further deliberate attempt on the part of the regime to depoliticize, if not to dethrone, Islam.[201]

For all of the above reasons, it was not surprising that the major opposition to the New Order regime, peaceful or otherwise, had frequently come from the leaders and activists of political Islam. As suggested before, suffice it to describe their political relationship as characterized by mutual hostility. The fact that this uneasy relationship remained intact throughout the 1970s and up to the mid-1980s provoked several fragmentary movements which were often waged under the banner of Islam.

In 1978 an unknown named Warman appointed himself as the inheritor of the spirit of Kartosuwirjo, the leader of West Java's Darul Islam movement executed for treason against the state in 1962. Supported by a handful of radicals, his movement endorsed violent measures.[202] In 1981 a young fanatic named Imran Muhammad Zein emerged to inflame the spirit of Islamic revolution in Indonesia. His activities included physical confrontation with local military officers (Cicendo, West Java) and the infamous hijacking of a domestic airliner (Garuda Woyla).[203]

It was largely these religious-political discontents that led to a number of violent incidents associated with Muslim activism in the mid-1980s (for example, the bombing of the Chinese-owned Bank Central Asia and the bombing of the Borobudur temple in Central Java). Most shocking was the bloody incident in Tanjung Priok — a destitute port area in the northern part of Jakarta — on 12 September 1984. In this case, as a response to two Military Sub-District Command (Koramil) officers' disrespectful acts (that is, entering As Sa'adah prayer house without taking off their shoes and smearing gutter water on the mosque wall) and arbitrary detainment of the local mosque activists, Muslims in the area staged a massive demonstration. Led by Amir Biki, an early supporter of the New Order and notable informal leader of the area, the crowd was met with the military's automatic weapons. No precise number of the toll is known. But "[e]stimates ran as many as 63 killed and more than 100 severely wounded. Families subsequently reported 171 as missing."[204] Following these incidents a number of Muslim figures such as Abdul Qadir Djaelani, H.M. Sanusi, Mawardi Noer, Salim Qadar, Usman Alhamidy, and A.M. Fatwa, to name only the most prominent ones, were incarcerated. They were charged, directly or otherwise, with inciting the affair.[205]

CONCLUDING REMARKS

From the lengthy discussion presented above, it is safe to argue that the antagonism between political Islam and the state was largely due to the former's legalistic and formalistic idealism and activism. The latter's political substance, conceptualized in a national-unitary construct of the state with Pancasila as its ideology, was perceived as a secular political arrangement. It is the formalistic expression of political Islam, as will be discussed in the next several chapters, that the new generation of Muslim intellectuals have tried to transform.

Notes

1.   Robert N. Bellah, "Islamic Tradition and the Problems of Modernization", *Beyond Belief: Essays on Religion in a Post-Traditionalist World* (Berkeley and Los Angeles: University of California Press, 1991), p. 162.

2.   The concept of "deconfessionalization" was introduced by C.A.O. Van Nieuwenhuijze. Drawn from the accommodationist tendency of the Netherlands' socio-cultural and political groupings, this concept calls for a "creative interpreta-tion of Islamic principles, in such a way as to reestablish their relevance for

twentieth-century life in Indonesia". More especially, deconfessionalization is a concept utilized to enhance the general acceptability of Muslim concepts to all parties involved "on the basis of common humane consideration". In short, with this concept, Muslims, in their interaction with other actors, are prepared to disentangle "their formal, [and] strictly dogmatic" orientations. And as such is "to give them a more general appeal and, at the same time, to guarantee that Muslims will still recognize them for what they are". See C.A.O. Van Nieuwenhuijze, "The Indonesian State and 'Deconfessionalized' Muslim Concepts", in his *Aspects of Islam in Post-Colonial Indonesia* (The Hague and Bandung: W. van Hoeve Ltd., 1958), pp. 180–243.

3.   According to Clifford Geertz, "*[a]bangan*, representing a stress on the animistic aspects of the over-all Javanese syncretism and broadly related to the peasant element in the population; *santri*, representing a stress on the Islamic aspects of the syncretism and generally related to the trading element (and to certain elements in the peasantry as well); ... ." See his *Religion of Java* (Chicago and London: University of Chicago Press, 1976), p. 6. In general, however, people tend to see *abangan* as a syncretist or less devout Muslim; and *santri* as an orthodox and devout Muslim. For different perceptions of this *abangan–santri* concept see Zamakhsyari Dhofier, "Santri–Abangan dalam Kehidupan Orang Jawa: Teropong dari Pesantren", *Prisma* 7, no. 5 (1978): 48–63; Mark R. Woodward, *Islam in Java: Normative Piety and Mysticism in the Sultanate of Yogyakarta* (Tucson: University of Arizona Press, 1989).

4.   See Muhammad Iqbal, *The Reconstruction of Religious Thought in Islam* (Lahore: Muhammad Ashraf, 1962).

5.   See H.A.R. Gibb, ed., *Whither Islam?: A Survey of Modern Movements in the Moslem World* (London: Victor Gollancz Ltd., 1932), p. 12.

6.   See Taha Abd al-Baqi Surur, *Dawla al-Qur'an* (Cairo: Daru al-Nadha Misr, 1972), p. 80; Muhammad Yusuf Musa, *Nizam al-Hukm fi al-Islam* (Cairo: Dar al-Kitab al-Arabi, 1963), p. 18. Cited from Ahmad Syafii Maarif, "Islam as the Basis of State: A Study of the Islamic Political Ideas as Reflected in the Constituent Assembly Debates in Indonesia" (Ph.D. dissertation, University of Chicago, 1983), p. 21. See also his *Islam dan Masalah Kenegaraan: Studi Tentang Percaturan dalam Konstituante* (Jakarta: LP3ES, 1985), p. 15.

7.   George Mc.T. Kahin, *Nationalism and Revolution in Indonesia* (Ithaca: Cornell University Press, 1952), p. 38.

8.   Fred R. von der Mehden, "Islam and the Rise of Nationalism in Indonesia" (Ph.D. dissertation, University of California Berkeley, 1957), p. 34.

9.   See Kahin, op. cit.; Mehden, op. cit.; Harry J. Benda, *The Crescent and the Rising Sun: Indonesian Islam under the Japanese Occupation 1942-1945* (The Hague and Bandung: W. van Hoeve Ltd., 1958); Ahmad Timur Jaylani, "The Sarekat Islam Movement: Its Contribution to Indonesian Nationalism" (M.A. thesis, McGill University, 1959); Robert Van Niel, *The Emergence of the Modern Indonesian Elite* (The Hague: W. van Hoeve, Ltd., 1960); Deliar Noer, *The Modernist Muslim Movement in Indonesia 1900–1942* (Oxford, New York, and Jakarta: Oxford University Press, 1978).

10. Kahin, op. cit., pp. 65–66.

11. According to Kahin, within four years of its existence, Sarekat Islam had registered 360,000 members. By 1919 the membership had reached almost two and a half million. See his *Nationalism and Revolution in Indonesia*, pp. 65–66.

12. Benda, op. cit., pp. 41–42.

13. Ruth McVey, "Faith as the Outsider: Islam in Indonesian Politics", in *Islam in the Political Process*, edited by James P. Piscatori (Cambridge: Cambridge University Press, 1983), p. 200.

14. See Mehden, op. cit., pp. 163–95; Benda, op. cit., pp. 54–60; Noer, op. cit., pp. 112–53, 247–75.

15. For a further account, see Mehden, op. cit., pp. 157–62. See also Noer, op. cit., pp. 119-26.

16. Kahin, op. cit., p. 70.

17. Kahin, op. cit., p. 71. See also Mehden, op. cit., p. 126; Noer, op. cit., pp. 121–22.

18. Bernard H.M. Vlekke, *Nusantara: A History of Indonesia* (The Hague and Bandung: W. van Hoeve Ltd., 1959), p. 353.

19. Kahin, op. cit., p. 71.

20. Kahin, op. cit., p. 71.

21. Maarif, "Islam as the Basis of State", p. 135. See also his *Islam dan Masalah Kenegaraan*, p. 87.

22. Vlekke, op. cit., pp. 355–56.

23. Kahin, op. cit., p. 73.

24. Kahin, op. cit., pp. 72–73; Mehden, op. cit., pp. 108–11, 129-30, 150-55; Vlekke, op. cit., p. 359.

25. Mehden, op. cit., pp. 139-56.

26. Mehden, op. cit., p. 155; Vlekke, op. cit., p. 359; Noer, op. cit., p. 125.

27. Mehden, op. cit., p. 124.

28. Mehden, op. cit., p. 156.

29. Noer, op. cit., pp. 132–33.

30. Noer, op. cit., pp. 139-40.

31. Noer, op. cit., pp. 136–37.

32. Noer, op. cit., pp. 142–46.

33. See Mehden, op. cit., pp. 163–95.

34. Kahin, op. cit., p. 90.

35. Kahin, op. cit., p. 90.

36. Given the historical circumstances and the fact that the primary leaders (if not the majority of the members) of the *kebangsaan* group consisted of Muslim individuals, I tend to see these two groups in the light of political (not religious) categories.

Many, however, as suggested in chapter 1, are inclined to view these two groups in a religious light, by alternating the terms "Islamic" and "nationalist" with *santri* (devout Muslim) and *abangan* (less devout Muslim); thereby, characterizing Mohammad Natsir as *santri* and Soekarno as *abangan*. In my view, the fundamental differences between the Muslims who aspired for the development of Islam as a political category and the Muslims who favoured Islam as a moral or ethical underpinning in their ideological-political ventures lay not so much on the degree of religious devotion (or faith), but on the way they interpreted and understood the messages of Islam. Considering the polyinterpretability of Islam, this is perfectly legitimate. Therefore, even having to reject the idea of an Islamic state, individuals like Soekarno and Hatta were no less Islamic than their Muslim counterparts who strived for an Islamic state.

37. *Fadjar Asia*, 18 and 20 August 1928. Cited from Noer, op. cit., p. 253. See also Bernhard Dahm, *Sukarno and the Struggle for Indonesian Independence* (Ithaca and London: Cornell University Press, 1969), p. 68.

38. Soekarno, *Nationalism, Islam and Marxism*, translated by Karel H. Warouw and Peter D. Weldon, with an introduction by Ruth McVey (Ithaca: Modern Indonesia Project, Southeast Asia Program, Cornell University, 1984), p. 39.

39. Noer, op. cit., pp. 253–57; Dahm, op. cit., p. 175.

40. For a treatment of Persatuan Islam, see Howard M. Federspiel, *Persatuan Islam: Islamic Reform in Twentieth Century Indonesia* (Ithaca: Modern Indonesia Project, Southeast Asia Program, Cornell University, 1970).

41. Noer, op. cit., p. 259.

42. Natsir attended Hollandsch Inlansche School (HIS, Dutch native school), Meer Unitgebreid Lager Onderwijs (MULO, extended primary education, junior high school), and Algemeene Middlebare School (AMS, public secondary school). See Peter Burns, *Revelation and Revolution: Natsir and the Pancasila* (Townsville: Southeast Asian Monograph Series no. 9, Committee of South-East Asian Studies, James Cook University of North Queensland, 1981), p. 3.

43. *Pandji Islam* 6, no. 4 (23 January 1939). Cited from Noer, op. cit., p. 276.

44. *Pembela Islam,* no. 41 (January 1932). Cited from Noer, op. cit., p. 263.

45. *Pembela Islam*, no. 36 (October 1931). Cited from Noer, op. cit., p. 260.

46. *Pembela Islam*, no. 42 (January 1932). Cited from Federspiel, op. cit., p. 89.

47. Noer, op. cit., p. 276.

48. Soekarno, op. cit., p. 42. See also Noer, op. cit., p. 255; Dahm, op. cit., pp. 68–69.

49. Dahm, op. cit., p. 176.

50. Soekarno, op. cit., p. 41.

51. Under the leadership of Iljas Ja'kub and Muchtar Luthfi of West Sumatra, this organization based its nationalist movement on Islam and *kebangsaan*. See Noer, op. cit., p. 263.

52. Noer, op. cit., p. 264.

53. His relevant essays included: "Memudakan Pengertian Islam" [Rejuvenating our understanding of Islam]; "Apa Sebab Turki Memisah Agama dari Negara?" [What makes Turkey separate religion from the state?]; "Saya Kurang Dinamis" [I am not dynamic enough]; "Masyarakat Onta dan Masyarakat Kapal Udara" [Camel society and aircraft society]; "Islam Sontolojo" [Despicable Islam]. Reprinted in Soekarno's *Dibawah Bendera Revolusi*, vol. 1 (Jakarta: Panitia Penerbitan Dibawah Bendera Revolusi, 1964), pp. 369–500.

54. Soekarno, "Saya Kurang Dinamis", *Dibawah Bendera Revolusi*, p. 452.

55. Ibid., p. 453.

56. Ibid., p. 452.

57. See his "Apa Sebab Turki Memisah Agama dari Negara?", *Dibawah Bendera Revolusi*, pp. 407–8.

58. Initially published by Persatuan Islam in 1936. Reprinted in *Dibawah Bendera Revolusi*, pp. 325–44. Consisting of twelve letters, it originated from his religious-political correspondence with Persis leader Ahmad Hassan between December 1934 and October 1936 while he was on exile in the remote island of Endeh as the result of his nationalist activities. During this time, thanks to such communication coupled with intensive readings of Islamic literatures, Soekarno converted himself from "a soul which is only superficially Islamic into a convinced one" (his last letter to Ahmad Hassan, dated 17 October 1936).

59. Soekarno, *Dibawah Bendera Revolusi*, p. 334.

60. Soekarno was particularly impressed with Ameer Ali's *Spirit of Islam*, a historical treatise on the evolution of the ideals of Islam, published in the early 1920s.

61. For a fuller account, see Soekarno's "Memudakan Pengertian Islam", *Dibawah Bendera Revolusi*, pp. 369-402. See also his "Masyarakat Onta dan Masyarakat Kapal Udara" and "Islam Sontolojo", *Dibawah Bendera Revolusi*, pp. 483–91, 493–500.

62. Soekarno, "Apa Sebab Turki Memisah Agama dari Negara", *Dibawah Bendera Revolusi*, pp. 404–7.

63. Beirut: Dar Maktabah al-Hayah, 1966.

64. Soekarno, "Apa Sebab Turki Memisah Agama dari Negara", *Dibawah Bendera Revolusi*, p. 407.

65. See Mohammad Natsir, "Persatuan Agama dengan Negara", *Capita Selecta*, (Jakarta: Bulan Bintang, 1973), pp. 429-95.

66. See Mohammad Natsir, "Islam dan Kebudayaan", *Capita Selecta*, p. 15. For Gibb's viewpoint, see his *Whither Islam?*, p. 12.

67. See his "Persatuan Agama dengan Negara", *Capita Selecta*, pp. 436–37.

68. Mohammad Natsir, "Arti Agama dalam Negara", *Capita Selecta*, p. 437.

69. Ibid., p. 441.

70. Ibid., p. 437.

71. Ibid., p. 442.

72. Mohammad Natsir, "Islam 'Demokrasi'?", *Capita Selecta*, p. 452.

73. Mohammad Natsir, "Mungkinkah Qur'an Mengatur Negara?", *Capita Selecta*, pp. 447–55.

74. Noer, op. cit., p. 323.

75. Benda, op. cit., p. 198.

76. Daniel S. Lev, *Islamic Courts in Indonesia: A Study in the Political Bases of Legal Institutions* (Berkeley, Los Angeles, and London: University of California Press, 1972), p. 34.

77. Ibid., p. 34.

78. Benda, op. cit., p. 201.

79. B.J. Boland, *The Struggle of Islam in Modern Indonesia* (The Hague: Martinus Nijhoff, 1971), p. 9.

80. Benda, op. cit., p. 202.

81. Lev, op. cit., p. 34.

82. M.A. Aziz, *Japan's Colonialism and Indonesia* (The Hague: Martinus Nijhoff, 1955), p. 206.

83. Functioning as "an embryonic Cabinet", its members included Abikusno Tjokrosujoso, Buntaran Martoatmodjo, Ki Hadjar Dewantara, M. Hatta, Rasjid, Samsi, R.M. Sartono, Singgih, Soekardjo, Soewandi, Supomo, and Woerjaningrat. They were responsible for providing answers to the administration's questions on issues related to Islamic affairs. According to Lev, the majority of these individuals were from the *kebangsaan* group. See his *Islamic Courts in Indonesia*, p. 35.

84. As of May 1945, this committee consisted of sixty-two members. Out of this number, at most only eleven seemed to represent the Islamic group. They included Ki Bagus Hadikusumo, Abdul Kahar Muzakkir, H. Agus Salim, K.H. Abdul Halim, K.H. Masjkur, H. Ahmad Sanusi, K.H. Mas Mansjur, Abikusno Tjokrosujoso, Sukiman, K.H.A. Wachid Hasjim, and A. Baswedan. For a fuller list, see Muhammad Yamin, *Naskah Persiapan Undang-Undang Dasar 1945*, vol. 1 (Jakarta: Yayasan Prapanca, 1959), p. 60.

85. Lev, op. cit., pp. 34–41.

86. Ibid., p. 39.

87. Quoted from Lev, op. cit., p. 40.

88. Boland, op. cit., p. 20.

89. Ibid., p. 20.

90. Ibid., p. 20.

91. Ibid., p. 21. Italics are added.

92. Ibid., pp. 21–22. On the origins of Soekarno's Pancasila see his *The Birth of Pancasila: An Outline of the Five Principles of the Indonesian State* (Jakarta: Ministry of Information, 1958).

93. The first eight members were Muslims with different political outlook. The first four were from the *kebangsaan* group, while the latter four were from the Islamic group. Maramis was a Christian who shared the ideological inclination of the *kebangsaan* group.

94. For a full treatment on the Jakarta Charter, see Saifuddin Anshari, *The Jakarta Charter 1945: The Struggle for an Islamic Constitution in Indonesia* (Kuala Lumpur: Muslim Youth Movement of Malaysia [ABIM], 1979).

95. The phrase is from Lev, op. cit., p. 42.

96. Boland, op. cit., p. 30; Anshari, op. cit., p. 21.

97. Boland, op. cit., p. 31.

98. Ibid., p. 30.

99. Ibid., p. 33.

100. Deliar Noer, *Partai Islam di Pentas Nasional 1945–1965* (Jakarta: Pustaka Utama Grafiti, 1987), p. 40. See also Mohammad Hatta, *Sekitar Proklamasi* (Jakarta: Tintamas, 1969), pp. 57–59.

101. Boland, op. cit., p. 36. See also Anshari, op. cit., p. 30; Noer, *Partai Islam di Pentas Nasional*, pp. 40-41.

102. Noer, *Partai Islam di Pentas Nasional*, p. 41.

103. Mavis Rose, *Indonesia Free: A Political Biography of Mohammad Hatta* (Ithaca: Cornell Modern Indonesia Project, Southeast Asia Program, Cornell University, 1987), p. 112.

104. Noer, *Partai Islam di Pentas Nasional*, p. 43.

105. *Risalah Perundingan 1957* (n.p.: Konstituante Republik Indonesia, n.d.), p. 325. Cited from Adnan Buyung Nasution, *The Aspiration for Constitutional Government in Indonesia: A Socio-legal Study of the Indonesian Konstituante 1956–1959* (Jakarta: Pustaka Sinar Harapan, 1992), p. 106.

106. Herbert Feith, *The Decline of Constitutional Democracy in Indonesia* (Ithaca: Cornell University Press, 1962), p. 284.

107. The origin of Masyumi remains a matter of controversy. Some have argued that it was simply a continuation of the Japanese-sponsored Masyumi. (See, for instance, Harold Crouch, "Indonesia", in *The Politics of Islamic Reassertion*, edited by Mohammed Ayoob (London: Croom Helm, 1981), p. 193; Boland, op. cit., p. 42.) Others, despite the obvious duplication in name, considered it a "new and distinct organization". (See, for instance, Kahin, op. cit., p. 156; Noer, *Partai Islam di Pentas Nasional*, p. 47.)

108. W.F. Wertheim, "Islam before and after the Election", in *Indonesia after the 1971 Elections,* edited by Lee Oey Hong (London and Kuala Lumpur: Hull Monograph Series on Southeast Asia, no. 5, Oxford University Press, 1974), p. 91. See also his "Indonesian Moslems under Sukarno and Suharto: Majority with Minority Mentality", in *Studies on Indonesian Islam* (Townsville: Occasional Paper no. 19, Centre for Southeast Asian Studies, James Cook University of North Queensland, 1986), p. 15.

109.   Feith, op. cit., pp. 274–75.

110.   Ibid., pp. 122–28, 146–55, and 434–35.

111.   Ibid., p. 284.

112.   Mohammad Natsir, *Some Observations Concerning the Role of Islam in National and International Affairs* (Ithaca: Southeast Asia Program, Department of Far Eastern Studies, Cornell University, 1954), p. 1.

113.   See Benedict R.O'G. Anderson, "Old State, New Society: Indonesia's New Order in Comparative Historical Perspective", *Journal of Asian Studies* 42, no. 3 (May 1983): 480-86; R. William Liddle, "Soeharto's Indonesia: Personal Rule and Political Institutions", *Pacific Affairs* 58, no. 1 (Spring 1985): 71–85; Arief Budiman, "The Emergence of Bureaucratic Capitalist State in Indonesia", in *Reflections on Development in Southeast Asia*, edited by Lim Teck Ghee (Singapore: Institute of Southeast Asian Studies, 1988), pp. 115–18.

114.   Joel S. Migdal, *Strong Societies and Weak States: State-Society Relations and State Capabilities in the Third World* (Princeton: Princeton University Press, 1988), p. 261.

115.   The terms within quotes are from ibid., p. 4.

116.   For a treatment on these insurgencies, see Herbert Feith and Daniel S. Lev, "The End of Indonesian Rebellion", *Pacific Affairs* 36, no. 1 (Spring 1963); John D. Legge, *Central Authority and Regional Autonomy in Indonesia* (Ithaca: Cornell University Press, 1961); Audrey Kahin, ed., *Regional Dynamics of the Indonesian Revolution: Unity from Diversity* (Honolulu: Hawaii University Press, 1985); Nazaruddin Sjamsuddin, *The Republican Revolt: A Study of the Acehnese Rebellion* (Singapore: Institute of Southeast Asian Studies, 1985); C. van Dijk, *Rebellion under the Banner of Islam: The Darul Islam in Indonesia* (The Hague: Martinus Nijhoff, 1981); Eric Eugene Morris, "Islam and Politics in Aceh: A Study of Center-Periphery Relations in Indonesia" (Ph.D. dissertation, Cornell University, 1983); Barbara S. Harvey, *Permesta: Half A Rebellion* (Ithaca: Southeast Asia Program, Cornell University, 1977); Ichlasul Amal, *Regional and Central Government in Indonesian Politics: West Sumatra and South Sulawesi 1949-1979* (Yogyakarta: Gadjah Mada University Press, 1992).

117.   Boland, op. cit., p. 57. See also Karl D. Jackson, *Traditional Authority, Islam, and Rebellion: A Study of Indonesian Political Behavior* (Berkeley, Los Angeles, and London: University of California Press, 1980), pp. 9–10.

118.   Jackson, op. cit., p. 10.

119.   Ibid., p. 10.

120.   C.A.O. Van Nieuwenhuijze, "The Dar ul-Islam Movement in Western Java Till 1949", *Aspects of Islam in Post-Colonial Indonesia* (The Hague and Bandung: W. van Hoeve Ltd., 1958), pp. 168–71. See also Boland, op. cit., p. 58; Jackson, op. cit., pp. 10-11.

121.   Nieuwenhuijze, op. cit., p. 173. See also Jackson, op. cit., pp. 11–12.

122.   Boland, op. cit., p. 59.

123.   Jackson, op. cit., p. 12.

124.   Ibid., p. 15.

125.   Boland, op. cit., pp. 63–64.

126.   Ibid., p. 65.

127.   In his study on the Acehnese rebellion, Nazaruddin Sjamsuddin noted that "[t]he national revolution had made it possible for the Acehnese to regain autonomy in the social, economic, and political fields, because the revolutionary Central Government was incapable of interfering in Acehnese local affairs". And "[t]he fact that the Acehnese had succeeded in preventing Dutch reoccupation of their region reinforced their sense of autonomy". See his *The Republican Revolt*, p. 2.

128.   Boland, op. cit., p. 72.

129.   Ibid., p. 72.

130.   Sjamsuddin, op. cit., p. 2.

131.   For a full treatment on this line of argument, see Morris, op. cit., especially pp. 1–18.

132.   Boland, op. cit., p. 74.

133.   Natsir, *Some Observations Concerning the Role of Islam in National and International Affairs*, p. 1.

134.   Feith, op. cit., p. 273.

135.   Ibid., pp. 424–37. For a fuller account on general elections, see Herbert Feith, *The Indonesian Elections of 1955* (Ithaca: Modern Indonesia Project, Southeast Asia Program, Cornell University, 1957).

136.   Feith, *The Decline of Constitutional Democracy in Indonesia*, pp. 274–75.

137.   *Sin Po*, 19 April 1952. Cited from Feith, *The Decline of Constitutional Democracy in Indonesia*, p. 275.

138.   *Antara*, 29 January 1953. Cited from Feith, *The Decline of Constitutional Democracy in Indonesia*, p. 281. See also Noer, *Partai Islam di Pentas Nasional*, pp. 264–65.

139.   Feith, *The Decline of Constitutional Democracy in Indonesia*, pp. 281–82.

140.   Herbert Feith, "Dynamics of Guided Democracy", in *Indonesia*, edited by Ruth McVey (New Haven: Southeast Asia Studies, Yale University, by arrangement with Human Relations Area Files Press, 1963), p. 317.

141.   Feith, *The Decline of Constitutional Democracy in Indonesia,* p. 282.

142.   Ibid., p. 282.

143.   Josef A. Mestenhauser, "Ideologies in Conflict in Indonesia, 1945–1955" (Ph.D. dissertation, University of Minnesota, 1960), p. 144. Cited from Feith, *The Decline of Constitutional Democracy in Indonesia*, pp. 284–85.

144.   Feith, "Dynamics of Guided Democracy", p. 317.

145.   For a further account, see Feith, *The Indonesian Elections of 1955*, pp. 1–37.

146. See, for instance, Anshari, *The Jakarta Charter 1945;* Maarif, "Islam as the Basis of State"; Nasution, *The Aspiration for Constitutional Government in Indonesia.*

147. See Noer, *Partai Islam di Pentas Nasional*, pp. 266–67. Revealing their conversations with Prawoto Mangkusasmito, a former chairman of Masyumi, a number of my interviewees in Jakarta and Bandung confirmed this viewpoint.

148. From 1945 to about 1959, Indonesia experienced three different forms of state as well as constitutional arrangements. (1) From 1945–49 Indonesia was a national unitary state under the 1945 Constitution. (2) Following the transfer of sovereignty from the Dutch in 1949, Indonesia became a federal state under the name of the Republic of the United State of Indonesia (RUSI) with the 1949 Constitution. (3) The unitarist move in 1950 made Indonesia once again a national unitary state under the 1950 Constitution. See Kahin, *Nationalism and Revolution in Indonesia*, pp. 446–69; Feith, *The Decline of Constitutional Democracy in Indonesia*, pp. 1–99.

149. This was based on a statement made by the chairman of the Constituent Assembly, Wilopo. See Muhammad Yamin, *Naskah Persiapan Undang-Undang Dasar 1945*, vol. 2 (Jakarta: Yayasan Prapanca, 1959), p. 510. See also Noer, *Partai Islam di Pentas Nasional*, pp. 265 and 267.

150. Nasution, op. cit., pp. 42–44.

151. Ibid., p. 41.

152. The confrontation of ideas between proponents of Islam and Pancasila was recorded in *Tentang Dasar Negara Republik Indonesia dalam Konstituante*, vols. 1–3 (Bandung: no publisher, 1958).

153. All the Islamic political parties, such as Masyumi, NU, PSII, and Perti, advocated the idea of an Islamic state signified by the adoption of Islam as the ideological basis of the state. In spite of this, they differed in the degree and intensity. Comparing the political attitude of Masyumi and NU, some had argued that the former was more intent than the latter. See Daniel S. Lev, *The Transition to Guided Democracy: Indonesian Politics 1957–1959* (Ithaca: Modern Indonesia Project, Southeast Asia Program, Cornell University, 1966), pp. 123–32.

154. See *Tentang Dasar Negara Republik Indonesia dalam Konstituante*, vol. 1, pp. 113–29 and 365. See also Mohammad Natsir, *Islam Sebagai Dasar Negara* (Bandung: Pimpinan Fraksi Masyumi dalam Konstituante, 1957).

155. See *Tentang Dasar Negara Republik Indonesia dalam Konstituante*, vol. 1. Cited from Herbert Feith and Lance Castles, eds., *Indonesian Political Thinking 1945–1965* (Ithaca and London: Cornell University Press, 1970), p. 219.

156. *Tentang Dasar Negara Republik Indonesia dalam Konstituante*, vol. 3, pp. 348–72.

157. *Tentang Dasar Negara Republik Indonesia dalam Konstituante*, vol. 2, pp. 343–50.

158. See, for instance, a speech by Atmodarminto in the Constituent Assembly. *Tentang Dasar Negara Republik Indonesia dalam Konstituante*, vol. 1, p. 68.

159. See, for instance, Karkono Partokusumo's address in the Constituent Assembly. *Tentang Dasar Negara Republik Indonesia dalam Konstituante*, vol. 1, p. 99.

160. *Tentang Dasar Negara Republik Indonesia dalam Konstituante,* vol. 2, p. 352.

161. Twice the Assembly conducted a vote on the Jakarta Charter. The results were 268 to 210 and 265 to 201 against the Jakarta Charter. See Boland, *The Struggle of Islam in Modern Indonesia,* p. 98.

162. The results of three times voting were 269, 264, and 263 for the return, and 199, 204, and 203 against the return to the 1945 Constitution. Ibid., p. 99; Noer, *Partai Islam di Pentas Nasional,* p. 270.

163. For a fuller account on Soekarno's alliance with the army to end the work of the Constituent Assembly, see Nasution, op. cit., pp. 255–401.

164. Because of this NU was often perceived as an opportunistic party. Its leaders maintained, however, that their involvement in the Guided Democracy regime was to balance the increasingly dominant position of PKI.

165. This was a political manifesto which called for (1) the return to the 1945 Constitution; (2) Indonesian socialism; (3) guided democracy; (4) guided economy; and (5) the Indonesian identity. See Boland, op. cit., pp. 101–2.

166. For a fuller account, see Ahmad Syafii Maarif, "Islamic Politics under Guided Democracy in Indonesia, 1959-1965" (M.A. thesis, Ohio University, 1980). See also his *Islam dan Politik di Indonesia Pada Masa Demokrasi Terpimpin (1959-1965)* (Yogyakarta: IAIN Sunan Kalijaga Press, 1988). See also Noer, *Partai Islam di Pentas Nasional,* pp. 349-457.

167. For a further treatment see, for instance, Boland, op. cit., pp. 135–49.

168. Allan A. Samson, "Islam in Indonesian Politics", *Asian Survey* 8, no. 12 (December 1968): 1005.

169. Crouch, "Indonesia", p. 201.

170. Ibid., p. 200.

171. Samson, op. cit., pp. 1005–7.

172. For a detailed account on the foundation of Parmusi, see Kenneth E. Ward, *The Foundation of the Partai Muslimin Indonesia* (Ithaca: Modern Indonesia Project, Southeast Asia Program, Cornell University, 1970).

173. Ibid., pp. 41–54.

174. Harold Crouch, *The Army and Politics in Indonesia* (Ithaca and London: Cornell University Press, 1978), p. 262.

175. Harold Crouch, "Indonesia", p. 202. See also his *The Army and Politics in Indonesia,* pp. 261–62. In his student days Mintaredja was a chairman of Himpunan Mahasiswa Islam (Islamic University Student Association). In addition, he was a notable Muhammadiyah activist.

176. See Samson, op. cit., pp. 1012–13; Ward, op. cit., pp. 44–49; Boland, op. cit., p. 153; Crouch, "Indonesia", p. 201; Deliar Noer, "Contemporary Political Dimensions of Islam", in *Islam in South-East Asia,* edited by M.B. Hooker (Leiden: E.J. Brill, 1983), p. 192.

177. In fact, according to Justus M. van der Kroef, "[e]specially in NU and some PSII circles a conviction arose that Suharto, in implementing the New Order, was

relying altogether too much on the leaders of the Christian parties for support". Justus M. van der Kroef, *Indonesia after Sukarno* (Vancouver: University of British Columbia Press, 1971), p. 57.

178. Samson, op. cit., pp. 1013–17; Boland, op. cit., pp. 154–56.

179. Crouch, "Indonesia", p. 202. For further accounts on the holding of the 1971 general election, see Masashi Nishihara, *Golkar and the Indonesian Elections of 1971* (Ithaca: Monograph Series, Modern Indonesia Project, Cornell University, 1972); Ken Ward, *The 1971 Election in Indonesia: An East Java Case Study* (Clayton: Monash Papers on Southeast Asia, no. 2, Centre of Southeast Asian Studies, Monash University, 1974); Lee Oey Hong, ed., *Indonesia after the 1971 Elections* (London and Kuala Lumpur: Hull Monograph Series on Southeast Asia, no. 5, Oxford University Press, 1974).

180. Ward, *The 1971 Election in Indonesia*, p. 11.

181. Ibid., p. 12.

182. Ibid., p. 12; Crouch, *The Army and Politics in Indonesia*, p. 267.

183. R. William Liddle, "Evolution from above: National Development and Local Leadership in Indonesia", *Journal of Asian Studies*, no. 32 (February 1973), p. 299. See also Wertheim, "Indonesian Moslems under Sukarno and Suharto", p. 24; Ward, *The 1971 Election in Indonesia*, pp. 165–66.

184. On the issue of candidate selection, Ken Ward observed that "[t]he Kopkamtib [the Command of the Operation for the Restoration of Security and Order] commanders at each level were empowered to disqualify any candidate without being obliged to explain precisely why". See his *The 1971 Election in Indonesia*, p. 15.

185. Modified from Feith, *The Indonesian Elections of 1955;* and Nishihara, *Golkar and the Indonesian Elections of 1971.*

186. For further accounts, see Umaidi Radi, *Strategi PPP 1973–1982: Suatu Studi Tentang Kekuatan Politik Islam Tingkat Nasional* (Jakarta: Integrita Press, 1984); Syaifuddin Zuhri et al., *PPP, NU dan MI: Gejolak Wadah Politik Islam* (Jakarta: Integrita Press, 1984).

187. See "Pondok-Pondok Yang Berpaling", *Tempo*, 21 February 1987, pp. 20-28; "Pasang Surut Hubungan Islam-Beringin", *Tempo*, 21 September 1991, pp. 22–33.

188. The voting percentages are taken from Leo Suryadinata, *Military Ascendancy and Political Culture: A Study of Indonesia's Golkar* (Athens: Monograph Series in International Studies, Southeast Asia Series, no. 85, Ohio University, 1989), pp. 159–60. The significant decline of PPP's electoral gain in the 1987 general elections was mainly due to the withdrawal of NU (the major element in PPP) from PPP. On the withdrawal of NU from PPP, see Bahtiar Effendy, "The 'Nine Stars' and Politics: A Study of the Nahdlatul Ulama's Acceptance of Asas Tunggal and Its Withdrawal from Politics" (M.A. thesis, Ohio University, 1988), especially pp. 219-64.

189. This policy was "designed to contribute funds to the capital's improvement". Kroef, op. cit., p. 57.

190. For a further account of the 1973 marriage bill, see Muhammad Kamal Hassan, *Muslim Intellectual Responses to "New Order" Modernization in Indonesia*

(Kuala Lumpur: Dewan Bahasa dan Pustaka Kementerian Pelajaran Malaysia, 1982), pp. 145–55.

191. On the reaction of Muslim leaders, see *Sikap Majelis Ulama dan Pemimpin-Pemimpin Islam Indonesia Terhadap Aliran Kepercayaan* (no author, no publisher, no date).

192. See Nurcholish Madjid, "Islam in Indonesia: Challenges and Opportunities", in *Islam in the Contemporary World*, edited by Cyriac K. Pullapilly (Notre Dame: Cross Roads Books, 1980), p. 346.

193. These efforts were carried out through the (1) incorporation of Pancasila in the educational curriculum; and (2) Pedoman Penghayatan dan Pengamalan Pancasila (P4, Guide to Understanding and Implementing Pancasila) training. See *Himpunan Ketetapan-Ketetapan MPR 1978* (Jakarta: no publisher, 1978), pp. 49-58, 112–14.

194. See *Kompas*, 8 April 1980.

195. David Jenkins, *Suharto and His Generals: Indonesian Military Politics 1975–1983* (Ithaca: Monograph Series, Publication no. 64, Cornell Modern Indonesia Project, Southeast Asia Program, Cornell University, 1984), p. 158.

196. The Lapangan Banteng Affair refers to the turbulent campaign rally of Golkar on 18 March 1982 in Jakarta. There was a violent physical clash between supporters of PPP and Golkar. For a fuller account see, for instance, *Tempo*, 27 March, 3 April, and 10 April 1982.

197. See Soeharto, *Amanat Kenegaraan IV 1982–1985* (Jakarta: Inti Idayu Press, 1985), p. 11.

198. See M. Nasir Tamara, "Sejarah Politik Islam Order Baru", *Prisma*, no. 5 (1988), p. 49.

199. See Lukman-Harun, *Muhammadiyah dan Asas Pancasila* (Jakarta: Pustaka Panjimas, 1986); Saleh Harun and Abdul Munir Mulkhan, *Latar Belakang Ummat Islam Menerima Pancasila Sebagai Asas Tunggal* (Yogyakarta: Aquarius, 1987); Effendy, "The 'Nine Stars' and Politics", pp. 58–128.

200. The phrase originated from the meeting of reformist Muslim leaders on 1 June 1972, as quoted by Hassan in his *Muslim Intellectual Responses to "New Order" Modernization in Indonesia*, p. 121. See also McVey, "Faith as the Outsider: Islam in Indonesian Politics", p. 199.

201. See "Robohnya Dinding Politik Islam", *Tempo*, 29 December 1984, pp. 12–16.

202. See "Dari Syak Wasangka dan Sengketa", *Tempo*, 6 July 1991, p. 32.

203. Ibid., p. 32. For a further account of Imran, see *Dari Cicendo ke Meja Hijau: Imran Imam Jamaah* (no author, Solo: C. V. Mayasari, 1982).

204. John Bresnan, *Managing Indonesia: The Modern Political Economy* (New York: Columbia University Press, 1993), pp. 223–24.

205. See *Indonesia Report*, 15 January 1985, p. 9. See also M. Nasir Tamara, *Indonesia in the Wake of Islam: 1965–1985* (Kuala Lumpur: Institute of Strategic and International Studies, 1986), pp. 20–22.

3

Emergence of the New Islamic Intellectualism
Three Schools of Thought

> If Islam is to be preserved as a social and political force in Indonesia, someone will have to serve as cultural mediator between that Islam and the new national culture of Indonesia.
>
> Leonard Binder[1]

The development of Indonesia's new Islamic intellectualism over the past two decades can be considered crisis-determined. Its general tone has been influenced and shaped by the debilitating situation of political Islam and the devastating repercussions this has had on its thinkers and activists. These unfavourable circumstances have emerged mainly, though not wholly, due to the poor political relationship between Islam and the state and the resulting socio-cultural and political synthesis of Islam within the framework of the state.

For reasons discussed below, the rise of this new Islamic intellectualism can be seen as representing a promising attempt to remedy the discouraging disjunction between Islam and the state. So far, these efforts have been primarily carried out through enunciations of new Islamic political thoughts and actions which are perceived to be more compatible with Indonesia's socio-cultural and religious heterogeneity.

These intellectual endeavours have been led by a new generation of Islamic thinkers and activists who, since the early 1970s, have sought to develop a new format for political Islam in which substance, rather than form, serves as the primary orientation. In the model which these new intellectuals espouse, the notion of "Islamic-ness" and "Indonesia-ness" — two important elements which provide cultural as well as structural legitimacy to the construct of Indonesia's "national unitary state" — is harmoniously synthesized and integrated.[2]

As indicated in their intellectual discourse, this agenda requires (1) re-examination of the theological or philosophical underpinnings of political Islam; (2) redefinition of the political objectives of Islam; and (3) reassessment of the ways by which those political ideals can be effectively realized.

The main tasks of this chapter and the following two chapters are as follows: chapter 3 will describe the pronouncements of the new Islamic intellectualism. The broad tenets of this idealism and activism can be categorized as revolving around three important areas: (1) theological/religious renewal; (2) political/bureaucratic reform; and (3) social transformation.[3]

In spite of the fact that these three spheres of renewal operate in different social arenas, they have been combined in a serious campaign for a new articulation of Islamic political ideas and practices. Based on such a perspective, chapter 4 will explore the implications of the new Islamic intellectualism for the efforts to promote a political reconciliation between Islam and the state. More specifically, it will examine the extent to which these new ideas and practices contribute to the shaping of a new, contextually sound model of political Islam, especially regarding its construct, goals, and tactical approaches. The latter issue (that is, the approach of political Islam) will be discussed specifically in chapter 5.

THEOLOGICAL RENEWAL: A CALL FOR DESACRALIZATION, REACTUALIZATION, AND INDIGENIZATION

From the perspective of the new Islamic intellectualism, the problems confronting political Islam do not solely concern practical issues. In spite of the fact that the problems, as described in the preceding chapter, emerged rather exclusively in the form of a chronicle of political havoc, there has been a widely held belief that the crux of the matter went beyond these practical domains.

Observing the intellectual discourse of Indonesia's Islamic political thinking, particularly with regard to the ideas concerning the proper relationship between Islam and the state, proponents of this new Islamic intellectualism have concluded that the problems are related to, if not rooted in, the theological or philosophical dimensions of political Islam. In their view these theological or philosophical underpinnings — which in themselves were products of Muslims' understanding of their religious doctrines — influenced and shaped the ideas and practices of political Muslims, particularly those of the earlier generation.

As Indonesia's post-colonial politics unfolded, it appeared that political Muslims experienced great difficulties in synthesizing their theological or philosophical foundations with the existing socio-cultural and political realities. This was particularly the case with regard to their attempt to formulate nationally acceptable linkages between Islam and the state. Numerous political episodes have indicated that efforts to establish a formalistic and legalistic connection between Islam and the country's political system ended up with an impasse, sharp ideological and political animosity, or violence.

As a result of this difficult and uneasy dialogue, the political ideas and practices of the earlier generation of political Muslims grew to a seemingly unbridgeable gap between them and their nationalist counterparts. Even though the latter included substantial number of Muslims, they have never been in favour of the idea of a formalistic and legalistic bond between Islam and the state. Throughout the course of Indonesia's modern political history, they have rejected the notion of an Islamic state, or Islam as the ideological basis of the state. This ideological political conflict created hostilities between these two groups.

When the position of political Islam appeared to be worsening, particularly following the New Order's manoeuvre to restructure Indonesia's political format, many of its leaders became increasingly reactionary. In the view of some observers of Indonesian political Islam, this was a sign of the inability of Islamic political thinkers and activists to structure intelligent religious-political responses pertinent to these challenges.[4] Therefore, despite the fact that their political agendas in the early years of the Soeharto regime (that is, pressing for the legalization of the Jakarta Charter; demanding the rehabilitation of the proscribed Masyumi; and striving for direct involvement of the former Masyumi leaders in the newly established Parmusi) were rejected by the New Order, defenders of the past format of political Islam remained virtually unchanged, making their orientation towards politics and religion practically rigid. Many have interpreted this persistently inflexible religious-political behaviour as an indication of their inability to relinquish their formalistic and legalistic approach in politics.[5]

There is no doubt that their resoluteness was deeply motivated. Simply put, it was based on religious belief derived chiefly from their understanding of the holistic nature of Islam. But, given the country's socio-religious heterogeneity, it was nonetheless not well conceived. Primarily because of this, in the view of some younger Muslim leaders and activists, associated mainly with Himpunan Mahasiswa Islam (HMI, Islamic

University Student Association) and Pelajar Islam Indonesia (PII, Islamic Student Association), Islamic political elites — particularly their modernist wing — "suffered from inflexibility, almost dogmatism, in practical considerations".[6] They questioned the soundness of the overall strategy, tactics, and goals of political Islam as defined by the older elites. In fact, many of them even directly challenged the notion of Islam as an ideology; or the idea that the state is an extension (or integral part) of Islam.[7] "Although Islam, as a religion, does contain socio-political teachings," argued M. Dawam Rahardjo, an important figure in the new Islamic intellectual movement, "it is not in itself an ideology." Thus, "[an] 'Islamic Ideology' does not exist".[8] In the meantime, in the attempt to relate Islam and the state more appropriately, Djohan Effendi, another notable participant in the new Islamic intellectualism, as recalled by Ahmad Wahib, suggested on various occasions that the prophet Muhammad himself did not actually proclaim an Islamic state.[9]

In the light of these religious-political and intellectual developments, advocates of the new Islamic intellectualism believe that the heart of the problem lies in a specific mode of theological expression common among many Muslim political thinkers and activists. At some point of their historical experiences, the perceptions of the older leaders and activists of political Islam fixed a religious view of worldly affairs (that is, politics) that was too formalistic, legalistic, or scripturalistic in orientation. In the opinion of the emerging generation of new Muslim intellectuals, unless such a mode of theological formulation is transformed or at least becomes more flexible and adaptive, it seems unlikely that a viable synthesis between Islam and the state can be established.

Against this background, the new Muslim intellectuals have called for the refurbishment of Islamic thought and the rejuvenation of religious understanding. In the context of modern Indonesian Islam this is not entirely a novel agenda. Some of the basic propositions resemble concerns expressed by Soekarno, who in the 1930s voiced the opinion that Indonesian Muslims should rediscover the "*api Islam*" (the "fire of Islam") rather than simply grasping the messages of Islam in its literal or textual sense.[10]

What the new intellectuals want to convey with these reinvigorative religious-political themes, although often misunderstood by their critics, is not a proposal to revise the doctrines of Islam. Like all other Muslims, they believe that Islam is permanent. But they are also convinced that Muslims' understanding or interpretation of the Qur'an and Sunnah, the two primary sources of Islamic teachings, is subject to change.

Accordingly, comparable to the profound concerns of many other past prominent Islamic reformers and thinkers (for example, Jamal al-Din al-Afghani, Muhammad Abduh, Rashid Ridha) whose influences are still palpable in the Muslim world, they simply want to urge their fellow Muslims to rethink their understanding and interpretation of Islam as societal circumstances warrant.[11]

By doing so, it is expected that Muslims' comprehension of their religious messages will not stagnate. More importantly, reflecting the belief that Islam is timeless and universal (*al-Islam shalih li kull-i zaman wa makan*),[12] Muslims should not lose their grip on the demands of modernity. Rather, they should be able to conduct a productive and intelligent dialogue between the universality of Islamic teachings and the necessity of — in this particular case — Indonesia's spatial-temporal peculiarities. Included in this sociological framework are the heterogeneous characteristics of the archipelago's socio-religious structures as well as its political orientations.

As stated earlier, from the late 1960s to the mid-1970s this theological concern was particularly, though not exclusively, strong among some activists in some Islamic student organizations, such as HMI or PII. Being one of the most renowned Islamic student associations in the country, HMI was probably the best organization to be affiliated with to cultivate familiarity with numerous important issues pertinent to the Muslims as well as to Indonesian society at large.[13] Though this agenda for renewal was never adopted as an official policy of the organization — thanks to the differing opinions among the organization's members concerning the nature and substance of the reform movement on the one hand, and the history of political Islam on the other — many of its influential leaders and activists became the intellectual actors of the reform movement.[14]

In Yogyakarta, where HMI was formed in 1947, this theological renewal was centred around the younger figures such as Djohan Effendi, Manshur Hamid, Ahmad Wahib, and — to some extent — M. Dawam Rahardjo. These individuals, in addition to being HMI activists, were also regular participants of the Limited Group (1967–71).[15] As reflected in Ahmad Wahib's controversial diary, *Pergolakan Pemikiran Islam*, this was an open discussion forum primarily focused on religious, social, cultural, and political affairs.[16] Being liberal as it was, the Limited Group provided ample opportunities for its members to express their ideas without fear of being construed as stepping beyond the boundary of religious or theological appropriateness.[17] Throughout its existence, this forum was under the direction of A. Mukti Ali, a professor in the field of comparative study of religion at Yogyakarta's Institut Agama Islam Negeri (IAIN, State Institute for Islamic Studies), who was also Minister of Religion from 1971 to 1978.[18]

Through lengthy and intense discussions, conducted within both HMI circles and the Limited Group, they came to a number of theologically focused conclusions. Though claiming no originality, as many other individuals also shared similar findings, they reasserted several important propositions nonetheless and packaged these propositions into a new religious-political perspective on the relationship between Islam and the state.

First, in their view there is no clear-cut evidence that the Qur'an and Sunnah oblige Muslims to establish an Islamic state. According to their observations, Muhammad's political experimentation did not include the proclamation of an Islamic state. Because of this, they reject the political agenda of earlier leaders and activists of political Islam that seems to demand the formation of an Islamic state or a state based on Islamic ideology.[19]

Second, they recognize that Islam does contain a set of socio-political principles. Even so, they view that Islam is not an ideology. Therefore, in their opinion, an Islamic ideology does not exist.[20] In fact, according to some of them, the ideologization of Islam can be considered as reductionism of Islam.[21]

Third, since Islam is perceived as timeless and universal, Muslims' understanding of it should not be confined to its formal and legal sense, particularly that drawn from a specific time or place. Instead, it should be based on thorough interpretations which apply its textual or doctrinal denotation to its contemporary situation and context. This viewpoint, in turn, at least according to Ahmad Wahib, necessitates the transformation of Islam into a contemporary set of principles and practices.[22]

Fourth, they strongly believe that only Allah possesses the absolute truth. Thus, it is virtually impossible for mankind to grasp the absolute reality of Islam. In their judgment, Muslims' comprehension of their religious doctrines remains essentially relative in value and therefore subject to change. Given this polyinterpretability of Islam on the one hand, and the fact that Islam recognizes no religious priesthood (*la rahbaniyyah fi al-Islam*) on the other, there should be no individual who can claim that his or her understanding of Islam is truer and more authoritative than that of others. Accordingly, it is imperative for Muslims to foster religious tolerance, internally as well as externally.[23]

With these fundamental premises in mind, the new intellectuals have campaigned for the more substantive — less symbolical — nature of the

Islamic political struggle, in which programmes rather than partisan ideology serve as the primary orientation. Shifting their focus away from structure and in an attempt to end the hostility between political Islam and the state, they see no reason not to accept the current form of the state. In fact, they restated the position of HMI and other Islamic organizations, which as early as 1969 suggested that Pancasila be accepted as their political ideal. And finally, they assert that Muslims should make their primary commitment to Islam (that is, Islamic values) and not to institutions or organizations (that is, Islamic parties).[24]

The watershed of this theological renewal movement, however, originated with Nurcholish Madjid, a graduate from IAIN Jakarta, who for two consecutive periods served as the national chairman of HMI (1966–69 and 1969–71). It was not that his ideas were substantively better than those of his counterparts in Yogyakarta, but what appears to have led many observers of Indonesia's contemporary Islam to construe Nurcholish's ideas as the intellectual paradigm of this theological renewal movement was simply the fact that he more articulately and deliberately formulated the ideas of the group. In addition, his unique stature as national chairman of HMI (that is, the fact that, so far, he is the only individual who has led HMI for two consecutive periods) undoubtedly also served to give additional weights to his views and statements.

On 2 January 1970 he delivered a speech to a gathering of four Islamic organizations: HMI, PII, Gerakan Pemuda Islam Indonesia (GPII, Indonesian Islamic Student Movement), and Persatuan Sarjana Muslim Indonesia (Persami, Indonesian Muslim Scholar Association).[25] In his paper, "Keharusan Pembaharuan Pemikiran Islam dan Masalah Integrasi Ummat" (The Necessity of Renewal of Islamic Thought and the Problem of Integration of the Islamic Community), Nurcholish offered the straightforward observation that Indonesian Muslims suffered stagnation in religious thinking and had lost the "psychological striking force" in their struggle.[26] An important indication of this intellectually disarticulated Indonesian Islam, as observed by Nurcholish, was the inability of the vast majority of Muslims to differentiate values which were transcendental from those which were temporal. In fact, he pointed out further that the hierarchy of values was often the reverse; transcendental values were conceived as temporal and *vice versa*. Everything was likely to be perceived as transcendental, and therefore, without exception, valued as divine. As a result of this mode of religiosity, "Islam is [viewed as] equal in value as tradition; and becoming Islamic is comparable to being traditionalist".[27]

Reform of this situation is possible provided that Muslims are prepared to undertake a path of renewal — even if the choice is at the expense of the integration of the *umat*. To undergo this religious renewal, he suggested that Muslims *liberate* themselves from the tendency to transcend values, which are supposedly profane, into the domain of divinity. As a consequence to the belief that Islam is timeless and universal, there is an inherent obligation for Muslims to initiate creative thinking relevant to the demands of the modern age.

According to Nurcholish, this endeavour can only be realized if Muslims enjoy some degree of confidence to allow any ideas, however unconventional they may be, to be expressed and communicated freely. More importantly, given the fact that Islam conceives human beings as naturally oriented towards truthfulness (*hanief*), Muslims need to be open-minded. Furthermore, they should accept and absorb any ideas, regardless of their origins, provided they objectively speak of truth.[28]

Nurcholish's fundamental viewpoints derived from his radical understanding of two basic principles in Islam: (1) the concept of *al-tawhid* (oneness of God); and (2) the notion that men are the vicegerents of God (*khalifat al-Allah fi al-ardh*). From these two principles he formulated his theological premises which suggest that only Allah possesses absolute transcendency and divinity. As a consequence to their acceptance of this monotheistic principle, quite naturally Muslims should perceive the world and its temporal affairs (social, cultural, or political) as they are. Viewing the world and its objects in a sacred or transcendental manner can be theologically considered to be contradictory to the very notion of Islamic monotheism.[29]

But, unlike his previous writings, which were loaded with Qur'anic references,[30] in this paper Nurcholish wrapped his ideas in a highly controversial jargon, that is, *sekularisasi* (secularization). This concept, as indicated in his paper, was borrowed from Harvey Cox, a respected American theologian. In his *magnum opus, The Secular City: Secularization and Urbanization in Theological Perspective*, Cox defines secularization as "the liberation of man from religious and metaphysical tutelage, the turning of his attention away from other worlds and toward this one".[31] Yet, he maintains that secularization is different from secularism. In his own words:

> In any case, secularization as a descriptive term has a wide and inclusive significance. It appears in many different guises, depending on the religious and political history of the area concerned. But whatever it appears, it should be carefully

distinguished from secular*ism*. Secularization implies a historical process, almost certainly irreversible, in which society and culture are delivered from tutelage to religious control and closed metaphysical world-views. We have argued that it is basically a liberating development. Secularism, on the other hand, is the name for an ideology, a new closed world-view which functions very much like a new religion.[32]

It was the notion of "liberating development" as well as the "clear distinction between secularization and secularism" which Nurcholish employed in articulating his ideas concerning the logical consequences of Islamic monotheism (*al-tawhid*). As he put it in his paper:

> Secularization is not meant as the implementation of secularism, because *secularism is the name for an ideology, a new closed world view which functions very much like a new religion*. In this case, what is meant [by secularization] is every form of *liberating development*. ... [nor is it] to convert Muslims to become secularists. Rather, it is meant to temporalize worldly values, and to liberate [Muslims] from the tendency of making those values transcendental.[33]

With this statement, he not only provided an explanation of what he meant by secularization, but at the same time he also reconfirmed his "original position" opposing the notion of "secularism".

In 1968, two years prior to his speech, he engaged in discussions with a number of Indonesia's "secular modernizing intellectuals" concerning the issue of modernization.[34] In his view it appeared that the underlying messages behind the rhetoric of modernization as promulgated by those intellectuals in the early period of the New Order regime were belittling — not to say anti — religious values. According to Nurcholish, some of them even depicted the calls to Islamic prayer using audio devices as "electronic terrors".[35] In this debate he argued very strongly that modernization is neither the implementation of secularism nor the emulation of Western cultural values. Rather, in his view, "modernization is rationalization".[36] As recorded by Muhammad Kamal Hassan in his dissertation, this was an intellectual position which earned him the title of the "new Mohammad Natsir".[37]

The term "secularization" was meant as a necessary process that would enable the Islamic community to distinguish between transcendental and temporal values. For Nurcholish, "secularization", understood as a process of liberating development, is also a *conditio sine qua non* to facilitate Muslims — in accordance with their function as vicegerents of God (*khalifat al-Allah fi al-ardh*) — in their endeavours to relate the universalism of Islam to today's Indonesia.[38]

This "secularization" agenda was heavily criticized. Surprisingly enough, the majority of the criticisms came from the modernist circles — Nurcholish's very own natural acquaintances.[39] For the most part, these criticisms were triggered by the use of the term "secularization" — regardless of the fact that the intentional use of the term was part of a "shock therapy" plan.

Since the 1980s, following his return from the University of Chicago, where he obtained his doctoral degree in Islamic studies under the guidance of a prominent Pakistani Islamic thinker of the neo-modernist stream, Prof. Fazlur Rahman, he has remained faithful to the substance of his renewal ideas.[40] But it is important to note that Nurcholish no longer employs the controversial term "secularization".[41] Thanks to the indirect intellectual encouragement of similar understanding of "secularization", as promulgated by a number of prominent and influential sociologists, such as Talcott Parsons[42] and — more importantly — Robert N. Bellah,[43] he has been able to smoothly rephrase the term "secularization" as "radical devaluation" or "desacralization".[44]

According to Bellah, this notion of radical devaluation had its origins in the historical processes of early Islam. In fact, it was one of the most important structural elements in Muhammad's time when he built the religious-political community of Medina. Explaining the development of radical devaluation in the early history of Islam, he wrote:

> Let us consider the structural elements of early Islam that are relevant to our argument. First was a conception of a transcendent monotheistic God standing outside the natural universe and related to it as creator and judge. Second was the call to selfhood and decision from such a God through the preaching of his prophet to every individual human being. Third was the radical devaluation, one might legitimately say secularization, of all existing social structures in the face of this central God-man relationship. This meant above all the removal of kinship, which had been the chief locus of the sacred in pre-Islamic Arabia, from its central significance.[45]

The implications of such theological pronouncements, in Nurcholish's view, are that there is nothing sacred about the matters of an Islamic state,

Islamic political parties, or an Islamic ideology.[46] Accordingly, Muslims — again primarily because of the logical consequences of their adherence to the principle of *al-tawhid* — should be able to "secularize" or "desacralize" their perceptions on those worldly issues. In the light of this, he introduced the phrase: "*Islam Yes, Partai Islam No*" (Islam Yes, Islamic Party No).[47] With such jargon, among other things, he encouraged his fellow Muslims to direct their commitment to Islamic values and not to institutions, even those of Islamic origin such as Islamic parties.

Other Islamic thinkers such as Harun Nasution, Abdurrahman Wahid, and Munawir Syadzali sketched many theologically similar thoughts. Their ideas are generally focused on reinforcing the fact that the Qur'an, in particular, does not contain everything, let alone a detailed blueprint of life. This position suggests the importance of the concept of *ijtihad* as a way to reinterpret or to reactualize the doctrines of Islam as societal circumstances necessitate. In this case Muslims must take into account the significance of local, contextual, and temporal particularities.

The first proposition is particularly strong in Harun Nasution's theological thinking. He holds a doctoral degree from McGill University's Institute of Islamic Studies. He is also an ardent student of Mu'tazilism — the most notable rationality-centred perspective in the historical discourse of Islamic thought.[48] He disclaims the arguments which suggest that Islam contains everything. Even though he recognizes the fact that there are some verses which seem to imply the encompassing or pan-explanatory nature of the Qur'an,[49] he is nonetheless of the opinion that the assumption does not conform to the reality in the Qur'an.

Relying on the examinations of some prominent Egyptian Muslim scholars,[50] Harun maintains the argument that the vast majority of Qur'anic verses are basically prophetic accounts of events prior to the coming of Muhammad's Islam. Out of 6,236 verses in the Qur'an, approximately only 500 verses address theological, ritual, and societal issues. Since these doctrines were intended to serve as universal and permanent guidelines, it is logical that they were formulated only in a very general manner, without further explanations as to how they should be actually realized or implemented.[51]

Thus, for Harun Nasution, interpretation becomes a crucial part in Islam. Because of the fact that the Qur'an does not go into detail, the implementation of its doctrines requires thorough interpretations. In early Islam explanations to the generality of the Qur'an derived chiefly — though not wholly — from Muhammad. In post-Muhammad Islam it is the *ulama* who generally provide further interpretations in accordance with the demands of their own times.

Related to his emphasis on the idea of generality-requires-interpretation, Harun, whose theological quest has been primarily promulgated in the academic circles, with IAIN Jakarta — where he served as rector from 1973 to 1984 — as the principal base, also reinforces the Janus-face of Islamic doctrines: the absolute (*qath'i*) and the relative (*dhanni*). He asserts that 95 per cent of Islamic teachings are products of human interpretation, while only 5 per cent originated from the Qur'an.[52] The former is subject to change, while the latter — being the absolute — remains the source and arena of interpretive enterprises. Thus, in his view, religious renewal in Islam is basically an endeavour to reinterpret the absolute component of Islamic doctrines in conformity with the needs of the changing situation.[53]

There are more virtues to the idea of generality of the Qur'an other than simply depicting it as an indication of its incompleteness. Among them is the notion of flexibility. This line of thought is generally associated with a widely accepted proposition regarding the timeless and universal nature of Islamic values. This means that Muslims' understanding of their religion's social (not ritual) doctrines should reflect a response to the needs of their own time and place. As societal circumstances develop and change across time, Muslims are required to re-examine their religious understandings so that their "Islamic-ness" can rise to the demands of modernity. As such they can only be realized if the Qur'an reveals its guidelines in a general way, thus providing room for further interpretations.

In connection with this particular issue, Abdurrahman Wahid addresses the necessity of Islam accepting plurality and accommodating indigenous and local circumstances. He is a grandson of the founding father of Indonesia's largest Islamic traditional organization (Nahdlatul Ulama [NU]), Hasyim Asy'ari; and a son of the organization's "most beloved figure", Wachid Hasyim — a former Minister of Religion in the early years of the Republic. Abdurrahman's understanding of Islam was enriched by years of study in Cairo and Baghdad in the 1960s. He is currently the national chairman of NU.

In the context of his indigenization agendas, Abdurrahman Wahid advocates the notions of (1) Islam as a complementary factor in Indonesia's socio-cultural and political life;[54] and (2) the indigenization of Islam (*pribumisasi Islam*).[55]

The first aspect of his idea is a call to dissuade fellow Muslims from making Islam an alternative ideology to the current construct of the

Indonesian nation state. In his view, as a principal component of Indonesia's social structure, Islam should not be put in a contending position *vis-à-vis* other components (for example, the national unitary framework of Indonesia's socio-political arrangement). Instead, Islam should be presented as a complementary element in the formation of the country's social, cultural, and political fabric. Primarily due to the heterogeneous characteristics of the archipelago's social, cultural, and political community, making Islam an alternative ideology or the "sole colour giver" will only be divisive to society as a whole.[56]

This, however, does not mean that Abdurrahman Wahid discourages Islam from playing a role in the state. In this particular case his main concern is actually about the equality of rights and obligations among Indonesia's existing socio-political groupings. In his view, with Pancasila as the nation's ideological compromise, each socio-religious grouping (that is, Islam, Protestantism, Catholicism, Hinduism, and Buddhism) has equal rights to contribute to Indonesia's nation state with its own values. Therefore, despite his insistence that Islam should not be a "sole colour giver", he believes that Muslims have the equal right to shape the course of direction of the state according to their own religious injunctions. In his own words:

> Now [having accepted Pancasila as our national ideology] there must be a follow up, what would NU do with this state? And that [the state] must be furnished with Islamic visions. This is our right, in the same manner as any body else who also enjoys a similar right to fill [the state] with their own visions.[57]

The second aspect of his proposal is a reminder concerning the necessity of taking local circumstances into account in the course of the realization or implementation of Islamic teachings. By doing so, it is expected that (Indonesian) Islam will not be uprooted from its own local context (that is, culture, tradition, etc.). This agenda requires that Islamic doctrines be understood in a manner in which contextual factors are taken into serious consideration. In its simplest form, this includes the need to take account of local (religious) terms. In this case Abdurrahman Wahid rhetorically asks: "why must [we] use the [Arabic] term *shalat* [Islamic praying], if the [Indonesian] term *sembahyang* is no less true [than the former in meaning]?"[58] On another occasion he argues for the socio-cultural comparability of the Arabic's *assalamu'alaikum* with local greetings such as *selamat pagi/siang/malam* (good morning/afternoon/evening).[59]

But Abdurrahman Wahid also throws in a word of caution. In his view in the process of indigenization the mixture between Islam and local culture must be controlled so that the indigenous does not predominate over the very nature of Islam. In spite of the fact that Islam should be contextually understood, nonetheless the characteristics of Islam must be preserved in their original form (for example, the chanting of the Qur'an in the observance of religious rituals, such as in prayers, must remain in Arabic).[60]

Elucidating what he means by the indigenization of Islam, he writes:

> The indigenization of Islam is neither '*Jawanisasi*' (Javanization) nor syncretization. The indigenization of Islam is merely to take local [Indonesia] necessities into account in formulating religious laws, without having to alter the construct of the laws themselves. It is not an attempt to put aside [religious] norms for the sake of culture, but simply to ensure that those norms accommodate the necessities of culture by using the opportunity provided by variations in understanding the [Qur'anic] texts, ...[61]

To shed further light on what he meant by this concept, he portrays Islam as a big river and Indonesia's socio-cultural particularities as a sub-river. The two shall meet to form an even bigger river. The coming of this sub-river undoubtedly brings new water, which in turn may change, or in fact contaminate, the colour of the earlier water. In spite of this, it remains the same river with the same old water nonetheless. In Abdurrahman Wahid's words:

> The indigenization of Islam is part of the history of Islam. ... [The above] illustration is meant to say that the interaction process of Islam with historical realities does not change Islam [*per se*]. Instead, it simply changes the manifestation of Islamic religion in life.[62]

In another essay he has written:

> What is being 'indigenized' is only the manifestation of Islam. Not the doctrines which contain the essence of belief and formal rituals. There is no need to have a 'Batak Qur'an' nor a 'Javanese Hadits.' Islam must remain Islam wherever it might be. But, it does not mean that its 'external forms' should all be homogenized.[63]

In the meantime Munawir Syadzali, a long-time senior officer in the Department of Foreign Affairs, who for two consecutive periods (1983–93) served as the Minister of Religion, suggests the necessity for the reactualization of Islamic teachings.[64] In the reform movement Munawir is actually a latecomer. Unlike his younger counterparts, who began to take up the renewal agenda in the 1970s, his ideas concerning religious reactualization were virtually unknown prior to his appointment as the Minister of Religion. His long years of service in the Department of Foreign Affairs (1950s to 1983) had prevented him from taking an active role in the initial discourse on the new Islamic intellectualism. But it was a blessing in disguise. The disengagement, as he himself recognized, had provided him with ample opportunities to observe, and think about, Indonesian Islam more objectively.[65]

The central point of his message is to encourage Muslims to take up religious *ijtihad* (deliberate independent judgment) honestly, to make Islam more responsive to the needs of Indonesia's local and temporal circumstances.[66] In this regard one of his most often discussed topics is the principle of Islamic inheritance. On this matter the Qur'an stipulates that sons inherit twice as much as daughters. Drawing from, among others, his own personal experiences, he concludes that in some circumstances this particular regulation appears to be contradictory to the very notion of justice. According to Munawir, many *ulama* have realized the issue, but have been unwilling to resolve the matter conclusively. Instead, like many other Muslims, they prefer to take pre-emptive moves by substantially reducing the amount of the assets to be inherited. By and large, these practices are carried out in a manner in which properties are distributed (*hibbah*) to their children, on their own terms, before their death.[67]

The significance of Munawir's reactualization agenda lies beyond the rhetoric of the inheritance issue. A closer look at the framework of his theological thought seems to suggest that he is inclined to argue that there are some Qur'anic stipulations — associated particularly with societal, not ritual, affairs — which are no longer compatible with the demands of the present era (for example, inheritance law, slavery issue). In these cases he relies mostly, but not exclusively, on the practices and examples of the second Caliph, Umar ibn al-Khattab. According to Munawir, due to the changing social circumstances, Umar carried out policies which were not in full compliance with the stipulations laid down by the Qur'an and the traditions of the Prophet. Most notable was his policy concerning the distribution of the spoils of war.

Inspired by the courageous and honest *ijtihad* of Umar, Munawir suggests that there should be aggressive and candid measures to deal with Islamic doctrines. Believing in the dynamism and vitality of Islamic law, he proposes that Muslims should undertake a reactualization agenda to make Islam more suitable to Indonesia's own local and temporal particularities.[68]

POLITICAL/BUREAUCRATIC REFORM:
BRIDGING THE IDEOLOGICAL GAP BETWEEN POLITICAL
ISLAM AND THE STATE

Muslim intellectuals who hold this position generally believe that the problem of the uneasy relationship between political Islam and the state as well as the implications it has for political Muslims can be gradually eradicated by their becoming directly involved and participating in the mainstream of the political and bureaucratic processes of the state.[69] Though few proponents of this political reform have the luxury to dwell on the issues in a manner in which the previous school experienced, nonetheless this perspective developed from several theological as well as political considerations.

First, it is the view of this intellectual stream that Islam should not take an antagonistic position with the state. In this case it is especially important not to make Pancasila contradictory with Islam. Instead, the two should be complementary. This particular view originated from a religious-political understanding that each of the five Pancasila principles (that is, belief in One God, humanitarianism, nationalism, democracy, and social justice) is in accordance with the teachings of Islam.[70] Thus, in their view it is neither necessary nor religiously obligatory for proponents of political Islam to question the legitimacy of the Indonesian state which is formally based on a non-religious — though by no means irreligious, much less anti-religious — ideology.

Subsequently, this viewpoint necessitates a reassessment concerning the objectives of political Muslims. Like their colleagues from different intellectual streams (for example, theological renewal and social trans-formation, the latter to be discussed in the following section), they do not see the making of Islam as a basis of the state an aspiration for which Muslims need to fight. Instead, partly influenced by the thoughts of the theological school, they believe it is the formation of socio-political arrangements of the state so that Muslims can freely exercise their religious beliefs, that needs to be secured. In their view this goal is achievable, though perhaps with greater effectiveness, under existing political and ideological arrangements.

The rationale behind this assumption is that this approach does not place Islam in a confrontational position *vis-à-vis* the state. Accordingly, they argue that Islam's struggle in contemporary Indonesian politics should not emphasize its formal ideological character, especially in the sense that it is perceived, as in the past discourse of political Islam, as an "imperative demand".[71]

Second, throughout the history of modern Indonesian politics, political Muslims have not been able to develop a strong tradition of governing. With the exception of the 1950s era, when many of its leaders were appointed to head Cabinets and a number of important bureaucracies (especially in the Department of Religion), political Islam has played no significant role in state institutions and bureaucratic agencies.[72] This phenomenon not only provides a partial explanation for the peripheral position of activists of political Islam in the state institutions and bureaucratic agencies, but also sheds some light on their relative detachment from the state. Sociologically speaking, simply by being one of the major parties, there ought to be an intrinsic necessity for political Muslims to play a significant part in the process of governing or policy-making.

To overcome these discrepancies (that is, to cultivate the tradition of governing, to develop a fair basis in the state political as well as technocratic representation, and — more importantly — to eliminate the "myth" of *santri* detachment from, if not hostility towards, the state), it is necessary for the leaders and activists of political Islam to remain in contact with the existing political and bureaucratic institutions. It has been generally argued by proponents of this school that only by entering these formal political and bureaucratic institutions will leaders and activists of political Islam become effectively involved in the decision-making processes of the state. More especially, it will eliminate the perception of Islamic hostility towards the state and its bureaucratic agencies. In short, in the view of the proponents of this intellectual current, these are important steps to ensure the realization of an Islamic society as well as the administering of Islam in the framework of a nationally accepted socio-political and ideological arrangement.[73]

Third, all of these approaches and strategies are imperative measures to restore the esteem of political Muslims, who are generally perceived as subjects, outsiders, or minorities in Indonesia's political process. More significantly, these strategies are also important for reviving the Muslim sense of involvement in a wide range of state affairs, which has declined partly as a result of their political debacles.[74]

With these considerations in mind, it is the hope of this intellectual stream that political renewal and bureaucratic participation will be able to overcome the uneasy relationship between Islam and the state. Furthermore, by strengthening political and ideological proximity, it is expected that unnecessary confrontations — politically as well as ideologically — can be gradually reduced, if not entirely eliminated. It is in this particular context, as noted by Wahib, that proponents of this intellectual stream can be regarded as the political arm of the theological school.[75]

One of the early initiators of this political renewal was Dahlan Ranuwihardjo, a graduate of the Faculty of Law at the University of Indonesia. From 1951 to 1953 he was the national chairman of HMI. In the late 1950s he was an important leader of the Gerakan Pemuda Islam Indonesia (GPII, Indonesian Islamic Youth Movement), a close affiliate of Masyumi.[76] As early as the 1950s Dahlan had adopted a political stance against the juxtaposition of Islam and Pancasila. Like many other Muslim individuals who share such a point of view, this political attitude basically originated from a deep conviction that Pancasila, as mentioned before, is in accordance with the teachings of Islam. Mainly due to this perspective, in the eyes of Dahlan there are always opportunities and openings to uphold and implement the basic principles of Islam within the framework of the Pancasila state. Accordingly, he saw no reason to develop negative attitudes towards the state and its policies.[77]

Based on these perceptions, regardless of his formal affiliation with Islamic organizations (that is, HMI and more importantly GPII), Dahlan shared the "national unitary" construct of the state. In the mid-1950s, in the wake of the re-emerging controversies concerning the issue of the "Islamic state" versus the "national state", he clearly supported the latter.[78] He also supported the general policy of the state under Soekarno's Guided Democracy regime, even with Manipol Usdek (Political Manifesto) as its principal platform. Moreover, at a time when many leaders and activists of political Islam — particularly the "idealist" individuals in the modernist wing — began to detach themselves, or were being pushed aside, from participating in the mainstream of Indonesia's political and bureaucratic processes, he accepted his appointment from Soekarno to serve in the parliament (Dewan Perwakilan Rakyat Gotong Royong, DPRGR).[79]

It is important to note, however, that this political renewal, particularly its practical dimensions (that is, practical politics), did not exclusively originate from the accommodationist faction of the Islamic "modernism" group. Following the dissolution of the Constituent Assembly in the late 1950s, with the exception of the idealist camp within Masyumi circles, there was growing support among various leaders and activists of political Islam to pursue and develop a policy of reconciliation.[80] Included in this group was the traditionalist NU, which claimed a substantial number of members in the rural areas. In fact, this socio-political organization emerged as one of the most dominant actors in the early stages of political reconciliation between Islam and the state.

Given the political aura of Soekarno's Guided Democracy, it seems reasonable to argue that the success story of NU in this early politics of reconciliation to a large extent was due to its institutional and "solidarity-making" approach.[81] This approach was possible because Soekarno was attempting to create a regime in which the uproars of partisan and mass politics were inseparable parts.[82]

With the dramatic changes in Indonesian politics in the mid-1960s, NU's role in these reconciliatory processes declined rapidly. For the most part, this was due to Soeharto's earlier "search for a (new) political format" which showed a strong inclination to dismantle the practices of partisan and mass politics at the behest of political stability (order) and economic development (growth). The New Order regime's emphasis on these twin goals ultimately contributed to the disappearance of the "plausibility structure" (that is, the overtones of party and mass politics), upon which NU had comfortably based its political approach for so many years.

While this political approach had to be terminated, NU was unable to replace it with a more suitable mechanism for dealing with the New Order. This may represent a partial explanation of the fact that NU, as a political organization, before and after its fusion into Partai Persatuan Pembangunan (PPP) in 1973, transformed itself into a fervent and bold critic of the New Order regime, replicating Masyumi's role during Soekarno's early "years of living dangerously".[83]

Considering the social and structural characteristics of the bases of NU's supporters at that time (for example, traditionalist, rural oriented, limited exposure to modern education), it is logical to assume that NU would be very unlikely to take the path of the individual and problem-solving approach as practised by its modernist counterparts. This latter group, mainly because of its modern educational background, in the wake of the New Order's political stability and economic development programmes, was able to cultivate a more technocratic-bureaucratic or developmentalist approach in politics. Accordingly, during the first fifteen years of the Soeharto period the discourse of the reconciliatory politics was largely, but not entirely, dominated by the new generation of Muslim intellectuals and activists rooted within the tradition of Islamic modernism.

From the party politics perspective, this reform movement was especially centred on the younger Muslim political thinkers and activists. Like their colleagues from different schools, they were disenchanted with the development of Islamic political ventures in the late 1950s and the 1960s. During this period they saw that the political struggles of Islam were generally characterized by at least three dominant features: (1) emphasis on the formal ideological struggle of political Islam; (2) a limited view of the political meaning of Islam which subsequently resulted in the choice of parliament as its primary playing field; and (3) focus on partisan interests which led to, among other things, the development of a communalistic viewpoint of Islam (that is, a narrow definition of *umat*, denoting only those who are associated with Islamic socio-political organizations).

In the view of the new intellectual stream, these characteristics had served as important ingredients for the development of the politics of exclusivism among the leaders and activists of political Islam. And ultimately, as proponents of this intellectual school argued, they contributed to the decline of Islam as a political force.[84]

In the early 1970s Mintaredja and Sulastomo, respectively the general chairman and secretary general of Parmusi, were among the notable actors of this political renewal movement. During their college years both Mintaredja and Sulastomo were activists of HMI. In fact, during different periods, they each served as the national chairman of the association. In the early period of the Soeharto regime, Mintaredja held a Cabinet post as Minister of Social Affairs. In the meantime Sulastomo, holding a medical degree from the University of Indonesia, pursued his career mostly in the state bureaucracy.

Seeking to reverse the continuing disenfranchisement of political Islam, both Mintaredja and Sulastomo were of the opinion that political Islam in modern Indonesia should struggle on a broader playing field. More importantly, political Islam should work on novel agendas relevant not only to its interests, but also to the demands of Indonesian society at large.[85] One way to put this idea into operation was to participate in the mainstream of Indonesia's political processes. Another was to join hands with the existing political institutions as well as the state bureaucratic agencies.[86] Partly encouraged by the composition of his party candidates for the 1971 election, which consisted of a significant number of tertiary education degree holders (that is, engineering, law, and economics), Sulastomo even suggested the suitability of Parmusi as "a partner for the technocratic-led Golkar".[87]

Although views such as those of Mintaredja and Sulastomo never came to dominate the perspective of the broader segment of the Indonesian Muslim community, many others had actually shared similar concerns, particularly the necessity of bridging the ideological and political gap between Islam and the state by joining the state bureaucratic agencies. In the early years of the New Order administration, this strategic step was carried out by a number of ex-HMI and Persami activists, including Sularso, Bintoro Tjokroamidjojo, Barli Halim, Bustanul Arifin, Madjid Ibrahim, Norman Razak, Zainul Yasni, Omar Tusin, Sya'dillah Mursid, Mar'ie Muhammad, and Hariry Hadi. These individuals pursued their technocratic and bureaucratic careers in the Badan Perencanaan Pembangunan Nasional (Bappenas, National Development Planning Board), and other related economic and development agencies. More importantly, many of them were under the professional (and perhaps political) patronage of Widjojo Nitisastro — the czar of the New Order's market-oriented economic policy.[88]

Unlike their colleagues from different renewal streams, who to some extent indulged themselves in the intellectual or theoretical discourse of Islam in its relationship with broader social and political affairs, these individuals were more apt to be immediately involved in the state and its bureaucratic institutions. Partly because of this, coupled with the nature of the country's bureaucratic polity which — among other things — demands monolithic loyalty from its apparatus, many of these reformers were often perceived as relatively detached from the *umat*. In spite of this, however, they have played significant roles in the attempts to build a more amicable political relationship between Islam and the state. In its simplest form their mere participation in the bureaucratic process has contributed greatly to the evaporation of a perceived hostility or detachment of political Muslims towards the state bureaucratic agencies.

In the meantime, with the increasing number of the offsprings of the defenders of political Islam entering the state bureaucracy since the 1970s, thanks to their relatively easy access to modern higher education, they have played major roles in shaping the course of action and direction of the state. In this particular context, the growing process of what since the early 1980s has been called the "Islamization of the state bureaucracy" (to be discussed in a later chapter) can be partially attributed to the work of these political and bureaucratic reformers.[89]

SOCIAL TRANSFORMATION:
DIVERSIFYING THE POLITICAL MEANING OF ISLAM

Seen from the reconciliatory perspective of the renewal movement, the intellectual pronouncements of the social transformation school are more complex — thus more difficult — to describe. First, the complexity lies in the choice of the agenda, which is populist and society-oriented in character. Second, it also rests in its political overtones which appear to lead to the formation of a strong society *vis-à-vis* the state, rather than simply directed at the process of political reconciliation between Islam and the state.

With this kind of political nuance, it is difficult to imagine that the intellectual paradigms as well as the courses of action of this school would be characteristically docile to the state. As its place in Indonesia's intellectual discourse unfolds, it appears that this social transformatory school represents an important segment of what some observers have called "radical critical pluralists" within the Indonesian political community.[90] Since the late 1970s the critical attitude of this stream can be identified most conspicuously from the intellectual perspective of some of its leading figures, who have tended to see the New Order's development policies in the light of critical school and dependency theory.[91]

This, however, does not necessarily suggest that they always oppose any policies initiated by the state; much less imply that they are detached from the state bureaucracy. In fact, in undertaking their transformatory agendas, they often cultivate a degree of co-operation with the relevant governmental or state agencies.[92]

Nonetheless, given the hegemonic and exclusionary nature of the New Order state, such a critical stance may instigate questions concerning the coherence of the strategy of this new intellectual movement (that is, in promoting a better relationship between political Islam and the state). The critical attitude of this transformatory school presumably runs counter to the approach of the theological and political-bureaucratic streams which appear to be less critical and more accommodating in their orientations.

A closer look at the general ideas and practices of this transformatory school, as this section will try to elucidate, will calm the above appre-hensions. Like their counterparts from different currents, proponents of this intellectual stream are generally aware of the perennial problems confronted by political Islam. However, they do not consider the notion of the uneasy relationship between political Islam and the state as their primary intellectual concern. Instead, they are compelled to address the more tangible or immediate problems confronted by Indonesian society at large, the majority of which is Muslim. In this case, they are more interested in dealing with the socio-economic and political impacts of the regime's policy which puts too heavy a weight on stability and growth at the expense of popular participation and distribution. In tackling those pressing issues, they employ empirical and non-confrontational approaches. Partly because of this, in spite of its critical stance, this society-oriented perspective complements the idea of political reconciliation between Islam and the state.

Perhaps the linkage of this social transformatory movement with the efforts to promote a viable relationship between political Islam and the state can be explained as follows:

First, the concern of this intellectual stream has been primarily the egalitarian and emancipatory transformation of society.[93] Considering the scope of their agenda, it is hardly conceivable that proponents of this intellectual stream would adhere to a partisan approach. Moreover, given the complexity of social transformation processes, it is reasonable to argue that the realization of this idea requires more diversified programmes, strategies, and playing fields in order to succeed.[94]

Second, it has been widely observed that the state under the New Order regime is indisputably strong. Compared to the nature of the state under the previous regimes (that is, liberalism and Guided Democracy), the present situation of the state is by far more capable of "penetrating" society, "regulating" relationships between existing social and political groupings, and "extracting" and "appropriating" both human and natural resources in more or less determined ways.[95] Included in these capabilities is the ability of the state to function as the most dominant actor in Indonesia's socio-economic and political development. Given this particular context and coupled with the complexity of social transformatory processes, proponents of this intellectual stream need to work closely with the state (that is, relevant bureaucratic agencies) as well as other similar — though not necessarily of Islamic background — organizations to implement their programmes.[96]

Keeping these perspectives in mind, this intellectual stream actually has called for: (1) the adherence to a broader meaning of politics, which in its truest sense consists of more diversified programmes, strategies, and playing fields instead of fighting for partisan interests with parliament as its sole battleground; (2) the cultivation of meaningful relationships with the state as well as other organizations, preferably of similar concerns; and (3) the reformulation and redefinition of the political objectives of Islam, which are inclusionary in nature, to synthesize (rather than to contradict) the dimensions of Islamic-ness and Indonesia-ness.[97]

In the early 1970s Sudjoko Prasodjo and Dawam Rahardjo were among the leading individuals who initiated these social transformation programmes.[98] Both were HMI activists in Yogyakarta, who later moved to Jakarta to pursue their professional careers.

In Jakarta Sudjoko was actively involved in, among others, Pendidikan Tinggi Dakwah Islam (PTDI, Higher Education for Islamic Preaching). In the meantime Dawam — who graduated from the Faculty of Economics at the University of Gadjah Mada — cultivated his early career at the Bank of America before finally affiliating himself with the Lembaga Penelitian, Pendidikan dan Penerangan Ekonomi dan Sosial (LP3ES, Institute for Economic and Social Research, Education and Information). Basically, it was through this research institute that he introduced his social transformatory ideas. In later years he also undertook similar activities through a number of non-governmental organizations (NGOs) which he and his colleagues jointly established.[99]

Towards the later part of the 1970s Adi Sasono, a renowned HMI activist and student leader at Institut Teknologi Bandung (ITB, Bandung Institute of Technology), followed suit. Formerly, Adi was a successful general manager of PT Krama Yudha, one of the most well-known automotive assembly plants in the country. Determined to orient his intellectual call to politics in its broadest sense, with social transformation as his central focus, he resigned from the company. In 1978, together with his colleagues, Adi formed Lembaga Studi Pembangunan (LSP, Institute for Development Studies).[100] Like Dawam in LP3ES, he launched his social agendas primarily from LSP, beginning by undertaking a series of research and policy studies relevant to programmes he aspired to implement.[101]

The nature of this transformatory school was basically political. In fact, one of its principal objectives was to create a strong political infrastructure, more specifically, the formation of a real political basis at the grass-roots level, capable of supporting more or less a participatory political system.

To realize these goals, the approach of this intellectual stream has been primarily to develop the capability and consciousness of society at large.

This particular strategy is ultimately aimed at the formation of an autonomous middle class — the core element in the making of a relatively strong society in its relationship with the state. Within the theoretical framework of both society-centred as well as state-centred perspectives, the existence of an autonomous middle class or strong civil society represents an important determinant for the development of a democratic political system.[102]

This political overtone is acknowledged by Dawam Rahardjo.[103] Observing the venture of political Islam, especially that of Masyumi in the 1950s, he offers the intriguing assessment that political Islam has no solid basis of power. His understanding of the socio-economic fabric of the *umat*, particularly at the grass-roots level, led him to conclude that the social basis of the Islamic group had been generally permeable. Mainly because of the lack of solid and genuine social bases, they failed to provide the necessary support for the development of (1) a strong tradition of governing; and (2) the articulation of more rational — that is, less ideological — political ideas and practices.[104]

Based on these viewpoints, together with Sudjoko Prasodjo and his other colleagues, such as Tawang Alun, in the mid-1970s Dawam undertook a number of activities related to the social transformatory agenda. Included in these were community development programmes designed to create small-scale industries and to improve the quality of Islamic traditional schools with *pesantren,* or traditional Islamic schools, as their primary pilot project.[105]

These activities could not be implemented through a partisan approach. Rather, their success was determined by the ability of their initiators to muster the necessary support from institutions as well as individuals. Thus, Dawam sought co-operation with appropriate bureaucratic agencies to ensure the success of his programmes. Among the agencies involved in undertaking these community development programmes were the Departments of Industry, Co-operatives, and Religion. In fact, he was able to persuade the Department of Religion, which at that time was under the leadership of A. Mukti Ali, his former mentor in the Limited Group, to take up the *pesantren* development programme as a national project.[106]

Since *pesantren* institutions, particularly in Java, are largely identified as the educational enterprises of traditionalist Islam, promoters of this programme were also aware of the significance of cultivating meaningful co-operation with individuals associated with NU, the organization *par excellence* of Indonesia's Islamic traditionalism.[107] While the impact of this collaborative venture in bridging the differences between Islamic modernism and traditionalism — theologically as well as socio-politically — had its ups and downs, unquestionably it drew the latter camp into joining the renewal bandwagon. One of its most important representatives to take part in this cause was Abdurrahman Wahid.[108] In the 1980s, with his ideas already described above, Abdurrahman not only played an important role in this new intellectual movement, but also emerged as one of its major players.

Basically, Adi Sasono has operated under the same intellectual paradigms and approaches as those of his colleagues (Sudjoko Prasodjo and Dawam Rahardjo, in particular). Like those of his counterparts, his social transformation agenda was strongly influenced and shaped by an ethos of social emancipation. This explains his obsessions, as expressed in a number of his writings, with the defence of the oppressed (*mustadz'afin*), egalitarianism, social justice, and economics as well as political democratization.

But, different from Sudjoko and Dawam, whose intellectual concerns are, to some extent, oriented towards rural community development, as exemplified by their *pesantren* programmes, Adi's socio-political ideas and practices seem to be pointed more at issues pertinent to the interests of urban and city dwellers.[109] In this particular case, his concerns encompass a long list of problems, ranging from mass poverty and urban unemployment to social and political oppression.[110] In short, his main interests stem from opposition to the New Order's preference for political stability and economic growth at the expense of popular participation and distribution.

In addition to what has been suggested earlier, there are at least two other factors that have influenced the course of Adi's political thought and actions. These include: (1) recognition of the pluralist nature of the social and religious formation of the Indonesian community; and (2) the marginal position of political Islam, partly as the result of its debilitating venture in the politics of ideological symbolism.[111]

Seeing the heterogeneity of the social and religious orientations of Indonesian society, Adi has focused his intellectual discourse towards less symbolic goals. For the most part, his actions have been aimed at the development of a more substantive or rational politics. Accordingly, he argues that the "struggle of Islam in modern Indonesia" should be nationalistic in character. In this respect, he has repeatedly argued that social emancipation, popular participation, and economic distribution are the key issues for the realization of the social and political goals of Islam.[112]

Notes

1. Leonard Binder, "Islamic Tradition and Politics: The Kijaji and the Alim", a commentary to Clifford Geertz's "The Javanese Kijaji: The Changing Role of a Cultural Broker", *Comparative Studies in Society and History* 2 (October 1959–July 1960): 256.

2. For a concise account of the integration of Islamic-ness and Indonesia-ness, see Nurcholish Madjid, "Integrasi Keislaman dalam Keindonesiaan Untuk Menatap Masa Depan Bangsa" (Speech delivered at the opening of the Paramadina's Religious Study Club, Jakarta, 1986).

3. I am indebted to M. Dawam Rahardjo for pointing me to these three areas of the new Islamic intellectualism. Interview with Dawam Rahardjo in Jakarta, 20 August 1991. For a useful comparison, see Djohan Effendi and Ismet Natsir, eds., *Pergolakan Pemikiran Islam: Catatan Harian Ahmad Wahib* (Jakarta: LP3ES, 1981), pp. 172–74.

4. See Allan Samson, "Islam and Politics in Indonesia" (Ph.D. dissertation, University of California, 1972).

5. For a further analysis on this issue, see Allan Samson, "Islam in Indonesian Politics", *Asian Survey* 8, no. 12 (December 1968): 1001–17; see also his "Indonesian Islam since the New Order", in *Readings on Islam in Southeast Asia*, edited by Ahmad Ibrahim, Sharon Siddique, and Yasmin Hussain (Singapore: Institute of Southeast Asian Studies, 1985), pp. 165–70.

6. See Nurcholish Madjid, "The Issue of Modernization among Muslims in Indonesia: From a Participant's Point of View", in *Readings on Islam in Southeast Asia,* edited by Ahmad Ibrahim, Sharon Siddique, and Yasmin Hussain (Singapore: Institute of Southest Asian Studies, 1985), p. 383.

7. This observation refers to Ahmad Wahib's recollections of a discussion between a number of HMI activists and a former leader of Masyumi, Prawoto Mangkusasmito. See Effendi and Natsir, op. cit., especially pp. 145–46 and 150.

8. M. Dawam Rahardjo, "Tujuan Perjuangan Politik Ummat Islam di Indonesia", *Panji Masyarakat*, no. 85 (August 1971). Cited from Muhammad Kamal Hassan, *Muslim Intellectual Responses to "New Order" Modernization in Indonesia* (Kuala Lumpur: Dewan Bahasa dan Pustaka Kementrian Pelajaran Malaysia, 1982), p. 101.

9. Effendi and Natsir, op. cit., p. 149.

10. For Soekarno's views on Islam, see *Surat-Surat Islam dari Endeh* (Bandung: Persatuan Islam, 1936). Reprinted in Soekarno's *Dibawah Bendera Revolusi*, vol. 1 (Jakarta: Panitia Penerbitan Dibawah Bendera Revolusi, 1964), pp. 325–44. See also M. Thalib and Haris Fajar, eds., *Pembaharuan Faham Islam di Indonesia: Dialog Bung Karno–A. Hassan* (Yogyakarta: Sumber Ilmu, 1985).

11. It is generally believed that Islamic teaching is permanent in nature. To understand its messages, however, particularly in the post-Muhammad era, requires a thorough interpretation and reinterpretation as circumstances warrant. Within the intellectual

tradition of Islam, this endeavour is called *ijtihad*. This is an act to acquire a deliberate independent judgment which is not only meant to uncover the meaning of the doctrines of Islam, but also to reveal their general principles.

12. The phrase is taken from Nurcholish Madjid's "Masalah Tradisi dan Inovasi Keislaman dalam Bidang Pemikiran serta Tantangan dan Harapannya di Indonesia" (Paper delivered at the Istiqlal Festival, Jakarta, 21–24 October 1991), p. 4.

13. On the position of HMI in Indonesia's Islamic ideological and political discourse, see Victor Tanja's "Himpunan Mahasiswa Islam: Its History and Its Place among Muslim Reformist Movement in Indonesia" (Ph.D. dissertation, Hartford Seminary Foundation, 1979). See also his *Himpunan Mahasiswa Islam: Sejarah dan Kedudukannya di Tengah Gerakan Muslim Pembaharu di Indonesia* (Jakarta: Sinar Harapan, 1982).

14. Effendi and Natsir, op. cit., pp. 144–74.

15. Among other members of this discussion group were Syu'bah Asa, Saifullah Mahyuddin, Djauhari Muhsin, Kuntowijoyo, Syamsuddin Abdullah, Muin Umar, Kamal Muchtar, Simuh, and Wadjiz Anwar. See Mukti Ali's foreword in Effendi and Natsir, op.cit., p. vii. Part of this information was also obtained from my interviews with Kuntowijoyo, Ichlasul Amal, Djohan Effendi, and Dawam Rahardjo conducted in Yogyakarta and Jakarta between July and August 1991.

16. Effendi and Natsir op. cit., especially pp. 1–193.

17. See Mukti Ali's foreword in Effendi and Natsir, op. cit., p. viii.

18. For a concise account on Mukti Ali's socio-intellectual origins, see Howard M. Federspiel, *Muslim Intellectuals and National Development in Indonesia* (New York: Nova Science Publishers Inc., 1992), pp. 19–22.

19. Interview with Djohan Effendi in Jakarta, 26–27 August 1991. See also Effendi and Natsir, op. cit., pp. 149 and 155.

20. Rahardjo, op. cit.

21. Effendi and Natsir, op. cit., pp. 146 and 150.

22. Effendi and Natsir, op. cit., pp. 19–20, 69, 110–11, 121–26.

23. Effendi and Natsir, op. cit., pp. 33–43, 46–48, 90–91. See also Djohan Effendi, "Pluralisme Pemahaman dalam Perspektif Theologi Islam", in *Teologi Pembangunan: Paradigma Baru Pemikiran Islam*, edited by M. Masyhur Amin (Yogyakarta: LKPSM NU DIY, 1989), pp. 149–52; Djohan Effendi, "Pluralisme Pemikiran dalam Islam" (Unpublished paper, August 1987); Djohan Effendi, "Persekusi Ataukah Persuasi?" (Unpublished paper, February 1986).

24. Interview with Djohan Effendi in Jakarta, 26–27 August 1991. See also Effendi and Natsir, op. cit., pp. 144–56.

25. The event was organized by Utomo Dananjaya and Usep Fathuddin, respectively the national chairman and secretary general of PII. On this occasion, Nurcholish actually was a substitute for Alfian, a new graduate from the University of Wisconsin, whose

doctoral dissertation discusses the issue of Islamic modernism in Indonesian politics during the Dutch colonial period with Muhammadiyah as its special case. (Interview with Nurcholish Madjid in Montreal, 3 November 1991.) Alfian's dissertation is "Islamic Modernism in Indonesian Politics: The Muhammadiyah Movement during the Dutch Colonial Period" (Ph.D. dissertation, University of Wisconsin, 1969). In 1989 this dissertation was published by Gadjah Mada University Press under the title *Muhammadiyah: The Political Behavior of a Muslim Modernist Organization under Dutch Colonialism.*

26. Nurcholish Madjid, "Keharusan Pembaharuan Pemikiran Islam dan Masalah Integrasi Ummat", in *Pembaharuan Pemikiran Islam*, edited by Nurcholish Madjid et al. (Jakarta: Islamic Research Centre, 1970), pp. 1–12.

27. Ibid., p. 4.

28. Ibid., pp. 4–9.

29. According to Nurcholish his understanding of the Islamic monotheist principle (*al-tawhid*) was largely shaped by his experiences accumulated during his visits to a number of Muslim countries, particularly Saudi Arabia, in the late 1960s. Because of the country's orientation to the Wahabiate theological school, which is obsessed with religious purification, the vast majority of its inhabitants adhere to a radical understanding of *al-tawhid*. This roughly means that nothing is sacred except Allah. In 1969, following his return from the trips, he articulated this radical notion of Islamic monotheism in his *Nilai-Nilai Dasar Perjuangan (NDP)*. Later, after undergoing minor revisions with the help of Endang Saifuddin Anshari and Sakib Mahmud, it became the ideological manual of HMI. (Interview with Nurcholish in Montreal, 3 November 1991.) Now, while its content remains largely the same, the title has been changed to *Nilai Identitas Kader (NIK)*. For this, see *Hasil-Hasil Ketetapan Kongres Himpunan Mahasiswa Islam ke-16*, March 1986, especially pp. 74–123. It is important to note, however, that while Saudi Arabia does not seem to expand such a perception to the socio-political domains, Nurcholish does. Because of this, Saudi Arabia virtually adheres to the idea of legal/formal unity between Islam and the state.

30. See particularly his *Pokok-Pokok Islamisme* and *Nilai-Nilai Dasar Perjuangan*.

31. Harvey Cox, *The Secular City: Secularization and Urbanization in Theological Perspective* (New York: Macmillan Company, 1966), p. 17.

32. Ibid., pp. 20–21.

33. Madjid, "Keharusan Pembaharuan Pemikiran Islam dan Masalah Integrasi Ummat", pp. 4–5. The quotations in italics are from Cox, op. cit., pp. 20–21.

34. A brief expose on this group of intellectuals can be found in R. William Liddle, "Modernizing Indonesian Politics", in *Political Participation in Modern Indonesia,* edited by R. William Liddle (New Haven: Southeast Asia Studies, Yale University, 1973), pp. 177–206.

35. Interview with Nurcholish Madjid in Montreal, 3 November 1991.

36. On the issue of modernization is rationalization, see his *Modernisasi Adalah Rasionalisasi Bukan Westernisasi* (Bandung: Mimbar Demokrasi, 1968).

37. Hassan, *Muslim Intellectual Responses to "New Order" Modernization in Indonesia*, p. 117.

38. This notion of "secularization" can also be found in Nurcholish's four other articles, written during 1970–73. These include: "Beberapa Catatan Sekitar Masalah Pembaharuan Pemikiran dalam Islam", "Sekali Lagi Tentang Sekularisasi", "Perspektif Pembaharuan Pemikiran Islam", and "Menyegarkan Paham Keagamaan di Kalangan Umat Islam Indonesia". All these essays are included in his *Islam Kemoderenan dan Keindonesiaan* (Bandung: Mizan, 1987), pp. 215–56.

39. For a range of criticism of his ideas, see Madjid et al., *Pembaharuan Pemikiran Islam*, pp. 13–72; Endang Saifuddin Anshari, *Kritik Atas Faham dan Gerakan "Pembaharuan" Drs. Nurcholish Madjid* (Bandung: Bulan Sabit, 1973); H.M. Rasjidi, *Koreksi Terhadap Drs. Nurcholish Madjid tentang Sekularisasi* (Jakarta: Bulan Bintang, 1972).

40. For a brief assessment on the extent of the impact of Fazlur Rahman's ideas on Indonesia's new Islamic intellectualism, see Greg Barton, "The International Context of the Emergence of Islamic Neo Modernism in Indonesia", in *Islam in the Indonesian Social Context*, edited by M.C. Ricklefs (Clayton: Annual Indonesian Lectures Series, no. 15, Monash University, 1991), pp. 69–82.

41. Interview with Nurcholish Madjid in Montreal, 3 November 1991. This matter was also expressed in his essay honouring Prof. Rasjidi, one of his most ardent critics, entitled "Sekitar Usaha Membangkitkan Etos Intelektualisme Islam di Indonesia", in *70 Tahun Prof. Dr. H.M. Rasjidi*, edited by Endang Basri Ananda (Jakarta: Pelita, 1985), pp. 215–25.

42. See Talcott Parsons, Edward Shils, Kaspar D. Naegelle, and Jesse R. Pitts, eds., *Theories of Society: Foundations of Modern Sociological Theory* (New York: Free Press of Glencoe, 1961), pp. 249–51, 256–63.

43. See his "Islamic Traditions and the Problems of Modernization", *Beyond Belief: Essays on Religion in a Post-Traditionalist World* (Berkeley and Los Angeles: University of California Press, 1991), pp. 146–67.

44. Interview with Nurcholish Madjid in Montreal, 3 November 1991. See also "Nurcholish yang Menarik Gerbong", *Tempo*, 14 June 1986, pp. 60–62. See also his post-1970s writings, *Islam Doktrin dan Peradaban: Sebuah Telaah Kritis Tentang Masalah Keimanan, Kemanusiaan, dan Keindonesiaan* (Jakarta: Yayasan Wakaf Paramadina, 1992).

45. Bellah, op. cit., p. 151.

46. Interview with Nurcholish Madjid in Montreal, 3 November 1991. See also "Nurcholish yang Menarik Gerbong", *Tempo*, 14 June 1986, pp. 60–62.

47. Madjid, "Keharusan Pembaharuan Pemikiran Islam dan Masalah Integrasi Ummat", p. 2.

48. His dissertation is about the place of reason in Muhammad Abduh's theological thought. In this work he concludes that Abduh was indeed a Mu'tazilate in

orientation. See his "The Place of Reason in Abduh's Theology: Its Impact on His Theological System and Views" (Ph.D. dissertation, McGill University, 1968). For a series of appraisals on his position in the discourse of Indonesia's Islamic thinking, see *Refleksi Pembaharuan Pemikiran Islam: 70 Tahun Harun Nasution* (Jakarta: Lembaga Studi Agama dan Filsafat, 1989).

49. See for instance, Qur'an 6:38: "We have neglected nothing in the Book (of Our decrees)"; Qur'an 16:89: "And We reveal the Scripture unto thee as an exposition of all things". The translations are from Marmaduke Pickthall, *The Glorious Koran*, a bilingual edition with English translation, introduction, and notes (Albany: State University of New York Press, 1976).

50. Among them: Abd al-Wahab al-Khalaf and Muhammad 'Izzah Darwazah. See Harun Nasution, "Islam dan Sistem Pemerintahan dalam Perkembangan Sejarah", *Nuansa*, December 1984, p. 5.

51. See, for instance, Nasution, "Islam dan Sistem Pemerintahan dalam Perkembangan Sejarah", pp. 4–5. See also his *Islam Ditinjau dari Berbagai Aspeknya*, 2 vols. (Jakarta: UI Press, 1984).

52. The percentage is based on his comparative perception of the basic teachings of the Qur'an *vis-à-vis* voluminous interpretative or explanatory works of *ulama*. See "Menanyakan Kembali Pemikiran Islam", *Tempo*, 22 September 1990, p. 101.

53. Ibid., pp. 101–2.

54. Abdurrahman Wahid, "Massa Islam dalam Kehidupan Bernegara dan Berbangsa", *Prisma*, extra edition, 1984, pp. 3–9.

55. Abdurrahman Wahid, "Pribumisasi Islam", in *Islam Indonesia Menatap Masa Depan*, edited by Muntaha Azhari and Abdul Mun'im Saleh (Jakarta: P3M, 1989), pp. 81–96.

56. Wahid, "Massa Islam dalam Kehidupan Bernegara dan Berbangsa", p. 8.

57. Abdurrahman Wahid, "Merumuskan Hubungan Ideologi Nasional dan Agama", *Aula*, May 1985, p. 31.

58. Abdurrahman Wahid, "Salahkah Jika Dipribumikan?", *Tempo*, 16 July 1991, p. 19.

59. See "Merelevansikan Bukannya Menghilangkan Salam", *Amanah*, no. 22 (8–21 May 1987).

60. Wahid, "Pribumisasi Islam", pp. 82–83.

61. Ibid., p. 83.

62. Ibid., p. 83.

63. Wahid, "Salahkah Jika Dipribumikan?", p. 19.

64. His familiarity with Islamic scholarship went back to his teenage years when he was a student at Mambaul Ulum, a notable *pesantren* in Solo, Central Java. Though later on he completed his graduate work at Georgetown University's Department of

Political Science, where he wrote an M.A. thesis on "Indonesia's Muslim Parties and Their Political Concept" (1959), his interest in Islamic subjects never ceased. In this regard he is an autodidact, taking full advantage of his easy access to Islamic classical as well as contemporary literatures. He collected many works while he was ambassador to the United Arab Emirates from 1976 to 1980. (Interview with Munawir Syadzali in Jakarta, 6 September 1991.)

65. Interview with Munawir Syadzali in Jakarta, 6 September 1991.

66. See "Pembaharuan: Aplikasi Tanpa Kehilangan Esensi", *Panji Masyarakat*, no. 436 (1 July 1984), pp. 12–13.

67. Munawir Syadzali, "Reaktualisasi Ajaran Islam", in *Polemik Reaktualisasi Ajaran Islam*, edited by Iqbal Abdurrauf Saimima (Jakarta: Pustaka Panjimas, 1988), pp. 1–11.

68. See Munawir Syadzali, "Dinamika dan Vitalitas Hukum Islam", *Panji Masyarakat*, no. 459 (21 February 1985), pp. 25–28. See also his "Shari'a: A Dynamic Legal System" (Paper presented at a conference on Shari'a and Codification, Colombo, Sri Lanka, December 1985); and his "Gejala Krisis Integritas Ilmiah di Kalangan Ilmuwan Islam", *Pelita*, 24 and 25 July 1987.

69. My analysis on this intellectual stream is primarily based on interviews with M. Dawam Rahardjo (Jakarta, 20 August 1991), Djohan Effendi (Jakarta, 26–27 August 1991), Hartono Mardjono (Jakarta, 28 August 1991), Sulastomo (Jakarta, 10 September 1991), and Ridwan Saidi (Jakarta, 21 August 1991). In addition, my observation is also based on a number of relevant works. These include: H.M.S. Mintaredja, *Renungan Pembaharuan Pemikiran Masyarakat Islam dan Politik di Indonesia* (Jakarta: Permata, 1971); M. Dawam Rahardjo, "Basis Sosial Pemikiran Islam di Indonesia Sejak Orde Baru", *Prisma*, no. 3 (March 1991), pp. 3–15; M. Dawam Rahardjo, "Pluriformitas dalam Perkembangan Islam di Indonesia dan Kebangkitan Agama-Agama" (Unpublished paper, n.d.); M. Dawam Rahardjo, "Menilai Sejarah Ummat Islam dari Sudut Al-Qur'an", *Panji Masyarakat*, nos. 441 and 442 (27 August and 1 September 1984); and Hassan, *Muslim Intellectual Responses to "New Order" Modernization in Indonesia*, especially pp. 78–115.

70. In a way this argument is reminiscent to that of Mohammad Natsir. In his famous speech before the Pakistan Institute of World Affairs in Karachi in 1952, Natsir suggested that Pancasila was in accordance with Islam. In fact, he also equated Indonesia with Pakistan as an Islamic country primarily because of the former's adoption of Pancasila as the state ideology. See Mohammad Natsir, *Some Observations Concerning the Role of Islam in National and International Affairs* (Ithaca: Southeast Asia Program, Department of Far Eastern Studies, Cornell University, 1954). See also his "Bertetangankah Pancasila dengan Al-Qur'an", *Hikmah*, 29 May 1954.

71. See, for instance, Mintaredja, op. cit. The term ideology as an "imperative demand" is from Allan Samson. See his "Conceptions of Politics, Power, and Ideology in Contemporary Indonesian Islam", in *Political Power and Communications in Indonesia*, edited by Karl Jackson and Lucian Pye (Berkeley, Los Angeles, and London: University of California Press, 1978), pp. 196–226.

72. For further accounts on this issue, see Donald K. Emmerson, "The Bureaucracy in Political Context: Weakness in Strength", in *Political Power and Communications in Indonesia*, edited by Karl Jackson and Lucian Pye (Berkeley, Los Angeles, and London: University of California Press, 1978), pp. 82–136; see also his *Indonesia's Elite: Political Culture and Cultural Politics* (Ithaca and London: Cornell University Press, 1976).

73. For a useful description of the administration of Islam in modern Indonesia, see Deliar Noer, *Administration of Islam in Indonesia* (Ithaca: Modern Indonesia Project, Cornell University, 1978); see also its Indonesian version, *Administrasi Islam di Indonesia* (Jakarta: Rajawali, 1982).

74. In the 1970s the most pressing problems confronting Indonesian society at large, political Islam in particular, were issues of modernization and economic development. These issues had created significant polarization among Muslim intellectuals, particularly with regard to their possible participation in the process. For a detailed account on the unofficial blueprint of Indonesia's modernization and economic development strategy, see Ali Moertopo, *Dasar-Dasar Pemikiran Tentang Akselerasi Modernisasi Pembangunan 25 Tahun*, Centre for Strategic and International Studies (Jakarta: Yayasan Proklamasi, 1973). On the differing responses of the Islamic group to these issues, see Hassan, *Muslim Intellectual Responses to "New Order" Modernization in Indonesia*.

75. Effendi and Natsir, *Pergolakan Pemikiran Islam*, p. 173.

76. Deliar Noer, *Partai Islam di Pentas Nasional 1945–1965* (Jakarta: Pustaka Utama Grafiti, 1987), p. 370.

77. In the early 1960s Dahlan criticized GPII for its tendency to always develop negative attitudes towards the state. See "Pembubaran GPII Saya Terima Dengan Ikhlas", *Duta Masyarakat*, 13 August 1963. Cited from Noer, *Partai Islam di Pentas Nasional*, p. 371.

78. Dahlan perceived that to a large extent the uneasy synthesis between Islam and the state — a phenomenon which he characterized as *probleemstelling* — was due to semantic confusions. This is particularly true with regard to the widely used terms "national state" and "Islamic state" which resurfaced into the public debate as a result of Soekarno's "Amuntai speech" in the early 1953. In an attempt to end the controversy, he wrote a letter to President Soekarno asking for further explanations concerning the relationship between Pancasila and the ideals of Islam in Indonesia's socio-cultural and political life. See Soekarno, "Negara Nasional dan Cita-Cita Islam" (Lecture delivered at the University of Indonesia, 7 May 1953).

79. Noer, *Partai Islam di Pentas Nasional*, pp. 370–71, 450.

80. For a useful description of Islamic political ventures during this period, see Ahmad Syafii Maarif, "Islamic Politics under Guided Democracy in Indonesia, 1959–1965" (M.A. thesis, Ohio University, 1980). See also his *Islam dan Politik di Indonesia Pada Masa Demokrasi Terpimpin (1959–1965)* (Yogyakarta: IAIN Sunan Kalijaga Press, 1988); Noer, *Partai Islam di Pentas Nasional*, pp. 349–424.

81. The term "solidarity-making" originated from Herbert Feith's description of the prevailing bipolar models in Indonesia's early political leadership. Generally, the model refers to Soekarno's "solidarity-making" style *vis-à-vis* Hatta's "problem-solving" tendency. See Herbert Feith, *The Decline of Constitutional Democracy in Indonesia* (Ithaca: Cornell University Press, 1962).

82. In the forefront of NU's reconciliatory politics were Idham Chalid and Saifuddin Zuhri, the party's two most important political leaders. Different from those of Islamic modernism, NU's theological underpinning in its attempt to maintain a close proximity with the regime was basically based on a well-known legal maxim: *ma la yudrak kulluh la yutrak kulluh* (what cannot be done totally should not be left out totally). Though generally supportive of Soekarno's policy, NU — and many other segments of political Muslims — remained critical to communism, with PKI as its primary embodiment. References to NU's support of Soekarno can be found in, among others, Idham Chalid, *Islam dan Demokrasi Terpimpin* (Jakarta: Lembaga Penggali dan Penghimpun Sejarah Revolusi Indonesia, 1965). See also his *Mendajung Dalam Taufan* (Jakarta: Endang dan Api Islam, 1966).

83. On NU's political radicalism in the 1970s, see Mitsuo Nakamura, "The Radical Traditionalism of the Nahdlatul Ulama in Indonesia: A Personal Account of the 26th National Congress, June 1979, Semarang", *Southeast Asian Studies* 19, no. 12 (September 1981): 187–204. On the polemics of NU's political role during these two periods, see Saifuddin Zuhri et al., *PPP, NU dan MI: Gejolak Wadah Politik Islam* (Jakarta: Integrita Press, 1984).

84. Mintaredja, *Renungan Pembaharuan Pemikiran Masyarakat Islam dan Politik di Indonesia*, pp. 7–15. His political and ideological disenchantment with the past ventures of political Islam was also publicly disclosed during the campaign for the 1971 general election. For this account, see Ken Ward, *The 1971 Election in Indonesia: An East Java Case Study* (Clayton: Monash Papers on Southeast Asia, no. 2, Centre of Southeast Asian Studies, Monash University, 1974), pp. 114–33.

85. Interview with Sulastomo in Jakarta, 10 September 1991. See also Mintaredja, op. cit.

86. Some observers have interpreted this viewpoint as accommodationistic in nature. See, for instance, Samson, "Indonesian Islam since the New Order", p. 166. See also Hassan, *Muslim Intellectual Responses to "New Order" Modernization in Indonesia*, pp. 78–115.

87. In this case the percentage of Parmusi's degree holder candidates was second only to Golkar. Out of its 327 candidates, 112 individuals (34 per cent) were degree holders in various fields. On the other hand, out of Golkar's 538 candidates, 212 (39 per cent) had university degrees. See Ward, op. cit., p. 128.

88. According to Dawam Rahardjo, they formed the second layer to the generation of Widjojo's first economic team which included Ali Wardhana, Subroto, Emil Salim, Sumarlin, and so forth. Interview with Dawam Rahardjo in Jakarta, 20 August 1991. See also his "Basis Sosial Pemikiran Islam di Indonesia Sejak Orde Baru", p. 9.

89. Some have suggested otherwise, that it is the "bureaucratization or etatization of Islam". Either way, this phenomenon suggests the growing proximity between the

Islamic group and the nationalist group which dominate the state. Even in a less optimistic fashion, it still indicates the melting of a traditionally mutual hostility between these two political factions. An interesting observation of this issue can be found in Rahardjo, "Pluriformitas dalam Perkembangan Islam di Indonesia dan Kebangkitan Agama-Agama". See also "Islamisasi Birokrasi atau Birokratisasi Islam?", *Media Dakwah*, July 1991. For a local context, see Robert Hefner, "Islamizing Java?: Religion and Politics in Rural East Java", *Journal of Asian Studies* 46, no. 3 (August 1987): 533–54.

90. See the introductory remarks of Herbert Feith and Lance Castles to the Indonesian version of their *Indonesian Political Thinking 1945–1965*, Herbert Feith and Lance Castles, eds., *Pemikiran Politik Indonesia 1945–1965* (Jakarta: LP3ES, 1988), pp. xvii–xxxvii.

91. See, for instance, M. Dawam Rahardjo, *Esei-Esei Ekonomi Politik* (Jakarta: LP3ES, 1983); Adi Sasono and Sritua Arif, *Indonesia: Ketergantungan dan Keterbelakangan* (Jakarta: Lembaga Studi Pembangunan, 1981) [Its English version is published under the title *Indonesia: Dependency and Underdevelopment* (Kuala Lumpur: Meta, 1981)]; Adi Sasono and Achmad Rofi'ie, *People's Economy* (Jakarta: Southeast Asian Forum for Development Alternatives, 1988).

92. According to Adi Sasono, the political proximity of some Muslim intellectuals to the state is not the issue. In this case he tends to see the political proximity in terms of function. As long as it creates positive impacts, such as on the development of democratization or social justice, there is nothing wrong in maintaining a close relationship with the state. (Interview with Adi Sasono in Jakarta, 4 September 1991.)

93. This pronouncement is particularly strong in Adi Sasono's intellectual discourse. For a range of his ideas on this particular issue, see his "Moral Agama dan Masalah Kemiskinan" (Unpublished discussion paper, 21 April 1985); "Usaha Pengembangan Emansipasi Sosial: Beberapa Catatan", in *Perspektif Islam dalam Pembangunan Bangsa*, edited by A. Rifa'i Hasan and Amrullah Achmad (Yogyakarta: PLP2M, 1986), pp. 323–35; "Peta Permasalahan Sosial Umat Islam dan Pokok-Pokok Pemikiran Usaha Pengembangannya: Beberapa Catatan" (Unpublished discussion paper, 28–30 May 1984).

94. This notion is expressed, among others, by Dawam Rahardjo in his criticism of the mode of Islamic struggle in the past. See his "Umat Islam dan Pembaharuan Teologi", in *Aspirasi Umat Islam Indonesia*, edited by Bosco Carvallo and Dasrizal (Jakarta: Leppenas, 1983), pp. 117–32.

95. These characteristics of the strength of the state are taken from Joel S. Migdal, *Strong Societies and Weak States: State-Society Relations and State Capabilities in the Third World* (Princeton: Princeton University Press, 1988).

96. Interview with Dawam Rahardjo in Jakarta, 20 August 1991. See also his "LSM dan Program-Program Pengembangan Masyarakat" (Unpublished paper, n.d.); "Metode Pelibatan Partisipasi Masyarakat dalam Pembangunan Pedesaan" (Unpublished paper, n.d.).

97.   Interview with Adi Sasono in Jakarta, 4 September 1991. See also his "Islam dan Sosialisme Religius", in *Aspirasi Umat Islam Indonesia*, edited by Bosco Carvallo and Dasrizal (Jakarta: Leppenas, 1983), pp. 109–16.

98.   Though his interest is primarily in the field of social transformation, to some extent Dawam also shares the intellectual concerns of the theological school. For a range of his interests in conventional Islamic thinking, see his reader on *Insan Kamil: Konsepsi Manusia Menurut Islam* (Jakarta: Pustaka Grafitipers, 1985). See also his regular columns in *Ulumul Qur'an* — an Islamic quarterly journal which he and his peers publish — in which he writes a series of encyclopedic themes on the Qur'an.

99.   Among the respected research study institutes the formations of which Dawam participated in were LSP; Pusat Pengembangan Agribisnis (PPA, Centre for Agribusiness Development); Perhimpunan Pengembangan Pesantren dan Masyarakat (P3M, Association for Pesantren and Community Development); Lembaga Studi Agama dan Filsafat (LSAF, Institute for the Study of Religion and Philosophy); and Pusat Pengembangan Sumberdaya Wanita (PPSW, Centre for Women Resources Development).

100.   Among the founders of LSP were Dawam Rahardjo, Tawang Alun, Badir Munir, Listianto, and Sritua Arif. See "Adi Sasono: Pembela Mustadz'afin", *Media Dakwah*, December 1989, pp. 44–47. Many observers have characterized LSP as an organization with "high level politics" and "grass-roots mobilization". See Philip Eldridge, *NGOs in Indonesia: Popular Movement or Arm of Government* (Clayton: Working Paper no. 55, Centre of Southeast Asian Studies, Monash University, 1989).

101.   Fachry Ali and Bahtiar Effendy, *Merambah Jalan Baru Islam: Rekonstruksi Pemikiran Islam Indonesia Masa Order Baru* (Bandung: Mizan, 1986), pp. 165, 217.

102.   For the Indonesian case, a brief sketch of this issue has been raised by among others, Herbert Feith. See his "Democratization and the Indonesian Intellectuals: Some Perspective" (Outline paper delivered at a conference on the State and Civil Society in Contemporary Indonesia, Monash University, November 1988).

103.   Interview with Dawam Rahardjo in Jakarta, 20 August 1991. See also his "Basis Sosial Pemikiran Islam di Indonesia Sejak Order Baru", p. 9.

104.   This viewpoint is strongly expressed by Dawam in his "Umat Islam dan Pembaharuan Teologi", pp. 117–32.

105.   Interview with Dawam Rahardjo in Jakarta, 20 August 1991. For a report on their collaborative work on *pesantren*, see Sudjoko Prasodjo et al., *Profil Pesantren: Laporan Hasil Penelitian Pesantren Al-Falak dan Delapan Pesantren Lain di Bogor* (Jakarta: LP3ES, 1974). For a range of Dawam's ideas on *pesantren*, see his "Dunia Pesantren dalam Peta Pembaharuan", in *Pesantren dan Pembaharuan*, edited by M. Dawam Rahardjo (Jakarta: LP3ES, 1974), pp. 1–38; "Kyai, Pesantren dan Desa", *Prisma*, no. 4 (August 1973), pp. 80–95; "Gambaran

Pemuda Santri: Penglihatan dari Jendela Pesantren di Pabelan", in *Pemuda dan Perubahan Sosial*, edited by Taufik Abdullah (Jakarta: LP3ES, 1974), pp. 90–112.

106.   Interview with Dawam Rahardjo in Jakarta, 20 August 1991. In the mid-1970s, the Department of Religion launched a series of vocational training programmes involving a large number of *pesantren* throughout the country as part of its renewal agendas in Islamic education. For an official blueprint of *pesantren* educational reform, see H. Kafrawi, *Pembaharuan Sistem Pendidikan Pondok Pesantren* (Jakarta: Cemara Indah, 1978).

107.   The best study on the genealogical as well as intellectual relationship between *pesantren* and Indonesia's Islamic traditionalism is Zamakhsyari Dhofier, *Tradisi Pesantren: Studi Tentang Pandangan Hidup Kyai* (Jakarta: LP3ES, 1982).

108.   Ali and Effendy, op. cit., p. 164.

109.   Ibid., p. 165. Among Adi Sasono's most recent urban projects, carried out in conjunction with many other institutions, was transforming a slum area in Samarinda, South Kalimantan, into a representative business establishment. In 1989 this Citra Niaga project received the Aga Khan architectural award. See "Adi Sasono: Pembela Mustadz'afin", *Media Dakwah*, December 1989, pp. 44–47.

110.   See his "Moral Agama dan Masalah Kemiskinan" (Unpublished discussion paper, 21 April 1985).

111.   See his "Islam dan Sosialisme Religius", p. 113.

112.   See his "Islam dan Sosialisme Religius", p. 110.

4

Implications of the New Islamic Intellectualism
Ideas and Practices

Now is the time to conduct a rational and functional politics, in the sense of managing [Indonesia's] common concern, namely: welfare, justice, and democracy. This new political discourse must be developed within Muslim community. A new [mode of] politics, which takes sociological changes into account, must be initiated. Without this, there will be a gap between institution and social base. Indonesia is no longer a field for elite political alliance. To begin a new political tradition is not an easy task. There will always be forces which try to reintroduce the old political bases.

Kuntowijoyo[1]

In chapter 3 I described at length the general pronouncements of the new Islamic intellectualism. To better understand the nature of this intellectual movement, I examined the case in the light of its socio-political context. Wherever necessary, I also discussed — albeit briefly — the social origins of its key actors and precursors, particularly concerning their intellectual background. And finally, I also attempted to throw some light on — but did not fully illuminate — the kind of impact the new intellectualism has on the contemporary expression of Islamic political ideas and practices.

This and the following chapters address the latter issue more fully. Based on the variety of the intellectual preferences described above, I will explore the implications of the new intellectualism on the current expression of Indonesia's Islamic political thoughts and actions under three major themes: (1) reformulation of the theological or philosophical underpinning of political Islam; (2) redefinition of the political objectives of Islam; and (3) reassessment of the political approach of Islam. The first two of these themes will be treated in this chapter, while the third is given a chapter of its own. In my view, as will be demonstrated in the following discussion, it is in terms of these three interlocking themes that the significance of the intellectual transformation of Islamic political ideas and practices in today's Indonesian political Islam must be understood.

REFORMULATING THE THEOLOGICAL UNDERPINNING OF POLITICAL ISLAM

Recalling our earlier discussion in chapter 2, I suggested that the chief, though not the only, problem which had inhibited a viable synthesis between Islam and the state was the difficulty of finding a nationally acceptable linkage between them. A number of historical episodes have demonstrated that, due to the heterogeneous nature of the sociological and cultural contours of the Indonesian community, a formalistic or legalistic connection between Islam and the state was not acceptable to all. As is widely known, the ultimate embodiment of this model was the attempt of the earlier leaders and activists of political Islam to make Islam the ideological basis of the state. The softer variation of this quest can be attributed to their endeavours — through their efforts to press for the legalization of the Jakarta Charter — to authorize the state to exercise control over the implementation of Islamic *shari'a* by its adherents. As it turned out, these ventures not only resulted in a political impasse, but also contributed to the peripheral and weakened position of its political activists.

As discussed at the beginning of chapter 3, there were theological or philosophical underpinnings behind the determination of political Muslims to advocate a formalistic or legalistic bond between Islam and the state. To a large extent, these theological underpinnings were shaped and influenced by their perceptions of Islam.

Briefly reiterated, the nucleus of this theological underpinning was a belief in the holistic nature of Islam.[2] This religious premise was perceived as an indication that Islam provides knowledge about every aspect of life. In fact, this particular viewpoint became the chief basis for an understanding that Islam recognizes no separation between religion and the state, between the transcendental and the temporal.

Many leaders and activists of the 1950s and 1960s used this tenet to establish and further their social and political agendas. Included was a perception that Islam furnishes its adherents with a full-fledged concept of the state or system of governing. Additionally, some of them even maintained that the state is in fact an integral part, or extension, of Islam. This is a religious-political stance which, in some quarters of the Islamic world, is popularly phrased as *inna al-Islam al-din wa al-dawlah* — that Islam is both a religion and the state. From this perspective, they insisted that it was appropriate for them to propose that Islam be adopted as the ideological basis of the state.[3]

The new emerging generation of Islamic thinkers and activists, especially those whose main interest has been in the field of religious (or theological) renewal, also earnestly believe in the notion of Islamic holism. Nonetheless, they reject the conclusion of the earlier generation of Islamic thinkers and activists, drawn from such a religious precept. They assert that the holistic nature of Islam does not necessarily require a mixture between the divine (that is, Islamic values) and the profane (that is, state, political organization, ideology, etc.). Nor does it imply an understanding that these two different realms should be placed on the same level. In their view, though Islam does not acknowledge the notion of partition between these two domains, they can — and in fact must — be differentiated. Placing these two domains in parallel will only lead to confusion in the structure and hierarchy of Islamic values (such as portraying the form of state, ideology, or political party as sacred objects). This in turn, as argued strongly by the strong advocate of Indonesia's contemporary Islamic religious reform, Nurcholish Madjid, may contradict the very principle of Islamic monotheism (*tawhid*).[4]

In addition, they are also of the opinion that in spite of the fact that Islam is holistic in nature, in itself Islam does not actually regulate every aspect of life. Instead, they believe that as far as the societal (not ritual) doctrines of Islam are concerned, it appears that Islam, as suggested by Harun Nasution, only provides moral values which serve as the basic and general guidelines for human life.[5]

This theological stance, as articulated under the themes of "desacralization", "reactualization", and "indigenization of Islam", has implications for the political ideas and practices of the new emerging Muslim thinkers and activists who have been writing since the 1970s. This is especially the case with regard to their (1) perceptions towards the state and its ideology (Pancasila), (2) socio-political aspirations, and (3) strategies and tactics.

There are two paradigmatic religious-political propositions which can be directly associated with their theological thinking. First, as a consequence of the belief that only Allah possesses absolute transcendency (sacredness), they consider every aspect of worldly matters temporal and relative in value. By implication, this statement suggests that there is nothing sacred or absolute concerning the nature of the state, ideology, party, or any other socio-political affairs.

Second, given the holistic nature of Islam, it is imperative that political institutions (for example, the state, parties) and their system of governing reflect the basic injunctions as laid out by the Qur'an as well as the traditions of Muhammad (*sunnah*). But, since Islam — perhaps because of its timeless and universal character — speaks of societal (again not ritual) matters in highly general principles, it is, therefore, their opinion that the implementation of those general principles is at the discretion of its adherents. In other words, practical considerations or preferences in the realization of those particular values should be at the volition of its thinkers (*ulama*) and activists (*umara*, literally meaning rulers) to devise.

It is important to note that the hallmark of this religious renewal has been the will and skill of the new generation in critically examining the stipulations of the Qur'an and *sunnah* concerning the position of Islam *vis-à-vis* the state in particular and politics in general. Their intellectual ventures have been oriented towards doctrinal as well as empirical inquiries. They have tried to investigate and determine whether or not Islam does indeed lay down an explicit concept (or simply a set of general principles) of the state, politics, and system of governing. In addition, given Islam's centuries-long encounter with those issues, both in terms of thoughts and actions, they have also revisited the theoretical statements of a number of prominent classical (for example, Al-Mawardi, Ibn Taymiyyah) as well as modern (for example, Ali Abd al-Raziq, Abu al-A'la al-Maududi, Sayyid Qutb) Islamic thinkers on the particular subject of the political relationship between Islam and the state.[6]

In this intellectual quest this new emerging generation of Muslim intellectuals, especially those whose main concern is to reformulate their theological underpinnings, find no clear indications that Islam has a profound interest in regulating issues pertinent to the affairs of the state. From the Qur'an, the primary source of Islamic messages, they see no doctrines which specifically discuss the issue. In fact, given the significance of the matter, it is astonishing that the term "state" (*dawlah*) does not even appear in the Qur'an. Furthermore, to support their belief that the question of an Islamic state (*dawlah Islamiyah*) is in fact a modern phenomenon, a product of the encounter of the Muslim world with Western colonialism, they argue that a formal declaration of an Islamic state had never been actually made during the period of classical or medieval Islam.[7]

It is, therefore, their opinion that Islam does not oblige its adherents to form a state. Rather, because of the fact that a substantial number of Qur'anic doctrines address societal issues more frequently than transcendental ones, they tend to believe that the emphasis of Islam is on the formation of a good society, that is, a society which reflects the substance of Islamic universal messages (*rahmah li al-'alamin*).[8] Thus, for some Muslim thinkers, like Nurcholish Madjid, the idea of an Islamic state or Islamic ideology, as once strongly proposed by earlier leaders and activists of political Islam, was only "a form of apologetical tendency". More specifically, it represented an apologia to (1) the dominant position of Western ideologies such as liberal-democracy, socialism, and capitalism; and (2) the legalistic tendencies of many Muslims in their understanding of Islamic religious tenets.[9]

Similarly, they do not see enough evidence that the traditions of Muhammad (*sunnah*) deal with the question of state or politics in a more comprehensive fashion. In their view, the *sunnah* — like the Qur'an — does not set forth a detailed model of how a state should be actually organized. In fact, in their opinion, Muhammad himself did not even provide a clear indication that what he created in Medina was actually a political institution which could be labelled a state.

This viewpoint, as expressed in the writings of — to name only a few of them — Nurcholish Madjid, Harun Nasution, Abdurrahman Wahid, and Munawir Syadzali, was partly drawn from the fact that a fixed mechanism for leadership succession and transfer of power/authority was absent in the early days of Islamic political history. Both the theoretical (doctrinal) as well as empirical (historical) Islam indicated that the Prophet Muhammad did not formulate such a necessary procedure for the management of the state. On these particular issues (that is, leadership succession and transfer of power/authority), the only recognized mechanism (in fact, it had become some kind of rule of thumb) was simply an obligation to apply the principle of *syura* (consultation).[10]

There is no question concerning the applicability of the principle of *syura* in the process of leadership succession and transfer of power/authority. However, it is important to note that the practices of leadership succession — especially in the early period of Islam — varied from time to time. During the time of Muhammad, at least according to Sunni historical accounts,[11] there had been a widely held belief that he did not select a political successor. Abu Bakr, one of his closest companions, became the first Caliph through a limited election; Umar ibn al-Khattab, the second Caliph, was appointed by Abu Bakr to succeed him; Utsman ibn Affan was elevated to the office of the caliphate, to become the third Caliph, by a committee formed under the executive order of Umar; and Ali ibn Abi Thalib became the fourth Caliph through a different form of election.[12]

Accordingly, for some proponents of Indonesia's new Islamic intellectualism, such as Abdurrahman Wahid, the lack of a uniformly accepted mechanism for leadership succession indicates that Muhammad did not deliberately or intentionally aspire to the creation of an Islamic state. In his journalistic column he asked rhetorically:

> If it is true that the Prophet aspired for the formation of an 'Islamic State' it is impossible that the issues of leadership succession and transfer of power were not formally formulated. [In this case] the Prophet simply ordered [the Muslim community] to 'consult in matters.' [It was amazing that] issues of such great significance were not concretely institutionalized, rather it sufficed for him to regulate those issues in a single dictum: 'their affairs should be consulted among them.' Is there a state in such a form?[13]

Despite the lack of a clear conceptual construct, advocates of this new Islamic intellectualism find that both the Qur'an and *sunnah* do provide a set of ethical principles relevant to administering the state and its governing mechanism. They point out that the Qur'an repeatedly mentions the normative ideas of consultation (*syura*), justice (*'adl*), and egalitarianism (*musawah*).[14] These were the very principles which were applied and demonstrated vigorously in the political traditions of early Islam, particularly during Muhammad's time. Because of this, some proponents of the new intellectualism like Nurcholish Madjid — by way of quoting Robert Bellah — share the notion which characterizes Muhammad's city state of Medina as "a very type of equalitarian participant nationalism".[15]

The best expression of this set of ethical values (that is, the principles of consultation, justice, and egalitarianism), according to many defenders of the new intellectualism, was Muhammad's Constitution of Medina (*Mitsaq al-Madinah*). This Constitution, as they perceive it, was the governing formula which regulated the socio-political relationships among members of the Medinan community. At that time this single political community, described by Muhammad as an *ummah*, consisted of a number of different religious groups, such as Muslims, Jews, and tribal-pagans.[16]

In the view of Ahmad Syafii Maarif, a graduate of the University of Chicago's Department of Near Eastern Languages and Civilization and an earnest disciple of Fazlur Rahman, whose major intellectual interest is in the political relationship between Islam and the state,[17] these political tenets can be considered to be a common platform which enabled the process of socio-political convergence to take place among the subjects of a political community with different religious backgrounds.[18] Others recognize the Constitution of Medina as a political document which provides a basic model for the relationship between Islam and politics, and Islam and the state.[19]

In spite of the different perceptions of this Constitution, in the eyes of many proponents of the new Islamic intellectualism, the significance of this political document rests primarily on its emphasis on the principles of justice, participation, consultation, and egalitarianism.[20] This perception, at least according to Munawir Syadzali, is reinforced by the fact that, regardless of the majority position of Muslims in the composition of Medina's political community, this Constitution did not mention Islam as the formal religion of the state. In his widely read *Islam dan Tata Negara* (Islam and the Administration of the State), Munawir wrote:

> One thing which should be noted is that the Constitution of Medina, which is perceived by many students of politics as the constitution of the first Islamic state, did not mention [Islam as] the religion of the state.[21]

This point is important for Munawir because he considers the mentioning of a certain religious belief as the religion of the state as a necessary condition for the existence of a theocratic state (*negara agama*). Therefore, in his view, the fact that the Constitution of Medina did not mention Islam as the religion of the state suggests that Muhammad did not actually call for the establishment of a theocratic state in which Islam would have served as its sole basis.[22]

Based on this examination, there are at least two important propositions discernible. First, it can be strongly argued that Islam does not have any particular conceptual or theoretical preferences concerning the nature or construct of the state and its system of governing. Furthermore, it can also be suggested that Islam does not specifically oblige its adherents to establish a state, let alone a theocratic one. Second, in spite of the absence of a full-fledged concept of the state or politics in Islam, nonetheless Islam does possess a set of ethical values or political principles, such as justice, consultation, and egalitarianism. It is the substantive implementation — as once demonstrated by the political practices of Muhammad — of these particular injunctions which is compulsory in Islam.

With these theological-political perceptions, this new generation of Muslim intellectuals are actually advancing a middle way of Islamic political theorizing. In this respect, they do not share the formalistic, legalistic, or scripturalistic interpretation of Islamic holism, as articulated most notably by Abu al-A'la al-Maududi who argues that the state is in fact an integral part (or even extension) of Islam.[23] At the same time they also reject the secular version of Ali Abd al-Raziq's political ideas which suggest a complete partition between Islam and the affairs of the state.[24]

In the view of Indonesia's current Islamic thinkers and activists, these two differing theoretical models have major weaknesses. Maududi's theoretical error lies primarily in his failure to recognize the fact that Islam does not actually offer a definite or fixed mechanism to regulate political succession or transfer of power/authority — an important element in the construction of a theory of the political administration of the state.[25]

By contrast, the defect in Ali Abd al-Raziq's political theory is his perception that the state, as a political instrument, should be separated from any religious (Islamic) stipulations. This idea not only denies any possible connection (linkage) between Islam and the state, but also rejects *in toto* the normative aspects of Islam in the socio-political processes and the governing mechanism of the state.[26] These theologically driven political ideas have undoubtedly played decisive roles in shaping the perceptions of this new generation of Islamic thinkers and activists on (1) the nature of Indonesia's nation state; and (2) the position of Pancasila as the national ideology of the state.

Given the character of their theological values on the one hand, and the make-up of Indonesia's socio-religious and cultural situation on the other, it is obvious that the new generation of Muslim intellectuals share the notion of a national unitary construct of the state. Within those limits, they actually see the current form and structure of the state as the best imaginable model. Therefore, they unequivocally support and accept it. Some of them, such as Abdurrahman Wahid and Munawir Syadzali, even ardently assert that the present ideological construct of the state should be regarded as the final goal for Indonesian Muslims.[27]

Other than the aforementioned theological considerations, there are a number of important factors which serve as the direct bases for their acceptance of Indonesia's national unitary construct of the state. These include the facts that (1) the state guarantees freedom for Muslims to implement their religious teachings; (2) the majority of the archipelago's population is Muslim; and (3) the state Constitution does not contradict — in fact to some extent it even reflects — the substance of Islamic principles.[28] Put together, these factors represent an undeniable reality that, simply by virtue of the fact that the majority of the country's inhabitants are Muslims, the basic contour of its governing principles is in tune with, if not in fact influenced by, Islamic values. Within this framework, at least theoretically, the state will not implement laws and policies which are in direct conflict with Islamic teachings.

This seems to be the case with the nature of Indonesia's nation state. It is gradually evolving as a religious state, that is, a state which is concerned with the implementation and development of religious values, without having to become a theocratic state which is constitutionally based on certain formal religious institutions.[29] In this context, as state officials themselves have acknowledged publicly, religion does provide a spiritual, ethical, and moral basis for Indonesia's national development.[30] Primarily because of this, many defenders of the new Islamic intellectualism believe that Indonesia's national unitary state deserves religious-political legitimacy and acceptance among Muslims.

It is fair to say that the principal factor in their acceptance of Indonesia's nation state boils down to the fact that the state provides ample opportunities for Muslims to implement their religious teachings. Historically, this position has been especially popular among the disciples of Indonesia's Islamic traditionalism. Already in 1935, Nahdlatul Ulama (NU) had issued a religious instruction (*fatwa*) suggesting that it was religiously obligatory (*wajib*) to defend the Dutch Indies — that is, Indonesia under the colonial tutelage of the Netherlands — from external attacks. The basis for the issuance of this religious *fatwa* was purely the fact that the state — even though its administrators obviously were not followers of Islam — guaranteed freedom for Muslims to perform their religious duties.[31]

To some extent, their acceptance of the current form of the state has also been strengthened by their perception of Pancasila ideology and the 1945 Constitution. In their opinion both the ideological and constitutional foundations of the state are in accordance with the teachings of Islam. More especially, each of the five principles of Pancasila — particularly the notions of transcendental monotheism, consultation, and social justice — are considered to reflect the substance of Islamic teachings. For these reasons, a number of Muslim intellectuals like Munawir Syadzali, Nurcholish Madjid, Syafii Maarif, Dawam Rahardjo, and Djohan Effendi, have come forward to advance an intriguing proposition which suggests that Pancasila is in fact comparable to — though by no means exactly the same as — the Constitution of Medina.

On this issue their argument is based on two major premises: (1) substantively, both the Constitution of Medina and Pancasila recognize the connection between religious values and the affairs of the state; and (2) functionally, these two political formulas represent common platforms (*kalimah al-sawa'*), serving as the governing principle for a socio-religiously diversified political community.[32]

This complementary juxtaposition between the Constitution of Medina and Pancasila has further socio-political implications, especially in the way they see other segments of Indonesia's political community of different religious backgrounds. From the previous discussion, it will be recalled that an important part of the new intellectualism is the idea of pluralism or inclusivism. Internally, this concept enlarges the tent of Indonesia's Muslim community. More importantly, it also reinforces the notion of Islamic brotherhood (*ukhuwwah Islamiyah*), in which the concept of *umat Islam* is no longer defined in terms of socio-political orientations and associations. Instead, their perception of the community of *umat Islam* is simply based on being a Muslim.

Externally, this idea represents a serious effort to further develop the notion of a national brotherhood (*ukhuwwah wathaniyah*).[33] With this concept the new Muslim intellectuals perceive other segments of Indonesia's political community as equal counterparts — rather than as religious-political adversaries — for the accomplishment of common socio-political objectives that include the formation of a just, egalitarian, and participatory Indonesian state and society. Viewed from the historical perspective of Indonesia's parliamentary democracy era, this was actually one of the most idealized common political goals among some modernist factions of the country's political parties (that is, Masyumi, Partai Sosialis Indonesia [PSI], Parkindo, and Partai Katolik) in the early 1950s.

Based on such a lengthy and critical discourse, which the protagonists of this new Islamic intellectualism have conducted with the principal ingredients of Islamic doctrines as well as with the diversity of Indonesia's social fabric, they call for the development of a new political meaning for Islam. As has been repeatedly suggested, in this particular framework substance — rather than formality or legality — becomes an "imperative demand", religiously as well as sociologically.

Accordingly, it is fair to conclude that the kind of theological or philosophical underpinning of political Islam which this new emerging generation of Muslim thinkers and activists have been trying to redefine and shape during the last two decades can be labelled as substantialism. In this conception Islam in politics is no longer based on scripture focused on ideological symbolism. Instead, congruent with the increasing exposure of Muslim youth — particularly those who have some sort of cultural or emotional linkage with Indonesia's earlier Islamic political movement — to modern tertiary education as well as to economic development, the expression of political Islam is carried out in a less symbolic or ideological fashion. In this model the substantive values of political Islam — identified earlier as justice, consultation, and egalitarianism — serve as its core orientation.[34]

REDEFINING THE SOCIO-POLITICAL OBJECTIVES OF ISLAM

Seen from a broader religious perspective, there are actually no major differences between the aspirations of the earlier leaders of political Islam and those of the new emerging generation of Islamic political thinkers and activists. Comparable with the circumstances of the Calvinists, whose pathways to economic capitalism are motivated by the principle of *beruf* (religious calling),[35] to a large extent the political ventures of these two different Muslim generations are driven by the same Islamic religious precepts, such as the notion of *ya'muru bi al-ma'ruf wa yanhauna 'an al-munkar* (to enjoin right conduct and forbid indecency).[36] In addition, it can also be suggested that their ultimate goals, as expressed in their socio-political thoughts and actions, seem to refer to the realization of Qur'anic dictums, most notably the idea of *baldatun thayyibatun wa rabbun ghafur* (a fair land and an indulgent Lord).[37] From this particular context, it can be said that both generations of Muslim intellectuals — at least theoretically — are Qur'anic-centred in the sense that their political ideas and practices are connected to, if not rooted in, Islamic values.[38]

However, it is in the implementation of this general objective that they differ markedly. As indicated in the preceding chapters, in the process of spelling out this general goal the earlier generation of Islamic thinkers and activists tended to be scripturalistically oriented. They were obsessed with relating Islam and the state formally and legally, which drove many of them to maintain the idea of creating an Islamic state as their central political objective. In their view the above general goal (that is, *baldatun thayyibatun wa rabbun ghafur*) could not be inherently accomplished in a state which was not formally based on Islam as its ideology and/or official religion.[39]

On the contrary, the new emerging generation of Muslim intellectuals appear to adhere to a substantialist approach to the societal doctrines of Islam. By emphasizing the substantive side of politics, they reject the formalistic and legalistic character of Islamic political goals. Therefore, as a point of departure, they do not aspire to the establishment of an Islamic state. In fact, as discussed earlier, based on their understanding of Islamic doctrines as well as the sociological contours of Indonesian society, they oppose the notion of Islam as the ideological basis of the state. Instead, their primary concern is the development of a socio-political system which reflects, or is in tune with, the general principles of Islamic political values.

In spite of the absence of the formalistic or legalistic political connection between Islam and the state, they strongly believe that the current form of Indonesia's nation state — with Pancasila as its ideological basis — is sufficient to accommodate the realization of those Islamic socio-political injunctions.[40] In other words, the state — at least theoretically — provides opportunities for the implementation of the socio-political idealism of Islam.

The fact that those socio-political objectives — which are essentially democratic in nature — have not been fully realized or implemented, perhaps with some exceptions during the liberal democracy period in the 1950s, must be considered common concerns for all Indonesians. Concomitant with such a viewpoint, it is very much the opinion of this new generation of Muslim thinkers and activists that this particular problem (and many other problems of the state for that matter) should not be construed as a legitimate ground to transform the national unitary character of the state. Instead, efforts to reinstate those democratic principles (or to remedy any other of Indonesia's socio-political problems) ought to be carried out within the framework of the present ideological construct of the state.[41]

It can be suggested that the pronouncements of the new Islamic intellectualism, as described at some length in the preceding section, represent an elaborated version of the above socio-political objectives. Regardless of the differences that exist among the champions of the new Islamic intellectualism, both in terms of approach and area of interest, it is evident that their thoughts and actions express relatively unified socio-political concerns. In this regard, given the present situation confronting political Muslims in particular and Indonesia's Muslim community in general, it is safe to conclude that attempts to redefine the new socio-political aspirations of Islam fall into two important headings: (1) the development of egalitarian and democratic political arrangements; and (2) the inception of equitable economic processes. Seen from the plight of political Islam and its constituents in contemporary Indonesian politics, these two goals are not only relevant, but also remedial to their debilitating condition.

From the previous discussions concerning the uneasy relationship between Islam and the state, it is noticeable that one of the most serious implications of this inimical situation has been the withering of the former's political role. Included in this dismal predicament are the diminishing opportunities for political Muslims, particularly during the 1970s and 1980s, to participate fully in the country's political development. Contrary to their earlier experiences, especially at a time when Indonesia was still adhering to a liberal democratic political arrangement (1950–57), their current involvement in the political process is only peripheral. As a result of these discouraging circumstances, coupled with the New Order's determination to establish political order and stability at the expense of popular participation, it is fair to say that political Islam, both at the legislative and executive-bureaucratic levels, has not been proportionally represented.[42]

It is against this political backdrop that the socio-political objectives of Islam, especially with regard to the idea of more egalitarian political arrangements, are enunciated. As reflected in the intellectual discourse of the new generation of Muslim thinkers and activists, all of their endeavours are directed towards re-entry into politics.

There are at least two strategic elements embedded in this redefined political objective. First, from the value-oriented perspective, the idea of an egalitarian or democratic political arrangement reflects the basic political principles of Islam (for example, *al-'adl*, *al-musawah*, *syura*). In spite of the fact that it represents Islamic political idealism, different from the earlier political aspirations where the notion of an Islamic state or Islamic ideology served as the central point, this political objective is considered to be neither threatening nor irritating to the unitary construct of Indonesia's nation state.

The basis of this encouraging perception has been the conventional wisdom that an egalitarian or democratic political arrangement is inclusive in character, shared virtually by all champions of modern politics regardless of their religious affiliations. In the context of Indonesian politics, this viewpoint was exemplified by the fact that in the early 1950s such political idealism had once served as a common platform for the development of a relatively smooth political relationship between Islamic (that is, Masyumi) and non-Islamic political groupings (that is, Socialist and Christian parties).[43]

Second, from the goal-oriented perspective, by advancing this kind of socio-political objective and rejecting the formalistic idea of an Islamic state or Islamic ideology, it paves the way for integration in the mainstream of national politics, thereby, at least theoretically, increasing opportunities for its participants to become fully involved in the discourse of the country's politics. This may lead to their eventual proportional representation, at both the parliamentarian and executive-bureaucratic levels. In other words, from a practical politics point of view, the nature of these socio-political goals, as imagined by Amien Rais, will enhance the possibility of the current leaders of activists of political Islam to have a say in determining the future of Indonesia.[44] Or as argued by Nurcholish Madjid, it has the potential to serve as a necessary, though by no means sufficient, groundwork for the foundation of a new political equilibrium in which the majority of the country's religious community can fully participate in national development.[45]

This framework of analysis is equally useful in understanding the rationale behind the promulgation of the second major objective of political Islam, that is, an agenda dealing with the issues of the distributive economy, recognizing that the calamitous political relationship between Islam and the state has shrunk the former's economic opportunities. As suggested by Deliar Noer, this has been signified by the failure of a number of important resources, both in terms of policy and organization, perceived as potential for the enhancement of Muslim economic bases.[46]

During the liberal democracy period, the participation of the earlier political Muslims in the executive and bureaucratic offices was strong. Beginning with the premiership of Natsir and Sukiman, this strategic position was used to reinforce, among other things, the politics of economic nationalism.[47] Other than nationalizing such an important economic infrastructure such as De Javasch Bank,[48] operating under Sumitro Djojohadikusumo's Economic Urgency Programme, those Islamic political activists, with Sjafruddin Prawiranegara and Jusuf Wibisono at the forefront,[49] were determined to strengthen the position of indigenous entrepreneurs *vis-à-vis* their foreign counterparts.[50]

During Soekarno's guided democracy era, the influence of political Muslims in Indonesia's economic and political development began to erode significantly. It is not an exaggeration to say that their actual leverage to power did not go beyond the office of the Department of Religious Affairs, which was still very much in the control of NU. This political gap, coupled with Soekarno's deliberate adoption of a radical self-help economic policy, contributed to the collapse of the previous economic policy, which greatly hampered further expansion of strong indigenous entrepreneurship in such industries as cigarette and *batik*.[51]

Given the country's demographic make-up, quite naturally it was Muslim entrepreneurs who largely suffered from the breakdown of this early economic policy. During the New Order period this dismal state of affairs had been signified by their continued declining role in those industrial commodities. One major case in point is the downfall of the once powerful Gabungan Koperasi Batik Indonesia (GKBI, Association of Indonesian Batik Co-operatives) due to the difficulty in acquiring additional capital.[52]

If we put this uneasy-political-relationship-leads-to-economic-disadvantage perspective aside, perhaps the greatest factor promoting the idea of a distributive economy has been the state's prevailing economic policy, which tends to give more emphasis to growth than to distribution. This tendency, as expressed in many studies concerning the downside of the New Order government's growth-oriented economic policy, has contributed to the widening gap between the have and have-not. Moreover, it also has its significant share in the making of economic exclusivism, which has led to the monopolization of virtually every economic sector.[53]

These undemocratic realities have undoubtedly placed most Indonesians in an unfavourable economic position. This unbalanced situation is detrimental to a substantial part of the population, and it is a potential source of societal discontent. As has been frequently noted, the occurrence of a number of instances of significant socio-political unrest in the country has always had dissenting economic overtones.[54]

Accordingly, since the early development of the new Islamic intellectualism in the 1970s, emerging Muslim thinkers and activists like Nurcholish Madjid, Djohan Effendi, Ahmad Wahib, Utomo Dananjaya, Usep Fathuddin (all concerned with religious renewal); Mintaredja, Sulastomo, Bintoro Tjokroamidjojo, Sa'dillah Mursid, Ridwan Saidi, Akbar Tanjung (proponents of political/bureaucratic reform); Sudjoko Prasodjo, M. Dawam Rahardjo, Tawang Alun, Adi Sasono, and Ekky Syachruddin (advocates of social transformation) have emphasized the strategic meanings of these two primary objectives. Along with their younger (not necessarily in the sense of generational age) counterparts in the 1980s, including Munawir Syadzali, Abdurrahman Wahid, Imaduddin Abdurrahim, Aswab Mahasin, Amin Aziz, A.M. Saefuddin, Amien Rais,

Kuntowijoyo, Watik Pratiknya, Yahya Muhaimin, Halide, Jalaluddin Rakhmat, and Fuad Amsyari, they have organized various discussion forums relevant for further development of the idea of securing more egalitarian political arrangements as well as more equitable economic distribution.

What has been accomplished, in both theoretical as well as practical sense, by these new Muslim intellectuals in the past two decades has pointed towards a possible realization of these two main objectives. The political and bureaucratic breakthrough initiated by Muslim political reformers can be read as an important strategy to pave the way to an integrative and substantive re-entry of political Islam into the country's political discourse. Likewise, the activism of Muslim social transformers is designed to pursue relevant emancipation agendas aimed at the formation of a relatively strong civil society, economically as well as politically. This will enable society to function as participant, rather than subject of Indonesia's political community.

These socio-economic and political overtones are well represented in the idealism and activism of the new generation of Muslim intellectuals. Though by no means covering the whole spectrum of aspirations of the Indonesian Islamic community, the publication of *Aspirasi Umat Islam Indonesia* (Aspiration of the Indonesian Islamic Community) expresses textually their determination to reject the earlier formalistic and legalistic objectivism of political Islam, and reassert their commitment towards political and economic democracy.[55] Through a series of national gatherings and limited discussion groups, those agendas were developed further.[56] They expect that the foundation of Ikatan Cendekiawan Muslim Se-Indonesia (ICMI, Union of Indonesian Muslim Intellectuals) in December 1990 can serve as a national forum where Muslim intellectuals and activists are able to develop the goal of economic and political democratization into its relevant components.[57]

Notes

1. "Kiblat Baru Politik Kaum Santri", *Pesan*, no. 1 (1992), p. 24.

2. There are a number of Qur'anic verses which can be used to support this statement. The most fashionably referred to is Qur'an 16:89 which reads: "And We reveal the Scripture unto thee as an exposition of all things, and a guidance and a mercy and good tidings for those who have surrendered (to Allah)." Translation is from Marmaduke Pickthall, *The Glorious Koran* (Albany: State University of New York Press, 1976).

3. For a useful description of their political ideas, see, among others, Munawir Syadzali, "Indonesia's Muslim Parties and Their Political Concepts" (M.A. thesis, Georgetown University, 1959); Harun Nasution, "The Islamic State in Indonesia: The Rise of the Ideology, the Movement for Its Creation and the Theory of the Masyumi" (M.A. thesis, McGill University, 1965); Ahmad Syafii Maarif, "Islam as the Basis of State: A Study of the Islamic Political Ideas as Reflected in the Constituent Assembly Debates in Indonesia," (Ph.D. dissertation, University of Chicago, 1983). See also Ahmad Syafii Maarif, *Islam dan Masalah Kenegaraan: Studi Tentang Percaturan dalam Konstituante* (Jakarta: LP3ES, 1985).

4. Nurcholish Madjid, "Keharusan Pembaharuan Pemikiran Islam dan Masalah Integrasi Ummat", Nurcholish Madjid et al., *Pembaharuan Pemikiran Islam* (Jakarta: Islamic Research Centre, 1970), p. 4.

5. Harun Nasution, "Islam dan Sistem Pemerintahan dalam Perkembangan Sejarah", *Nuansa*, December 1984, pp. 4–12.

6. See, for instance, Nasution, "Islam dan Sistem Pemerintahan dalam Perkembangan Sejarah", pp. 4–12; Nurcholish Madjid, "Agama dan Negara dalam Islam: Sebuah Telaah atas Fiqh Siyasi Sunni" (Paper delivered at Paramadina Religious Study Club, Jakarta, 1991); Abdurrahman Wahid, "Islam, Ideologi dan Etos Kerja di Indonesia" (Discussion paper presented to Paramadina Religious Study Club, 1990; Abdurrahman Wahid, "Islam, the State, and Development in Indonesia" in *Ethical Dilemmas of Development in Asia*, edited by Godfrey Gunatilleke, Neelan Tiruchelvam, and Radhika Coomaraswamy (Lexington: Lexington Books, 1983), pp. 41–68; Munawir Syadzali, *Islam dan Tata Negara: Ajaran, Sejarah dan Pemikiran* (Jakarta: UI Press, 1990); Ahmad Syafii Maarif, "Kedudukan Negara dalam Perspektif Doktrin Islam" (Paper presented at a conference on the concept of the state in Islam, Universitas Islam Indonesia (UII), Yogyakarta, 18 October 1987); M. Dawam Rahardjo, "Critical Islamic View of the State", *Mizan* 3, no. 2 (1990): 39–48.

7. According to Nurcholish, the term "Islamic state" (*dawlah Islamiyah*), as initiated by Pakistan, does not have a strong foothold in the political history of Islam. The historical discourse of political Islam recognizes the term *dawlah* Abasiyah (the Abbasiate dynasty) or *dawlah* Umawiyah (the Umawiyate dynasty). During the Ottoman empire the term *dawlah* was simply used to denote "cycle", suggesting that human beings are determined by a "wheel of fortune" that has its ups and downs. The up side of the cycle refers to the occupation of power or authority. It was the idea of controlling power or authority which was known as *dawlah*. See "Islam Punya Konsep Kenegaraan?", *Tempo*, 29 December 1984, p. 17.

8. Nurcholish Madjid, "Khilafah dan Perkembangannya", *Nuansa*, December 1984, p. 31. See also a gallery of opinions in "Islam Punya Konsep Kenegaraan?", *Tempo*, 29 December 1984, pp. 12–19.

9. Nurcholish Madjid, "Menyegarkan Paham Keagamaan Di Kalangan Ummat Islam", *Islam: Kemoderenan dan Keindonesiaan* (Bandung: Mizan, 1987), pp. 253–56.

10. See Madjid, "Agama dan Negara dalam Islam". See also his viewpoint on this issue in "Islam Punya Konsep Kenegaraan?", *Tempo*, 29 December 1984, pp. 17–18; See

Abdurrahman Wahid's statements in "Islam tak Punya Konsep Baku Mengenai Negara", *Kompas*, 24 November 1986; "Masih Relevankah Teori Kenegaraan Islam: Tinjauan Kontemporer Atas Prinsip-Prinsip Rekonstruksinya" (Discussion paper on Islamic Concept of the State, Universitas Islam Indonesia, Yogyakarta, 7 February 1988); and "Tidak Terdapat Bukti Kuat Islam Punya Konsep Negara", *Media Indonesia*, 8 August 1991. See also Nasution, "Islam dan Sistem Pemerintahan dalam Perkembangan Sejarah"; Munawir Syadzali, *Islam dan Tata Negara: Ajaran, Sejarah dan Pemikiran* (Jakarta: UI Press, 1990).

11. Based on their interpretation of Muhammad's farewell speech, the Syi'i claimed that the Prophet had actually indicated publicly that Ali ibn Abi Thalib, his cousin and son-in-law, should succeed his political leadership. For a concise account on this issue, see Seyyed Hossein Nasr, *Muhammad: Man of Allah* (London: Muhammadi Trust, 1982).

12. Syadzali, *Islam dan Tata Negara*, pp. 21–28. See also "Kita ini Kurang Berani", *Tempo*, 20 October 1990, pp. 96–97.

13. Abdurrahman Wahid, "Islam: Punyakah Konsep Kenegaraan?", *Tempo*, 26 March 1983.

14. See, for instance, Qur'an 3:159; 42:38; 6:115; 42:15.

15. See, among others, Madjid's "Agama dan Negara dalam Islam", p. 18. The quotation is from Robert Bellah, "Islamic Tradition and the Problems of Modernization", *Beyond Belief: Essays on Religion in a Post-Traditionalist World* (Berkeley and Los Angeles: University of California Press, 1991), p. 151.

16. On the Constitution of Medina, see Muhammad Husayn Haykal, *The Life of Muhammad*, translated by Isma'il Ragi al-Faruqi (North American Publications, 1976), pp. 180–83; Ibn Hisham, *The Life of Muhammad*, a translation of Ishaq's Sirat al-Rasul Allah, with introduction and notes by A. Guillaume (Lahore, Karachi, and Dacca: Oxford University Press, 1970), pp. 231–33; W. Montgomery Watt, *Muhammad at Medina* (Oxford: Clarendon Press, 1956), pp. 221–28.

17. His doctoral dissertation was on "Islam as the Basis of State: A Study of the Islamic Political Ideas as Reflected in the Constituent Assembly Debates in Indonesia" (1983). Prior to his Ph.D. candidacy at the University of Chicago, he was a student at Ohio University's Department of History. He wrote an M.A. thesis on "Islamic Politics under Guided Democracy in Indonesia" (1980).

18. See Ahmad Syafii Maarif, "Piagam Madinah dan Konvergensi Sosial", an appendix to his *Islam dan Politik di Indonesia Pada Masa Demokrasi Terpimpin (1959–1965)* (Yogyakarta: IAIN Sunan Kalijaga Press, 1988), pp. 149–63.

19. See, for instance, Madjid, "Agama dan Negara dalam Islam", pp. 11–18. If this particular essay is any indication, it is obvious that Nurcholish's view on the Constitution of Medina, to some extent, is shaped by the perceptions of a number of prominent scholars like Muhammad Arkoun, Muhammad al-Dawalibi, and Robert Bellah.

20. See, for instance, Madjid, "Agama dan Negara dalam Islam", pp. 11–18; Maarif, "Piagam Madinah dan Konvergensi Sosial", pp. 149–228.

21. Syadzali, *Islam dan Tata Negara*, p. 16.

22. According to Munawir Syadzali, other parameters of a theocratic state include (1) the making of the Holy Scriptures as the source of the law of the land; and (2) the state leadership being in the hands of religious leaders. These parameters must converge all together in a state for it to be called a theocratic state. For details on this account, see his "Negara Pancasila Bukan Negara Agama dan Bukan Negara Sekuler" (Unpublished paper, n.d).

23. On the political theory of Maududi, see his *The Islamic Law and Constitution*, translated and edited by Khurshid Ahmed (Lahore: Islamic Publications, 1977).

24. On the political theory of Ali ibn Abd al-Raziq, see his *Al-Islam wa Ushul al-Hukm* (Beirut: Dar Maktabah al-Hayah, 1966); see also his *Al-Islam wa Qawa'id al-Sulthan*.

25. For a further criticism of Maududi's political ideas, see Syadzali, *Islam dan Tata Negara*, pp. 157–79; see also "Kita ini Kurang Berani", *Tempo*, 20 October 1990, p. 96–97.

26. Wahid, "Islam, Ideologi dan Etos Kerja di Indonesia", pp. 5–7; Syadzali, *Islam dan Tata Negara*, pp.137–45; see also "Kita ini Kurang Berani", *Tempo*, 20 October 1990, pp. 96–97.

27. The idea of the finality of the current form of the Indonesian state originated from Nahdlatul Ulama (NU). In 1984, following the organization's twenty-seventh conference, NU declared publicly that the Republic of Indonesia was the final goal for Indonesian Muslims in their ventures to devise the best possible form of the state. It was widely believed that the intellectual figures behind this pronouncement were the late Achmad Siddiq and Abdurrahman Wahid. See, for instance, "Pimpinan PB NU Bertemu Presiden: Negara RI adalah Bentuk Final", *Kompas*, 15 February 1985. See also Munawir Syadzali, "Wawasan Perjuangan Muslim Indonesia" (Paper delivered at the commemoration of HMI's forty-third *dies natalis*, Yogyakarta, 4 February 1990), p. 2.

28. These factors have been employed by Hasbullah Bakri, a former professor at IAIN Yogyakarta and Jakarta, to argue that Indonesia can actually be considered as a non-constitutional Islamic state. This is in the sense that, given the nature of Pancasila, which is in tune with Islamic principles, the state would not embrace a policy which contradicts Islamic values. See his "Lima Dalil Republik Indonesia Bisa Disebut Negara Islam Non-Konstitusional", *Panji Masyarakat*, no. 439 (1 August 1984), pp. 28–31. This article also appeared in *Merdeka*, 23 August 1984.

29. In a similar tone, the state repeatedly proclaims that Indonesia is neither a theocratic state (*negara agama*) nor a secular one. The articulation of this phrase is particularly given by the Minister of Religion, Munawir Syadzali. See his "Negara Pancasila Bukan Negara Agama dan Bukan Negara Sekuler" (Unpublished official speech, n.d).

30. Some leaders of the pre-New Order state, most notably Soekarno, had frequently echoed this religious-political sentiment. For a fuller account on this issue, see his ideas concerning the relationship between religion (Islam) and the state as reflected

in his scattered writings, such as "Negara Nasional dan Cita-Cita Islam", *Bung Karno dan Islam: Kumpulan Pidato tentang Islam 1953–1966* (Jakarta: Haji Masagung, 1990). For contemporary articulations on this subject, see Soeharto, *Agama dalam Pembangunan Nasional: Himpunan Sambutan Presiden Soeharto* (Jakarta: Pustaka Biru, 1981); Alamsyah Ratu Perwiranegara, *Islam dan Pembangunan Politik di Indonesia* (Jakarta: Haji Masagung, 1987); Munawir Syadzali, "Agama Sebagai Landasan Spiritual, Etik dan Moral Pembangunan" (Keynote address delivered at the Manggala Training Forum, Bogor, 12 June 1990).

31. According to Abdurrahman Wahid, this *fatwa* was based on a well-known Islamic classical text *Bughya al-Mustarsyidin*. (Interview with Abdurrahman Wahid in Jakarta, 10 May 1988.) See also his "Islam, Ideologi dan Etos Kerja di Indonesia", pp. 1–2.

32. See Syadzali, "Wawasan Perjuangan Muslim Indonesia"; Nurcholish Madjid, "Cita-Cita Politik Kita", in *Aspirasi Umat Islam Indonesia*, edited by Bosco Carvallo and Dasrizal (Jakarta: Leppenas, 1983), pp. 10–16; Maarif, "Piagam Madinah dan Konvergensi Sosial", pp. 160–63; M. Dawam Rahardjo, "Menilai Sejarah Ummat Islam dari Sudut Al-Qur'an", *Panji Masyarakat*, nos. 441 and 442 (27 August and 1 September 1984); Djohan Effendi, "Agama, Ideologi dan Politik dalam Negara Pancasila", in T.B. Simatupang et al., *Peranan Agama-Agama dan Kepercayaan Terhadap Tuhan Yang Maha Esa dalam Negara Pancasila yang Membangun* (Jakarta: BPK Gunung Mulia, 1987), pp. 149–56.

33. This concept was best articulated by the late Achmad Siddiq, the former general chairman of NU's consultative body (*Syuriah*). See Bahtiar Effendy, "The 'Nine Stars' and Politics: A Study of the Nahdlatul Ulama's Acceptance of Asas Tunggal and Its Withdrawal from Politics" (M.A. thesis, Ohio University, 1988), p. 268.

34. See, for instance, Nurcholish Madjid, "Suatu Tatapan Islam Terhadap Masa Depan Politik Indonesia", *Prisma*, extra ed. (1984), pp. 10–22; "Jilid Dua Orde Baru: Islam Hanya Soal Nilai", *Panji Masyarakat*, no. 537 (1988), pp. 26–31. See also a dialogue on "Pemahaman yang Lebih Substantif dan Budaya Politik Partisipasi", *Prisma* 17, no. 5 (1988): 64–82.

35. See Max Weber, *The Protestant Ethic and the Spirit of Capitalism*, translated by Talcott Parsons (London: George Allen and Unwin Ltd., 1985).

36. The phrase is from Qur'an 3:104, 110, and 114. The translations are from Pickthall's *The Glorious Koran*.

37. The expression is from Qur'an 34:15; 7:58; and 14:35. The translations are from Pickthall's *The Glorious Koran*. Compare this with the Javanese idea of a *negeri subur makmur gemah ripah loh jinawi toto tentrem kertoraharjo*, which stresses the importance of a safe and prosperous state and society.

38. Many observers of Indonesian politics tend to overlook this side of the relationship between Islam and politics. That is, the fact that politics is also utilized for the pursuit of religious objectives (that is, the realization of Islamic teachings). On the contrary, many of them, as suggested by Anderson, are accustomed to seeing leaders of political Islam using religion for their own political purposes. See his "Religion and

Politics in Indonesia Since Independence", in Benedict R.O'G Anderson, *Religion and Social Ethos in Indonesia* (Clayton: Monash University, 1977), p. 22. This is not, however, to suggest that the entire discourse of Indonesian political Islam is purely religious in nature.

39. See, for instance, Munawir Syadzali's discussion concerning the philosophy and programmes of Indonesia's past in his "Indonesia's Muslim Parties and Their Political Concepts", pp. 59–83.

40. See, for instance, Madjid's "Cita-Cita Politik Kita", Ahmad Syafii Maarif's "Islam, Politik dan Demokrasi di Indonesia", and Dawam Rahardjo's "Umat Islam dan Pembaharuan Teologi", in *Aspirasi Umat Islam Indonesia*, edited by Bosco Carvallo and Dasrizal (Jakarta: Leppenas, 1983), pp. 1–36, 37–63, 117–32.

41. See, for instance, Madjid, "Cita-Cita Politik Kita", pp. 7–36; Syadzali, "Wawasan Perjuangan Muslim Indonesia"; Abdurrahman Wahid, "Peranan Ummat dalam Berbagai Pendekatan", *Universalisme Islam dan Kosmopolitanisme Peradaban Islam*, limited ed. (n.p., 1991), pp. 30–42.

42. Like many other observers, virtually all of my interviewees share this view of the weakened situation of political Islam.

43. Interview with M. Dawam Rahardjo in Jakarta, 20 August 1991. Interview with Nurcholish Madjid in Montreal, 3 November 1991.

44. Interview with Amien Rais in Yogyakarta, 24 July 1991.

45. Interview with Nurcholish Madjid in Montreal, 3 November 1991. See also his "Islam dan Birokrasi", *Tempo*, 28 December 1991, pp. 28–29.

46. Interview with Deliar Noer in Jakarta, 11 September 1991. To some extent, such a viewpoint is also shared by Halide, an economics professor at the University of Hasanuddin, Ujung Pandang, South Sulawesi. See, for instance, his "Potensi dan Permasalahan Usahawan Muslim" (Paper delivered at the first meeting of Muslim intellectuals at the PKBI building, Jakarta, 26–28 December 1984).

47. For further study on this issue, see John O. Sutter, *Indonesianisasi: Politics in a Changing Economy, 1940–1955* (Ithaca: Southeast Asia Program, Cornell University, 1959).

48. See, for instance, Sjafruddin Prawiranegara, "Nasionalisasi De Javasch Bank", *Ekonomi dan Keuangan, Makna Ekonomi Islam: Kumpulan Karangan Terpilih 2* (Jakarta: Haji Masagung, 1986), pp. 74–84.

49. Known as leaders of Masyumi, both can actually be considered to be early Muslim economic theorists. Following the transformation of De Javasch Bank into the Indonesian Central Bank, Sjafruddin Prawiranegara was its governor. Prawiranegara and Wibisono subsequently served as Natsir's and Sukiman's economic ministers respectively.

50. As summarized by Herbert Feith, this programme "provided for the promotion of small industries in rural areas in such fields as leatherware, umbrella making, brick- and tile-making, and ceramics. In addition, medium- and large-scale industries were

to be established — printing plants, rubber remilling plants, a cement plant, a tile factory, and some other units on a short-term plan, and as long-term projects, a caustic soda factory, a fertilizer plant, an aluminium plant, a paper factory, spinning and knitting mills, and several other plants." Quoted from his *The Decline of Constitutional Democracy in Indonesia* (Ithaca: Cornell University Press, 1962), p. 174.

51. For a further account, especially on the cigarette industry, see Lance Castles, *Religion, Politics, and Economic Behavior in Java: The Kudus Cigarette Industry* (New Haven: Cultural Report Series no. 15, Southeast Asia Studies, Yale University, 1967).

52. Interview with Deliar Noer in Jakarta, 11 September 1991.

53. See, for instance, Halide, "Potensi dan Permasalahan Usahawan Muslim"; M. Dawam Rahardjo, "Eklusivisme Kelompok dan Perekonomian Nasional", *Media Indonesia*, 20 August 1990; M. Dawam Rahardjo, "Demokrasi Ekonomi, Revolusi Manajerial dan Peranan Perguruan Tinggi Islam", *Media Dakwah*, October 1990, pp. 64–66.

54. To name several of them, these include university student demonstrations in the 1970s; the Tanjung Priok and Lampung incidents in the 1980s which involved bloody clashes between Muslim activists and the military apparatus; and various strikes launched by disgruntled workers.

55. It contains only the thoughts of Nurcholish Madjid, Ahmad Syafii Maarif, Adi Sasono, Hidayat Nataatmadja, Dawam Rahardjo, and Amien Rais.

56. In December 1984 a number of individuals associated with Lembaga Penelitian, Pendidikan dan Penerangan Ekonomi dan Sosial (Dawam Rahardjo), Lembaga Studi Pembangunan (Adi Sasono), Pusat Pengembangan Agribisnis (Amin Aziz), Universitas Ibnu Khaldun (A.M. Saefuddin), and Majelis Ulama Indonesia (Hasan Basri) organized a national gathering of Muslim intellectuals. This meeting was directed to explore the strategic role of Islam in the course of national development. Issues such as development ethos, culture, technology, economy, and other sociopolitical affairs were discussed as part of the strength-weakness-opportunities-threat identification strategy. For a further account, see Ahmad Rifa'i Hassan and Amrullah Achmad, eds., *Perspektif Islam dalam Pembangunan Bangsa* (Yogyakarta: PLP2M, 1984). Through a number of follow-up meetings, involving a larger segment of Muslim intellectuals, they formed Forum Komunikasi Pembangunan Indonesia (FKPI, Indonesian Development Communication Forum) in 1986 under the chairmanship of Ahmad Tirtosudiro, a retired army general and former ambassador to Saudi Arabia. On the establishment of FKPI, see A. Rifa'i Hasan and Sri Marhaeni, "Sejarah Forum Komunikasi Pembangunan Indonesia" (Sekretariat Eksekutif FKPI, December 1986).

57. On the foundation of ICMI, see "Simposium Nasional Cendekiawan Muslim", Universitas Brawijaya, Malang, 6–8 December 1990. See also M. Syafi'i Anwar, "Islam, Negara, dan Formasi Sosial dalam Order Baru: Menguak Dimensi Sosio-Historis Kelahiran dan Perkembangan ICMI", *Ulumul Qur'an* 3, no. 3 (Supplement 1992): 1–28.

5

Beyond Parties and Parliament
Reassessing the Political Approach of Islam

In the old days, Islamic parties were often considered as representing the Muslim community. Thus, the aspiration of the
Muslim community was perceived as identical with that of the
parties. This should not have been the case as only some
Muslims joined political parties based on Islam. Now that
three existing socio-political organizations such as PPP,
Golkar and PDI have accepted Pancasila as their [ideological]
basis, formally there are no longer any parties which wave an
Islamic flag. The aspiration of the Muslim community can
now be articulated through various socio-political groups.

Lukman Harun[1]

ISLAMIC STRATEGY IN THE PAST

Based on the previous discussion, it can be suggested that at some point
the history of Indonesia's political Islam was characterized by two dominant features. To achieve their desired goals, the earlier leaders and
activists of political Islam relied mostly on (1) non-integrative or partisan
politics and (2) parliament as the only playing field.

The partisan politics approach was directly related to the grouping of
Islam as political forces (that is, Masyumi, later to be succeeded by
Parmusi, Nahdlatul Ulama [NU], Partai Sarekat Islam Indonesia [PSII],
and Perti. What was then known as political Islam appeared to become
the sole enterprise of Islamic parties. In other words, political Islam
emerged to become an exclusive project and venture of these parties to
envision and fulfil.

It is arguable that under such political groupings Islam gained relative
clarity with respect to its formal and institutional role in politics. In fact,

there had been a growing inclination to perceive the mere presence of these parties as evidence of the dynamism and vitality of political Islam. This made their existence seem to be theologically and politically imperative.[2]

However, given the severity of the ideological polarization among the existing political parties, especially during the liberal as well as Guided Democracy periods, it became apparent that these political groupings had further religious-political consequences. They posed some constraints to Islam as a single religious entity.

One of the most noticeable implications of these groupings was that they had contributed to the contraction of the concept of *umat Islam*. In this regard, because of the sharp ideological-political differences between political Muslims and their nationalist counterparts, recognition of an individual's Islamic-ness was not simply determined by virtue of the fact that he or she was a Muslim. Instead, it was defined and measured by his or her association with Islamic socio-political organizations and commitment to certain political ideals perceived as Islamic.

For these reasons, Muslims who did not share the political goals of Islamic parties were usually portrayed as secular or hypocritical. Moreover, due to their political association with non-Islamic groups (that is, Partai Nasional Indonesia [PNI], Partai Sosialis Indonesia [PSI], etc.), they were also considered as not representing the socio-political aspiration of Islam. In short, suffice it to say that the political representation of Islam (or the vision of political Islam) was rendered exclusively in the hands of Islamic political parties. This made political Islam, usually with the religion of Islam as its natural extension, a communalistic concept and claim.[3]

This reductionist tendency in the conceptualization of what constitutes an Islamic community had subsequently led, or at least encouraged, the Islamic group to foster a number of socio-political objectives which were by nature non-integrative or partisan. Their exclusive goals included (1) establishing Islam as the ideological basis of the state and (2) pressing for the legalization of the Jakarta Charter.

In a situation such as the liberal period, in which ideological symbolism was an inseparable part of its political format, the substantive aspect of those partisan political ideals was never highlighted. The uproar of the ideological struggle among Indonesia's post-revolutionary socio-political forces had driven many leaders and activists of political Islam (and those of other political parties) to translate their programmes in language which was appealing only to their own political constituencies.[4] Thus, it was not surprising that the notion of *baldatun thayyibatun wa rabbun ghafur*, the nucleus of Islamic socio-political objectives, was expressed in terms of making Islam the ideological basis of the state.

In the meantime, it also appeared that the doctrine of *al-amr bi al-ma'ruf wa al-nahyu 'an al-munkar*, the theological cornerstone of the involvement of many Muslims in the socio-political affairs of the state, was frequently expressed in terms of negative oppositionalism. This dissenting ideological and political sentiment, in turn, led some of the earlier leaders and activists of political Islam to operate — overtly or otherwise — outside the mainstream of the country's governing political formula. Given these perspectives, it is safe to conclude that the failure of political Islam to marshal the necessary support for the realization of its socio-political agenda lay in part in its inability to deconstruct and explain its religious precepts in political language which was acceptable to the broader segment of the Indonesian Muslim community. Thus, the idea of an Islamic state was presented and perceived as introducing *shari'a* as the law of the land, instead of aspiring for a just, egalitarian, and participatory system of governing.

The second feature referred to the fact that the approach of political Islam in the past (the 1950s and 1960s) was basically monolithic. This was especially true with regard to the fact that the earlier leaders and activists of political Islam considered parliament as the sole arena for the articulation and realization of the socio-religious and political goals of Islam. In this case, it is not an exaggeration to say that, practically speaking, other possible means and avenues were never cultivated.

It was true that while engaging in the practices of party politics, political Muslims still maintained the socio-religious and educational functions of their own non-governmental organizations such as Muhammadiyah and NU. In fact, their involvement in party politics and the bureaucracy to some extent had been instrumental in the development of these organizations in carrying out socio-religious and educational programmes.[5] Nonetheless, the inclination of many of their leaders and activists to define politics in a narrow sense, that is, exclusively in terms of party politics, contributed greatly to the neglect of the political impact of these two organizations.

With this limited perception of politics, it was understandable that the practices of Muhammadiyah and NU, beyond the confinement of party politics, appeared to be lacking in political significance. It was only recently, at a time when these two prominent organizations formally relinquished their partisan political roles,[6] that the political significance of their involvement in various socio-religious and educational activities had been given serious expression.[7]

One way to put some political weights on the socio-religious agenda of these two organizations, as reflected in the ideas and practices of their younger leaders and activists, is by providing macro-oriented perspectives to their respective programmes. By so doing, in spite of their formal status as non-political organizations, Muhammadiyah and NU remain potential corporatist brokers for the articulation and aggregation of Islamic socio-political aspirations. Without a macro-oriented agenda, as some have suggested, both Muhammadiyah and NU would only be playing roles as agents of socio-religious works, not knowing the real goals they actually want to accomplish.[8]

Partly because of such an orientational shift, that is, the changing nature of the organizations' respective programmes from micro- to macro-oriented agendas, coupled with the ability of their younger leaders and activists to create the necessary socio-political spaces in their relationship with the state, since the 1980s there have been some suggestions to see Muhammadiyah and NU in the light of a civil society perspective.[9] In the long run, in spite of the staggering evidence that the state under the New Order regime is indisputably strong, this analysis indicates the relative political significance of these two organizations *vis-à-vis* the state.

At this juncture it is fair to suggest that in spite of the claim by many Muslim activists as well as some observers of contemporary Indonesian politics that the New Order's Islam is becoming more cultural than political,[10] in actuality the archipelago's Islam remains characteristically — but not exclusively — political. In line with the central premise of this study, it can be said that it is only the format or formula of political Islam — consisting of mainly (1) the theological or philosophical underpinning of political Islam, (2) the political objectives of Islam, and (3) the political approach of Islam — which is now actually being transformed, from the politics of legal-formalism to substantialism, or from the politics of exclusivism to inclusivism.

THE NEW INTELLECTUAL: BEYOND PARTIES AND PARLIAMENT

Today's political approach of Islam, as currently being developed by the new emerging generation of Muslim intellectuals and activists, tends to be more inclusive or integrative. The inclusive or integrative nature of the approach is particularly evident in (1) the way the present thinkers and activists of political Islam express their socio-political ideas; and (2) how they endeavour to realize the socio-political objectives of Islam.

It has been a fairly noticeable phenomenon that from the 1970s the precursors of the new intellectualism ventured to formulate the political aspirations of Islam in a less subjective and ideological way. Corresponding to the relentless efforts of the current generation of Muslim intellectuals to redefine the socio-political goals of Islam, the present agenda of the Islamic group is articulated in a more inclusive and pragmatic fashion. In this regard the political aspirations of Islam are designed in such a way so that they do not necessarily clash with those of Indonesians *en masse*. Thus, it assures a relatively easy relationship between Islamic-ness and Indonesia-ness.

If the many works written by today's Muslim intellectuals are any indication, it is obvious that the current socio-political objectives of Islam are beginning to be synthesized and integrated with the concerns and ideals of Indonesian society at large.[11] This drive represents an intelligent approach to ensure the incorporation of Islamic-ness with Indonesia-ness — two important elements which had often been contradictorily juxtaposed in the course of Indonesia's socio-political development.

Thus, the new generation of Muslim intellectuals like Nurcholish Madjid, Abdurrahman Wahid, Dawam Rahardjo, Djohan Effendi, Adi Sasono, Ahmad Syafii Maarif, Kuntowijoyo, and Amien Rais, to name only some of them, do not share the formalistic and legalistic pronouncement of the socio-political goals of Islam. On the contrary, they are more interested in issues which will have a tangible impact on the well-being of the archipelago's political community as a whole. As reflected in the general contents of their writings, it is clear that they have put more emphasis on themes which are inclusive and objective in nature. Furthermore, they also espouse their socio-political agenda in a language which is understood and shared by the Indonesian society at large.

From this particular viewpoint, it can be concluded that the notions of *baldatun thayyibatun wa rabbun ghafur* and *al-amr bi al-ma'ruf wa al-nahyu 'an al-munkar* in today's Indonesian political Islam are no longer articulated in the context of ideological and symbolic subjectivism (that is, Islamic state or Islamic ideology). Instead, they are translated and decoded into several agendas pertinent to the interests of the Indonesian society in general, including a number of broader issues such as democratization,[12] religious and political tolerance,[13] socio-economic egalitarianism, and political emancipation.[14]

With this approach they believe that the expression of the political objectives of Islam will no longer be perceived as peripheral. More importantly, they also anticipate that such political thoughts and actions would not be construed as threatening to the national unitary outlook of Indonesia's nation state. This is because the substance of their socio-political programme is objective and integrative to the concerns of many Indonesians as a nation. In other words, because of their encompassing qualities, the political aspirations of Islam recognize no religious or partisan boundaries.

Other than being inclusive or integrative, the current approach of political Islam is also more diversified. This is in the sense that party politics, with Islamic parties at the forefront, is no longer considered as the sole avenue and playing field for the articulation and realization of Islamic socio-political objectives. In fact, for reasons largely rooted in (1) the structural elements of the New Order state (that is, the emphasis on order and stability at the expense of popular participation); (2) the changing nature of the socio-cultural basis of Indonesian Muslims; and (3) the substantive inclination of the contemporary Islamic socio-political agenda (that is, justice, democracy, egalitarianism, and participation), the party politics approach no longer occupies the centre stage in the struggle of political Islam in contemporary Indonesia.[15]

Thus, since the mid-1970s, coinciding with the New Order regime's politics of restructuring (1973), which led to the reduction in the number of political parties to only three different groups (PPP, Golkar, and PDI), there has been a growing determination among the new generation of Muslim thinkers and activists to articulate the notion of political Islam through much wider mechanisms. In this case the most popularly utilized additional channels include non-governmental organizations, mass media, publishing houses, state agencies, and other pertinent power centres.

Using these institutions as instruments to accomplish the socio-political objectives of Islam is a logical step. As such, it actually represents a natural consequence of the growth of this new intellectualism. Because the emerging generation of Muslim thinkers and activists is prepared to engage in a new discourse on political Islam, the cultivation of different possible pathways (other than political parties) is largely based on a mechanism which has an immediate affinity with their own socio-intellectual basis. Increasing exposure to modern tertiary education and communications coupled with the political structure of the New Order regime contributed directly to the choices for these diversified socio-political vehicles.

Muslim intellectuals, whose primary concern is to bring about social transformation, became actively involved in various Lembaga Swadaya

Masyarakat (LSM, self-reliant community development organizations). In the 1970s, with the Lembaga Penelitian, Pendidikan dan Penerangan Ekonomi dan Sosial (LP3ES) as their home base, many advocates of the new intellectualism like Dawam Rahardjo, Tawang Alun, and Sudjoko Prasodjo launched their social transformatory agenda.[16] In conjunction with a number of state agencies (especially with the Department of Religion) and several important figures associated directly with Islamic traditional boarding schools (for example, Abdurrahman Wahid, Yusuf Hasyim, Hamam Dja'far, and Soleh Widodo), they introduced community development programmes. With Adi Sasono joining the movement, they formed Lembaga Studi Pembangunan (LSP) — a more urban project-oriented research development institute. In the 1980s, as the needs and interests to develop the quality of *pesantren* education grew further, together with some influential *pesantren* leaders as well as Institut Agama Islam Negeri (IAIN) graduates, they established Perhimpunan Pengembangan Pesantren dan Masyarakat (P3M, Association for Pesantren and Community Development).[17]

All of these social transformatory institutions are action (or praxis) oriented. Virtually all of their social agendas are empirically based. Accordingly, their emphases have always been on the practical dimensions of their community development programmes. They designed a number of plans which have concrete bearings on the socio-economic and political well-being of their targeted groups, particularly those at the grass-roots level. Their transformatory activities include the development of small-scale (or home) industry; animal husbandry; vocational training; appropriate technology; health and nutrition; co-operative works; and those in the informal sector.[18]

To channel their ideas which are more intellectually or speculatively inclined (though in the long run they may have practical implications as well), the emerging generation of Muslim intellectuals organized various relevant study groups. For instance, Nurcholish Madjid sponsored the creation of Yayasan Wakaf Paramadina (Paramadina Foundation).[19] In a similar fashion, in fact prior to the development of Paramadina, Dawam Rahardjo had already established the foundation of Lembaga Studi Agama dan Filsafat (LSAF, Institute for the Study of Religion and Philosophy).[20] In Yogyakarta Amien Rais and Watik Pratiknya formed Pusat Pengkajian Strategi dan Kebijakan (PPSK, Centre for Strategic and Policy Studies) — a more politically oriented research institution.[21] Others, especially those who serve as members of the academic teaching staff, such as Ahmad Sadali and Imaduddin Abdurrahim of the Bandung

Institute of Technology, Sjahirul Alim of Gadjah Mada University, and Fuad Amsyari of Airlangga University, have pioneered the establishment of various Islamic study groups at their respective campuses.[22]

In addition to these newly opened avenues, proponents of the new Islamic intellectualism have also utilized major Islamic organizations such as Muhammadiyah, NU, and Majelis Ulama Indonesia (MUI, Indonesian Ulama Council).[23] They saw great potentials in these socio-religious organizations, both as interest aggregating and articulating bodies as well as viable institutions in the pursuit of their socio-economic and political ideals.

There are two main reasons behind this assumption. First, from the perspective of Islamic interest representation, these organizations, especially Muhammadiyah and NU, can be considered as the two most authoritative institutions which symbolize the collective aspirations of Indonesian Muslims. With roughly 60 million members scattered throughout the archipelago's rural and urban areas, undoubtedly they do represent a sizeable bulk of the nation's Muslim community.[24]

Second, with their organizational chains stretching down to the village level, Muhammadiyah, NU, and — to some extent — MUI provide solid institutional networks of *ulama* and *kyai* (*pesantren* leaders). Arguably, given the still influential character of the traditional authority relationship model in Indonesia, where followers often look up to charismatic leaders for advice and guidance, this socio-religious networking makes further efforts to socialize and realize Islamic socio-political agendas more effective.[25]

Keeping these considerations in mind, in the early 1980s many proponents of the new Islamic intellectualism started to penetrate the national and regional leadership of Muhammadiyah, NU, and MUI.[26] In so doing, their primary goal has been to take an active role in the efforts to redirect the actions of these organizations. More specifically, their presence has offered fresh ideas pertinent to the organizations' efforts to confront various problems faced by Muslims in particular and Indonesians in general. With the blessing and support of some prominent leaders like A.R. Fakhruddin (Muhammadiyah), Achmad Siddiq (NU), and Hasan Basri (MUI), they were able to persuade the leadership of these organizations to accept a number of their macro-oriented ideas. Muhammadiyah, NU, and MUI have thus become important interest and pressure groups.

At NU Abdurrahman Wahid, who became the organization's national chairman in 1984, replacing its long-time political leader Idham Chalid, emerged as the most relentless individual to bring this organization in line with the core ideas of the new Islamic intellectualism. In this regard, with the support of NU's renowned leaders such as As'ad Syamsul Arifin,[27] Ali Maksum, and Achmad Siddiq, his primary objective has been to develop the notion of an Indonesian Islam. That is, as he perceives it, an "Islam which emphasizes more on national integration".[28]

To make this idea work, there were two major issues which had to be addressed by NU and other Islamic socio-religious organizations. First, the still uneasy relationship between Islam and the state ideology (Pancasila) had to be resolved. Second, the old style of political Islam had to be transformed from partisan or party politics to a more inclusive, integrative, and diversified approach.

NU's 1984 Muktamar (national congress), held at Pesantren Salafiyah Syafiiyah in East Java, was basically designed to deal with these particular agenda items. In an attempt to ease the political relationship between Islam and the state, Abdurrahman Wahid, together with Achmad Siddiq, led the way to NU's declaration concerning the "finality" of the current form of Indonesia's nation state with Pancasila as its ideology. On the grounds that Pancasila does not contradict the teachings of Islam, they also pioneered NU's acceptance of Pancasila as its organizational basis.

In the meantime, in an effort to broaden NU's political space, both these individuals also played key roles in the organization's determination to relinquish its partisan or parliamentarian political role. This particular manoeuvre ended NU's long time (since 1952) role as a political organization as well as its political affiliation with PPP (since 1973). Thus, NU returned to its original character (*khittah*) as a socio-religious organization, but with a macro-oriented agenda.[29]

There was no doubt that NU's withdrawal from party politics had important implications. On the surface, as evident in the 1987 and 1992 general elections, it allowed its members to cast their votes for any political party of their choice. At a much deeper level, however, it actually reflected the general trend of the current Islamic socio-political idealism and activism which stresses the substance rather than the form of struggle. This is in the sense that the struggle for Islam can always take a variety of routes (not necessarily formally Islamic ones), as long as they are not in opposition to Islamic principles.

From the perspective of NU's internal leadership, as expressed by Abdurrahman Wahid on various occasions, this new development has liberated the organization from the syndrome of "political minority" status. It also has enabled NU and its members to enter the mainstream of Indonesia's political dynamism, that is, a national politics (*politik kebangsaan*) instead of a partisan (that is, Islamic) one. Furthermore, having to treat the existing political parties (PPP, Golkar, and PDI) indiscriminately, as a logical consequence of NU's self-proscription as a political organization, it provided ample opportunities for this organization to become an inherent part of the nation in its truest sense.[30]

Being officially a non-political organization, and yet functioning as one of the largest Islamic self-reliant community development organizations in the country, since the mid-1980s NU has been shifting its focus to new socio-economic and political transformatory programmes. In addition to the recent persistent campaigns of its leaders, especially Abdurrahman Wahid, to voice the necessity of the state and society to uphold democratic principles, NU has been paying more attention to issues related to the economic well-being of its members. In 1990 this particular concern led this organization to pioneer the establishment of a number of credit institutions — branches of Bank Perkreditan Rakyat (BPR, People's Credit Bank) — which provide loans to small entrepreneurs. Interestingly, this programme has been carried out in conjunction with one of the country's most prominent Chinese tycoons, Edward Suryadjaja — owner of the recently collapsed Summa Bank.[31]

With some variations, Muhammadiyah and MUI also engage in similar activities. The current generation of Muslim intellectuals, especially those who have direct ties with this organization, believe that Muhammadiyah is indeed a valuable asset and instrument for the articulation and realization of new Islamic socio-religious and political ideas.

However, considering the circumstances which have beset Muhammadiyah for the last two decades, younger figures such as Amien Rais, Watik Pratiknya, Kuntowijoyo, Ahmad Syafii Maarif, and Yahya Muhaimin have had to lay the necessary groundwork to enable this organization to function viably. In this regard, suffice it to say that their primary approaches have been (1) to redirect the organization's overall course of actions; (2) to redefine its socio-political functions, which so far have simply been defined in terms of practical deeds (*amal usaha*); and, more importantly, (3) to rejuvenate its commitment to the spirit of *tajdid* (renewal) — the trade-mark feature of Muhammadiyah's own history.[32]

For this, the key strategy of these Muslim activists has been to devise a new theological underpinning as an inspirational basis for Muhammadiyah's socio-religious struggles.[33] By doing so, it is expected that this organization can be more sensitive to the nation's common problems such as poverty and social justice — two important segments of the current Islamic socio-political agenda.[34]

Thanks to the direct participation of the younger generation, since its national congress in late 1990, it has been increasingly noticeable that Muhammadiyah has shown more concern for a wide range of Indonesia's socio-economic issues. In this case, though less ambitious than NU, it also shares the goal of developing small and medium-sized financial credit institutions such as BPR. In addition, co-operating with a number of Chinese-owned commercial enterprises (for example, Matahari Group, Hero Super Market, and Lippo Group), Muhammadiyah has organized internship and training programmes for its members to improve their technical and managerial skills in trade and business activities.[35]

In the meantime, it appears that MUI also acts on this line of concern. With the active participation of many younger Muslim intellectuals like Adi Sasono, Amin Aziz, and Quraish Shihab in the national leadership, directly or otherwise, in recent years this organization has taken numerous efforts to make its functions more socio-politically diversified. Thus, while it remains one of the most important organizations to issue religious decrees (*fatwa*) on a variety of socio-economic and political issues,[36] MUI also tries to serve as a potential interest aggregating and articulating body for Indonesian Muslims.[37] In this regard, the most recent celebrated case in point has been MUI's central role in the founding of the first Indonesian Islamic bank (Bank Muamalat Indonesia or BMI) in 1991.[38] Other than to help develop and mobilize the economic resources of the Indonesian Muslims, the establishment of BMI is also meant to accommodate those who, for religious reasons, do not conduct business or financial transactions with common banks which offer and charge interest.[39]

NEW INTELLECTUAL AND POLITICAL PARTIES

Discussing these institutions and their diversified routes for the articulation and realization of Islamic socio-political ideas at such length does not suggest that the party politics approach has been totally left out. It is true that, for the reasons already mentioned, the emphasis in Islamic political discourse on party politics has decreased considerably. Yet, by default the party politics approach is still considered an important avenue because of its law-ratifying or adjudicating function, with parliament serving as its primary embodiment.

Since the early campaign of this new Islamic intellectualism in the 1970s, there had been some important figures in the movement who were determined to work within the framework of a party politics approach.

Gradually, and particularly in the last ten years or so, this party politics approach has attracted many other Muslim contemporaries to follow suit.

In spite of the fact that the party politics approach is still considered a viable outlet, the discourse of political Islam in this particular arena is not without significant changes. The younger generation of Muslim activists realizes that for the party politics approach to work effectively it requires a fundamental transformation, especially in terms of agenda formulation (that is, rational and realistic political programmes instead of ideological and utopian ones) as well as party affiliation model (that is, a diversified party alliance rather than being limited to a formal Islamic party).

Based on this viewpoint, in addition to their endeavours to redefine the socio-political objectives of Islam, this new generation of Muslim reformers also tries to develop a much broader and inclusive political relationship with the existing political parties. In this respect, there are those who choose to struggle under the flag of an Islamic political party such as PPP (for example, Mintaredja, Hartono Mardjono, and Ridwan Saidi). On the other hand, there are those who decide to affiliate themselves politically with the ruling party of Golkar (Akbar Tanjung, Fahmi Idris, and others). More recently, some have even initiated a political association with PDI — the amalgam of the Nationalist and Christian parties — by becoming its candidates in the 1992 general election (for example, Sugeng Saryadi). Under this new approach, the socio-political aspirations of Islam are voiced through all of the existing political organizations, cutting across their inherent ideological cleavages.

This political diversification has become a model in the practice of the New Order's political Islam which employs party politics as its complementary approach. It is interesting to note, however, that in this discourse Golkar appears to be at the leading edge. Since the early 1980s, there has been a growing trend to channel the socio-political objectives of Islam through this ruling political party. This, undoubtedly, represents an important development which has influenced many other Muslim leaders, both in the urban and rural areas, to join the country's largest political organization.[40]

There are several reasons behind this strategic move, especially with regard to selecting Golkar as the most favourable political outlet to represent the socio-political interests of Islam. At the philosophical level there has been a widely shared notion among this new generation of Muslim political thinkers and activists that the socio-political aspirations of Islam are the concerns of all Indonesian Muslims, regardless of their socio-political affiliations. Accordingly, they should not be construed as the sole prerogative of political parties which formally or symbolically bear an Islamic identity to envision and realize (for example, PPP). Considering the fact that many Muslims — who for socio-cultural, practical, or ideological reasons decline to be represented by Islamic parties — are constituents of non-Islamic socio-political organizations, other political parties such as Golkar and PDI should also enjoy a similar right to articulate and represent the socio-political interests of Indonesian Muslims.

At the practical level it can be equally argued that this new party politics approach basically developed from pragmatic considerations. In this regard, the cultural and structural features of PPP (that is, its origins, orientation, and political relationship with the state) *vis-à-vis* those of the others, especially Golkar, may serve as the chief ingredients. Nonetheless, in essence, everything seems to boil down to one crucial issue: effectiveness in channelling the socio-political aspirations of Islam.

To date, it is safe to argue that the political discourse of PPP as a potential articulator of the Islamic socio-political agenda has not been fully effective. Several reasons underlie this assessment. One of the most widely accepted arguments on this issue has been the hegemonic nature of the state. This is in the sense that in the attempt to aggrandize its power and influence the state has often applied coercive measures against other existing strong socio-political forces.[41] While there is no reason to dispute this view, other relevant factors deserve highlighting nonetheless.

First, during the first fifteen years of PPP's existence the political emphasis of its activists was not wholly directed to aggregating and articulating Islamic socio-political interests. Being an amalgam of political parties, the political actions of its leaders, particularly those of its younger generation, were primarily aimed at reorienting the party's ideological and political world view, from the politics of formal-legalism to substantialism.

Obviously, this is so as an attempt (1) to eradicate the uneasy relationship between Islam and the state, and — more importantly — (2) to enable PPP to adapt itself to the New Order's demands for order, stability, and development. For these reasons, the initial concerns of some prominent Muslim political activists, such as Mintaredja, Sulastomo, Hartono Mardjono, and Ridwan Saidi, had been directed more towards modernizing the party (including programmes, orientation, and party constituents) than simply striving for Islamic socio-economic and political interests.

There are some cases in point. In the early 1970s while leading Parmusi, an important party element in PPP, Mintaredja[42] and Sulastomo[43] were compelled to campaign for a more rational approach to politics instead of an ideological one. Comparably, in the first half of the 1980s, PPP's notable figures such as Hartono Mardjono[44] and Ridwan Saidi[45] had to argue that Islam should not be treated simply as a political commodity or issue. Furthermore, to bring the party's modernization programme into its fullest extent, Ridwan Saidi even proposed that PPP become an open party for all Indonesians regardless of their racial and religious origins. Apparently, his intention was not to throw away PPP's Islamic character, but — at least as he perceived it — to prove that the party had accepted Pancasila as its ideological basis.[46]

Second, when the New Order government introduced its policy of party restructuring in 1973, four Islamic parties (that is, NU, Parmusi, PSII, and Perti) were unified into a single political entity — PPP. Shortly thereafter, it became obvious that a complete and thorough political fusion was not possible. As a result, the party was never able to act effectively as a single unit.[47]

From the initial inception of PPP up to the mid-1980s, the party was continually preoccupied with prolonged internal conflicts among party elements, especially between NU and Parmusi. Typically, the points of contention which plagued the political life of PPP ranged from issues concerning the composition of party leadership to the process of party nominating candidates.[48] This disheartening situation not only hindered PPP's ability to serve as an able articulator of Islamic socio-political aspirations, but also brought about a negative image to the party from its very own natural constituents, the Muslims.[49] Partly because of this, a large segment of the Muslim community, including many of its influential leaders and activists, decided to voice their socio-political aspirations through the more effective political organization, Golkar.[50]

It is only recently that PPP — under the new leadership of Ismail Hassan Metareum, a less flamboyant political figure than his predecessor, John Naro — has been able to improve its political image. Though this political upturn had no significant impact on PPP's voting results in the 1992 general election, it nonetheless enabled the party leadership to cultivate a far more positive relationship with a wider segment of the Muslim community, particularly its intellectuals, who previously had remained aloof from the party's political discourse. As a starter, in a gathering held in Jakarta in August 1991, a number of Muslim intellectuals were solicited to contribute their ideas pertinent to the development of PPP.[51] Some of them were then asked to join the party. In fact, many of them even became PPP's leading candidates in the 1992 and 1997 general elections.[52]

In the meantime Golkar had remained free of such political problems. Though there had been some internal squabbles among its supporting groups, particularly between the military and bureaucratic streams, it nonetheless remained Indonesia's most viable political organization for aggregating and articulating the interests of its political constituents.[53] For many Muslims, Golkar's power of attraction as a political vehicle seemed to rest in several concrete situations.

First, Golkar was by far the largest and most powerful political organization in the country. If the general elections were any indications, the dominating position of the New Order's Golkar in the parliament had been demonstrated through its five consecutive landslide victories.[54] But, being the governing party, its political dominance actually went well beyond the legislative arena. It is conspicuous that its political networking reached every existing agency of the state. In fact, it can be said that all of the state apparatus, from President Soeharto and many of his Cabinet ministers who occupied positions on Golkar's advisory council, were members of this political organization. With political resources of this magnitude, it was imperative for Muslims to cultivate the support of Golkar to ensure the realization of their interests.

Second, being the ruling party, Golkar provided an opportunity for Muslim activists to express and articulate their interests in the sense that their views expressed in Golkar, though characteristically Islamic, did not arouse suspicion on the part of the state. Unlike those of their Muslim counterparts who were determined to work within the boundaries of Islamic socio-political organizations, their ideas represented an inherent part of the overall programmes of Golkar.

Third, there were strong indications that the struggle for the Islamic cause was, by and large, compatible with the socio-economic and political agenda of Golkar. In this regard it is worth noting that unlike the other two political organizations (that is, PPP and PDI), Golkar did not actually grow out of mass constituents. Rather, it had been originally supported by functional groups.[55] In the early years of the New Order administration, particularly in the 1970s, through the doctrine of monoloyalty, its primary support derived from the military and bureaucratic apparatus. During this period, as many have argued, its parliamentary successes were primarily due to the regime's coercive and persuasive (or co-optative) measures.[56]

Part of this latter strategy (that is, persuasive and co-optative measures) had been to accommodate and develop the notion of Islamic aspirations and themes. This was not only to attract Muslim voters, especially during the election years, but also to further solidify Golkar's own position as a political organization *vis-à-vis* its (Muslim) political constituents. Included in this design were the attempts to (1) politically tap a number of prominent Muslim leaders and activists to join the organization; and (2) channel funds to various Islamic institutions (for example, mosques, educational institutes), and organizations.[57] Obviously, it is for these reasons that Golkar formed a number of Islamic socio-religious organizations, such as: Gabungan Usaha Perbaikan Pendidikan Islam (GUPPI, Joint Effort to Improve Islamic Education); Majelis Dakwah Islamiyah (MDI, Islamic Missionary Council); Tarbiyah Islamiyah (Islamic Education); Persatuan Tarekat Islam (Union of Islamic Sufism); Satkar Ulama (Ulama Association); and Pengajian Al-Hidayah.[58]

It is through these various routes that the current generation of Muslim thinkers and activists are striving for the articulation and realization of Islamic socio-political ideals. It is beyond the scope of this study to assess the extent to which these ideals have been actually accomplished. However, with respect to the original position of this new Islamic intellectualism, that is, in terms of developing a viable synthesis between political Islam and the state as well as redeeming the political role of Islam, it can be stated that this new Islamic political activism appears to have resulted in a number of positive outcomes.

Since the last two general elections, for instance, it has been widely noted that more and more Muslim political thinkers and activists have been able to participate in the process of policy decision-making, within both the executive and legislative branches. Many former Himpunan Mahasiswa Islam (HMI) activists have been recruited to occupy important ministerial posts.[59] And in recent years, there has been an increase in the number of Islamic representatives in the parliament, although not necessarily through Islamic parties such as PPP.[60]

Moreover, since the last five years or so, there has been a growing political will on the part of the state to accommodate the socio-religious, economic, and political interests of Islam. The acts include the passing of the education law which stipulates the obligatory nature of religious instruction (1988); the passing of a religious court law which strengthens the position of Islamic courts in adjudicating marriage, divorce, reconciliation, and inheritance issues (1989); the establishment of ICMI (1990); a compilation of Islamic law (1991); a joint ministerial decision concerning the *zakat* (religious alms) collection and distribution agency, Bazis (1991); the reversal of a policy which prohibited Muslim female high school students from wearing the *jilbab,* an Islamic head covering (1991); the holding of an Islamic cultural festival — Festival Istiqlal (1991 and 1995); the establishment of BMI (1992); the annulment of Sumbangan Dermawan Sosial Berhadiah (SDSB), a form of national lottery (1993); the development of religious infrastructure, such as mosques and religious educational institutions; the teaching of the Arabic language on national television; and the sending of Muslim religious preachers to the remote transmigration areas. Interestingly enough, though it often goes unnoticed, many of these ideas are congruent with those of the earlier generation of Islamic political leaders and activists.

All of these new developments represent important steps forward in the changing nature of the political relationship between Islam and the state. More importantly, they serve as key determinants in the process of cessation of traditional hostility between political Islam and the state which had been in existence for so many years, and they may well signify the withering away of what Kuntowijoyo calls the myth of Islamic hostility and antagonism towards the state and bureaucracy.[61]

Notes

1. See "Mulai Ditinggalkan, Aspirasi Umat Islam Lewat Kelembagaan Formal", *Kompas,* 22 October 1986.

2. Therefore, it was not surprising that many exponents of Islamic political parties tended to perceive the amalgamation of the four Islamic political parties into the single entity of Partai Persatuan Pembangunan (PPP) — regardless of the fact that the nationalist and Christian parties were also instructed to merge into Partai Demokrasi Indonesia (PDI) — as an indication of the depoliticization of Islam, rather than a hegemonic manoeuvre to solidify and strengthen the position of the state. For a journalistic account of this popular perception, see "Robohnya Dinding Politik Islam", *Tempo,* 29 December 1984, pp. 12–16. See also "Setelah Depolitisasi Islam", *Panji Masyarakat,* 21–30 June 1991, pp. 20–24.

3. Some proponents of the new Islamic intellectualism re-echo this sentiment as the arrogance of *santri* religiosity. For this, Munawir Syadzali assesses: "They consider themselves as true Muslims. With such arrogance they doubt others' commitment to Islam. Then they struggle [for Islam] exclusively. ... Let us be honest. For example, those who became the leading supporters of Islamic court bills (Rencana Undang-Undang Peradilan Agama, RUU-PA) are not Rahmat or Munawir [Arabic, presumably indicating *santri*-ness] by names, but Sugiono and also Temon [Javanese, thus implying non-*santri*-ness]. Their commitment to Islam is not less than ours." See "Jihad Melawan Nafsu", *Tempo,* 17 February 1990, pp. 102–3. See also "Islam Milik Semua", *Tempo,* 6 July 1991.

4. This analysis is partially influenced by two intriguing works on (1) the political language of Islam and (2) the languages of Indonesian politics. On the former, see

Bernard Lewis, *The Political Language of Islam* (Chicago: University of Chicago Press, 1988). On the latter, see Benedict Anderson, "The Languages of Indonesian Politics", *Indonesia*, no. 1 (April 1966), pp. 89–116.

5. This was particularly true in the case of NU. Its long-time dominance over the Department of Religion had contributed greatly to the mushrooming of NU's religious schools. (Interview with Hasyim Latif, an East Javanese NU leader, in Surabaya, 4 April 1988.)

6. As we have already known, Muhammadiyah never became a political party. Nonetheless, it was one of the most important backbones of the Masyumi party. With the banning of the Masyumi in 1960, and the fusion of Parmusi (the widely perceived successor of Masyumi) in Partai Persatuan Penbangunan (PPP) in 1973, Muhammadiyah decided to focus its activities on socio-religious programmes. On the other hand, NU became a political party in 1952, following its departure from Masyumi in that year. In 1984, having experienced a series of political blows, particularly after its amalgamation with PPP, NU withdrew its formal affiliation with PPP.

7. There are now growing tendencies to see the trade-marking activities of Muhammadiyah in the field of religious preaching and education in the light of "allocative politics". For a further account on this issue, see M. Sirajuddin Syamsuddin, "Religion and Politics in Islam: The Case of Muhammadiyah in Indonesia's New Order" (Ph.D. dissertation, University of California Los Angeles, 1991). Likewise, the withdrawal of NU from PPP in the mid-1980s to return to its original function has also been seen by many students of Indonesian (political) Islam as an ingenious move or strategy to enable the organization to engage in a broader meaning of politics. On the political transformation of NU, see Bahtiar Effendy, "The 'Nine Stars' and Politics: A Study of the Nahdlatul Ulama's Acceptance of Asas Tunggal and Its Withdrawal from Politics" (M.A. thesis, Ohio University, 1988).

8. This argument is strongly advanced by, among others, Kuntowijoyo. (Interview with Kuntowijoyo in Yogyakarta, 25 July 1991.) See also "Budaya Partisipasi dalam Islam", *Prisma*, no. 2 (1988), pp. 79–82.

9. See, for instance, Aswab Mahasin, "NGOs show strength in nation's socio-political development", *The Jakarta Post*, 12 August 1988; Philip Eldridge, "NGOs and the State in Indonesia", *State and Civil Society in Indonesia*, edited by Arief Budiman (Clayton: Monash Papers on Southeast Asia, no. 22, Centre of Southeast Asian Studies, Monash University, 1990), pp. 503–38; M. Dawam Rahardjo, "LSM dalam sistem politik Indonesia", *Berita Buana*, 19 and 20 February 1991; R. William Liddle, "Indonesia's Democratic Past and Future", *Comparative Politics*, no. 24 (July 1992), pp. 443–62.

10. See, for instance, Sudirman Tebba, "Islam di Indonesia: Dari Minoritas Politik Menuju Mayoritas Budaya", *Jurnal Ilmu Politik*, no. 4 (1989), pp. 53–65; Robert Hefner, "Islam Lebih Berkembang di Bidang Kebudayaan", *Pelita*, 15 September 1991; Abdurrahman Wahid, "Peranan Ummat dalam Berbagai Pendekatan", *Universalisme Islam dan Kosmopolitanisme Peradaban Islam* (limited ed., no publisher, 1991), pp. 30–42; Donald K. Emmerson, "Islam in Modern Indonesia: Political Impasse, Cultural Opportunity", in *Change and the Muslim World*, edited by Philip H. Stoddard et al. (Syracuse: Syracuse University Press, 1981), pp. 159–68.

11. See, for instance, Abdurrahman Wahid, *Muslim di Tengah Pergumulan* (Jakarta: Leppenas, 1981); Amien Rais, ed., *Islam di Indonesia: Suatu Ikhtiar Mengaca Diri* (Jakarta: C.V. Rajawali, 1986); A. Rifa'i Hasan and Amrullah Achmad, eds., *Perspektif Islam dalam Pembangunan Bangsa* (Yogyakarta: PLP2M, 1987); Muntaha Azhari and Abdul Mun'im Saleh, eds., *Islam Indonesia Menatap Masa Depan* (Jakarta: P3M, 1989); Masyhur Amin, ed., *Teologi Pembangunan: Paradigma Baru Pemikiran Islam* (Yogyakarta: LKPSM NU DIY, 1989); Nurcholish Madjid, *Islam Doktrin dan Peradaban: Sebuah Telaah Kritis Tentang Masalah Keimanan, Kemanusiaan, dan Keindonesiaan* (Jakarta: Yayasan Wakaf Paramadina, 1992).

12. See, for instance, Nurcholish Madjid's "Cita-Cita Politik Kita", Ahmad Syafii Maarif's "Islam, Politik dan Demokrasi di Indonesia", and Amien Rais' "Islam dan Demokrasi", in *Aspirasi Umat Islam Indonesia*, edited by Bosco Carvallo and Dasrizal (Jakarta: Leppenas, 1983), pp. 1–78.

13. See, for instance, Dawam Rahardjo's "Umat Islam dan Pembaharuan Teologi", in *Aspirasi Umat Islam Indonesia*, edited by Bosco Carvallo and Dasrizal (Jakarta: Leppenas, 1983), pp. 117–32. See also Djohan Effendi, "Pluralisme Pemahaman dalam Perspektif Teologi Islam", in *Teologi Pembangunan: Paradigma Baru Pemikiran Islam*, edited by M. Masyhur Amin (Yogyakarta: LKPSM NU DIY, 1989), pp. 149–52; Abdurrahman Wahid, "Massa Islam dalam Kehidupan Bernegara dan Berbangsa", *Prisma*, extra ed., 1984, pp. 3–9.

14. See, for instance, Adi Sasono, "Islam dan Sosialisme Religius", in *Aspirasi Umat Islam Indonesia*, edited by Bosco Carvallo and Dasrizal (Jakarta: Leppenas, 1983), pp. 109–16. See also his "Keadilan Sosial Tema Abadi", in *Islam Indonesia Menatap Masa Depan*, edited by Muntaha Azhari and Abdul Mun'im Saleh (Jakarta: P3M, 1989), pp. 108–18; and "Usaha Pengembangan Emansipasi Sosial: Beberapa Catatan", in *Perspektif Islam dalam Pembangunan Bangsa*, edited by A. Rifa'i Hasan and Amrullah Achmad (Yogyakarta: PLP2M, 1987), pp. 322–35.

15. See, for instance, an account of a conversation with Abdurrahman Wahid, Lukman Harun, and Moeslim Abdurrahman, in "Mulai Ditinggalkan, Aspirasi Umat Lewat Kelembagaan Formal", *Kompas*, 22 October 1986.

16. This is not to suggest that LP3ES is an Islamic NGO. Nonetheless, it is important to note that many of its staff members are activist Muslims. Politically, as suggested by one of its former leading figures, many of its prominent individuals share the common ideals of an Indonesian state as perceived by Masyumi and PSI in the early 1950s (for example, the idea of a democratic and egalitarian state). On this latter statement, see R. William Liddle, "RMS", *Tempo*, 10 April 1993, p. 104.

17. For an overview of P3M activities, see a number of related essays in Manfred Oepen and Wolfgang Karcher, eds., *The Impact of Pesantren in Education and Community Development in Indonesia* (Jakarta: P3M, 1988).

18. For a fuller treatment, see M. Dawam Rahardjo, "LSM dan Program-Program Pengembangan Masyarakat" (Unpublished paper, n.d.). See also Adi Sasono, "Peta Permasalahan Sosial Umat Islam dan Pokok-Pokok Pemikiran Usaha

Pengembangannya: Beberapa Catatan" (Paper delivered at the BKS PTIS third annual meeting, Jakarta, 28–30 May 1984); and "Usaha Pengembangan Emansipasi Sosial: Beberapa Catatan", in *Perspektif Islam dalam Pembangunan Bangsa*, edited by A. Rifa'i Hasan and Amrullah Achmad (Yogyakarta: PLP2M, 1987).

19. Paramadina's primary concern has been to preach and develop the notion of an inclusive and tolerant Islam. To serve this purpose, Paramadina offers a series of intensive courses on classical as well as contemporary Islam across different religious schools (*madzhab*), within both the *sunni* and *syi'i* traditions. In addition, a monthly general forum is organized to address religious issues pertinent to the interests of its members. Unlike many existing similar religious foundations, however, Paramadina appears to cater to the spiritual needs of the (formerly unnoticed) Muslim upper middle class who reside in Jakarta and beyond. (Personal observation in Jakarta between July and September 1991.) For a good summary on Paramadina's ideological-intellectual position, see Nurcholish Madjid, "Integrasi Keislaman dalam Keindonesiaan Untuk Menatap Masa Depan Bangsa" (Speech delivered at the opening of the Paramadina's Religious Study Club, Jakarta, 1986).

20. During its initial inception, LSAF was under the directorship of Dawam's younger contemporaries. In the late 1980s, following his departure from LP3ES, Dawan assumed the LSAF directorship. The stress of LSAF has been to conduct a regular and open forum to discuss religious and philosophical issues. This study institute also publishes a quarterly journal, *Ulumul Qur'an*.

21. PPSK is organized by a number of Ph.D. degree holders in social sciences. Many of them are graduates of American universities. Since its inception, the primary interest of this forum has been to assess Indonesia's contemporary socio-political and cultural issues. Other than holding regular discussion meetings, this institution also publishes a quarterly journal, *Prospektif*. (Personal observation in Yogyakarta, 24 July 1991.)

22. It is interesting to note that these religious study groups flourish in many prominent secular universities, most notably in Jakarta (University of Indonesia, UI), Bogor (Bogor Institute of Agriculture, IPB), Bandung (Bandung Institute of Technology, ITB), Yogyakarta (Gadjah Mada University, UGM), Surabaya (Airlangga University, Unair), Ujung Pandang (Hasanuddin University, Unhas), and Medan (Northern Sumatra University, USU). Since the beginning, their primary interests have been to study the fundamental teachings of Islam. Their course materials are compiled in, among others, Imaduddin Abdurrahim's *Kuliah Tauhid* (Bandung: Pustaka Salman, 1979). For a further account on these religious study groups, see "Islam Sebagai Baju Zirah di Kalangan Muda", *Tempo*, 13 May 1989, pp. 74–84. For the case of ITB's Salman mosque, see "Gerakan Kaum Muda Islam Mesjid Salman", in *Gerakan Islam Kontemporer di Indonesia*, edited by Abdul Aziz, Imam Tolkhah, and Soetarman (Jakarta: Pustaka Firdaus, 1989), pp. 207–81.

23. Formed in 1975, MUI is a state-sponsored institution. It is an autonomous body outside the state agency, and often critical to a number of government policies towards Islam. As widely noted, however, its creation was at the behest of the New Order regime. One of the chief functions of MUI, especially during its earlier years,

has been to cultivate a more positive relationship between *ulama* (religious leaders) and *umara* (state leaders).

24. No exact figure is available with regard to the membership of both Muhammadiyah and NU. The number cited here is based on claims by each respective organization. For evidence of the representativeness of these two organization, see reports in *Tempo*, 2 December 1989 and 15 December 1990. See also Abdurrahman Wahid's statement at the event of NU's grand gathering in Jakarta as reported in *Tempo*, March 1992 and *Panji Masyarakat*, 1–10 March 1992.

25. For a general treatment on the significance of *ulama* and *kyai*, see Zamakhsyari Dhofier, *Tradisi Pesantren: Studi Tentang Pandangan Hidup Kyai* (Jakarta: LP3ES, 1982). On the strategic position of this networking of *ulama*, see Dawam Rahardjo, "Lembaga Keulamaan" (No publisher, n.d.). For a comparison, see Taufik Abdullah, "Pola Kepemimpinan Islam di Indonesia", *Islam dan Masyarakat: Pantulan Sejarah Indonesia* (Jakarta: LP3ES, 1987), pp. 54–87.

26. To name only some of them: Abdurrahman Wahid (NU); Amien Rais, Watik Pratikmya, Kuntowijoyo, Yahya Muhaimin, Ahmad Syafii Maarif, M. Dawam Rahardjo (Muhammadiyah); Quraish Shihab, Adi Sasono, M. Amin Aziz (MUI).

27. Later As'ad Syamsul Arifin, a charismatic *kyai* of an East Javanese *pesantren* Salafiyah Syafiiyah, withdrew his support for Abdurrahman Wahid. In fact, the former disengaged (*mufaraqah*) himself from the latter's leadership. As'ad was furious with a number of Abdurrahman Wahid's controversial ideas and practices. Most notably they concerned (1) his notion of socio-cultural affinity between the greetings of "*assalamualaikum*" and "good morning/afternoon/evening" and (2) his willingness (in spite of his status as general chairman of NU) to become a judge in Indonesia's film festival. See "Gus Dur Sam'an wa Tha'atan", *Aula*, October 1987, pp. 8–17. See also "Saya Akan Salat Sendiri", *Tempo*, 2 December 1989, p. 31; "Kyai As'ad: Saya Tak Makmum Kepada Imam yang Kentut", *Panji Masyarakat*, 21–31 December 1989, p. 17.

28. See "NU: Menuju Islam Indonesia", *Tempo*, 8 December 1984, p. 13. For a further account, see also Abdurrahman Wahid, "The Nahdlatul Ulama and Islam in Present Day Indonesia", in *Islam and Society in Southeast Asia*, edited by Taufik Abdullah and Sharon Siddique (Singapore: Institute of Southeast Asian Studies, 1986), pp. 175–83.

29. On the new character of NU, see Arief Mudatsir's preliminary notes, "Dari Situbondo Menuju NU Baru: Sebuah Catatan Awal", *Prisma*, extra ed., 1984, pp. 130–42.

30. For a fuller account, see Abdurrahman Wahid, "NU dan Politik", *Kompas*, 24 June 1987. See also "Umat Islam Tidak Lagi Di Kandang Sempit", *Tempo*, 11 April 1987, p. 15; "Politik Ma'rifat NU", *Tempo*, 11 April 1987, pp. 12–15.

31. See "Pernikahan NU dengan Bank Summa", *Aula*, June 1990, pp. 12–25. NU's initial plan was to build 2,000 BPRs within a twenty-year span. With the collapse of Edward Suryadjaja's financial empire, it is not clear how NU will carry out this programme further.

32. There has been a lot of criticism, especially from younger thinkers and activists, that Muhammadiyah has been emphasizing more on its *amal usaha* than its original mission as a religious renewal (*tajdid*) movement. (Reportedly, Muhammadiyah currently owns nineteen hospitals, seventy higher educational institutions, and thousands of schools. See "Di Mana Diperlukan Pembaruan?", *Tempo*, 15 December 1990, p. 28.) This tendency, as perceived by many, has led to a serious intellectual stagnation within the organization. Being so, it inhibits the ability of Muhammadiyah to contribute to the formulation of alternative ideas relevant to the nation's socio-religious, economic, and political problems. For criticism of Muhammadiyah, see Ahmad Syafii Maarif, "Gejala Kemandegan Muhammadiyah dalam Pembaharuan Pemikiran Islam di Indonesia: Mitos Atau Realitas" (Discussion paper, November 1985); M. Din Syamsuddin, ed., *Muhammadiyah Kini dan Esok* (Jakarta: Pustaka Panjimas, 1990).

33. This idea is proposed by Amien Rais and Watik Pratiknya. It is still not clear what is meant by a new theological underpinning in this respect. Nonetheless, there are indications which suggest that this is some sort of a mundane or down-to-earth social ideology which directs the individual's or organization's course of actions. In a way, this notion of theology resembles the idea of transformatory (transformative) theology, which has been introduced and developed by other activists such as Moeslim Abdurrahman. With this new theology, it is expected that Muhammadiyah would side with those who are socio-economically deprived (*dhuafa*). Both Amien Rais and Watik Pratiknya are of the opinion that theology does not just refer to the science of divinity. In their view, theology should also relate to various aspects of life, which include socio-economic, scientific, and technological matters. See their viewpoints as expressed in "Di Mana Diperlukan Pembaruan?", *Tempo*, 15 December 1990, p. 30.

34. See "Di Mana Diperlukan Pembaruan?", *Tempo*, 15 December 1990, p. 30. See also Fahmy Chatib, "Kaum Dhuafa, Ekonomi Pasar dan Muhammadiyah", *Panji Masyarakat*, 21–30 December 1990.

35. See "Konglomerat Tanpa Dasi", *Tempo*, 15 December 1990, pp. 33–34. For a critical view of this account, see "Kerjasama Ormas Islam dan Konglomerat: Siapa Yang Untung?", *Panji Masyarakat*, 21–31 October 1991, pp. 17–24.

36. The *fatwa* of MUI are considered to be non-binding. In general, they serve as important guidance. But the implementation of these *fatwa* is very much dependent on the individuals' religious inclination. For a good study on the *fatwa* of MUI, see M. Atho Mudzhar, "Fatwas of the Council of Indonesian Ulama: A Study of Islamic Legal Thought in Indonesia, 1975–1988" (Ph.D. dissertation, University of California Los Angeles, 1990). For a preliminary compilation of the council's *fatwa*, see *Kumpulan Fatwa Majelis Ulama Indonesia* (Jakarta: Pustaka Panjimas, 1984).

37. This has been signified, among other things, by MUI's recent involvement with several Islamic socio-religious study institutes to collaborate in certain relevant projects. In 1984, in conjunction with a number of Islamic research and study institutes (for example, LSP, Pusat Pengembangan Agribisnis, Universitas Islam Assyafi'iyah, Universitas Ibnu Khaldun, and Lembaga Studi Agama dan Filsafat), MUI was involved in organizing the first national gathering of Muslim intellectuals,

and the formation of Forum Komunikasi Pembangunan Indonesia (FKPI, Indonesian Communication Development Forum) in 1986. Through its organizational network, this forum — as many have perceived — had substantial precursorial impacts on the eventual establishment of the Association of Indonesian Muslim Intellectuals (Ikatan Cendekiawan Muslim Se-Indonesia, or ICMI) in 1990. (Interview with Dawam Rahardjo in Jakarta, 20 August 1991.)

38. Actually, MUI was not the initial promoter of Islamic banking. The idea to have an Islamic bank had been in the air since 1973. Because of the still growing hostilities between some proponents of political Islam, particularly those who aspire to having a formal political relationship between Islam and the state, and the New Order regime, such an idea could not be realized any sooner. For further information on the genealogy of BMI, see "Bank Islam, Atau Bunga 0%", *Tempo*, 6 April 1991, p. 19; "Bank Dengan Agunan Amanah", *Tempo*, 9 November 1991; "Mengapa Baru Sekarang BMI Berdiri", *Prospek*, 2 November 1991, pp. 72–81; "Bank Istimewa, Tanpa Bunga", *Editor*, 9 November 1991, pp. 75–76. For a preliminary analysis, see Robert W. Hefner, "Islamizing Capitalism: On the Founding of Indonesia's First Islamic Bank" (Paper presented at the conference on Intellectual Development in Indonesian Islam, Arizona State University, 19–21 February 1993).

39. There are Muslims who consider interest to be a form of *riba* (usury). It is true that the doctrine of Islam prohibits *riba*. However, what is meant by *riba* is still (and will continue to be) a polemical issue, as in the Islamic world there is no single unified interpretation of *riba*. Accordingly, there will always be tugs of war among Muslims concerning what constitutes *riba*; between those who regard interest as *riba* and those who perceive otherwise. A workshop held by MUI in August 1990 to address this issue reconfirmed the bipolarity of the problem of interest and banking in Islam. (See "Dari Bogor, Terserah Masing-Masing", *Tempo*, 1 September 1990, pp. 100–1.) Yet, it is interesting to note that such an important figure as Sjafruddin Prawiranegara, a former leader of the proscribed Masyumi and governor of Bank of Indonesia, did not view interest as *riba*. For a fuller treatment of his thoughts on the relationship between Islam and the economy, see Sjafruddin Prawiranegara, *Ekonomi dan Keuangan, Makna Ekonomi Islam: Kumpulan Karangan Terpilih 2* (Jakarta: Haji Masagung, 1986).

40. For some interesting accounts, see "Robohnya Dinding Politik Islam", *Tempo*, 29 December 1984, pp. 12–16; "Pondok-Pondok Yang Berpaling", *Tempo*, 12 February 1987, pp. 20–28; "Aspirasi Islam: Ke Mana Kini?", *Tempo*, 9 May 1987, pp. 20–25; "Golkar dan Pemilih Islam", *Tempo*, 21 September 1991, pp. 21–33.

41. In this case, the state originally relied on the Opsus (Operasi Khusus, or Special Operation) agency. Following its termination in the mid-1970s, Kopkamtib (Komando Pemulihan Keamanan dan Ketertiban, or the Operational Command for the Restoration of Order and Security) resumed a similar function until its dissolution in 1988. For fuller treatment of this issue, see a range of essays in Lee Oey Hong, ed., *Indonesia after the 1971 Elections* (London and Kuala Lumpur: Hull Monograph Series on Southeast Asia, no. 5, Oxford University Press, 1974). See also a number of articles in Arief Budiman, ed., *State and Civil Society in*

Indonesia (Clayton: Monash Papers on Southeast Asia, no. 22, Centre of Southeast Asian Studies, Monash University, 1990), chapters 6–10, pp. 115–288.

42. See H.M.S. Mintaredja, *Renungan Pembaharuan Pemikiran Masyarakat Islam dan Politik di Indonesia* (Jakarta: Penerbit Permata, 1971). See also Ken Ward's treatment of Parmusi in his *The 1971 Election in Indonesia: An East Java Case Study* (Clayton: Monash Papers on Southeast Asia, no. 2, Centre of Southeast Asian Studies, Monash University, 1974), pp. 114–33.

43. Interview with Sulastomo in Jakarta, 10 September 1991.

44. Interview with Hartono Mardjono in Jakarta, 28 August 1991.

45. Interview with Ridwan Saidi in Jakarta, 21 August 1991. See also his political statements which appeared in "Harus Dicegah, Agama Islam Dijadikan Komoditi Politik", *Kompas*, 23 August 1986 and "Saya Tidak Membuang Islam", *Tempo*, 30 August 1986. For further accounts of Ridwan Saidi's political thinking, see, for instance, his *Islam: Pembangunan Politik dan Politik Pembangunan* (Jakarta: Pustaka Panjimas, 1983); and *Islam dan Moralitas Pembangunan* (Jakarta: Pustaka Panjimas, 1984).

46. Ridwan Saidi's idea concerning PPP as an open political party stirred conflict between himself and the party's central leadership, particularly John Naro and Mardinsyah — respectively, then the general chairman and secretary general of PPP. This, in turn, led to his dismissal from PPP in October 1986. Currently, Ridwan Saidi is a member of the Southern Jakarta branch of Golkar. For a further account on this issue, see "Saya tidak Membuang Islam", *Tempo*, 30 August 1986, pp. 12–13. See also "Ijtihad Politik Ridwan Saidi", *Panji Masyarakat*, 1–10 June 1988, pp. 46–47.

47. This problem is not unique to PPP. The political discourse of PDI has also suffered a comparable predicament. For its latest accounts, see "Soerjadi Mengapa Dihabisi", *Tempo*, 24 July 1993, pp. 21–29.

48. For a documentary treatment, see Saifuddin Zuhri et al., *PPP, NU dan MI: Gejolak Wadah Politik Islam* (Jakarta: Integrita Press, 1984). See also Machrus Irsyam, *Ulama dan Partai Politik: Upaya Mengatasi Krisis* (Jakarta: Yayasan Perkhidmatan, 1984); Abdul Basit Adnan, *Ada Apa di PPP* (Solo: Mayasari, 1982). For a general treatment of PPP, see Umaidi Radi, *Strategi PPP 1973–1982: Suatu Studi Tentang Kekuatan Politik Islam Tingkat Nasional* (Jakarta: Integrita Press, 1984).

49. Disappointment over PPP's political discourse had been voiced by many prominent Muslim leaders. See, for instance, the statements of Lukman Harun, Yunan Nasution, Syafruddin Prawiranegara, and Hamam Dja'far in "Ujung Tanduk Perjalanan Partai Islam", *Tempo*, 9 May 1987, pp. 24–25.

50. The watershed of this political move was represented by NU's withdrawal from PPP in 1984. As a result, in the 1987 general elections PPP won only 15.97 per cent of the votes — a drop of nearly 12 per cent from the 1982 result (27.78 per cent). In the meantime, Golkar and PDI increased their votes by almost 9 per cent and 3 per cent respectively. Figures are modified from Leo Suryadinata, *Military Ascendancy*

and Political Culture: A Study of Indonesia's Golkar (Athens: Monograph in International Studies, Southeast Asia Series, no. 85, Ohio University, 1989), pp. 159–60.

51. Among those who were invited to the gathering: Burhan Magenda, A.M. Saefuddin, Daud Ali, Amien Rais, Sri Bintang Pamungkas, Dipo Alam, Afan Gaffar, Hadimulyo, and Saleh Khalid. For a fuller account of the event, see "Ruh Islam di PPP", *Panji Masyarakat*, 1–10 September 1991, pp. 15–24. On the implications of this new development, see Bahtiar Effendy, "Islam dan Aktualisasi Politik PPP", *Panji Masyarakat*, 1–10 September 1991, pp. 25–26.

52. They included A.M. Saefuddin, Muchtar Naim, Sri Bintang Pamungkas, Rusydi Hamka, Saleh Khalid, and Hadimulyo.

53. On the origins and development of Golkar, see David Reeve, *Golkar of Indonesia: An Alternative to the Party System* (Singapore: Oxford University Press, 1985). See also Suryadinata, op. cit.

54. Respectively, 62.80 per cent (1971), 62.11 per cent (1977), 64.34 per cent (1982), 73.16 per cent (1987), 68 per cent (1992), and 74.51 per cent (1997). With the exception of the 1992 and 1997 results, figures are from Suryadinata, op. cit., pp. 159–60. The 1992 result is from *Tempo*, 20 June 1992, pp. 21–31; and the 1997 result is from *The Jakarta Post*, 24 June 1997.

55. For detailed lists of Golkar's supporting groups, see Suryadinata, op. cit., pp. 184–97.

56. An argument of this sort can be found in Afan Gaffar, *The Javanese Voters: A Case Study of Election under a Hegemonic Party System* (Yogyakarta: Gadjah Mada University Press, 1992).

57. See "Pondok-Pondok yang Berpaling", *Tempo*, 21 February 1987, pp. 20–24; "Santri di Antara Beringin dan Bintang", *Tempo*, 21 February 1987, pp. 24–28; "Pasang Surut Hubungan Islam — Beringin", *Tempo*, 21 September 1991, pp. 22–27.

58. See "Menyingkap Sayap Islam di Golkar", *Panji Masyarakat*, 1–10 March 1990, pp. 26–27.

59. At least eight former HMI activists occupied ministerial posts (1987–92). They included Saleh Afif, Azwar Anas, Hasrul Harahap, Akbar Tanjung, Arifin Siregar, Syamsuddin Sumintapura, Sya'dilah Mursid, and Syarifuddin Baharsyah. (Interview with Dawam Rahardjo in Jakarta, 20 August 1991.) With a few changes, the composition of the 1993–98 Cabinet still indicated the accommodative nature of the regime towards Muslim political activists. It included: Saleh Afif, Azwar Anas, Akbar Tanjung, Sya'dilah Mursid, Mar'ie Muhammad, Ahmad Latief, and Tarmizi Taher.

60. See "Beringin Semakin Hijau", *Tempo*, 3 October 1992, pp. 21–31. See also *Tempo*, 20 June 1992, pp. 21–31.

61. Interview with Kuntowijoyo in Yogyakarta, 25 July 1991. For a fuller account, see Kuntowijoyo, "Serat Cebolek dan Mitos Pembangkangan Islam: Melacak Asal-Usul Ketegangan Antara Islam dan Birokrasi", *Paradigma Islam: Interpretasi Untuk Aksi* (Bandung: Mizan, 1991), pp. 123–37.

6

Reducing Hostility
The Accommodative
Responses of the State

To many observers, these moves amounted to what seemed an obvious gambit. The scenario-makers spun out a logical sub-plot: Suharto needed to enlist Muslim political support in the run-up to elections. With opposition to his re-election to a sixth term in 1993 under the threat from an increasingly disillusioned military camp, Suharto appeared to be clutching at the only card left in his much diminished hand; he let it be known that when he died, he would like the Muslims to pray for him.

Michael R.J. Vatikiotis[1]

In themselves these events do not point to a decisive break with the policies of the early New Order. They can be dismissed as symbolic gestures. But if they are symbolic, they are not "merely" symbolic. Rather, they point to an ongoing and unstable dialectic in which changes in society — in particular, the growing influence of Islam in the urban middle class — have led some in government to look at Islam in new ways.

Robert W. Hefner[2]

ACCOMMODATION BY THE STATE

As suggested in the preceding chapters, the idealism and activism of the earlier generation of political Muslims were characterized by formalism and legalism. The ultimate embodiment of their ideas and actions was their aspiration for the creation of an Islamic state, or a state based on Islamic ideology. Failure to accomplish this goal, partly due to the fact that not every Muslim shared the idea of Islamic statehood, led to an uneasy relationship between Islam and the Indonesian state.

The implications of this uneasy political relationship were far-reaching, culminating with shrinking access to the corridors of power and the declining stature of political Muslims, especially during the first twenty years of the New Order regime. Illustrative of the defeat of political Islam were the proscription of Masyumi (1960); the exclusion of its prominent figures in the leadership of the newly founded Parmusi (1968); the reduction of the number of Islamic political parties from four — Nahdlatul Ulama (NU), Muslimin Indonesia (MI), Partai Sarekat Islam Indonesia (PSII), and Persatuan Tarbiah Islam (Perti) — into a single Partai Persatuan Pembangunan (PPP) (1973); plummeting representation in the parliament as well as in the Cabinet; and the denial of Islam as the basis of Islamic social and political organization (1985). Most distressing, political Islam had become a convenient target of ideological distrust, suspected for its adherence to anti-state ideology.[3]

It is this kind of dismal political situation which the new generation of Muslim thinkers and activists, emerging after the early 1970s, intended to remedy. Their primary emphasis has been to transform the legalistic-formalistic and exclusive outlook of the earlier idealism and activism of political Muslims into a more substantive and integrative approach. By changing the format of political Islam, including a new theological underpinning, set of goals, and approach, it was believed that its stature — not so much in a categorical sense (that is, Islam as a political category), but more in its inspirational meaning — could be gradually raised. More importantly, it was also expected that with this kind of strategy a viable political synthesis between Islam and the state could be genuinely established. This would enable Islam to function as a benevolence (*rahmah*) not only for Muslims, but also for Indonesian society at large.

It appears that this sort of expectation is now in fact beginning to take shape. Though the ideal — that is, an amicable political relationship between Islam and the state — has not yet fully materialized, there have been a number of important signs which indicate a re-entrance of political Islam (in its new format) into the country's political life. Evidence of this new development has included the political relaxation of the state towards Islam during the last several years, signified by the former's adherence to a number of policies that accord with the latter's socio-economic and political interests. Given the nature of the political relationship between Islam and the state in the past, it can be said that these accommodative moves would have been very unlikely in the early years of the New Order up to the mid-1980s — a period when political Islam was still perceived, especially by the state, as ideologically non-integrative if not threatening.

It would be naive to argue that the current accommodative attitude of the state towards political Islam is attributable to only a single factor. The socio-political context in which this phenomenon is evolving is certainly contributory to its development. From the perspective of this study, I would argue, however, that it is the intellectual transformation of Islamic political ideas and practices which has led to the changing stance of the state towards Islam. Without such an intellectual shift, if political Muslims were still nurturing the idea of Islamic statehood or ideology, it is difficult to imagine that such accommodative responses would ever take place in the 1990s.

The primary task of this chapter is to identify some evidence which may indicate the emergence of accommodative state policies towards Islam. In addition, it will also examine the types and forms of accommodation to shed light on their actual significance and to speculate on their possible ramifications in the future. In line with the basic argument presented above, my approach is to assess the available body of evidence in the light of the intellectual transformation of Islamic political ideas and practices. By doing so, it is expected that this inquiry can demonstrate that these accommodative enterprises of the state serve not as moves to orient itself towards the direction of Mecca,[4] nor as *ad hoc* courtesies towards political Islam, but represent the establishment of a meaningful foundation, however symbolic it may be, for the development of an amicable political relationship between Islam and the state — a political milestone on a road which was tainted with animosity for so long.

EVIDENCE OF ACCOMMODATION

The evidence of the growing accommodative stance of the state towards Islam includes the adoption of a number of policies beneficial to the interests of Muslims. Broadly categorized, they can be classified into four different types: (1) structural; (2) legislative; (3) infrastructural; and (4) cultural. A detailed chronological account of the evidence is not necessary. Nevertheless, a brief sketch of these subjects is critical to shed light on the extent to which they shape our perceived notion of the accommodative behaviour of the state towards Islam.

Structural Accommodation

One of the most conspicuous forms of accommodation has been the recruitment of the new generation of Muslim political thinkers and activists into the executive-bureaucratic and legislative agencies of the state. This form of accommodation did not happen instantaneously. It started with the appointment of a handful of Muslim activists in state agencies and other bodies of the New Order's early economic and political entities such as Soeharto's economic team, Golkar, and Bappenas.[5] This process gradually developed in the 1970s. But it is only recently, beginning in the mid-1980s, that Muslim activists have been assigned to a number of important political and bureaucratic posts,[6] providing a relatively easy access to power pertinent for the realization of Islamic interests. There are at least two main reasons behind this phenomenon. One is sociological, the other political.

First, access to modern education and economic development in independent Indonesia, especially during the New Order era, has transformed the social basis of the Muslim community.[7] It has given the Muslims the large portion of the country's middle class and professional sectors.[8] If during the late colonial and early independence periods, Indonesia's modern intellectual community was dominated at least by the *priyayi* (indigenous aristocrats) and those who embraced the "metropolitan subculture",[9] today's intellectualism is characterized by the active participation of Muslim thinkers and activists.[10] Because of this sociological mobility, exacerbated by the return of many Muslim Ph.D. holders from about the 1970s to the 1980s, they can no longer be perceived as representing a backward and marginal group. Instead, they represent a new socio-political group with certain aspirations but also with considerable skills who need structural avenues to channel their interests.[11]

Second, it is practically this new group of Muslim intellectuals which has tried to shape the new format of Indonesia's political Islam. As has been suggested, these intellectuals do not share the idea of a formalistic association between Islam and the state, they no longer aspire to an Islamic state goal, and they no longer consider partisan politics, with parliament as the sole playing field, as the only approach to politics. Instead, they consider the realization of a just, participatory, and egalitarian construct of the state as their goal which should be fought for not only through Islamic parties, but through the bureaucracy, non-governmental organizations, and even the then ruling party (Golkar).[12]

All of this has reduced the suspicion of the state towards political Islam. This has led the former to provide the necessary structural mechanism to enable the latter to express and realize its interests. Thus, since the 1970s we have seen a limited bureaucratic accommodation offered to a number of Muslim intellectuals such as Sularso, Bintoro Tjokroamidjojo, Barli

Halim, Bustanul Arifin, Madjid Ibrahim, Zainul Yasni, Sya'dillah Mursid, and Mar'ie Muhammad.[13] Others, such as Mintaredja and Sulastomo, both of Himpunan Mahasiswa Islam (HMI) origin, were entrusted to lead Parmusi following the party's upheaval in its early inception.[14] Akbar Tanjung, another former HMI leader, who became the first chairman of the state-sponsored Komite Nasional Pemuda Indonesia (KNPI, Indonesian Youth National Committee) in the mid-1970s, and other Muslim religious leaders such as Thohir Wijaja and Muhammad Tarmudji were recruited to become members of the then ruling party Golkar.[15]

Since then, this structural accommodation has grown in number and substance. Not only were more Muslim activists recruited into the bureaucratic and political machinery, they were also promoted to higher posts. During this period individuals like Abdul Gafur, Akbar Tanjung, Bustanil Arifin, Saleh Afif, Azwar Anas, Hasrul Harahap, Arifin Siregar, Syamsuddin Sumintapura, Sya'dillah Mursid, and Syafruddin Baharsyah, who had an early association with Islamic student organizations such as HMI, were appointed as Cabinet ministers.[16] In the early 1990s Mar'ie Muhammad, who has had a long bureaucratic career in the Department of Finance, and Ahmad Latief, a successful entrepreneur, were appointed as Ministers of Finance and Manpower respectively, strengthening the structural position of Islam within the bureaucracy.

But most conspicuous has been the recruitment of Muslim leaders and activists in parliament, some of whom had been outside and alienated from the government, following the 1992 election. This has led to a public assessment of the parliament becoming "greener", the colour often, but not always, perceived as the colour symbol of Islam.[17]

Adding to this structural accommodation is the formation of ICMI (Indonesian Association of Muslim Intellectuals) under the leadership of B.J. Habibie — Soeharto's close confidant and Minister of Research and Technology as well as chairman of Badan Pengkajian dan Penerapan Teknologi (BPPT, Board for the Study and Implementation of Technology).[18] This organization, as suggested by Liddle, "is in large part a patron-client network of Muslim government bureaucrats, ... it has also reached out successfully to the large and growing group of Islamic intellectuals and educated *santri* Muslims who have been outside and often alienated from the government".[19] Though its structural significance, compared with the bureaucracy and Golkar, has yet to be seen, ICMI has often been perceived as bringing Muslim thinkers and activists a step closer to power. Again as implied by Liddle, "[t]he composition of the Golkar delegation to Parliament elected in 1992 and of the government controlled fractions in the 1993-1998 MPR evince a considerable ability to find places for his ICMI proteges and supporters".[20]

In short, suffice it to say that all of these changes and appointments represent structural accommodation for Muslims to articulate and aggregate their interests as well as to have a say in the decision-making process.[21]

Legislative Accommodation

There are at least five major events related to the legislative form of state accommodation towards Islam: (1) the passing of the education law (Undang-Undang Pendidikan Nasional, UUPN) in 1989; (2) the enactment of the religious court law (Undang-Undang Peradilan Agama, UUPA) in 1989 and the compilation of Islamic law in 1991 (Kompilasi Hukum Islam, KHI); (3) the reversal of policy on *jilbab* (head covering) in 1991; (4) the issuance of a joint-ministerial decision concerning Badan Amil Zakat, Infak dan Sadaqah (Bazis), a collecting and distributing agency of religious alms (*zakat*) and charities (*infaq* and *sadaqah*) in 1991; and (5) the annulment of Sumbangan Dermawan Sosial Berhadiah (SDSB), a form of national lottery, in 1993. The rulings on these subjects are favourable to the interests of many Muslims.

Education Law

The issue of religious education has always been a concern for Muslims. Stated or otherwise, they expect their children to receive enough religious learning to understand the fundamental teachings of Islam and practise its basic rituals. Traditionally, early exposure to this sort of religious training was carried out through non-formal channels, where parents taught their children or sent them to local religious tutors. With increasing access to modern educational institutions, especially since the post-colonial period, Muslim leaders and activists have endeavoured to expand the avenues for the socialization of Islamic values.

This matter does not seem to be an issue with regard to educational institutions categorized as Islamic, namely those which are administered by the Department of Religion or Islamic organizations such as Muhammadiyah and NU. Given the origins of these schools, intrinsically they would include religious instruction in their curricula. To expand the avenues for the socialization of Islamic values, Muslims expect that religious instruction be incorporated into the curricula of public as well as private vernacular schools under the auspices of the Department of Education and Culture.

In 1950 the state attempted to accommodate this concern. Through its first education law, enacted in that year, the state prescribed that religious instruction be given in all public schools. Nevertheless, this legislation fell short of making religious instruction mandatory. Article 20, Sections 1 and 2 of this law, No. 4/1950, clearly stated that attendance at the course was not compulsory, but subject to parents' decision. Adding to its voluntary nature was the explanation to the law that religious instruction did not in any way affect student grades.[22]

With the ascension of the New Order administration to power in the mid-1960s, partly due to the regime's resentment towards communist atheism,[23] religious instruction became a required course.[24] This, however, did not put Muslims' concern over religious instruction to rest. In spite of the changes that occurred in the government regulation over the status of religious instruction, the policy did not seem to guarantee the right of many Muslim students who attended Christian schools, particularly at the primary and secondary levels, to receive Islamic religious instruction. On the contrary, they were often solicited to take a religious course on Christianity — an unfortunate reality which underlies the traditional contention between Muslims and Christians in Indonesia.[25]

This sentiment was exacerbated later by an attempt to draft a new education law, introduced by the Department of Education and Culture, which seemed to deny the overt inclusion of religious instruction in the school curricula.[26] According to Article 40 of the draft, the curricula of education consist of only the fields of science, technology, and art. Though the draft did offer subjects pertinent to the development of students' piety and belief in One God (explanation to Article 13, Section 1), in the view of many Muslims this did not necessarily constitute religious instruction.[27]

It was only after intensive lobbying, particularly by Majelis Ulama Indonesia (MUI) and Muhammadiyah, that the new education law, enacted in March 1989, recognized explicitly the role of religious instruction at all levels of education,[28] as stated in Article 20, Section 2.[29] Moreover, the explanation to Article 28, Section 2, concerning the quality of the religious instructor, stipulated that the religious instructor must adhere to the same religion being taught as well as be in accord with the students' religion.[30]

There is no doubt that the final outcome of this legislation pleased many Muslims. This is not only due to the fact that the new bill incorporated religious instruction into the curricula of education, but by implication, it also guaranteed the right of Muslim students attending Christian schools to receive Islamic religious instruction. At least theoretically, it obliged Christian schools to provide Islamic religious instruction for their Muslim students. In so doing, they have been required to stop their practice of offering Christian religious instruction to Muslim students.[31]

It was this kind of ramification that eventually generated protests and criticism, largely from Christian circles. Voiced mainly through the Partai Demokrasi Indonesia (PDI), they demanded the nullification of the latter clause. While accepting the incorporation of religious instruction into the curricula of education, they strongly rejected the stipulation that the religious instructor must be an adherent of the religion being taught as well as of the students' religion.[32] In other words, they objected to the idea that they should provide Islamic religious instruction to their Muslim students.[33]

This constant rejection and criticism, even after the enactment of the law, did not result in the annulment of the clause, but severely hindered the possibility of its implementation. Evidently, the government regulations (PP Nos. 27, 28, 29, and 30/1990), upon which the implementation of this education law is actually based, do not provide further directives for the realization of the clause. In fact, one of its regulations (No. 29/1989) explicitly stated that secondary schools with a certain religious character are not required to provide religious instruction different from their own religion.[34] This released schools with certain religious orientations (for example, Catholic general schools) from the obligation to offer religious instruction different from their own religion.

Having said this, it is fair to conclude that there are at least two areas of significance for Muslims with regard to the passing of this education law. Symbolically, it represents an important recognition of the fact that the state, being neither theocratic nor secular, does recognize the pivotal role of religion, including in the field of education. Functionally, it reasserts the right of every Muslim student at public as well as private educational institutions to receive religious instruction according to his or her own belief. Even though it could not be implemented in schools with certain religious character, nonetheless, it should protect Muslim students from being urged, directly or otherwise, to participate in religious instruction different from their own religious adherence.

Religious Court Law

The passing of the religious court legislation (UUPA) in December 1989, presented to the parliament by the Department of Religion, provided further evidence concerning the recent accommodative attitudes of the state towards Islam. This is so as the bill restored and strengthened the status and function of religious courts (Peradilan Agama), administered by the Department of Religion, in adjudicating marriage, inheritance, and endowment issues for consenting Muslims.

From the perspective of history, there is nothing peculiar with respect to the enactment of this law. In Indonesia religious courts, in their simplest form and function, have been in existence for centuries. Following the rapid process of Islamization in the archipelago, culminating with the rise of a number of Islamic rulers in Java and the outer islands, indigenous Muslims generally have settled their disputes on matters related to civil issues such as marriage, inheritance, and endowment through these religiously based judicial institutions.[35]

In spite of this long standing, religious courts have suffered from a number of critical defects. This situation, in turn, has contributed to their weak position *vis-à-vis* other judicial institutions (that is, military, civil, and state administrative courts) in the contemporary Indonesian legal system. These major defects are:

Disuniformity in Name and Authority

The existence of Islamic religious courts survived during most of the colonial period. In fact, convinced of the fact that the most acceptable ordinances to the native population were those of religion (that is, Islamic law), the colonial government institutionalized the status and function of religious courts in Java and Madura in 1882 (Staatsblad No. 152). However, by the turn of the twentieth century, this accommodative stance had changed rather abruptly. Mainly because of the surging influence of customary *(adat)* law in the process of colonial policy-making, the role of religious courts was considerably circumscribed.[36] In 1937 their authority was confined to handling matters related only to marriage issues (Staatsblad No. 116).[37] Judicial cases associated with inheritance and endowment issues were to be settled in civil courts (*pengadilan negeri*).

Towards the end of the Japanese interregnum and during the early years of independence, political Muslims such as Abikusno Tjokrosujoso and Ki Bagus Hadikusumo tried to restore the status and function of religious courts to their original position. Yet this was to no avail due to the strong opposition of their nationalist counterparts, Sartono, Supomo, and Mohammad Hatta. In fact, there was a notion to abolish the religious courts. As evident in Sartono's statement:

> In the new State which will separate affairs of State from affairs of Religion, it is unnecessary to establish a special court

to try those affairs of Muslims closely connected with their Religion. It is sufficient for all cases to be tried by an ordinary court, which can ask the advice of a religious expert.[38]

Shadowed by the debates on the nature of the relationship between religion and the state in the mid-1940s, these restorative enterprises were seen by many nationalist leaders simply as a move towards the creation of Islamic statehood.[39]

Following Indonesia's independence, significant changes did finally occur, especially with regard to the institutional expansion of religious courts. In 1947 the state established religious courts in Aceh and North Sumatra. A decade later the state expanded the institution of religious courts throughout Indonesia (Government Regulation No. 45/1957).

Surprisingly enough, despite the fact that this regulation led to the formation of religious courts all over the country, it did not unify the status and function of the existing religious courts. On the contrary, it tended to exacerbate their disuniformity in name and authority. Different from the similar institutions in Java, Madura, and Kalimantan, these newly established religious courts were called Mahkamah Syariah (Council of Islamic Law), instead of Peradilan Agama. More significant was the fact that they enjoyed a broader role, which included the authority to handle inheritance and endowment as well as marriage issues.[40]

Lack of Legal Autonomy

Other than this administrative and functional heterogeneity, the defect of Indonesia's religious courts was also indicated by the fact that they possessed no legal autonomy. Their decisions had no legal status unless recognized or reconfirmed by civil courts. In addition, they enjoyed no authority to enforce their rulings. The power to execute their decisions rested in the hands of civil courts.[41]

The implications of this situation could be very far-reaching. First, it opened up opportunities for clients to defy the rulings of these judicial institutions. Second, since their decisions had to be validated and executed by civil courts, it might well prolong the process of legal settlement, thereby making it less effective and more expensive.[42]

Administrative Discrepancy

Another defect of religious courts was the fact that their judges did not have equal administrative status *vis-à-vis* other judges from the other judicial institutions such as civil, military, and state administrative courts. Judges in these latter institutions were considered state judges because they were appointed by the head of state. On the other hand, judges in religious courts were not regarded as state judges as they were designated by the Minister of Religion.

Functionally, this discrepancy in administrative status did not seem to have a significant impact with respect to their position as judges, since they administered cases different from the other judicial institutions. Administratively, however, the fact that judges in religious courts were not considered state judges, in theory (as implied in the supreme court law No. 14/1985) they did not hold equal footing with those of their counterparts from the other judicial institutions when it came to promotion to the highest position in the supreme court.[43]

Absence of a Unified Legal Reference

Finally, an important defect of religious courts was the lack of a unified legal reference. In spite of their centuries-long existence, it was an irony that judges in religious courts possessed no single legal reference upon which they could establish their legal judgment. Instead, in the attempt to arrive at legal decisions, they generally referred their rulings to a number of classical works on Islamic jurisprudence (*fiqh*) of their choice.[44]

This irony was not without consequence. Because of the diversity of the legal references being used, depending on the literature preference of the judges — a situation which might well express their religious school of thought — there was always a possibility that two cases of the same nature might receive different rulings. And this, as suggested by Munawir Syadzali, would eventually create uncertainties among those who seek justice in religious courts.[45] In addition, given the fact that these classical references may not always be compatible with the current needs and circumstances, many cases in religious courts are still pending.[46]

Basically, the passing of this religious court law is designed to remedy these defects. First, it restored the scope of authority of religious courts in Java, Madura, and South Kalimantan, re-establishing their authority, like that of religious courts in other regions, to handle matters related to marriage, inheritance, and endowment issues. Second, it provided the necessary legal autonomy to religious courts. Because of this their decisions are final and binding. Furthermore, it also enabled them to execute their own rulings without the intervention of civil courts.[47] Third, it created equality of status of religious court judges with that of their colleagues in the other judicial institutions. Like their counterparts in the civil, military, and state administrative courts, religious court judges are now appointed by the head of state, thus making them state — rather than departmental — judges.[48] In short, in the words of Munawir Syadzali, "[the passing of this legislation would terminate] the disuniformity in names, authority, and structure of religious courts, as the result of the legal policy of the Dutch colonial government".[49]

To equip religious courts with a unified legal reference, the state sponsored the compilation of Islamic law project which was completed in 1991. Consisting of three books on matters related to (1) marriage; (2) inheritance; and (3) endowment issues, this compilation of Islamic law (Kompilasi Hukum Islam or KHI) serves as a single legal reference for religious courts. With it, judges in religious courts no longer have to rely on classical works of Islamic jurisprudence for their rulings. In fact, they are required to base their decisions on this particular legal reference.[50]

Indisputably, the passing of this legislation and the completion of the compilation of Islamic law pleased the Muslim community. At the other end of the spectrum, however, it also generated alarm especially, but not exclusively, among non-Muslim circles.[51]

There are at least two fundamental concerns which underlay their objection to this law. First, whether or not the law, given the very nature of religious court law, which only regulates Muslims' legal issues such as marriage, inheritance, and endowment, is actually congruent with the principle of unification of law in Indonesia's legal system. Second, whether or not the law is a cloak for the Jakarta Charter which obliges Muslims to implement Islamic law (shari'a).[52]

Given the response of the state (that is, the Minister of Religious Affairs Munawir Syadzali) and many other Muslim scholars on Islamic law, such as Ismail Sunny and M. Daud Ali, that UUPA will neither jeopardize the country's principle of unification of law nor become a cloak for the Jakarta Charter,[53] it seems fair to suggest that actually their opposition to this law has nothing to do with the substance of UUPA. Rather, it is related to their traumatic stance with the venture of political Islam in the past. The absence of a comprehensive concept as to the position of religion (not only Islam) in the state, coupled with the recent growing attention of the state towards Islam, only exacerbates the socio-political apprehension of the minority groups, especially Christians, as to what their place in the Republic will be in the future.

Policy Reversal on Jilbab

In 1991 the government, through the Directorate General of Elementary and Secondary Education, issued a new regulation on student uniforms.

This decision allowed Muslim female students at secondary educational institutions to wear the *jilbab* while attending school. Accordingly, those who wish to wear the *jilbab,* because of their religious conviction, may do so without fear of being sanctioned (SK No. 100/C/Kep/D/1991).[54]

To a certain extent, the question of the *jilbab* had contributed to the estranged relationship between Islam and the state in New Order Indonesia. It reinforced suspicion in some segments of Indonesia's Muslim community that the state hindered the implementation of Islamic religious teachings. This was especially the case with regard to the fact that the state, through its bureaucratic agency at the Department of Education and Culture, formulated a policy in 1982 which prohibited Muslim female students at secondary general schools from wearing the *jilbab* during school hours on the ground that this violated the school uniform code (SK No. 052/C/Kep/D/1982).[55]

This injunction imposed sanctions. Though varying from one school to another, generally the disciplinary actions being inflicted upon the parties concerned ranged from educational seclusion, disallowance to attend classes, temporary dismissal, or ejection from schools.[56]

The Muslim community, particularly its younger activists, had responded to the regulation and its sanctions no less vigorously. For nearly a decade, they had demanded that Muslim female students at secondary schools be permitted to wear the *jilbab*. They did so primarily by staging countless numbers of demonstrations in Jakarta, Bogor, Bandung, and Yogyakarta and registering complaints to their representatives in the parliament both at the national and regional levels. In fact, those who were dismissed from the schools brought their cases to the courts to be settled legally.[57]

In itself the issue of *jilbab* is actually a religious matter. It represents certain expressions of faith with regard to the appropriate way of dressing for female Muslims. Originally known as *kerudung* (a far more loose model of head covering than the *jilbab*), it has always been part of Indonesia's Muslim female apparel (but not necessarily perceived as *wajib*, religiously required), worn especially on religious occasions. Many Islamic educational institutions, public as well as private (for example, *pesantren* and other schools administered by Muhammadiyah, NU, and the Department of Religion), require their female students to wear head covering in different variations as part of their school uniforms. In those years, it seems safe to say, head covering was hardly an issue, let alone of such a national magnitude.[58]

However, the circumstances in which the issue evolved made it difficult for it to be seen as a mere religious phenomenon. On the contrary, the question of *jilbab* seemed to have had significant political weight. Thus, understanding the case simply in its religious context would not bring us any closer to the underlying problem as to why the state prohibited Muslim female students at secondary schools from wearing the *jilbab*.

In the late 1970s the Islamic world was overwhelmed by the spectre of religious resurgence.[59] For a decade or so, this notion of Islamic revivalism had shaped the religious and political expression of Islam. Religiously, it reasserted the practical and legal dimension of Islam, stressing "what were seen as central Islamic themes, including veiling and regulating women and legislating various areas of individual morality". Politically, it renewed the traditional conflicts between Islam and the state. In its crudest fashion, as exemplified by a number of cases in the Islamic heartland, it was directed "at overthrowing states found insufficiently Islamic and at installing Islamic states". For many, the latter's success story was unquestionably the Iranian revolution led by Khomeini in 1979.[60]

Though the form and magnitude of this religious resurgence varied from one country to another, it appeared that they shared some basic traits. As John L. Esposito noted in his *Islamic Revivalism*, with reference to the Middle Eastern phenomenon,

> there are [always] certain recurrent themes: a sense that existing political, economic, and social systems have failed; a disenchantment with and even rejection of the West; a quest for identity and greater authenticity; and the conviction that Islam provides a self-sufficient ideology for state and society, a valid alternative to secular nationalism, socialism, and capitalism.[61]

To a certain degree, Indonesia's resurgent Islam seemed to display comparable features. In the religious domain one of its major elements has been a surging interest among a sizeable proportion of urban-educated Muslims to initiate widespread campaigns to rekindle the notion of Islamic piety and authenticism (not so much in an intellectual sense, but more in a practical one). Included in this venture was an attempt to reinvigorate public conviction that wearing the *jilbab* should be mandatory for Muslim women. Surprisingly, through a series of lectures on the basic values of Islam (Nilai-Nilai Dasar Islam) presented at various religious study clubs, this enterprise was especially popular among the university and high school students at general educational institutions.[62]

In the realm of politics, though it did not represent the mainstream of political Islam, there was fragmented activism which seemed to reinforce the contention between Islam and the state in terms of their political relationship (for example, the Warman case, the Imran case). The growing sense of political animosity was exacerbated by the action of the state to enforce Pancasila as the sole ideological basis of all socio-religious as well as political organizations. This, in turn, contributed to an outburst of violence such as the Tanjung Priok affair and the bombing incidents involving Muslim activists. All of these instances had led the state to react harshly, charging the parties involved as subversives and scrutinizing virtually all Islamic activism, including religious sermons. In short, suffice it to say that in those years, Islamic activism was still perceived as representing a threat to the ideological and constitutional construct of the state. In other words, the state was still at the height of its suspicious stage towards Islam.

Having said this, it seems logical to argue that it was largely due to such political circumstances that the wearing of *jilbab* by Muslim female students at secondary educational institutions during the school hours was prohibited. The historical timing of the emerging popularity of the *jilbab* had conditioned the state to associate this religious phenomenon with the political aspect of Islamic resurgence, nationally as well as internationally. While there was no reasonable ground to outlaw the wearing of *jilbab* at the university level as higher educational institutions do not regulate school uniform, at the secondary schools, particularly those under the administration of the Department of Education and Culture, the state found its basis in the student uniform code.

This deepening hostility did not last. With the increasing development of the new Islamic intellectualism, coupled with the acceptance of *asas tunggal* by the Muslim community, the perceived notion that Islam represented a threat to the state began to evaporate in the late 1980s or early 1990s. Accordingly, the question of *jilbab,* as with many other Islamic issues, no longer carried politically threatening weight.[63] Largely because of this changing circumstance, the state reversed its policy on *jilbab* — a decision which has pleased many Muslims.

Joint-Ministerial Decision Concerning Badan Amil Zakat, Infaq, and Sadaqah (Bazis)

In 1991 the Minister of Religion and the Minister of Home Affairs issued a joint-decision concerning Badan Amil Zakat, Infaq, and Sadaqah (Bazis), a collecting and distributing agency of religious alms (*zakat*) and charities (*infaq* and *sadaqah*). Considering the fact that this agency has been in existence since 1968 (regardless of its fragmented and regionally based format), this decision did not seem to constitute an entirely novel act. Judging from the contents of the decision, it was primarily designed to lend a hand (presumably through the gigantic bureaucratic networks of the Department of Home Affairs and Department of Religion) to the Muslim community in their effort to intensify the implementation of *zakat* collection and distribution.[64]

The question of *zakat*, especially from its management standpoint, had long been a concern for many Muslims. As one of the five pillars (*rukun*) of Islam,[65] *zakat* is considered to be the only principle which has an immediate distributive economic impact. In fact, it has often been perceived as a panacea to eradicate poverty problems.[66] Nevertheless, in spite of the obligatory nature of *zakat* (thus serving as an inner religious drive for Muslims to pay *zakat*), the remedial socio-economic function of *zakat* does not seem to materialize automatically. The realization of this particular impact, as many have argued, depends on a number of things. Most importantly, it is contingent upon how *zakat* is administered, especially with respect to its collection as well as distribution mechanism.[67]

In this case of the leaders and activists of the Muslim community have generally agreed that the traditional administration of *zakat*, signified by a direct transaction between *muzakki* (*zakat* payer) and *mustahiq* (*zakat* recipient), where the former gives his/her *zakat* to the latter, could no longer be preserved. Religiously, such a practice is permissible, provided that it complies with the doctrinal requirements of *zakat*. Socio-economically, however, this mode of mechanism does not generate a significant impact other than reducing the burden of the economically less-fortunate individuals for a very short time.[68] Accordingly, the government came to the conclusion that sound and institutionalized management was required to enable *zakat* to develop not simply in the context of individual fulfilment of his/her religious obligation, but also in the framework of a structural strategy to alleviate the affliction of socio-economic impoverishment.[69]

It was largely against this background that the state expressed interest in lending a hand to establish institutionalized agencies to collect and distribute *zakat*. In 1968 the Department of Religion issued regulations concerning the foundation of Bazis (No. 4/July/1968) and Baitul Mal, an Islamic treasury agency (No. 5/October/1968). However, these two instructions were immediately suspended, because the Minister of Finance rejected the idea of legislating *zakat*, drafted a year earlier by the

Department of Religion. Curiously enough, this act of deferment was taken regardless of the Minister of Finance's suggestion that a ministerial decision is sufficient to regulate the administration of *zakat*.[70]

In the meantime, in his speech commemorating the Isra' and Mi'raj (Prophet Muhammad's journey to Allah) celebration in 1968, President Soeharto urged that *zakat* be administered systematically. In doing so, as recorded by Taufik Abdullah, "he, as 'a private [Muslim] citizen', was willing to take charge of the 'massive national effort of *zakat* collection' and to submit annual reports on the collection and distribution of *zakat*". To put this idea into operation, "he officially instructed three high military officers [Major-General Alamsyah, Colonel Azwar Hamid, and Colonel Ali Afandi] to make all necessary preparation for a nationwide *zakat* collection drive".[71]

Ali Sadikin, then the governor of Jakarta, was the first state official to put Soeharto's suggestion into action. In 1968, through a gubernatorial decision, he pioneered the establishment of Bazis. The relative success of this project encouraged other regional governments such as those in Aceh, West and South Sumatra, West Java, East and South Kalimantan, and North and South Sulawesi to form similar institutions.[72]

There is no doubt that the foundation of Bazis has created an intitutional breakthrough with regard to the administration and management of *zakat*, especially in terms of its collection and distribution. As in the case of Jakarta, it not only has intensified the rate and magnitude of *zakat* collection and distribution,[73] but also diversified the "categories of *zakat*able properties and income".[74]

In spite of this encouraging development, the collection and distribution of *zakat* remain contentious issues in virtually every seminar and discussion forum on *zakat*. This is especially true with regard to the effectiveness of the other regions in collecting and distributing *zakat,* which does not seem to match the success of Jakarta. Moreover, unrealistic though it may be, the success of *zakat* collection and distribution is often measured against its ability to generate an immediate socio-economic impact, capable of advancing the quality of welfare of its recipients. The fact that the welfare of the community at large remains a distressing issue is often perceived as an indication that *zakat* has not been intensively implemented. "The implementation of *zakat* in Indonesia," writes an observer of *zakat* issues, "has long been in existence, but why has the social justice and welfare of Muslim community not materialized?"[75]

Many Muslim leaders and activists are inclined to take a "statist" view of the implementation of *zakat*. They expect a greater role for the state in the administration of *zakat*. To them this can be initiated by providing an authorized *zakat* agency,[76] by legislating a law on *zakat*,[77] and by instituting the head of state to serve as the national *amil* (agent) of *zakat*.[78]

The issuance of the joint-ministerial decision on Bazis was basically an attempt to accommodate these concerns. But in this case the state neither shared the necessity to legislate *zakat* into a law nor acknowledged the urgency of instituting its officials to function as national or regional *amil* of *zakat*. As suggested by Munawir Syadzali, the state (partly to avoid possible dualism between *zakat* and tax) has no intention of regulating or managing *zakat*. Instead, the state confines its role to the extent that it simply supervises and guides the implementation of *zakat*.[79]

Regardless of the limited involvement of the state, this joint-ministerial decision would undoubtedly play an important role in the development of *zakat* collection and distribution. Specifically, it would strengthen the structure and format of the already existing agencies of *zakat* (that is, Bazis). Though it would not change the regionally based format of Bazis, nonetheless it would reduce the fragmented nature of this agency. This is in the sense that Bazis remains operative on a regional basis, but its existence would be more spread out in every region. Given the fact that the administration of *zakat* can be relatively successful without the issuance of this joint-ministerial decision (that is, the Jakarta case), it seems fair to suggest that perhaps the primary significance of this move lies in the willingness of the state to renew its commitment to facilitate Muslims in implementing their religious duties.

Annulment of Sumbangan Dermawan Sosial Berhadiah (SDSB)

Last but not least, the regulatory form of accommodation of the state towards Islam is also signified by the annulment of SDSB, a form of lottery that operated under the guise of "philanthropic donation with prizes".[80]

Under a variety of names, this form of lottery had been in existence for quite some time. In the late 1970s this "philanthropic donation with prizes" was introduced as Porkas, Kupon Sumbangan Olah Raga Berhadiah (KSOB, Coupon for Sports Donation with Prizes), and Tanda Sumbangan Sosial Berhadiah (TSSB, Receipt for Social Donation with Prizes), before finally being instituted as SDSB in 1989. While its day-to-day operation was entrusted to the hands of private enterprise, the Department of Social Affairs was solely responsible for overseeing and licensing the administration of SDSB.

The introduction of SDSB was driven largely by economic motives. It was designed to raise a large sum of money to enable the state "to fund sporting events, welfare programs, and disaster relief efforts".[81] Other than that, perhaps to solidify its existence and to silence its critics, this lottery agency also offered generous contributions to a number of socio-religious organizations and educational institutions.[82]

Regardless of these "virtuous" activities, SDSB had long been a target of criticism by many Muslim leaders and activists who vigorously demanded its nullification. There were at least two major reasons behind the Muslim opposition to SDSB. First, SDSB was considered a form of gambling, a forbidden act in Islam. Second, SDSB had generated severe socio-economic impacts, exemplified by "the decline of purchasing power of the low-income populace, the influx of funds from periphery to centre, and the increasing number of crimes".[83] Most distressingly, as people trusted their economic fate more to the lottery than to hard work, it also had contributed to "the deterioration of the productive forces of the society".[84]

Despite the strong opposition, from both the Muslim and Christian circles, there were no indications that the state would back down and revoke SDSB. The fact that SDSB had bred detrimental socio-economic effects was responded to only with the rhetorical attempts of the state to reduce the negative impacts of SDSB. On the contrary, there were occasions when the state in fact allowed nine additional lottery drawings (in mid-1991),[85] and renewed the SDSB licence for operation on a three-year basis instead of one (in September 1993).[86]

Basically, the disinclination of the state to repeal SDSB can be attributed to the fact that this lottery agency was an effective money-generating machine. According to an estimate, SDSB was able to raise Rp. 23 billion at a time (normally held once a week).[87]

This economically driven attitude could not be perpetually defended, however. By late 1993 the state reluctantly agreed to terminate the operation of this "philanthropic donation with prizes". Given the long history of Muslim rejection of SDSB, it is safe to argue that it was a combination of various factors which finally changed the heart and mind of the state on SDSB. Perhaps most important were the escalating opposition (described by the Minister of the State Secretary, Moerdiono, as having "reached the symbols of the state") of Muslim leaders and activists on SDSB on the one hand, and the increasing tendency of the state to accommodate Muslim interests, on the other. Sustaining the operation of SDSB further in the midst of the growing amicable political relationship between Islam and the state would only create an unnecessary political embarrassment to the regime.

Infrastructural Accommodation

Basically, this type of accommodation is designed to provide the necessary infrastructure to enable Muslims to perform their religious duties. So far the most common realization of this mode of accommodation has been the construction of mosques under the sponsorship of the state. Initially, it was President Soekarno who laid the groundwork for this form of accommodation. This was symbolically the case when he commanded the establishment of a small state mosque in the palace compound (Baiturrahiem) and a grandiose one in the capital city of Jakarta (Istiqlal). Nevertheless, it was Soeharto who actually shaped and developed the format of this sort of infrastructural accommodation, engaging basically in a statist effort to provide for the need of the Muslim community for places of worship.

An important indication of this approach is manifested in the appropriation of the state budgetary spending to finance this "religious project". In its first Five-Year Development Plan (1969–74), the state allocated Rp. 475 million to fund the development of mosques. By the time the state launched its fourth Five-Year Development Plan (1984–89), this amount had grown to Rp. 29 billion.[88]

It is a mistake to assume that the state has been chiefly, let alone solely, responsible for the building of mosques. Muslims themselves have spent an enormous amount of funds, solicited from various private donations and endowments, to build countless number of mosques. Nonetheless, it seems fair to argue that the rise in state spending, specifically allotted to finance the construction of mosques, has contributed to the increasing number of mosques in the country. The growing number of mosques from 507,175 in 1985 to 550,676 in 1990 (an increase of about 8.6 per cent in a five-year span) was partly attributable to the dramatic increase in the budgetary fund.[89]

In the meantime President Soeharto also founded the Yayasan Amal Bakti Muslim Pancasila (YAMP) in 1982, a semi-state foundation initiated primarily to develop Muslim socio-religious infrastructure. The fact that this foundation operated under Soeharto's direction and that of current and/or former senior state officials attracted virtually all Muslim civil servants and members of the armed forces to become its regular contributors. For nearly ten years of its existence, YAMP had collected more than Rp. 83 billion (by 1991). Out of this amount, Rp. 49 billion had been used to build 449 mosques.[90]

In the early 1990s, at the request of the Indonesian Council of Ulama (MUI), this foundation also became committed — for a number of years — to support financially the dispatch of 1,000 *da'i* (Muslim preachers) to remote transmigration areas.[91]

The most phenomenal form of this infrastructural accommodation was the willingness of the state not only to permit, but also to assist in the foundation of an Islamic bank, Bank Muamalat Indonesia (BMI), in 1991.[92] Like the issues of *jilbab* and religious court law, the idea of an Islamic bank, introduced for the first time in 1973, was once perceived as embedded in the Islamic state controversy. Understandably, given the political relationship between Islam and the state at that time, the idea of an Islamic bank could not be realized any sooner. Now that the notion of Islam representing an ideological threat to the state is substantially evaporating, there are no longer any reasons for the state to thwart the establishment of such a bank.[93]

Since the beginning, the idea of establishing an Islamic bank has been driven by religious and economic motives. Religiously, it is intended to serve as an alternative financial institution for those who, because of their religious conviction, do not want to conduct business or financial transactions with common commercial banks which offer and charge interest because they consider interest as a form of *riba* (usury), which is prohibited in Islam. Regardless of the ongoing controversy of whether or not interest is actually a form of *riba*, the fact that some Muslims object to it necessitates the establishment of such an interest-free bank.[94]

Economically, it is designed to help develop and mobilize the economic resources of Indonesian Muslims. More specifically, it is meant to create new business opportunities by serving as an investor rather than a creditor or a lending institution. Operating under the basis of, among other things, a profit and loss sharing mechanism (*mudharabah*), BMI can actually invest its capital in Muslim entrepreneurs who are generally unable to secure loans from other commercial banks because of the lack of the required (material) collateral.[95]

Cultural Accommodation

In the broader context the cultural accommodation of the state towards Islam is not a novel phenomenon. It is in fact an ongoing discourse, resulting from the acculturation process between Islam and the specifics of Indonesian time and space. The outcomes of these cultural dialogues vary, depending largely on the degree of the reconciliatory capacity of the parties involved. But in general they range from partial (syncretic) to total (pure) accommodation.[96] Given the fact that "Islam had established itself

fairly rapidly, and on the whole peacefully, in the greater part of the archipelago",[97] it is safe to say that many aspects of Islamic culture have long
been relatively accommodated.

One of the most striking features of this form of accommodation,
which often goes unnoticed, has been the adoption of Islamic idioms in
the vocabulary of the political and ideological instruments of the state. In
the context of Indonesia's pre-modern state, especially in Islamic localities, such terms as *sultan* (ruler), *kalipatullah* (vicegerent of God), and
sayidin (master) were used as titles of rulership.[98] While these terms are
no longer employed to designate Indonesia's post-colonial state apparatus, the presence of Islamic idioms in the country's ideology and
Constitution, government regulations, and political institutions remains
highly prevalent.[99]

The linguistic formulation of Pancasila is one of the many cases in
point. Putting the grammatical prepositions and conjunctions aside, it can
be suggested that at least one-third of the words and phrases in Pancasila
consist of Islamic idioms. They include words such as *adil* (just), *adab*
(civilized), *rakyat* (people or the ruled), *hikmah* (wisdom), *musyawarah*
(deliberation), and *wakil* (representative).[100] The naming of a number of
state institutions such as Majelis Permusyawaratan Rakyat, Dewan
Perwakilan Rakyat, and Mahkamah Agung also indicates the adoption of
Islamic nomenclature.[101]

In the meantime it is also increasingly apparent that the Islamic greeting of *assalamualaikum* (peace be upon you) is unofficially becoming the
national greeting. This is so in the sense that a significant number of state
dignitaries, including the President, Cabinet ministers, and senior officials, begin their official speeches with such a greeting. Although this
cultural move may not necessarily generate substantial ramifications, it
nonetheless represents an important gesture, indicating the cultural
accommodation of the state towards Islam.

This mode of accommodation was reinforced by the holding of a
month-long grandiose Islamic cultural event, the Festival Istiqlal, in
Jakarta in 1991.[102] This event provided a rare opportunity which enabled
Islamic culture, including artwork, architecture, calligraphy, film, music,
and dance, to be exhibited nationally. Beyond the physical aspect of the
exposition, this festival carried a far greater symbolical significance.
Considering the encouraging circumstances of the late 1980s and early
1990s, which marked a new phase of the political relationship between
Islam and the state, it seems fair to argue that this cultural event was
designed to symbolize the appreciation of the state towards the cultural

dimensions of Islam. More importantly, as a confirming rejoinder to the growing new articulation of Islamic idealism and activism, it was also intended as overt support for the notion of an Indonesian cultural Islam and an impetus for its further development.

It is, among other things, through such cultural gestures that the state could play its role in the process of integration between Islam and the state in Indonesia. Islam is no longer perceived as an outsider, but, like many other socio-religious entities — Catholicism, Protestantism, Hinduism, and Buddhism — as a complementary factor that shapes the nature and construct of Indonesia's unitary nation state.

Having said this, it is obvious that there is nothing peculiar with regard to the growing accommodative stance of the state towards Islam. Not every form of accommodation is necessarily novel in substance. Many of them — the education law, religious court law, joint-ministerial decision on Bazis — represent extensions or continuances of already existing practices. Even though the foundation of ICMI, the often-perceived pinnacle of the state accommodation towards Islam, does provide a certain degree of structural leverage, it does not and probably will not outweigh the pivotal roles of other important avenues such as non-governmental organizations, Muhammadiyah, NU, MUI, Golkar, and the bureaucracy. It is not an exaggeration to say that the recent increasing representation of Islam in parliament as well as in the Cabinet, as described in the preceding chapters, is largely due to the diversifying approach of the new generation of Muslim political thinkers and activists in articulating and realizing Islamic socio-economic and political interests.

Given this perspective, it is safe to argue that in this case the state simply moves to strengthen and solidify the structural, infrastructural, and cultural avenues of Muslims to articulate and realize their socio-religious, economic, and political agendas. Nevertheless, considering the nature of the political relationship between Islam and the state in the past, these accommodative ventures unquestionably serve as important indications, however symbolic they may be, of the declining hostility of the state towards Islam in terms of their political relationship.

FORCES FOR ACCOMMODATION

What have been the main forces driving the state to initiate these accommodative moves? Many tend to see this phenomenon in terms of a personal rule type analysis, rather than in a broader sociological perspective, in the sense that the whole enterprise was perceived simply as Soeharto's political project, designed primarily to cultivate Muslim political support. More specifically, it was intended to "boost his own position in the run-up to the [1993] elections".[103]

There are at least two important arguments to support this viewpoint. First, the historical timing in which the initiative to undertake these accommodative enterprises evolved, one after another, in a five-year span (1988-93), a period which was characterized by the growing concern with succession. Because of this, given the President's interest to bid for the presidency in the 1993 elections (in spite of his previous statement that his appointment as President in 1988 was his last), such moves can be easily viewed as deliberate attempts to seek Muslim political support. Moreover, the fact that in September 1989 and May 1992 a number of prominent Muslim figures and Islamic socio-religious organizations, led by Alamsyah Ratu Perwiranegara (a former aide to the President, Minister of Religion, and Co-ordinating Minister of Politics and Security Affairs), echoed unequivocal support for the continuation of Soeharto's leadership only reinforced this sort of analysis.[104]

Second, perhaps the most important factor was the perceived notion of the weakening Soeharto's grip on the military — the backbone (along with the bureaucracy) of the New Order regime. As Liddle has observed,

> After a quarter-century, Soeharto's grip on power is beginning to show signs of weakening. The first important evidence of decline came in March 1988, when his nominee for vice-president [Sudharmono] was publicly and angrily opposed by the military delegates during a tumultuous session of the Assembly. In the end, Soeharto got his way, but he had been served notice that the military as a whole and the senior army generals in particular were looking ahead to a time when they, as individuals and as an institution, would still be players but he would not.[105]

As suggested, Soeharto finally prevailed. But the rift did not disappear with the ending of the General Assembly. Immediately following its completion, the armed forces moved to strengthen their political position by capturing Golkar's regional leadership. In fact, "[r]eportedly, the generals also began to encourage student activists in Bandung, Yogyakarta, and other cities to engage in protest on local issues"[106] and "calling for an end to Soeharto's rule".[107]

Soeharto's answer to the challenge was no less direct. In September 1989, returning from an overseas trip to Moscow and a Non-Aligned Movement summit in Belgrade, he responded by threatening to "clobber" (*gebug*) anyone who tried to remove him from power unconstitutionally. In various journalistic accounts he was reported to have said,

> Putting it bluntly I might die on my feet ... Perhaps that is what they want so that I can be replaced. But if they want to replace me with someone else in an unconstitutional way, I will punish them no matter whether they are politicians or generals.[108]

All of these circumstances sent a clear message regarding the possible existence of stumbling blocks that Soeharto would have to confront should he run (which he did) for his sixth presidential term in 1993. The military's tacit insubordination towards his leadership not only had cast serious doubt concerning their traditional support for his presidency, but had also created an impression that they themselves might represent a potential threat to his presidential aspirations. Primarily because of this, so ran the argument,

> the president [not only] maneuvered to recapture the army by putting relatives and former adjutants in key posts, [but also] extended a hand to an old adversary, Indonesia's Islamic political movement, with the apparent goal of offsetting his weakening support from the army.[109]

Complementing this viewpoint, many also regarded the President's religious homage (along with his family members) to Mecca in 1991 as a political pilgrimage, a perception which has irked many Muslims.[110]

Both of these factors (that is, the historical timing of the accommodation and Soeharto's weakening grip over the military) have provided a certain logic to the validity of the above analysis. However, treating Soeharto's weakening grip over the military as the catalyst or cause for the unfolding accommodative stance of the state towards Islam is not without serious weaknesses.

First, it is obvious that the above analysis centres primarily on the conflict among Indonesia's political leviathans (Soeharto and senior military officers). Being so, it tends to overlook the broader dimension of the issue. As implied before, the accommodative enterprise of the state was perceived as a countervailing project, instead of a sociologically driven political necessity in response to the development of the country's societal dynamism. Therefore, understandably, it does not take into account societal factors which may in fact serve as potential determinants for the recent accommodative endeavours of the state towards Islam.

Second, it is important to note that a crisis of this sort was by no means new to Soeharto. As some have observed, through the course of two and a half decades of his rule, there had been a number of similar occurrences (though varied in the degree of intensity), aimed — directly or otherwise — at undermining his leadership.[111] In the 1960s, immediately following his ascension to power, there were already several important military figures in the New Order regime who registered opposition to his rule. In the mid-1970s, cloaked in the form of student protest during a visit by Japanese Prime Minister Kakuei Tanaka in January 1974, there were rumors about the ambitions of some military generals to unseat him.[112] Finally, in the early 1980s, as a result of his speeches during his meeting with the armed forces commanders in Pekanbaru and with the Red Beret army's special forces (Kopassandha) in Cijantung concerning the necessity of the military to take sides in the defence of Pancasila ideology, he was met with sharp criticism from a number of retired officers affiliated with Yayasan Lembaga Kesadaran Berkonstitusi (YLKB, Institute for the Awareness to Act Constitutionally) and Forum Studi dan Komunikasi TNI-AD (FOSKO, Army Forum for Study and Communication). Together with a number of civilian figures critical of Soeharto's leadership, they formulated their criticism in the form of a Statement of Concern, and submitted it to parliament.[113]

It is interesting to note, however, that in confronting these crises none of Soeharto's strategies seemed to involve the building of an alliance with a mass group. Basically, he took a "tour of duty" approach. This scheme was carried out by transferring or promoting his critics to politically less important (or honorary) positions, or by completely relieving them of their duties. At the same time, as indicated earlier, he appointed those who were considered loyal and close to him to key posts. In addition, since many of his military critics "are in business and often depend on government contracts, the government cut its ties with companies owned or run by these men".[114]

Given this pattern of rebuttal, the view that the New Order regime's sympathetic responses to the aspirations of the Muslim community represented a way to attract the latter's political support in the attempt to offset the perceived notion of Soeharto's weakening grip over the military does not seem to have a solid basis.

Finally, if securing the bid for the sixth term of the presidency was the prime motive of this manoeuvring, considering the non-competitive nature of the election (and the New Order regime in general), theoretically Soeharto was in no immediate need for massive political support. In spite of the existing opposition from some military quarters, he was still in control of the state's paramount electoral machinery (that is, Golkar). Being the Head of the Supervisory Council of Golkar, he enjoyed an enormous amount of power which was influential, among other things, in the selection process of the party's parliamentary candidates. As indicated by *Tempo*'s report in the event of finalizing Golkar's list of candidates for the 1992 general election,

> The Central Executive Board of Golkar has to revise its candidate list at the request of the Head of the Supervisory Council of Golkar, Soeharto. ... Even though it is only a suggestion or request, or whatever the name is, since it comes from the Head of the Supervisory Council — which according to Golkar's statute enjoys an enormous amount of power — it must be taken into serious consideration by Golkar.[115]

Coupled with his prerogative to appoint a sizeable number of members of the MPR (the People's Consultative Assembly, which elects the President and Vice-President), his presidential aspiration was actually very much protected. Having said this, it is fair to argue that these accommodative enterprises did not appear to correlate directly with Soeharto's balancing act in the effort to guarantee his own position in the run-up to the 1993 presidential election.

Theoretically, it is imprudent to completely dismiss these two factors in the quest for a candid explanation concerning the impetus of the state's accommodation towards Islam. Taking the above analysis into account, perhaps they did serve as push factors (though by no means the determinant ones) with regard to these accommodative endeavours. Nonetheless, from the perspective of this study, I tend to see these accommodative enterprises in the light of two major ingredients which have characterized the sociological and political features of Indonesia's Muslim community in the last two decades or so.

First, in the last twenty years or so Muslims have experienced a rapid process of socio-economic and political mobilization. Largely as a result of Indonesia's economic development (especially under the New Order regime) and the broadening access to modern higher education (at home as well as abroad), Muslims have transformed themselves into an "intermediate" entity — socially, economically, and politically. In the current national setting, it is not an overstatement to say that they occupy the largest part (after the ethnic Chinese) in the configuration of the country's middle class, which has been primarily represented in the state bureaucracy, entrepreneurial, and professional sectors.[116] At this stage they can no longer be ridiculed, as Hadisubeno (a former chairman of Partai Nasional Indonesia [PNI]) once did, as *kaum sarungan* (sarong-wearers) — a socio-religious, economic, and political mockery which implies backwardness and marginality. Likewise, their interests cannot be taken for granted.

Being the most conspicuous group to emerge in this fashion, they share certain aspirations that require appropriate responses from the New Order regime for the enhancement of its own legitimacy. In this regard, considering the debilitating circumstances which the larger segment of the Muslim community had experienced in the past, it is safe to argue that they are in obvious need of avenues that would enable them to articulate and realize their socio-economic, religious, and political interests.

It is in this context, I believe, that the New Order administration initiated these forms of accommodation. Putting off these accommodative enterprises would only strengthen the image concerning the unresponsiveness of the regime towards societal demands. Moreover, it would also breed tensions, which might eventually undermine the legitimacy of the regime. On the contrary, adopting accommodative measures would generate support and enhance legitimacy. If, as many had implied, the legitimacy of the New Order government had been primarily built upon its relative successes in developing the country's economy and creating political stability, accommodating Islamic interests would provide it with substantial cultural as well as political legitimacy.

Second, perhaps the most decisive factor for the state to undertake such forms of accommodation has been the intellectual transformation of the new generation of Muslim political thinkers and activists. As discussed at length in chapters 4, 5, and 6 in the attempt to cultivate an amicable political relationship between Islam and the state they have undergone an intense process of intellectual transformation which has enabled them to develop the notion of substantialist rather than legalist-formalist Islamic political ideas and practices. Because of the integrative nature of this new intellectualism and activism, it has shown some promising signs that political Islam (in its new format) would not run counter to the unitary construct of Indonesia's nation state. In so doing, it has actually minimized, if not completely eliminated, the validity of a convention that political Islam necessarily represents a threat to the state or nation.

In light of this development, there are no longer legitimate grounds for the state to exclude political Islam from the country's national political processes. Accommodating the already transformed ideas and practices of political Islam thus becomes an imperative task for the state to undertake in the effort to avoid tensions on the one hand, and to enhance its own legitimacy on the other.

In short, as an analytical rejoinder to the prevailing viewpoint that these accommodative endeavours of the state as well as its political relaxation towards Islam were simply Soeharto's manoeuvres to secure his presidential bid in 1993, it can be plausibly contended that without such an intellectual transformation they would not have taken place one after the other. In other words, had Islam still retained its old political idealism and activism, in which the struggle for the establishment of an Islamic statehood or state based on Islamic ideology served as its prime goal, perhaps there would be neither accommodation nor political relaxation of this nature.

INTEGRATION OR SECTARIANISM: WHERE IS THE POLITICS OF ACCOMMODATION HEADING?

Not every Muslim thinker and activist is comfortable with the process of cultivating a viable synthesis between Islam and the state. There are at least two contending paradigms which seem to have posed serious challenges to a positive evaluation of the recent politics of accommodation, especially (1) the pessimistic view of Deliar Noer; and (2) the alarmist reaction of Abdurrahman Wahid.

Deliar Noer was basically of the opinion that nothing had changed with regard to the fundamental character of the New Order regime. Underscoring the passage quoted at the beginning of this chapter, this former staff member of President Soeharto (1968), who from the late 1970s had been consistently one of the boldest critics of the New Order regime,[117] argued that these accommodative enterprises did not actually represent a "decisive break with the policies of the early New Order". This is especially true with regard to the perception of certain figures that the government was still adamant — not necessarily in a religious-ideological sense, but more in a *realpolitik* one — towards political Islam (and any other dissenting forces for that matter). For him, through the course of its twenty-five years of governing, the New Order regime remained essentially non-inclusionary, obsessed with depoliticization programmes as a means of preserving rule. In Deliar's words,

> This program of depoliticization is far thicker than the regime's leniency toward Islam. ... It appears that depoliticization has not loosened. On the contrary, it is becoming tighter. In general, this is signified by the new process of screening [for the 1992 parliament candidates] which is known as Litsus (Penelitian Khusus, or Special Investigation).[118]

Deliar is correct in pointing out the exclusionary nature of the New Order regime. However, in so doing, he actually operates on a different analytical plane which does not seem to consider the political hostility between Islam and the state as a specific problem of the parties involved (that is, Islam and the state). Rather, though recognizing the "apologetic" character of the idealism and activism of the earlier Muslim political thinkers and activists,[119] he tends to see the regime's manoeuvring to hamper the development of political Islam not as a response to the formalistic and legalistic tendencies of Islamic political thoughts and actions, but only as part of its depoliticization agenda.

Because of the different analytical angle of Deliar's observation, there is no need to shed further light on the merit of his viewpoint. It is worth mentioning nonetheless, as it adds a word of caution against the early and exorbitant euphoria of many Muslims. In addition, it also serves as a reminder that attempts to lay the necessary groundwork for the establishment of a relatively inclusionary system of governing (one of the major objectives of the new generation of Muslim political thinkers and activists) has yet to be realized in a more substantial fashion.

Given the focus of this study, the alarmist view of Abdurrahman Wahid is in fact more relevant with respect to the question of where the politics of accommodation is actually heading. Also, whether or not it represents a shift in the direction of greater sectarianism or towards a broader integration.

In this case Abdurrahman Wahid, almost by himself, stands at the centre of the controversy. This general chairman of NU has emerged as the most notorious critic of the politics of accommodation. Basically, he considers the accommodative phenomenon as leaning towards sectarianism and exclusivism. He believes that, in spite of some substantial breakthroughs by the Muslim community, particularly its thinkers and activists, in the socio-economic and political configuration of the latter part of the New Order administration, there are indications that they still want to dominate the power discourse in the archipelago. In doing so, they overlook the fact that Indonesia consists of heterogeneous socio-religious and political groupings. Along with it, he also points out that there are some signs indicating the growing interest of some Muslims in waving an "Islamic flag" in the nation's very own yard.[120]

It is important to note, however, that such tendencies do not seem to develop by themselves. According to Abdurrahman Wahid, the state, to some extent, exacerbates these tendencies by involving itself in issues related to religious affairs, especially those which concern the interest of the Islamic majority. As he sees it, the most telling evidence of the deepening penetration of the state in religious life includes the enactment of the religious court law, the issuance of the joint-ministerial decision concerning Bazis, the establishment of ICMI, the foundation of BMI, the holding of the Festival Istiqlal, the teaching of the Arabic language on the state's television network, and the attention given by the state to the demands of some Muslim circles concerning the *halal-haram* (permitted-prohibited) labelling of packaged foods.[121]

For Abdurrahman Wahid, the ramifications of these practices could be very damaging. At stake is the upholding of the principles of pluralism and national integration. Elaborating on this alarming possibility, in a routine meeting of Majelis Reboan (Wednesday Gathering) in April 1991, organized by his colleagues such as Nurcholish Madjid, Soetjipto Wirosardjono, Aswab Mahasin, Utomo Dananjaya, and Jalaluddin Rakhmat, he was reported to have said:

> Other than representing a discriminatory move toward religions adhered to by the minority [groups], the excessive intervention [of the state in religion] could eventually weaken the integration of the nation. Indonesia is not a theocratic state. Accordingly, the ruling government must set *clear limits* in administrating and protecting religious life. The essential meaning of democracy is to protect and defend the rights of the minority. If for some reason the state or government is more concerned with the interest of a certain religion, or only accepting the truth from a certain religion, it suggests that the state is leaning toward sectarianism.[122]

It is the concern over the possibility of this political interplay between Islam and the state, which, according to Abdurrahman Wahid, has the potential of bringing about sectarianism and exclusivism, that has led him to display such a critical stance. In this context, more than anything else, his initiative in March 1991 to form the Forum Demokrasi, which consists of virtually all the "national elements", is intended to serve as a symbolical response to the perceived sectarianism of the state.[123]

Nonetheless, the question remains whether or not this politics of accommodation represents a sectarian or an exclusive tendency. On the surface, seen from the uproar it has generated, especially with respect to the socio-political circumstances in which the phenomenon is evolving, it tends to underline Abdurrahman Wahid's assessment. From the mid-1980s to the early 1990s, the state seemed to act, in one instance after another, at the behest of Islamic interests — adhering to a number of policies favourable only to Muslims.

At a deeper level, however, it appears to suggest otherwise. First, there is substantively nothing peculiar with these forms of accommodation. Most of the subjects of accommodation (for example, religious court law, national education law, *zakat* collecting and distributing agency) were enacted simply to reinforce the already existing practices and/or institutions related to those issues. They were initiated not to strengthen the degree of etatism (in the sense of putting *all* religious affairs in the hands of the state). Nor were they intended to bring about sectarianism or exclusivism. Rather, in line with the nature of the Indonesian state, being neither a theocratic nor a secular state, they were aimed at providing avenues for Muslims to implement their religious teachings — a viewpoint which is also shared by some Christian circles.[124] Should any other existing religious grouping display comparable needs, as has been often indicated, the state would respond similarly.[125]

Second, it is important to note that the politics of accommodation has evolved in the general context of a reconciliatory atmosphere between Islam and the state.[126] Given the circumstances, these function more as symbolic gestures which indicate the falling away of the mutually suspicious political relationship between Islam and the state, rather than an actual synthesis between Islam and the state. In this regard it can be considered as representing an integrative move to the extent that Islam is no longer perceived as an "outsider" which poses a religious-ideological threat to the state, but — like other existing religious groupings — as a participant in the country's socio-economic and political discourse.

Why then did such harsh criticism, especially that of Abdurrahman Wahid, arise? As reflected in various journalistic accounts, in the attempt to answer this question many have tended to focus their attention on Abdurrahman Wahid, who has often taken unpopular stands on matters related to Islamic socio-religious and political issues (for example, his idea of Islam as a complementary factor, his notion of the indigenization of Islam, his defence of the banning of a tabloid newspaper, *Monitor*, for publishing an opinion poll perceived as blasphemous by many Muslims, and his relative proximity to Christian circles).[127] In doing so, they actually only highlight the differences between the defenders and critics of the politics of accommodation, instead of explaining the crux of the matter.[128] Because of this, it is necessary to look at different factors. One way to realize it is by stressing the analysis of the discourse of the politics of accommodation, both in terms of its processes as well as in the way the Muslim community has reacted.

The fact that the idealism and activism of political Islam have changed (that is, from legal-formalism to substantialism) and that the state has responded positively does not automatically make the construct (or format) of the political relationship between Islam and the state transparent. In spite of the encouraging signs of this religious-political interplay, it so far offers no clear model (formula) as to how Islam (and any other exist-ing religion for that matter) and the Indonesian state should properly interact. So Abdurrahman's suspicions as to the direction in which the relationship might be heading are at least legitimate.

One possible explanation for this lack of a clear model is that the process of establishing an amicable political relationship between Islam and the state has evolved sporadically in the sense that the issues unfold without first being deliberated by the nation's religious-political elites. Thus, what has actually happened in the five years or so, from the mid-1980s to the early 1990s, was basically a spontaneous religious-political interplay, where the intellectual transformation of Islamic political thoughts and actions was matched by the willingness of the state to launch a number of policies perceived to be in accordance with Islamic interests. Given the circumstances, it is fair to say that the interplay occurs only in an *ad hoc* fashion. In other words, there is no "negotiated settle-ment"[129] among the country's religious-political elites as to how religion and the state should be appropriately associated.[130]

In the absence of a nationally accepted formula, it is difficult to assess what the future of the political interplay between Islam and the state will be like. In this situation the issue remains essentially puzzling, and it tends to create myths and speculation concerning the fact of the matter as well as its possible ramifications.

It is in this analytical framework that Abdurrahman Wahid's position can be more meaningfully understood. Judging from the spectrum of his overall religious-political thoughts, he is bothered not so much with the material forms of the state's accommodation towards Islam.[131] Rather, it is the uncertainty of the interplay which seems to have led him to embrace such a critical stance towards the whole discourse of the politics of accommodation.[132] In such a state of affairs "fear of the unknown" pertaining to the consequences of the interplay on other socio-religious groupings generates public apprehension. In the meantime the excessive euphoria of some Muslim activists who have asserted, among other things, a viewpoint that now the majority rules the minority in this highly uncertain context only strengthens the anxiety.

Within this context, Abdurrahman Wahid actually echoes a cautious reminder to his fellow Muslims. As he himself suggested:

> My friends are varied. Among them are socialists, nationalists, or the mix between the two, street vendors, ... *abangan* (less devout Muslim), and so forth. All of them are in [the state of] fear. They are concerned [with this new development]. Even the Confucianists are worried.[133]

But in spite of his harsh criticism, he is actually not in full disagreement with his Muslim colleagues who welcome the state's accommodative responses towards Islam. There is no doubt that he, like many of his Muslim colleagues, has been obsessed with the notion of Islam as "a social ethic that will guide the course of the life of the state and society". Yet, being rooted in the country's Islamic traditionalism, he is also aware that there are *some parts* of Islam (but not *in toto*) that can be bureaucratized without jeopardizing the principles of pluralism or national integration.[134]

To conclude this discussion, it can be safely pointed out that it is the sporadic process of the interplay, as a result of the absence of a "negotiated settlement", which has led Abdurrahman Wahid to voice such strong criticisms with respect to the accommodative responses of the state towards Islam. In his view, without a nationally accepted model, this process of interplay can be initiated almost with no limits. Should this be the case, given the heterogeneity of Indonesia's socio-religious entities, it would only create tensions.

Notes

1.   Michael R.J. Vatikiotis, *Indonesian Politics under Suharto: Order, Development, and Pressure for Change* (London and New York: Routledge, 1993), p. 132.

2.   Robert Hefner, "Islam, State, and Civil Society: I.C.M.I. and the Struggle for the Indonesian Middle Class" (Paper delivered at the conference on Islam and the Social

Construction of Identities: Comparative Perspectives on Southeast Asian Muslims, Center for Southeast Asian Studies, University of Hawaii, 4–6 August 1993), p. 36.

3. For a concise recapitulation on the defeat of political Islam, see, for instance, Donald K. Emmerson, "Islam and Regime in Indonesia: Who's Coopting Whom" (Paper delivered at the American Political Science Association annual meeting, Atlanta, Georgia, 31 August 1989).

4. Donald K. Emmerson, "Resurgence of Islam Is No Danger to Indonesia", *The Asian Wall Street Journal Weekly*, 11 October 1993, p. 12.

5. Interview with Dawam Rahardjo in Jakarta, 20 August 1991. See also his "Basis Sosial Pemikiran Islam di Indonesia Sejak Orde Baru", *Prisma*, no. 3 (March 1991), pp. 3–15.

6. See "Golkar dan Pemilih Islam", *Tempo*, 21 September 1991, pp. 21–33; "Mengapa Cendekiawan Islam", *Tempo*, 8 December 1990, pp. 25–37.

7. See Rahardjo, op. cit., pp. 3–15.

8. On the issue of Indonesia's intermediate class, see a range of essays in Richard Tanter and Kenneth Young, eds., *The Politics of Middle Class Indonesia* (Clayton: Monash Papers on Southeast Asia, no. 19, Centre of Southeast Asian Studies, Monash University, 1990).

9. See, for instance, Robert Van Niel, *The Emergence of the Modern Indonesian Elite* (The Hague: W. van Hoeve Ltd., 1960); Hildred Geertz, "Indonesian Cultures and Communities", in *Indonesia*, edited by Ruth McVey (New Haven: Southeast Asia Studies, Yale University, by arrangement with Human Relations Area Files Press, 1963), pp. 24–96; J.D. Legge, *Intellectuals and Nationalism in Indonesia: A Study of the Following Recruited by Sutan Syahrir in Occupation Jakarta* (Ithaca: Monograph Series, Cornell Modern Indonesia Project, 1988).

10. See, for instance, Howard M. Federspiel, *Muslim Intellectuals and National Development in Indonesia* (New York: Nova Science Publishers Inc., 1992).

11. See "Setelah Boom Sarjana Islam", *Tempo*, 8 December 1990, pp. 34–37. See also Ridwan Saidi, "Cendekiawan Muslim dan Struktur Politik", *Kompas*, 8 December 1990.

12. See the discussion in chapters 4, 5, and 6.

13. Interview with Dawam Rahardjo in Jakarta, 20 August 1991. See also Rahardjo, op. cit., p. 9.

14. See Kenneth Ward, *The Foundation of the Partai Muslimin Indonesia* (Ithaca: Modern Indonesia Project, Southeast Asia Program, Cornell University, 1970). See also his *The 1971 Election in Indonesia: An East Java Case Study* (Clayton: Monash Papers on Southeast Asia, no. 2, Centre of Southeast Asian Studies, Monash University, 1974), pp. 114–33.

15. See "Pasang-Surut Hubungan Islam-Beringin", *Tempo*, 21 September 1991, pp. 22–27; Leo Suryadinata, *Military Ascendancy and Political Culture: A Study of Indonesia's Golkar* (Athens: Monograph in International Studies, Southeast Asia Series, no. 85, Ohio University, 1989), p. 141.

16. Interview with Dawam Rahardjo in Jakarta, 20 August 1991.

17. See "Beringin Makin Hijau", *Tempo*, 3 October 1992, pp. 21–31. See also *Tempo, 20 June 1992*, pp. 21–31.

18. Other than these, Habibie held several other important positions. See "Marhaban, ya Habibie", *Tempo*, 8 December 1990, p. 33.

19. See R. William Liddle, "Politics 1992–1993: Sixth-term Adjustments in the Ruling Formula", in *Indonesia Assessment 1993*, edited by Chris Manning and Joan Hardjono (Canberra: Australian National University, 1993).

20. Ibid. It is important to note, however, that Habibie had only been able to find places for his ICMI protégés and supporters with BPPT background.

21. Interview with Amien Rais in Yogyakarta, 24 July 1991.

22. For historical accounts of the attempts to insert religious instruction in vernacular educational institutions, see Soegarda Poerbakawatja, *Pendidikan dalam Alam Indonesia Merdeka* (Jakarta, 1970); Karl A. Steenbrink, *Pesantren, Madrasah, Sekolah: Pendidikan Islam dalam Kurun Modern* (Jakarta: LP3ES, 1986), pp. 83–96; Machnun Husein, *Pendidikan Agama dalam Lintasan Sejarah* (Yogyakarta: Nur Cahaya, 1983).

23. Largely because of this, adherence to one of the five recognized religious groupings (Islam, Catholic, Protestant, Hindu, and Buddhist) is mandatory. See, for instance, M.L. Lyon, "The Hindu Revival in Java: Politics and Religious Identity", in *Indonesia: The Making of a Culture*, edited by James Fox (Canberra: Research School of Pacific Studies, Australian National University, 1980), pp. 205–20.

24. This change occurred with the decision of the (then Provisional) People's Advisory Council (Majelis Permusyawaratan Rakyat, MPR) in 1966. Since then, virtually all the Broad Outlines of State Directions (Garis-Garis Besar Haluan Negara, GBHN), which the MPR formulates once in every five years, stipulate that students at all levels of educational institutions are required to take religious instruction in accordance with their religious adherence.

25. This practice is usually carried out by sending out letters, to be signed by Muslim parents, suggesting no objections with regard to their children's receiving Christian religious instruction. See, for instance, "PP No. 29/1990 Harus Ditinjau Kembali", *Panji Masyarakat,* 11–20 October 1991, p. 74. For a further account, see Mohammad Natsir, "Sekali Lagi: Kerukunan Hidup Umat Beragama di Indonesia", *Islam dan Kristen di Indonesia* (Jakarta: Media Dakwah, 1978), pp. 50–71.

26. See "Buram yang Belum Tuntas", *Tempo*, 6 August 1988; "Faith in Teaching", *Far Eastern Economic Review*, 28 July 1988, p. 25.

27. Lukman Harun, *Muhammadiyah dan Undang-Undang Pendidikan* (Jakarta: Pustaka Panjimas, 1990), pp. 12–13.

28. See "Setelah Pertemuan Dua Setengah Jam", *Tempo,* 13 August 1988; "Dari Pertemuan Mendikbud dan Pimpinan Pusat Muhammadiyah", *Panji Masyarakat*, 11–20 August 1988. For a fuller account, see Harun, op. cit.

29. See "Undang-Undang Republik Indonesia Nomor 2 Tahun 1989 Tentang Sistem Pendidikan Nasional".

30. See "Penjelasan Atas Undang-Undang Republik Indonesia Nomor 2 Tahun 1989 Tentang Sistem Pendidikan Nasional".

31. According to a report, in Jakarta and its close vicinities (Tangerang and Bekasi) alone, there are at least 360 Catholic schools. Out of their 125,000 students, 65 per cent are non-Catholics. (*Tempo*, 18 February 1989.)

32. See, for instance, *Suara Pembaruan*, 3 and 13 March 1989; *Kompas*, 7 March 1989.

33. In fact, individuals like Djohan Effendi, who has a broad relationship with Christian circles, regret the denial of the right of Muslim students attending Christian schools to receive Islamic religious instruction. For him, any students of any schools should have the right to obtain religious instruction according to their religious beliefs. In his view, the fact that Christian circles refuse to provide such a right represents a departure from the classical practices of toleration as displayed by Ethiopian Christians who once offered their churches to early Muslim immigrants for them to hold their religious observances. (Interview with Djohan Effendi in Jakarta, 26–27 August 1991.)

34. See "PP No. 29/1990 Harus Ditinjau Kembali", *Panji Masyarakat*, 11–20 October 1991, pp. 71–74. See also Ismail Sunny, "Peraturan Perundangan Mengenai Pendidikan Agama", *Panji Masyarakat*, 21–31 October 1991, pp. 33–35.

35. The best study of Indonesian Islamic courts is still Daniel S. Lev, *Islamic Courts in Indonesia: A Study of the Political Bases of Legal Institutions* (Berkeley, Los Angeles, and London: University of California Press, 1972). In addition to this work, the following discussion is also based on "Pengadilan Serambi Milik Kita Bersama", *Tempo*, 4 February 1989, pp. 74–81; "Peradilan Agama: Kebutuhan atau Kecemasan", *Tempo*, 24 June 1989, pp. 22–30; "Perjalanan Gagasan Ibn Al-Muqaffa'", *Tempo*, 10 August 1991, pp. 38–39; "Sejarah Peradilan Agama", *Media Dakwah*, August 1989, pp. 15–17; M. Daud Ali, "Undang-Undang Peradilan Agama: Sistematik dan Garis-Garis Besar Isinya", *Media Dakwah,* April 1990, pp. 44–47; "UU-PA dan Toleransi Beragama", *Panji Masyarakat*, 1–10 July 1989, pp. 18–26; "Kompilasi Hukum Islam Hampir Final", *Panji Masyarakat*, 11–21 July 1991, pp. 56–57; and interview with Munawir Syadzali in Jakarta, 6 September 1991.

36. On the *adat* law, see B. ter Haar, *Adat Law in Indonesia*, edited and translated by E.A. Hoebel and A.A. Schiller (New York: Institute of Pacific Relations, 1948). On the emerging influence of the *adat* law in colonial policy-making, see Harry J. Benda, *The Crescent and the Rising Sun: Indonesian Islam under the Japanese Occupation 1942–1945* (The Hague and Bandung: W. van Hoeve Ltd., 1958), pp. 65–90.

37. It was in this year that the colonial government extended the institutionalization of religious courts to South Kalimantan.

38. Cited from Lev, op. cit., p. 39.

39. Lev, op. cit., pp. 33–43.

40. See "Masihkah Peradilan Agama Dipercaya", *Tempo*, 24 June 1989, pp. 29–30.

41. The fact that religious courts had no legal autonomy originated from the colonial era. Along with the decision to institutionalize the status and function of religious courts in Java and Madura in 1882, the Dutch colonial government also regulated that the decisions of these courts did not have legal status unless reconfirmed by public courts (*landraad*). This weak position continued well over the period of independence. The marriage law of 1974 seemed to strengthen the case by stipulating that the decisions of religious courts must be validated and reconfirmed by public courts (Article 63, Section 2). See "Antara Apriori dan Lapang Dada", *Panji Masyarakat*, 1–10 July 1989, p. 22; "Masihkah Peradilan Agama Dipercaya?", *Tempo*, 24 June 1989, p. 29; "Pengadilan Serambi Milik Kita Bersama", *Tempo,* 4 February 1989, p. 74.

42. It is important to note, however, that this defect did not *always* serve as an obstacle for religious courts to function. Despite the fact that their rulings were non-binding, many — but not all — Muslims who sought legal settlement on matters related to marriage, inheritance, and endowment issues voluntarily honoured the decisions of these judicial institutions. More importantly, regardless of their weak position in the country's judicial system, they remained a logical choice for many Muslims to settle their disputes on the above issues. Studies conducted by the Board of National Law Development (Badan Pembinaan Hukum Nasional, BPHN) in 1978 and 1979 indicate that 91 per cent and 83 per cent of their respective respondents (taken from Muslim communities in a number of cities in Java, Sumatra, Lombok, and Kalimantan) chose to settle their disputes on the above issues in religious courts. See "Masihkah Peradilan Agama Dipercaya?", *Tempo*, 24 June 1989, p. 30.

43. Interview with Munawir Syadzali in Jakarta, 6 September 1991. See also "Peradilan Agama Nggak 'Mbawang' Lagi", *Panji Masyarakat*, 21–30 July 1992, pp. 54–55.

44. There were at least thirteen classical works recognized as references by the Department of Religion. These included: *Al-Bajuri, Fath al-Mu'in, Syarh al-Tahrir, Qalyubi/Al-Mahalli, Fath al-Wahab, Al-Tuhfah, Al-Targhib al-Musytaq, Al-Qawanin al-Syar'iyyah li Said Dahlan, Syasuri fi al-Faraidh, Bughyat al-Musytarsyidin, Al-Fiqh 'ala al-Madzahib al-Arba'ah*, and *Mughni al-Muhtaj*. See "Sejarah Baru Hukum Islam Indonesia", *Panji Masyarakat*, 21–30 September 1992, p. 23.

45. See "Rancangan Setelah Seabad Tak Seragam", *Tempo*, 4 February 1989, p. 76. See also "Sejarah Baru Hukum Islam Indonesia", *Panji Masyarakat*, 21–30 September 1992, p. 24.

46. See "Si Bungsu Yang Ditunggu Bukan Hantu", *Tempo*, 4 February 1989, p. 81.

47. Consequently, the Department of Religion, among other things, has to prepare 304 bailiffs (equal to the number of religious courts) to be deployed at the existing religious courts throughout the country. (Interview with Munawir Syadzali in Jakarta, 6 September 1991.)

48. Interview with Munawir Syadzali in Jakarta, 6 September 1991.

49. See "Pengadilan Serambi Milik Kita Bersama", *Tempo*, 4 February 1989, p. 74.

50. For a fuller account on the historical process as well as the contents of the compilation of Islamic law, see "Perjalanan Gagasan Ibn Al-Muqaffa'", *Tempo*, 10 August

1991, pp. 38–39; "Hukum Islam *Made In* Indonesia", *Panji Masyarakat*, 21–30 September 1992, pp. 22–29.

51. On the alarm, see Franz Magnis Suseno, "Seputar Rencana UU Peradilan Agama", *Kompas*, 16 June 1989; "DPR Setujui RUU Peradilan Agama Disahkan Jadi UU", *Suara Pembaruan*, 16 December 1989. See also "Peradilan Agama: Kebutuhan atau Kecemasan", *Tempo*, 24 June 1989, pp. 22–25; "Antara Apriori dan Lapang Dada", *Panji Masyarakat,* 1–10 July 1989, pp. 18–23.

52. See "Peradilan Agama: Kebutuhan atau Kecemasan", *Tempo*, 24 June 1989, pp. 22–25.

53. See "Dari Piagam Jakarta ke Wawasan Nusantara", *Tempo*, 24 June 1989, pp. 27–28.

54. See "Resmi Berlaku, Penggunaan Seragam Khas di Sekolah", *Kompas*, 17 February 1991.

55. See "Alhamdulillah Jilbab Bebas", *Media Dakwah*, January 1991, pp. 42–45.

56. See "Seragam Harus, Jilbab Boleh", *Tempo,* 19 January 1991, pp. 76–77.

57. See "Desah Panjang Para Ulama", *Media Dakwah*, January 1991, pp. 46–47; "Bogor Dengan Jilbab Cantik", *Media Dakwah*, January 1991, p. 48.

58. This point is made based on my personal accounts as a Muslim who grew up in a devout Muslim family and studied in Islamic elementary (*madrasah*), secondary (*pesantren*), and tertiary (IAIN) educational institutions.

59. See, for instance, John L. Esposito, ed., *Voices of Resurgent Islam* (New York and Oxford: Oxford University Press, 1983).

60. Nikki R. Keddie, "The Revolt of Islam and Its Roots", *in Comparative Political Dynamics: Global Research Perspective*, edited by Dankwart A. Rustow and Kenneth Paul Erickson (New York: Harper Collins Publishers, 1991), p. 301.

61. John L. Esposito, *Islamic Revivalism* (Washington, D.C.: American Institute for Islamic Affairs, School of International Service, American University, 1985), p. 1.

62. See, for instance, "Islam di Kalangan Muda," *Tempo*, 13 May 1989, pp. 74–84.

63. In addition to what has been presented, the analysis that the issue of *jilbab* carried a political threat is based on the fact that on the verge of its reversal, the Directorate General of Elementary and Secondary Education consulted, among others, the state intelligence agency (Bakin). See "Resmi Berlaku, Penggunaan Seragam Khas di Sekolah", *Kompas*, 17 February 1991.

64. See "Soal Zakat, Sebelum Buka Puasa", *Tempo*, 23 March 1991; "Mendagri dan Menteri Agama Tandatangani SKB Bazis", *Kompas*, 20 March 1991.

65. Other pillars include profession of faith that there is no God but Allah and Muhammad is his messenger (*shahadah*); performing prayer five times a day (*salat*); fasting during the month of Ramadhan; and the pilgrimage to Mecca.

66. See, for instance, M. Raquibuz Zaman, ed., *Some Aspects of the Economics of Zakah* (Plainfield: American Trust Publication, 1979). For the Indonesian context, see M. Dawam Rahardjo, "Zakat: Titik Masuk Perkembangan Ekonomi Islam", *Perspektif Deklarasi Makkah: Menuju Ekonomi Islam* (Bandung: Mizan, 1987), p. 154.

67. See Taufik Abdullah, "*Zakat* Collection and Distribution in Indonesia", in *The Islamic Voluntary Sector in Southeast Asia*, edited by Mohamed Ariff (Singapore: Institute of Southeast Asian Studies, 1991), pp. 50–84; M. Dawam Rahardjo, "Mencari Konsep Zakat Dalam Alam Pembangunan", *Panji Masyarakat*, 21–30 July 1981, pp. 2–17.

68. More specifically, since *zakat* is usually due at the end of the fasting month (Ramadhan), these "unorganized" practices would only help those who are less fortunate to get by during the Idul Fithri celebration.

69. See *Rekomendasi dan Pedoman Pelaksanaan Zakat* (Jakarta: Bazis, 1978); *Pedoman Zakat* (Jakarta: Direktorat Jendral Bimas Islam dan Urusan Haji, Departemen Agama, 1984). See also Rahardjo, "Zakat: Titik Masuk Perkembangan Ekonomi Islam", pp. 154–66.

70. M. Dawam Rahardjo, "Pola Pelaksanaan Zakat: Studi-Studi Kasus", *Perspektif Deklarasi Makkah*, p. 188.

71. See Abdullah, op. cit., pp. 51 and 80.

72. Rahardjo, "Pola Pelaksanaan Zakat: Studi-Studi Kasus", p. 189; Abdullah, op. cit., p. 60.

73. For an illustration, see Rahardjo, "Pola Pelaksanaan Zakat: Studi-Studi Kasus", pp. 190–97.

74. A statement issued by the governor of Jakarta in 1976 identified "five categories of *zakat*able properties and income". They included: "domestic animals, food crops, gold and silver, enterprises (commerce, industries, services), and unexpected income, which is received without much effort". (Abdullah, op. cit., p. 65.)

75. See Jihad Hasballah, "Intensifikasi Pelaksanaan Zakat di Indonesia", *Panji Masyarakat*, 1–10 August 1991, pp. 51–53.

76. See Syechul Hadi Permono, "Pendayagunaan Sumber Dana Umat Islam", *Panji Masyarakat*, 1–10 May 1991, pp. 28–29.

77. See Hasballah, op. cit., p. 51.

78. As reiterated by the Minister of Religion, Munawir Syadzali, a number of *ulama* in the late 1980s appealed to President Soeharto to serve as the national *amil* of *zakat*. See "Apakah Zakat Diurus Negara?", *Tempo*, 23 March 1991, p. 74.

79. See "Soal Zakat, Sebelum Buka Puasa", *Tempo*, 23 March 1991, pp. 74–75. Some have speculated on the possibility of this joint-ministerial decision becoming a law. Provided that the operation of Bazis is a successful one, it would require the co-operation of the Department of Finance or Bank Indonesia (to decide where the assets of Bazis would be deposited) and the Department of Foreign Affairs (to tap Indonesian Muslims residing abroad). Should this be the case, a joint-ministerial decision would be insufficient to administer Bazis. At least, a Presidential Decision (if not a law) is needed to direct this inter-departmental venture. (Interview with Ridwan Saidi in Jakarta, 21 August 1991.) See also Ridwan Saidi, "Undang-Undang Untuk Siapa?", *Risalah*, June 1991, p. 66.

80. See "Akhir Tunjangan Rabu Malam", *Tempo*, 4 December 1993, pp. 38–39.

81. See "Religious Lottery", *Far Eastern Economic Review*, 21 November 1991, p. 24.

82. Initially, due to the contrasting opinions concerning the legal status of SDSB from the perspective of religion (Islam), several Islamic socio-religious organizations and educational institutions agreed to accept donations from SDSB. However, with the converging view of Muslim leaders and activists on SDSB, especially following Majelis Ulama Indonesia's (MUI) *fatwa* (religious decree) that SDSB is forbidden (*haram*), a number of Islamic organizations and schools such as Nahdlatul Ulama (NU), Muhammadiyah, Himpunan Mahasiswa Islam (HMI), and Universitas Islam Indonesia (UII), to name only some of them, turned down or returned the contributions. See "Memprotes Sang Pemecah Belah", *Tempo*, 16 November 1991, pp. 31–32.

83. See "Akhir Tunjangan Rabu Malam", *Tempo*, 4 December 1993, p. 39.

84. At this stage opposition to SDSB transcended religious boundaries. Like their Muslim counterparts, Christian intellectuals such as Franz Magnis Suseno also voiced their rejection of SDSB. See "SDSB Netral: Bisa Buruk, Bisa Baik?", *Tempo*, 23 November 1991, p. 36.

85. See "Agar Munyuk tak Tertawa", *Tempo*, 10 August 1991, p. 23.

86. See "Akhir Tunjangan Rabu Malam", *Tempo*, 4 December 1993, p. 39.

87. See "Ketembak Sekali, Rugi", *Tempo*, 10 August 1991, p. 22. See also "Religious Lottery", *Far Eastern Economic Review*, 21 November 1991, p. 24.

88. See "Sujud Syukur, Semoga Mabrur", *Tempo*, 6 July 1991, p. 28.

89. Ibid., p. 28.

90. See "Ratusan Masjid, Seribu Dai", *Tempo*, 6 July 1991.

91. See "1000 Dai untuk Transmigran", *Tempo*, 10 November 1990, p. 117.

92. At the Bogor Palace the President sponsored the mobilization of funds which reached the amount of more than Rp. 110 billion to be used as the initial operating capital of BMI. For a fuller account, see "Bank Dengan Agunan Amanah", *Tempo*, 9 November 1991, pp. 22–23; "Mengapa Baru Sekarang Berdiri", *Prospek*, 2 November 1991, pp. 72–74; and "Bank Istimewa, Tanpa Bunga", *Editor*, 9 November 1991, pp. 75–76.

93. See, for instance, M. Dawam Rahardjo, "Bank Muamalat", *Tempo*, 2 November 1991, p. 39.

94. The Indonesian law on banking stipulates that banks must offer and charge interest. Legally, the foundation of BMI has been made possible by the fact that it is considered as operating on the basis of a zero per cent interest. See "Bank Islam, atau Bunga 0%", *Tempo*, 6 April 1991.

95. See "Kiat-Kiat Menghindarkan Riba", *Tempo*, 9 November 1991, pp. 24–25; "Bukan Bank Amal, Tapi Sistem Bagi Hasil", *Prospek*, 2 November 1991, pp. 78–79.

96. This point is adapted from Benda's analysis on the process of Islamization in different parts of Indonesia. See Benda, *The Crescent and the Rising Sun,* pp. 11–12.

97. Ibid., p. 11.

98. The great king of a central Javanese Islamic kingdom of Mataram was named Sultan Agung. He assumed a religious-political title of *kalipatullah sayidin panatagama* (the vicegerent of God, master and regulator of religion). In a different context, a similar issue is also raised in Mark Woodward, *Islam in Java: Normative Piety and Mysticism in the Sultanate of Yogyakarta* (Tucson: University of Arizona Press, 1989), pp. 156–57.

99. For a further account, see Nurcholish Madjid, "Islam dan Birokrasi", *Tempo*, 28 December 1991.

100. I am indebted to M. Imadduddin Abdurrahim for suggesting this point. (Interview in Jakarta, 26 August 1991.)

101. The terminologies originated from Islamic vocabularies.

102. Reportedly, the cost of the festival, which amounted to Rp. 4 billion, was paid for by private donations. The involvement of the state in this event was signified by the participation of its senior officials (for example, the President, Cabinet ministers, governors) in the executive committee. See, for instance, "Sajian Akbar Budaya Islam", *Editor*, 26 October 1991, pp. 26–28; "Budaya Islam Bangkit Dari Indonesia", *Panji Masyarakat*, 1–10 November 1991, pp. 16–24.

103. See "Call to the Faithful", *Far Eastern Economic Review*, 14 December 1989, p. 34. See also "The Muslim Ticket", *Far Eastern Economic Review*, 20 December 1990, p. 10.

104. Under the co-ordination of Alamsyah, on 30 September 1989 twenty-one Muslim prominent figures issued an unpublicized statement endorsing Soeharto's bid for his sixth-term presidency in 1993. In the midst of the controversy concerning the appropriateness of such a political endorsement, given the fact that the election was still four years away, the move was enthusiastically supported by a number of *ulama* in East Java. (See "Halal-Haramnya Kebulatan Tekad", *Tempo*, 26 May 1990, pp. 22–28.) In a more grandiose fashion (in spite of the tacit objection of other Islamic organizations such as ICMI and Himpunan Mahasiswa Islam [HMI]), Alamsyah also led the way for the initiation of *doa bersama* (collective prayers) in May 1992 for the purpose of cultivating Muslim political support for the president. (See "Dua Halaman Doa untuk Mohammad Soeharto", *Tempo*, 9 May 1992, pp. 22–31.)

105. See R. William Liddle, "Indonesia's Threefold Crisis", *Journal of Democracy* 3, no. 4 (October 1992): 61.

106. Ibid., p. 62.

107. Vatikiotis, *Indonesian Politics under Suharto*, p. 143.

108. See "Succession Scenarios", *Far Eastern Economic Review*, 28 September 1989, p. 31.

109. Liddle, op. cit., p. 62.

110. For a fuller account, see "Sujud Syukur, Semoga Mabrur", *Tempo*, 6 July 1991, pp. 26–27. See also M. Dawam Rahardjo, "Mandito", *Tempo*, 6 July 1991, p. 36.

111. For a fuller treatment, see, for instance, David Jenkins, *Suharto and His Generals: Indonesian Military Politics 1975–1983* (Ithaca: Monograph Series, Publication no. 64, Cornell Modern Indonesia Project, Southeast Asia Program, Cornell University, 1984). See also Vatikiotis, op. cit., especially chapter 3, pp. 60–91.

112. Vatikiotis, op. cit., pp. 68–75.

113. See Ulf Sundhaussen, "Regime Crisis in Indonesia: Facts, Fiction, Predictions", *Asian Survey* 21, no. 8 (August 1981): 815–37.

114. Ibid., p. 828.

115. See, for instance, "Pasang Surut Hubungan Islam-Beringin", *Tempo*, 21 September 1991, p. 22.

116. For a further account, see Aswab Mahasin, "The Santri Middle Class: An Insider's View", in *The Politics of Middle Class Indonesia*, edited by Richard Tanter and Kenneth Young (Clayton: Monash Papers on Southeast Asia, no.19, Centre of Southeast Asian Studies, Monash University, 1990), pp. 138–44.

117. For a further account on his criticism of the regime, see Deliar Noer, *Ideologi, Politik dan Pembangunan* (Jakarta: Yayasan Perkhidmatan, 1983). See also his *Islam, Pancasila dan Asas Tunggal* (Jakarta: Yayasan Perkhidmatan, 1984).

118. Interview with Deliar Noer in Jakarta, 11 September 1991.

119. This is especially true with regard to his assessment of Mohamad Natsir's political writings in pre-independent Indonesia. See Deliar Noer, *The Modernist Muslim Movement in Indonesia: 1900–1942* (Oxford, New York, and Jakarta: Oxford University Press, 1978), p. 323.

120. See "1991: Umat Islam Masih Ruwet", *Tempo*, 29 December 1990, pp. 30–31.

121. See "Tak Cukup Dengan Sebuah Festival", *Tempo*, 28 December 1991, pp. 32–33; "Saya Presiden Taxi Saja Deh ... ", *Detik*, 2 November 1992, pp. 6–8; "Gus Dur, Islam, dan Demokrasi", *Tempo*, 28 September 1991, p. 39; "Demokrasinya Gus Dur", *Panji Masyarakat*, 1–10 May 1991, pp. 24–27; "1991: Umat Islam Masih Ruwet", *Tempo*, 29 December 1990, pp. 30–31.

122. See "Demokrasinya Gus Dur", *Panji Masyarakat*, 1–10 May 1991, p. 25. Italics are mine.

123. By "national elements" I mean that the forum consists of Muslim and Christian figures (though it does not necessarily mean that they represent their faiths). For a fuller account, see "Demokrasi Versi Mufakat Cibeureum", *Tempo*, 13 April 1991, pp. 18–27.

124. Victor Tanja, a notable Christian intellectual, is a case in point. He does not see the whole discourse as leaning towards sectarianism or exclusivism. He considers, among other things, the enactment of the religious court law as an appropriate move to enable Muslims to implement their religious teachings. (Interview with Victor Tanja in Jakarta, 2 August 1991.)

125. In the event of the issuance of ministerial decision concerning Bazis, in response to a question as to whether the state would react similarly should a comparable need arise from non-Muslim groups, the Minister of Home Affairs, Rudini,

said: "If they [non-Muslims] want to form a similar agency, and ask for our help to serve as a supervisor, they may do so." See "Soal Zakat, Sebelum Buka Puasa", *Tempo*, 23 March 1991, p. 75.

126. See "Kecurigaan itu Sudah Usai", *Tempo*, 6 July 1991, pp. 34–35.

127. See, for instance, "Charismatic Enigma", *Far Eastern Economic Review,* 12 November 1992, pp. 34–36.

128. See "Selama Ada NU, Gus Dur Sektarian Juga", *Detik*, 2 November 1992, p. 9; Bachrun Martosukarto, "Negara Versi Abdurrahman Wahid Versus Pancasila", *Media Dakwah*, October 1993, pp. 70–71; Ridwan Saidi, "Undang-Undang Untuk Siapa?", *Risalah,* June 1991, p. 66.

129. The term "negotiated settlement" came from the literature on democratic transition. For a fuller treatment, see Guillermo O'Donnell, Philippe C. Schmitter, and Laurence Whitehead, eds., *Transitions from Authoritarian Rule: Latin America* (Baltimore and London: Johns Hopkins University Press, 1986). See also Guillermo O'Donnell and Philippe C. Schmitter, *Transitions from Authoritarian Rule: Tentative Conclusions about Uncertain Democracies* (Baltimore and London: Johns Hopkins University Press, 1986).

130. Actually, the ideology and constitution of the state have laid out the basic principles concerning the relationship between religion and the state. So far, they are used only to echo a religious-political phrase that Indonesia is neither a secular nor a theocratic state. With this phrase, any initiatives of the state to accommodate religious interests can be seen as an attempt to facilitate religious adherents in the realization of their religious duties. But it does not set a clear limit regarding the extent to which the state should be involved in religious issues.

131. In an interview he deprecates the significance of a number of the forms of accommodation, such as the religious court law and the teaching of Arabic language through the television network. See "Gus Dur, Islam, dan Demokrasi", *Tempo*, 28 September 1991, p. 39.

132. Some have suggested that there is also a personal factor involved. Prior to the emergence of the new generation of Muslim thinkers and activists, Indonesian Islam was often understood in a bipolar fashion between traditionalism and modernism. With the emergence of the new intellectualism in the 1970s, this dichotomous perspective is often perceived to be out of date. This is true, however, only in the intellectual sense, and not in the organizational sense. Though there were a number of activities involving these two groups in the 1970s and the 1980s, institutional sentiments remain. In this context, reportedly Abdurrahman Wahid has been left out in a number of activities initiated by his modernist counterparts (for example, the foundation of Paramadina, the creation of Forum Komunikasi Pembangunan Indonesia). In fact, he was also excluded from the process in the establishment of ICMI, the watershed of the politics of accommodation. This has made the whole discourse of the interplay virtually a modernist endeavour.

133. See "Saya Presiden Taxi Saja Deh ...", *Detik*, 2 November 1992, p. 7.

134. See Abdurrahman Wahid, "Islam dan Masyarakat Bangsa", *Pelita*, 6 June 1986.

7

Conclusion
Towards an Integrated Political Relationship between Islam and the State

But one thing which is still tempting is where political Islam [is] heading, if an ideological stake no longer exists. Several answers have been proposed. From the intellectual circle we often hear the necessity of turning Islam into a scientific, philosophical, or grand paradigm. At the same time, there are those who aspire that Islam moves to the realm of culture or engage in societal development [programmes], without having to put the *umat* [Muslim community] at political risk. While those answers sound prestigious and noble, in practice it is difficult to imagine an Islam which is totally "absent" from politics. The deepening root of Islam in the mass[es] naturally generates some sort of "political value." There are many mediators who are willing to find an appropriate meeting point between supply and demand. Other than that, there are always groups aspiring for an immediate and concrete offer. For them, political Islam needs to transform itself from ideology to a more practical political discourse. Now they have ample opportunities to bring Islam into power politics. It is in that direction that political Islam is seeking its new format.

Aswab Mahasin[1]

In a broader perspective the foregoing pages have sought to answer the question of whether or not Islam is actually compatible with a modern political system, with the idea of the nation state as its major element. Given the polyinterpretability of Islam, as suggested in the introduction of this volume, the answer to such an inquiry can be either affirmative or negative, depending on what kind of Islam is being put forward in the limelight of analytical investigation. Likewise, the problem of the political relationship between Islam and the state in Indonesia, through the course of its political history, is contingent upon what kind of Islamic political discourse is being developed.

By way of deconstructing the venture of the country's political Islam during the revolutionary (mid-1940s), liberal (mid-1950s), and early New Order (late 1960s) periods, this study shows that the formalistic or legalistic articulations of Islam, especially in terms of its political idealism and activism, played a crucial role in the evolution of a highly strained relationship between Islam and the state with regard to Islam's political role. In those years the ideological aura of political Islam was at the height of its intensity, demanding, among other things, that Islam be adopted as the state ideology or religion along with its socio-political ramifications.

It is important to note, however, that Indonesian Islamic legalism and formalism did not evolve out of a vacuum. To a large extent, these thoughts and actions were driven by negative encounters with the West, most notably Dutch colonialism. There was no doubt that this long and penetrating process of colonial control had a devastating impact. For the large part of the Muslim community, this was particularly evident in the obstruction of their economic, educational, and political opportunities. This, in turn, contributed to the limited availability of choices for political Muslims to express their self-realization in modern Indonesia. Thus, like Jamal al-Din al-Afghani in Egypt, who waged an ideological-political campaign of Pan Islamism in the wake of the European encroachment, they inwardly sought refuge in the "holistic" nature of Islam for the purpose of countering Westernism.

Not all Indonesian Muslims supported this kind of politics. A large and powerful group of Indonesian political thinkers and activists, concerned mainly with the nature of Indonesia's nation state, rejected these ideas and worked hard to contain them in the 1950s. The relative success of this politics of containment left political Islam an outsider in the country's political process. Later, especially during the first twenty years of the New Order regime, political Islam had in fact become a principal target of ideological-political distrust and the state's exclusionary policies, because it was suspected of being inherently against the state ideology Pancasila.

It is this kind of dismal situation which the new generation of Muslim thinkers and activists, emerging in the early 1970s, intended to remedy. Operating with three different, but related and compatible, modes of intellectualism — theological/religious renewal, political/bureaucratic reform, and social transformation — their primary purpose has been to transform the earlier outlook of political Islam, from formal-legalism to substantialism.

With their pioneering moves, today's political Islam has found a new format. Its primary features, which include (1) the theological underpinning, (2) the goal, and (3) the approach of political Islam, are perceived to be congruent with the construct of Indonesia's unitary nation state. In terms of its theological underpinning, this new format of political Islam does not require a legalistic or formalistic connection between Islam and the state (or politics in general). As long as the state, ideologically as well as politically, operates on a value system which does not contradict Islamic teachings, it is sufficient for political Muslims to render their loyalty and support. This makes them at ease with Pancasila which, as they themselves suggest, is in accord with Islamic precepts.

With respect to its goal, it is also obvious that political Islam no longer aspires to the establishment of an Islamic state. Instead, based on their understanding of the Islamic doctrines as well as the sociological contours of Indonesian society, which are heterogeneous in nature, they are working for the development of a socio-political system which reflects, or is in tune with, the general principles of Islamic political values, including justice, consultation, egalitarianism, and participation.

Finally, as an approach to realize these goals, political Islam no longer emphasizes its efforts in partisan politics with the parliament as its primary playing field. Instead, it tries to broaden and diversify its political mechanism which includes various non-governmental organizations, such as Nahdlatul Ulama (NU), Muhammadiyah, and a wide range of other private organizations, the state bureaucracy, as well as the then ruling party Golkar along with the other parties.

Since the late 1980s this more integrative approach has shown some encouraging signs of success. Political Islam seems to have found ways to integrate itself into the discourse of Indonesia's national politics. In addition, there are also a number of indications which suggest that the state is beginning to see political Islam not as a threat, but as a complementary force in the country's national development.

Evidence of this new development has been the political relaxation of the state towards Islam, signified by the former's implementation of a number of policies perceived as in accord with the latter's socio-cultural and political interests. Included in these accommodative actions are the passing of an education law which stipulates the obligatory nature of religious instruction at all levels of education, public as well as private (1988); the passing of a religious court law which strengthens the position of Islamic courts in adjudicating marriage, divorce, reconciliation, inheritance, and endowment issues (1989); the foundation of ICMI which adds a structural entry to policy decision-making (1990); the compilation of Islamic law (1991); the issuance of a joint-ministerial decision concerning the *zakat* collection and distribution agency, Bazis (1991); the reversal of a long-standing policy which prohibited Muslim female high school students from wearing the *jilbab* (1991); the holding of an Islamic cultural festival (1991 and 1995); the establishment of an Islamic bank (1992); and the annulment of the national lottery (1993).

Actually, there is nothing peculiar with regard to these accommodative moves of the state towards Islam. From a lengthy discussion concerning the nature of these forms of accommodation, it is clear that not every form of accommodation is necessarily novel in substance. Many of them, such as the education law, the religious court law, and the joint-ministerial decision on Bazis represent more of an extension or continuance of already existing practices. Even the foundation of ICMI, the often perceived-watershed of the state's politics of accommodation towards Islam, has not (and most probably will not) outweighed the structural significance of Muhammadiyah, NU, Majelis Ulama Indonesia (MUI), Golkar, and the state bureaucracy in the realization of Islamic interests.

In spite of this, considering the nature of the political relationship between Islam and the state in the past, these accommodative actions indisputably represent an important change, especially in what they symbolize, in the changing nature of the political relationship between Islam and the state.

To conclude the discussion, there are several important points that need to be brought out with respect to this new development.

First, the fact that the idealism and activism of political Islam have changed from legal-formalism to substantialism and that the state has responded positively does not completely resolve the problem of the political relationship between Islam and the state. In other words, in spite of encouraging signs, it does not offer a clear model as to how Islam (and other existing religious groupings such as Catholicism, Protestantism, Hinduism, and Buddhism) and the Indonesian state should properly relate.

A possible explanation for this is that basically the new relationship has evolved in a sporadic or *ad hoc* fashion. Issues have emerged and been dealt with without first being deliberated systematically by the nation's political elite. Therefore, it is safe to argue that what has actually happened was basically a spontaneous interplay between Islam and the state, in which the intellectual transformation of Islamic political ideas and practices was matched by the willingness of the state to embrace a number of policies perceived as in accordance with the interests of the Muslims. In other words, there is no "negotiated settlement" among the country's religious-political elites to determine how religion and the state should be appropriately connected.

In the absence of a nationally accepted formula with regard to the appropriate political relationship between religion and the state, it is difficult to assess what the future of the interaction between Islam and the state will be like. This tends to produce myth and speculation concerning the fact of the matter as well as its possible ramifications. This uncertainty is likely to bring about fear of the unknown, which in turn generates public apprehension. And the euphoria of some political Muslims, suggesting that now the majority rules the minority, only reinforces the anxiety. In short, without the process of a "negotiated settlement", the new relationship will be perceived, especially by its potential adversaries, as sectarian and exclusive.

Second, the intellectual transformation of Islamic political ideas and practices has evolved in a situation of authoritarianism and exclusion of many groups. As such it generates speculation as to whether or not this reformed idealism and activism of political Muslims would hold firm should the regime allow the Pandora's box to open, in pursuit of a more inclusionary and participatory system of governing. In such a state, in which freedom of expression is guaranteed, it is likely that the new Islamic intellectualism would be matched by other streams of thought which are more inclined to maintain the earlier version of Islamic political ideas and practices.[2]

Given the development of Indonesia's Muslim community in general and its political thinkers and activists in particular, the re-emergence of the older ideas should not be of particular concern. Regardless of the possibility of the re-emergence of the earlier Muslim political discourse in a democratic form of government, one thing is clear. For the last two decades or so the general spectrum of Islamic political ideas and practices has changed. More specifically, with the changing nature of the sociological basis of the Muslim community (due to a rapid process of socio-economic and political mobilization), most Indonesian Muslims understand the distinction between substance and form, between Islam and Islamic political organization. In this situation there seem to be no clear indications that the formalistic or legalistic articulations of political Islam would flourish, much less enjoy a comparable percentage of support as it did in the liberal era of the 1950s.

Finally, considering the circumstances which surround the transformatory process of the political relationship between Islam and the state, from hostility into amicability, it is fair to conclude that this new phenomenon is still in a transition phase. The fact that it evolved rather spontaneously, without first being consciously deliberated by the country's political elites, only confirms this finding. In such a situation uncertainty is always present, especially with regard to the notion of its sustainability. Since it can go either way — becoming more hostile or more amicable — a speculation on its possible consolidation or breakdown is appropriate.

Taking into account the factors that have led to the hostility between Islam and the state, it is likely that the consolidation of this process is very much dependent upon (1) the proportional representation of Muslims in the existing political institutions of the state, and (2) the maintenance of national commitment that Indonesia is not a secular state. This makes recognition of religious values in the process of policy-making imperative.

In this context suffice it to say that the return to a formalistic or legalistic conception of political Islam is only likely with a growing sense of deprivation, socially, economically, and politically. As in the earlier experience, its thinkers and activists would seek refuge inwardly in the holistic or totalistic nature of Islam to counter an encroaching state.

Notes

1. Aswab Mahasin, "Islam 'Politik'", *Tempo*, 2 November 1991, p. 96.

2. This concern is also raised by R. William Liddle. See his "*Media Dakwah* Scripturalism: One Form of Islamic Political Thought and Action in New Order Indonesia" (Paper delivered at a conference on Intellectual Development in Indonesian Islam, Arizona State University, 20–21 February 1993).

8

Political Islam in Post-Soeharto Indonesia
A Postscript

> With the emergence of new political parties among Muslim communities, concerns are being raised about the possible hazard of using Islamic idioms and symbols for electoral purposes. If religious idioms and symbols are used to increase political support, religion will become a divisive issue among Muslims and sensitive, possibly non-negotiable, principles and beliefs will burden electoral politics.
>
> Amien Rais[1]

On 21 May 1998 President Soeharto relinquished power after thirty-two years. The move was quite sudden, despite the fact that demands for his resignation — spearheaded mostly by university students, prominent intellectuals, and political activists — were echoed all over the country. It was a sudden end in the sense that, powerful as he was, the public did not think that he would step down without making significant efforts, politically as well as militarily, to defend his presidency. Even though the signs were there, and quite obviously indicating that he was losing his grip on what used to be his sources of support — consisting of the bureaucracy, Golkar, and the military — many believed that Soeharto would not give up easily. This was especially so at a time when the country was plunged into unprecedented crises, socio-economically as well as politically. The monetary crisis that hit Indonesia hard, starting with the devaluation of the rupiah in August 1997, was the main reason for the collapse of the country's economy.[2] This was followed by bloodshed and enormous destruction in cities like Jakarta, Medan, Solo, Banyuwangi, Yogyakarta, Padang, and Surabaya.[3] The circumstances did not seem right for Soeharto — who often suggested that being a soldier, he was not a man to run away from problems (in Javanese, *tinggal glanggang colong playu*) — to quit. But, realizing the fact that he was eventually alone — deserted by his very own confidants and supporters who had backed him until as late as March 1998, when he was unanimously re-elected for a seventh term — forced him to abdicate.[4]

So, on that very day, he declared unilaterally his departure from the post he had occupied for more than three decades. And with such a "unilateral declaration" — a carefully chosen phrase which was deliberately intended to prevent certain legal or constitutional bearings — Vice-President B.J. Habibie ascended to the presidency.[5]

Soeharto's resignation caused tremendous and far-reaching impacts. For one thing, it generated changes. Even though post-Soeharto Indonesia — like many other countries experiencing a transitionary period — is plagued with uncertainties,[6] undoubtedly it has opened up the country's political Pandora's box. For so many years Indonesian politics had been too restricted a field for the society to be involved in. Politics had not been permitted to be played out competitively. Rather, it had become an arena enjoyed primarily by "the praetorian guard". As a result, not only did society become more and more depoliticized — in the sense that it could not develop any political ideas and practices other than those dictated by the state — it often faced confrontation and discouragement to the point where the realm of politics simply had to be avoided.[7]

The resignation of Soeharto overturned the above situation. Public euphoria was everywhere, and as such demystified the sacredness or remoteness of politics. Thus, quite suddenly, politics became a public sphere where everybody felt he had the right to be involved in. Waged under the spirit of — but often looking more like a guise — *reformasi* (reformation), a political phrase which has become very popular since 1998, and which may have contributed to the downfall of Soeharto, the public engaged in political activities with virtually no structural or socio-cultural barriers.

One of the most conspicuous indications of this political relaxation or liberalization was the emergence of an astonishing number of political parties, perhaps beyond anybody's imagination. As reported, between May and October 1998, in the midst of socio-economic and political uncertainties — signified among other things by economic collapse, bloodshed, and enormous destruction in a number of big cities — Indonesia witnessed the birth of 181 political parties.[8] Out of that number, forty-two parties can be categorized as Islamic, the majority of which use Islam as their symbol and/or ideological basis.[9]

This development brought about different and perhaps even conflicting — though not necessarily novel — perspectives with regard to the relationship between Islam and politics. There are those who believe that in the end, political Islam simply could not separate religion from politics. The fact that Islam is generally perceived as a divine instrument to understand the world means that Islam should provide "the right moral attitude for [virtually all] human action",[10] which includes in politics. Accordingly, and putting such a religious value aside, Islam can also be used and treated as a major political resource.

Others are of the opinion that the rebirth of political Islam is a logical phenomenon. Like many other political groupings which were marginalized by the New Order government, political Islam saw the downfall of Soeharto as an opportunity to develop its own and independent political thinking. As the nature of the Indonesian state, both under Soekarno and Soeharto, was practically hostile to Islam, Muslims had to adjust their thoughts and actions and hence adopted some kind of docile religious-political stance. As discussed at length in the previous chapters, it appears that for the last three decades, especially under the New Order administration, Muslim political thinkers and activists had to develop the notion of substantialist and less symbolical political Islam. The resignation of Soeharto and the implications it brought about had provoked — or perhaps returned the right of — many Muslims to formulate their political thoughts and actions which — for religious as well as political reasons — required the use of Islam as their symbol, identity, or ideological basis.

This chapter focuses not so much on the "politics of reformation" — a phrase many observers have often used to describe the political development of post-Soeharto Indonesia, at least during its immediate months — in general. Rather, it deals specifically with the new wave of political Islam, signified primarily by the emergence of numerous Islamic parties and its possible ramifications. This new development raises a number of questions: What does this phenomenon suggest with regard to the future development of political Islam? Where does this politics of Islamic symbolism lead to? Does it represent a backlash with respect to the transformation of Islamic political ideas and practices which have been in place since the 1970s? How do Muslims react to the formation of these political parties? All of these questions need to be answered to clarify the position of political Islam in Indonesia following the resignation of Soeharto.

THE RISE OF ISLAMIC POLITICAL PARTIES:
FRAGMENTATION OF MUSLIM POLITICAL ACTIVISTS

The (re)emergence of Islamic political parties is a phenomenon one could not help noticing in Indonesia's turbulent years of reformation in the late 1990s. In fact, other than political relaxation and liberalization, which appear to set the general tone of post-Soeharto Indonesia, one would quickly point out that the (re)birth of Islamic political parties is the most conspicuous feature of the reformation era — that is, if one would like to see the politics of reformation from the Islamic group perspective. The formation of forty-two Islamic political parties in a six-month period (May to October 1998), following the resignation of Soeharto, is too obvious an indication of the rising tide of political Islam. More importantly, it is also perceived as a sign of the resurgence of symbolical and ideological Islam, along with the possible ramifications of this.

This phenomenon has brought about some speculations. But the tendency has been to see this development as *déjà vu* — a recurrent attempt on the part of many Muslim political thinkers and activists to (re)politicize Islam or (re)assert Islamic interests in politics. At least, if the term "politicization of Islam" sounds pejorative, the resurgence of Islamic parties has been viewed as an indicator that for (many) Muslims — and perhaps for (many) other political practitioners as well — Islam can function as a political resource.[11] Though it is justifiable in a free society — in fact it is often considered as a natural right — nonetheless the formation of political parties based on Islam will always remind the public, non-Muslims in particular, of the historical stigma of bringing Islam to the forefront of Indonesian politics. As such it will always be perceived as an attempt to legally or constitutionally link Islam with politics or to establish a state based on Islamic principles.[12]

But the alarm did not come only from non-Muslim quarters. Some Muslims also voiced a similar apprehension for different reasons. Kuntowijoyo, a highly respected Yogyakarta-based Muslim intellectual, wrote a provocative essay outlining six arguments why Islamic political parties should not be formed.[13] Like many Muslims, he recognizes that during Soeharto's thirty-two years in power, Islam was politically marginalized in the sense that Muslim political activists could not express thoughts and actions other than those allowed by the state. Accordingly, only those who shared — and felt comfortable with — the New Order's socio-economic and political agenda, which emphasized stability and order, could participate in politics.

In spite of this, in the view of Kuntowijoyo — and perhaps for many other Muslims as well — the New Order's politics of marginalization was a blessing in disguise. In a situation in which politics was a forbidden realm for many Muslims, the *santri* community had managed to diversify the political meaning of Islam by deliberately focusing their potential and energy on areas of strategic interest such as human resource development. The Muslim intellectual boom, which Nurcholish Madjid epitomized in Indonesian Islam in the mid-1980s and early 1990s, was a direct result of that choice.[14]

Not least important was the fact that Muslims' involuntary retreat from politics in those years brought about major impacts on at least two important socio-religious phenomena. First, it played a pivotal role in establishing a relatively amicable relationship between Muhammadiyah and Nahdlatul Ulama (NU). Any student of Indonesian political Islam could not fail to notice that these two organizations shared irreconcilable theological-political differences, which affected the nature of the relationship between these two socio-religious leviathans. During the height of activism of Indonesian political Islam in the 1950s and early 1960s, whatever differences Muhammadiyah and NU had could easily be transformed into socio-religious and political conflicts.[15]

Second, it contributed to the religious-political convergence between the *santri* and *abangan* communities. As discussed in chapter 2, the dichotomy between *santri* and *abangan* had been associated mainly with differences in religious understanding as well as the application of Islamic tenets in the daily life of Javanese Muslims. Given the position of Islam in Indonesian politics, this *santri–abangan* socio-religious grouping spilled over into the realm of politics. In fact, it polarized the country's modern politics into two major cleavages or currents (*aliran*). While the *santri* were inclined to direct their political orientations towards Islamic political parties, the *abangan* were more apt to express their political associations within the nationalist or communist parties.[16]

This kind of interplay between religion and politics characterized and sharpened the schism between these two religious-cultural groupings. However, the absence of *aliran* politics in Soeharto's New Order administration enabled *santri* and *abangan* communities to converge religiously as well as politically. More importantly, it allowed Muslims to build a larger umbrella for the Islamic community under which religiosity was not measured by certain political ideas or ideological and party affiliations, but simply by exercising religious tenets.

Given the above perspectives, for Kuntowijoyo, the re-entrance of Islam into politics could jeopardize this favourable development. In his view, the establishment of political parties based on Islam would likely to (1) stop Muslim social mobility; (2) bring about disintegration within the Muslim community; (3) encourage Muslims to become myopic, emphasizing more short-term (political) objectives; (4) narrow Muslims' understanding of Islam; (5) cease the proliferation of key Muslim figures; and (6) alienate the younger Muslim generation.[17]

Kuntowijoyo is correct in suggesting that the establishment of an Islamic party may bring about certain implications not necessarily consistent or compatible with some of the achievements Muslims have already accomplished when they concentrated their potential and energies on issues related to non-political aspects of Islam. Nevertheless, many Muslims do not seem to share his opinion. In fact, not only did they establish Islamic parties, but they also created Islamic political institutions in large numbers, unprecedented in the history of the Muslim world. The existence of forty-two Islamic parties is indeed a clear challenge to his view.

His alarmism is correct in so far as it is placed in the context of the pre-New Order circumstances in which Islamic political ideas and practices were generally perceived to be legalistic and formalistic in character. There is no doubt that the development of the new Islamic intellectualism and activism in the past three decades has contributed to the transformation of a sizeable proportion of Muslim intellectuals and practitioners to adhere to a more tolerant and inclusive Islam. Even so, many believe that some Muslims still aspire to a certain political idealism and symbolism, such as the use of Islam as a party platform and identity. However, it is a mistake to assume that this is an indication that Muslim political thinkers and activists will always "orient Indonesia to the direction of Mecca". This viewpoint is only true in a certain historical period, such as in the 1950s or early 1960s, when the relationship between Islam and politics not only contributed to the birth of *aliran* politics, but also polarized the Muslim community into *santri* and *abangan* socio-religious groupings. Thus, arguing that using Islam as a party platform and identity is automatically identical to promoting the idea of Islam as the basis of the state requires a number of factors than simply relying on a stigmatic account of history.[18]

Nevertheless, it is important to note that in so far as this issue is concerned (that is, the relationship between Islam and politics), historical stigma — more than anything else — is still the primary popular basis of perception. Because of that, Kuntowijoyo is not alone in trying to convince or alarm the public into believing that the establishment of

Islamic parties could eventually resurrect the past — the (re)emergence of an antagonistic and polarized Muslim community with all of its possible ramifications. As quoted at the beginning of the chapter, even Amien Rais — an important disciple of Mohammad Natsir — shares a similar notion.[19] Partly because of such a conviction, he chose to form a religiously neutral party such as PAN, rather than an Islamic one.

If the use of Islam as a party platform and identity is not meant to entertain the idea of Islam as the basis of state, why then do some Muslim political practitioners remain committed to the idea of Islamic symbolism in politics? Furthermore, what are the most likely explanations for those who are still inclined to see the current emergence of Islamic symbolism in politics in light of the past? To answer these questions, one has to examine (1) the dynamics of the relationship between Islam and the state; and (2) the political relaxation and liberalization which the fall of Soeharto has brought about.

Recalling the discussion in the previous chapters, it is safe to say that finding a proper place for Islam — or any religion for that matter — in Indonesia's socio-cultural, economic, and political development is the crucial point in the whole construct of the relationship between Islam and the state. The earlier generation of Islamic political thinkers and activists were of the opinion that Islam should function as the constitutional and legal basis of the state. Many Muslims, however, disagreed with the idea of linking Islam with the state. Instead, they proposed the notion of a deconfessionalized state based on the ideology of Pancasila. This made Indonesia neither Islamic nor secular, but a religious state, in the sense that the state allowed and assisted its citizen to perform their religious obligations.

The idea of a deconfessionalized state may have been a viable compromise between the religious and the nationalist groups. However, the manner in which Pancasila as well as the 1945 Constitution were formulated, introduced, debated, and finally accepted as the two most important legal bases of the state seemed to have left the impression that the adoption was temporary in nature. At best, the acceptance was not based on genuine compromises, as pressure and *fait accompli* were part of the environment of the constitutional committee meetings. In this case, as the minutes of the meetings indicate, Soekarno repeatedly asked members of the committee, especially those from the Islamic circle, to immediately accept Pancasila and the 1945 Constitution if they really wanted independence to occur. In the view of Soekarno, a complete and revised version of the ideological as well as constitutional arrangement of the state could be formulated when the country was independent.[20]

Partly because of this, Muslims as well as other political forces debated the issue once again in the Constituent Assembly. The formation of the Constituent Assembly following the first general elections of 1955, with the sole duty of formulating the ideological and constitutional basis of the state, reasserted the temporary nature of Pancasila and the 1945 Constitution. The fact that all four Islamic parties — Masyumi, NU, PSII, and Perti — reintroduced Islam as the basis of the state was only an exercise of their constitutional duties based on their religious as well as political aspirations, which they perceived to be appropriate and necessary. As such, one should not argue that Muslim parties were absolutist with regard to their religious-political ambitions. Like their nationalist counterparts, Muslims expected to have meaningful discussions and be able to reach a viable compromise. Indeed, they had done so as their duty to formulate a much better constitution — with the exception of the question of the state ideology (that is, Pancasila or Islam). The fact that Soekarno, backed by the military at that time, did not wish to go the extra mile to enable a genuine compromise to take place, and chose instead to issue a presidential decree in June 1959, which abrogated the laborious work of the Constituent Assembly — thus putting Pancasila and the 1945 Constitution once again into effect — only proved that a truly negotiated settlement among the country's national elite on the two most important issues (that is, Pancasila and the 1945 Constitution) failed to occur.[21]

This remained the case for the next forty-nine years. Forces that contributed to the failure of the national elite to compromise on issues related to the socio-cultural, economic, and political life of the country became more apparent during Soekarno's seven years and Soeharto's thirty-two years of rule. Especially during Soeharto's rule, the ideological position of Pancasila and the 1945 Constitution was strengthened and reasserted. They were treated as the two most sacred documents, which no one could discuss, question, and interpret in any way other than what was dictated by the state. Complementary to this situation, political or ideological Islam was severely contained, leaving it as an outsider in the country's political dynamic. During the first twenty years of the New Order administration, political Islam became a principal target of the state's exclusionary politics as well as the focus of ideological and political distrust. More particularly, political Islam was suspected of being inherently against the state ideology of Pancasila.[22]

This was indeed a distressing situation. As described before, the new generation of Muslim political thinkers and activists that emerged from the 1970s onwards endeavoured to reverse the situation by adhering to more substantive socio-political ideas of Islam. They did not aspire to the notion of Islam as the basis of the state. In their view, as long as the state operated on a value system that did not contradict Islamic teachings, there was no religious obligation to question the existence of such a state. More importantly, they also believed that in essence, Pancasila was in accord with Islamic precepts.[23]

By the late 1980s, a meaningful transformation with regard to Islamic political ideas and practices began to evolve. Muslims seemed to be at ease with the idea that Indonesia is neither an Islamic nor a secular state. When the state reversed its treatment of Islam, leaning to a more accommodative stance towards Islamic aspirations, the hostility was substantially reduced. In a situation like this, there was no religious-political need to raise the question of Islam as the basis of the state.

One important question still remains, however. How genuine was the transformation of Islamic political ideas and practices? Or rather, how sincere was the accommodative response of the state towards Islam? In a situation in which the state was very much still exclusionary in nature, there was no way of knowing the degree of sincerity of both sides — the Muslims and the New Order state. This issue needs to be raised because of the view that, as mentioned in the earlier part of this study, the hegemonic and authoritarian nature of the state was the major weakness of the whole process of Islamic ideological and political transformation. The fact that the state contained political Islam did not actually leave much room for political Islam to manoeuvre in order to survive. Strong as it was, no single socio-cultural, economic, and political institution could escape the web of the influence of the New Order state.

Because of that, it is fair to suggest that there was always a dimension of religious-political expediency. To be sure, there were Muslims who, for religious or other reasons, believed that Islam does not oblige its adherents to form a theocratic state. The process of the transformation of Islamic political ideas and practices during the New Order administration strengthened this conviction, and increased the number of those who shared and supported such a viewpoint.[24] Nonetheless, it was equally true that not every Muslim was on the same wagon of Islamic intellectual transformation. There were those who saw the issue differently — tacitly or otherwise conserving an organic view of Islam–state relationship.[25] It was the nature of the New Order state which prevented many of them from voicing and developing their genuine Islamic political aspirations.

While the proper relationship between Islam and the state remains a debatable issue among Muslims, this was not the case with regards to the characteristics of the New Order state. Muslims generally believe that the New Order state was basically hegemonic, practising non-competitive politics, and leaving no space for the public to articulate their demands. Indeed, it was considered a "repressive-developmentalist" institution. When the pillars that had supported Soeharto's way of governing crumbled, quite a sudden opportunity to embrace long-overdue ideological and political aspirations emerged. Like many other political practitioners, politically active Muslims wanted to express their own ideas which differed from what was decreed by the state — an exclusionary political system; the existence of two docile parties (PPP and PDI) and one corporatist political institution (Golkar); and the adoption of Pancasila as the sole ideological basis of existing socio-religious and political organizations. The rise of Islamic political parties — like many other political parties — and the adoption of Islam — like many other ideologies — as party ideology and symbol should be viewed from this perspective.[26]

Thus, the political relaxation and liberalization, which Soeharto's sudden departure from power brought about, was the major factor in the emergence of political forces and the articulation of their own interests. With virtually no socio-cultural, political, and ideological barriers in the way, they were very much on their own course of action and determination.[27] Therefore, it is only a natural phenomenon that political Islam has re-emerged and adopted Islam as its party ideology, symbol, and platform.[28] As suggested by Nurcholish Madjid, "We have lost our freedom for more than thirty years. All of a sudden, the freedom is back in our hands, which of course makes us happy. From this perspective, creating a large number of parties is only a natural phenomenon. This is like children who just got new toys."[29]

The fact that such a development has aroused apprehension and alarm — not only from non-Muslim quarters, but also from many Muslims as well — is equally understandable. As in the past (1950s), democracy gave ample opportunity for Muslims to aggregate and articulate their interests. Ironically, it was in this liberal and democratic situation that the debate on the question of Islam as the basis of the state reached its height. The failure to seek compromises, especially with regard to the position of Islam in Indonesia's political and ideological construct, brought about certain historical stigma. Primarily because of that stigma, the birth of forty-two Islamic political parties was conceived in a manner in which modern Indonesian political history had evolved. And because of that stigma, the existence of Islamic political parties will always be associated with the idea of a theocratic state and/or the absorption of Islamic *shari'a* into the country's legal system.[30]

This stigmatic standpoint, however, does not seem to provide an accurate description of the characteristics and agendas of post-Soeharto era Islamic political parties. The inclination to generalize all Islamic parties as proponents of Islam as the basis of the state is clearly misleading. The newly formed Islamic political parties cannot be viewed as homogeneous entities. Monolithicism is certainly not a useful concept to apply in this case. This is especially true given the fact that not every Islamic political party uses Islam as its ideological basis. While Islamic nuances and fervour are undoubtedly present, even in the self-proclaimed nationalist parties such as PKB (with NU members as its core constituents and Islamic jurisprudence as the basis of the party platform) and PAN (with Muhammadiyah members as its only meaningful supporters), some took Pancasila — or a combination of Pancasila, Islam, and the 1945 Constitution — as their party basis.[31]

If party basis can be regarded as party ideology, the reality presented above is surely a strong indication that not all Islamic parties adhere to a single ideological orientation. Should this characteristic stand, it is equally true that not every existing Islamic party adopts a single, unified political aspiration. On the contrary, they seem to have different, often contradictory, political agendas. Other than the fact that all ten Islamic parties which gained one or more seats in the parliament — together holding 172 seats — agreed with Amien Rais to form an Islamic, or Central Axis, caucus with the sole purpose of making Abdurrahman Wahid Indonesia's fourth president, there were hardly any other aspirations shared by the existing Islamic parties.[32] Even such important issues as whether Article 29 of the Constitution should be amended — a process which opened up the possibility of inserting the Jakarta Charter into the Constitution — was not able to bring Muslim political thinkers and activists together, although it was often considered of great importance to Muslim interests.

When the process to amend the Constitution began in 1999, it was clear from the start that not all Islamic parties shared the same vision regarding the proper place of Islam in the state. This situation continued well until 2002, the year in which parliament was scheduled to complete its work to amend the Constitution. Throughout the process, Islamic political forces demonstrated the fact that they have different opinions concerning the matter. There were those who wanted to revive the Jakarta Charter and insert it into the Constitution, which would make the implementation of

Islamic *shari'a* mandatory for all Muslims. Others, while not necessarily against the idea of putting some Islamic precepts into the country's legal system, rejected that particular idea quite explicitly.

Given the existence of public apprehension and alarm towards political Islam, it is interesting to note that the support for inserting the Jakarta Charter into the Constitution was minimal. Out of the ten Islamic parties in the parliament, only PPP, PBB, and an amalgam of small parties called Perserikatan Daulatul Ummah (PDU, Union of the Sovereignty of the Muslim Ummah) — together occupying around 82 seats — supported the inclusion of the Jakarta Charter in the new Constitution.[33] Of course, these three parties had done their best to realize their objectives. Nonetheless, they did not seem to launch a political struggle like their predecessors did half a century ago in the Constituent Assembly debates. Although the likelihood is that these three Islamic parties would continue their efforts to have the Jakarta Charter included in the Constitution, they did not block the assembly decision to stick to the original formulation of Article 29 of the Constitution, which says that the state is based on one God.[34] The fact that the process to amend the Constitution was far from dead-locked, especially on issues related to the relationship between Islam and the state, is an indication that the historical stigma of the ideological debates that occurred in the mid-1940s and the late 1950s can no longer be employed as a reference point in analysing the existing Islamic politi-cal parties in post-Soeharto Indonesia.

As far as the idea of placing Islam in its appropriate position within the state is concerned, it is also important to note that unlike their struggle in the mid-1940s and 1950s, current Islamic parties do not aspire to Islam being the basis of the state. Unlike before, no single Islamic party has ever publicly proposed the idea of Islam as the basis of state. At best, as already mentioned, their aspirations have been reduced or modified to something like the revival of the Jakarta Charter. Coupled with the fact that the process of constitutional amendment did not end in deadlock, it is safe to argue that the religious-political circumstances have undoubt-edly changed. Putting that in perspective, there is no legitimate reason for seeing the rebirth of Islamic political parties in light of the past. Given what has evolved over the last fifty years or so, one should not expect that a perfect and complete transformation from Islamic political legalism and formalism to substantialism can ever occur. However, the fact that Islamic parties are by no means homogeneous is evidence that their emergence should not and cannot be perceived in a monolithic manner.[35]

ISLAMIC PARTIES AND ELECTIONS:
THE MYTH OF THE POLITICAL STRENGTH OF ISLAM

In June 1999, under the Habibie presidency, Indonesia held its second ever democratic general elections. The first was carried out in 1955 under the premiership of Burhanuddin Harahap. In so far as democratically organized elections are concerned, the country has experienced only two general elections. However, from 1971 to 1997, the New Order regime conducted six elections at regular intervals, once every five years. The major difference between those and the first two mentioned elections was that the latter were administered in an uncompetitive atmosphere where intimidation, coercion, deceit, and fraud were integral parts of the political show. In a situation like this, the ruling Golkar party always emerged triumphantly, becoming the only dominant political force.[36]

From the political Islam perspective, free and democratically run elections have always been perceived as the most preferred political instrument to bring their activists and practitioners to power. In spite of this, it is important to realize that the democratic system entails ambiguity with regards to the realization of the interests of Muslims. This viewpoint has nothing to do with the attitude of the Islamically oriented political activists towards democracy, but more to do with the opportunities democracy will bring to their advantage.

In rhetoric, Muslims have always argued that democracy will enable them to realize their interests and aspirations. This perception is based not so much on what democracy will or can offer to any political contestants seeking power and positions in public office, but more on the simple fact that Muslims enjoy a numerical majority in Indonesia. In their view, in a democratic system, this demographic might will automatically lead to support for Islamic political parties and interests. This is generally due to a strong belief that Muslims will always direct their support and loyalty to Islamic causes and institutions — socio-religiously, economically as well as politically. Because of this, even though the reality may suggest otherwise, Muslims often think and act in such a linear fashion in their attempts to establish a possible linkage between one reality (that is, religious orientation) and another (that is, political affiliation or support).

The perception that democracy will automatically lead to the realization of Islamic political interests has been proven wrong in the history of modern Indonesian politics. When the first general elections were held in 1955, the Muslims' political imagination was loaded with such a religious-political stance. Realizing the fact that 90 per cent of Indonesians were Muslims, they believed that the largest portion of the votes would go to political parties based on Islam — Masyumi, NU, PSII, and Perti.[37] In reality — here is where the ambiguity of the notion that democracy will lead to the realization of Islamic interests or that demographic strength will bring about political power comes in — the elections did not seem to support the linear conviction they held so strongly. Instead of gaining the sum of votes that reflected the demographic majority of Muslims, the existing four Islamic political parties received fewer votes than what had been expected. Put together, they enjoyed only 43.5 per cent of the votes. If Muslims constituted 90 per cent of the population, then it is fair to suggest that more than 50 per cent of Indonesian Muslims gave their votes to non-Islamic parties. This discrepancy should have made clear the fact that not all Muslims shared a single, unified political aspiration. Thus, adherence to Islamic faith could not be construed in an automatic fashion to correlate with or to be translated into support for Islamic parties and interests.

It is important to note, however, that the above linear religious-political attitude was not adhered to only by Muslim political activists. The secularists, the nationalists, and particularly the *abangan* politicians also adopted such a religious-political viewpoint. Their support of non-Islamic parties was basically due to their differences with Muslim activists pertaining to socio-religious and political issues. This reality provided substantial empirical ground for anthropologists such as Clifford Geertz and Robert Jay to develop the *aliran* concept, where socio-religious groupings is a major factor in the choice of party preferences or affiliations.[38]

It has been often suggested that *aliran* or partisan politics characterized the dynamic of Indonesia's liberal democracy of the 1950s. As such, it was able to take root in the country's religious-political development primarily because of the unexpected circumstances where democracy and religion were destined to meet in an unsuitable socio-cultural setting. The defining feature of democracy is that it allows its citizens to lend their support to political parties of their choice. In a situation in which religion is perceived to have organic impacts on the socio-economic and political preferences of its adherents, political or party affiliations tend to be influenced and shaped by religious orientations. Voters would likely give their support to parties perceived as compatible with their socio-religious preferences. As suggested by Geertz, the 1955 elections were marked by a tendency for *santri* to give their votes to Islamic parties (for example, Masyumi, NU, PSII, and Perti), whereas *abangan* and *priyayi* (indigenous aristocrats) gave theirs to nationalist or communist parties (for example, PNI and PKI).[39]

Though different in degree and intensity, the politics of *aliran* was still very much alive during the first three general elections (1971, 1977, and 1982) held under the New Order government. During the election campaigns Muslim leaders were adamant in reminding their fellow Muslims that it was religiously mandatory to cast votes for Muslim parties. Despite the fact that the elections were held in a non-democratic way, Islamic parties managed to enjoy 27.11 per cent (1971), 29.29 per cent (1977), and 27.78 per cent (1982) of the votes.[40]

Following the implementation of Pancasila as the sole basis for socio-religious and political organizations in 1984, the *aliran* fervour eroded gradually, at least in the legal and formal sense. Coupled with the development of new Islamic political ideas and practices since the early 1970s, which emphasized more the substantive dimension of Islam rather than its legal and formal outlook, many Muslims began to accept the idea that it was basically all right to associate themselves with non-Islamic parties. Partly because of such a theological understanding, many Muslim figures affiliated themselves with the rulers' party of Golkar, especially from the early 1980s. This was a clear indication of the decline of the politics of *aliran*.[41] As a result, for the next three general elections the Islamic party of PPP, having been forced to change its Islamic basis and symbol, suffered substantial losses. In these three general elections, PPP was only able to collect 15.97 per cent (1987), 17.0 per cent (1992), and 22.43 per cent (1997) of the votes.[42]

How genuine was the decline of *aliran* politics during the New Order regime? If religious orientations are believed to have a prevalent role in shaping and influencing party affiliation, then the answer is negative, though it is important to note that in some cases, the post-Soeharto *aliran* politics may not have been as strong as it was in the 1950s. But, in spite of the fact that a substantial transformation with regard to the political ideas and practices of Muslims had taken place over the three decades of the New Order period, many Muslim political activists still adhere to a formalistic and legalistic political Islam in the new democratic Indonesia. They regard the adoption of Islam as the party basis to be part of their democratic right. Likewise is their effort to insert the Jakarta Charter into the Constitution as well as Islamic *shari'a* into the country's legal system. During the 1999 election campaign, they also called for Muslims to give their votes to Islamic parties. Thus, comparable to the dynamic of politics during the liberal democracy of the 1950s, the collapse of Soeharto's authoritarian rule and the country's democratic euphoria have given rise to a legalistic and formalistic political Islam — more or less, the kind of political Islam which the New Order's authoritarian regime denied rights to.

It was within such a perspective — that democracy allows its citizens to express even their primordial interests and in fact considers it as part of their democratic right — that twenty Islamic political parties participated in the second democratic general elections in 1999. Out of that number, only ten Islamic parties gained one seat or more in the parliament. These include PPP (58 seats), PKB (51 seats), PAN (34 seats), PBB (13 seats), PK (7 seats), PNU (5 seats), PP (1 seat), PSII (1 seat), PPII Masyumi (1 seat), and PKU (1 seat).[43] Once again, the 1999 election results indicated that regardless of the fact that the majority of the Indonesians are Muslims, Islamic parties remained unable to marshal majority support. Put together, in this second democratic elections, they received only 37.5 per cent of the votes (172 seats), including PKB and PAN, which are reluctant to be identified as Islamic parties. Without these last two parties, they gained only 17.8 per cent of the votes (87 seats).[44]

The poor performance of Islamic parties and the fact that non-Islamic parties gained 62.5 per cent of the votes (290 seats) has been used by some to suggest that *aliran* politics has lost its importance in post-Soeharto Indonesian politics. Nurcholish Madjid, for instance, is of the opinion that there has been a big shift in the nation's political outlook, where political constituents look more for substance than symbol. For him, this is the defining factor which differentiates today's politics from that of the 1950s.[45]

If, on the one hand, better performance of the non-Islamic political parties and, on the other, poor performance of Islamic parties is to be treated as an important factor in determining the disappearance or existence of the politics of *aliran*, then it is also appropriate to regard the 1955 elections as characterized by non-partisan politics. It was so because — in spite of the fact that Muslims constituted 90 per cent of the population — non-Islamic parties did better than the Islamic ones. Apparently, a sizeable proportion of Muslims chose to give their votes to non-Islamic parties (that is, PNI, PSI, or perhaps even PKI). As already mentioned, four Islamic parties gained only 43.5 per cent of the votes, while non-Islamic parties received 55.3 per cent of the votes.

Still, students of Indonesian politics tend to see the liberal democracy politics in the light of *aliran* perspective. This is simply because of the fact that Islam was deliberately used as a political flag carrier for certain political parties. Though losing much of its significance, this was also the case during the New Order's first three general elections. It was only after the state prohibited the use of Islam as a political symbol that the politics of *aliran* began to wane, though not necessarily vanish in substance. And when the power which hindered the politics of *aliran* crumbled, it re-emerged with the use of Islam as a political symbol and ideology. Though the motivation is yet to be fully unfolded, many believe that the *raison d'être* for this is basically religious. The fact that PPP — immediately after the holding of the Majelis Permusyawaratan Rakyat (MPR) special session in 1998 — decided to replace Pancasila and the Star with Islam and the Ka'bah as its party basis and symbol only confirmed this line of argument.

The fact that Islam has been used as a party symbol and platform may have reduced the level of acceptance of Islamic parties in the eyes of the public. The poor performance of eighteen Islamic parties (minus PKB and PAN), which gained only 17.8 per cent of the votes in the 1999 general elections, could in part be attributed to the use of Islam as party ideology and platform. It is a mistake, however, to suggest that their poor performance was simply due to the fact that they used Islam as their political flag. If substance or party programmes were indeed the defining factors of the 1999 elections *vis-à-vis* the 1955 elections, there is great difficulty in viewing Partai Demokrasi Indonesia — Perjuangan's (PDI-P) triumph from such a perspective. Academically, there has been no single attempt to attribute PDI-P's gain of 33.73 per cent of the votes (153 seats) to substance or party programmes. Instead, many have argued that the New Order's ill-treatment of PDI (before its transformation into PDI-P) and the fact that this party is led by Soekarno's daughter were the main ingredients in its success.

Based on this line of argument, it is safe to say that the public did not see the 1999 elections in the light of substance or party programmes. Rather, they saw it more as a protest vote against the New Order's incumbents, and regarded Megawati as its primary adversarial or oppositional symbol.

How then is the poor performance of Islamic parties in the 1999 general elections to be explained? There are at least two important factors which may help our understanding of the disappointing results in the 1999 elections for the Islamic political groups. First is the flaw of the argument that religious adherence will automatically be translated into political affiliation. Time and again, this viewpoint has never materialized throughout Indonesia's political history. Even when the *aliran* politics was at its height, religious sentiments could not entirely be used to marshal majority support. The unwillingness to accept this very fact has led many Muslim political practitioners to take Islam *vis-à-vis* politics for granted, instead of focusing their energies and potential on factors — not necessarily related to programmes and substance — which will enable them to attract swinging as well as non-traditional voters. This requires a sufficient understanding of the demographic character and the socio-cultural and political orientations of the voters. Likewise is the need to understand public psychology given the fact that the nation is experiencing socio-economic and political changes unprecedented in history. Relying on religion as a political resource to mobilize supporters may not be necessarily useful. In fact, recalling the opinions of a number of Muslim figures prior to election day, it was proven to be counterproductive.

Secondly, even though it is a mistake to see Islamic parties in the light of the past, the fact remains that the historical stigma still haunted the 1999 general elections. The inability of Islamic parties to articulate themselves in a way which differed from other existing non-Islamic parties only intensified that stigma. Because of this, the mere existence of Islamic political parties would always be equated with the idea of Islamic state or the insertion of the *shari'a* into the country's legal system. This sentiment hardly dies and is likely to continue in the foreseeable future of Indonesia's political development.[46]

If one cares to examine the written platforms of any existing Islamic parties, one will find that the idea of Islam as the basis of the state is hardly mentioned.[47] During the transition to democracy period, no single Islamic party has ever publicly demonstrated its commitment to replacing Pancasila with Islam as the basis of the state. In fact, the idea of inserting the Jakarta Charter into Article 29 of the Constitution was entertained only after the parliamentary decision to amend the Constitution was taken in the MPR's 1999 general assembly.

Accordingly, it is only fair to argue that the so-called "politics of fear", with regard to what political Islam can actually bring about, has taken a firm root among significant segments of the Indonesian population. The failure of the Islamic parties to realize this fact and to respond to it in an honest and objective way has only intensified that fear. So it was only natural for many voters who did not seem to be able to overlook that particular stigma to give their support to parties compatible with their religious-ideological preferences.

Putting the historical stigma aside, in reality there is nothing to be afraid of with regard to the emergence of political Islam. In a democratic state it has been primarily manifested in the form of Islamic political parties using Islam as their ideological basis and symbol. Both the 1955 and 1999 democratic elections proved that, in spite of the fact that Muslims constitute a majority, Islamic parties could not collect the largest number of votes. Based on the lengthy discussion presented above, it suffices to say that Muslims are destined to have different — and sometimes even contradictory — political aspirations. In so far as they are diverse and unable to express and articulate the idea of political Islam in the light of public interests, then it will be very difficult for Islamic political parties to be a dominant force on Indonesia's political stage.

NON-PARTY POLITICAL ISLAM:
SHARI'A IMPLEMENTATION AND THE IDEA OF A
PAN-ISLAMIC WORLD?

But it is not only the emergence of Islamic political parties that has created apprehension and alarm. Besides what has been suggested, the New Order's departure was also followed by the rise of a number of Islamic organizations. Apparently, the opening of the Pandora's box did not only encourage the development of political parties, but also the emergence of various socio-religious organizations. In a situation in which politics seems to be the only game in town, these organizations regarded themselves as instruments to express and channel Islamic aspirations. In fact, more than the existing Islamic parties, they often articulated their interests in a strong and forceful way which made others see them in the light of radicalism. This is especially true with respect to their calls for *shari'a* implementation.

Thus, other than giving more weight to what has been addressed by several Islamic political parties, their existence has been viewed as a confirmation of "the rising tide of Indonesian (political) Islam".[48] Their blunt outlook and militant tendency in communicating Islam has led many to observe their resurgence in the light of the past. The context of a globalized world has also encouraged them to relate this new development to the worldwide trend of political Islam. This is not to suggest that these religious organizations have connections with the international Islamic movement, though they might share comparable ideas and thoughts.[49]

Unlike the Islamic parties, the birth of these organizations was not an immediate response to Indonesia's democratic transition. Instead, their development was more a reaction to the socio-religious and political circumstances which evolved during the period of transition, which in their view did not seem in accord with Islamic values or Muslim interests. The inability of the state to administer effectively and solve pressing problems that concern the lives of many Muslims (for example, socio-religious conflicts, law enforcement on gambling and prostitution, and regulation of alcoholic beverages) has triggered the emergence of these Islamic groups.[50] Similarly, the foreign policy of the United States towards the Islamic world, which is often perceived as uneven-handed, discriminatory, and unjust, especially concerning the Palestinian nation, has also contributed to their emergence.[51]

These Islamic organizations include, to name only the most prominent ones, Front Pembela Islam (FPI, Islamic Defenders Front); Forum Komunikasi Ahlus Sunnah Wal Jamaah (FKASWJ, Ahl al-Sunnah wa al-Jama'ah Forum) along with its militia wing Lasykar Jihad (Jihad Brigade); Majelis Mujahidin Indonesia (MMI, Indonesian Mujahidin Council) along with its Lasykar Mujahidin (Mujahidin Brigade); Hizbu al-Tahrir (Independence Party); Hammas (Inter-Campus Muslim Students Association); Front Hizbullah (Hizbullah Front); Ikhwanul Muslimin; and the relatively much older organization Kisdi (Komite Indonesia untuk Solidaritas Dunia Islam, Indonesian Committee for Islamic World Solidarity).[52]

All of these groups seem to share the same concern — that is, that Islamic *shari'a* should have been taken more seriously by the state as well as the greater Muslim society. Such a viewpoint is based primarily on three important factors — theological, demographic, and socio-political. The first factor emphasizes the fact that Islam is perceived as a religion which offers guidance and solutions to all aspects of life — socio-cultural, economic, political, and so forth. This position has led them to believe that all Muslims are religiously obliged to base all aspects of their lives on Islamic values and teachings as outlined in the *shari'a*. The second factor refers to the fact that the majority of Indonesians are Muslims. Adherents of Islam constitute 87 per cent of the country's population. For the proponents of Islam this fact alone should function as socio-cultural and political legitimacy for making Islam the basis of the state — or at least to recognize Islamic *shari'a* as a core ingredient or an integral part of the Constitution.[53] The last factor points to the fact that the secular-positive law has not brought about socio-cultural, economic, legal, and political improvements for Muslims. In their view, for more than half a century, Indonesia has been plagued with a number of socio-economic and political misfortunes — with the recent multidimensional crises as its pinnacle — for which only Islam can serve as the ultimate solution.[54]

Should this be the case, then it is fair to argue that what these organizations aspire to is actually reminiscent of what had been articulated and aggregated by the Islamic groups in the 1940s and 1950s. This means that for more than a half century, Indonesia's national elite have not been able to come to terms with the position of Islam in this archipelagic nation state. As a result, the question of Islam — especially issues related to the implementation of Islamic *shari'a* — has tended to become a recurrent issue. Unless a negotiated settlement can be reached, it will always re-emerge in various forms, depending on the situation.

In spite of the fact that these new Islamic organizations share a common concern, one should not jump to the conclusion that they are in agreement on every aspect related to the implementation of Islamic *shari'a*. Like the Islamic groups in the past, they seem to have substantial differences of opinion on this matter. Precisely because of this, the issue of Islamic *shari'a* has never been discussed and exposed in great details — that is, what constitutes Islamic *shari'a*, how it is to be understood and interpreted, which interpretation should be adopted and followed, how it is to be applied, and so forth.

According to Aswar Hassan, the secretary general of the Committee for the Implementation of Islamic *Shari'a* (Komite Pelaksana Syariat Islam, KPSI), all of these issues are crucial. In fact, realizing the differences that these Islamic groups have, they might serve as a divisive factor for their movement and struggle.[55] Islam, as mentioned repeatedly earlier in this book, is one religion but its expressions and interpretations are many. The fact that Islam recognizes no religious priesthood that could provide a unified legal product that binds all Muslims is a major source of weakness in any attempt to institutionalize Islamic teachings in a single legal entity. All Muslims believe in the Qur'an and Sunnah, yet they differ greatly in their understanding of these two most important sources of Islam. (Un)fortunately, Islam does not give the right to anyone to claim that his or her religious understanding is better or truer than that of others. Expecting all Muslims to respect and follow the government's decisions on matters such as when the fasting month of Ramadhan begins and ends is already a difficult task, let alone binding them in a single, unified codification of Islamic law.

Realizing the difficulty of bringing all Muslims into the same fold in terms of an understanding of Islamic law has led these Islamic groups to express their views in a relatively general tone. Since the fall of the

Soeharto government, basically they only call for the need to implement Islamic *shari'a* in all aspects of life. This has been generally carried out in a peaceful manner, through the dissemination of ideas and thoughts, writings, and speaking.

A notable exception, however, should be attributed to FPI. This organization, other than calling for the implementation of Islamic *shari'a*, often took matters related to the regulations of gambling, pornography, prostitution, and the sale and consumption of alcoholic beverages into its own hands, which regretfully involved violence. As such, it has served as a spectre which haunted particularly those who worked in the gambling, pornographic, prostitution, and alcoholic beverages industries.[56] It is widely understood that Islam prohibits gambling, pornography, prostitution, and the consumption of alcoholic beverages. Even though Indonesia is not an Islamic state, there are legal provisions which prohibit gambling, pornography, and prostitution, except in localized areas — a policy which frequently invites criticism from many Muslim figures and institutions. In addition, there are also legal restrictions concerning the sale and production of alcoholic beverages. Because of this, it is fair to say that FPI — or any other Islamic organizations for that matter — actually has the right to voice opposition against gambling and prostitution practices as well as against the consumption of alcoholic beverages. This is in so far as it is carried out in full compliance with existing laws and regulations.

It is also worth mentioning that other than calling for the implementation of Islamic *shari'a*, FKASWJ sent its militia wing (Lasykar Jihad) to several conflict areas (for example, Ambon, Maluku, and Poso) with the main purpose of providing necessary assistance to their fellow Muslims who suffered attacks from non-Muslims. In their view, those who are by law responsible for establishing and keeping the peace were unable to provide safety and protection to Muslims. Out of solidarity, they have lent their strong hands to their Muslim counterparts in the conflict areas.[57] It was in one of these areas (that is, Ambon) that their strong commitment to implement Islamic *shari'a* was realized. One of its members (Abdullah) confessed to having committed adultery, and voluntarily requested to be stoned to death as a consequence of his belief in the *rajam* law.[58] Though the state guarantees freedom to its citizens to implement their religious practices, nevertheless putting such a law into effect contravenes the country's existing positive rules and regulations.

Adding to a general perception that the politics of Islamization is on the rise in the post-Soeharto years is the fact that many regions began to demand the implementation of Islamic *shari'a*. The decision of the central government to grant a wide range of autonomy to the regions has been viewed as an opportunity for the implementation of Islamic law. Even though religion, under government regulation No. 22/1999, is not a subject to be regulated regionally, nonetheless a number of regional governments took the necessary steps to implement what they perceived as Islamic *shari'a*. The districts of Pamekasan (East Java), Maros, Sinjai, and Gowa (South Sulawesi), Cianjur, Garut, and Indramayu (West Java) are now beginning to implement certain aspects of Islamic *shari'a*. They range from the wearing of Islamic dress, regulating the collection and distribution of *zakat* (religious alms), performing prayers and reciting the Qur'an, and allocating more time for religious subjects to be taught in schools.[59] The fact that Aceh, having been granted autonomous status by the central government, since 2000 has been officially administered by Islamic jurisprudence, only re-energized scattered efforts to implement Islamic *shari'a*.[60]

Besides the demand for the implementation of Islamic *shari'a*, these Islamic groups also frequently entertain the idea of an Islamic state. Though this remains infant in its development, they often refer to the idea of an Islamic state in the glorious history of Islam, from the classical period down to the early twentieth century, when the pan-Islamic world was governed under the caliphate (*khilafah*) system.[61] It is still not clear whether Indonesia would eventually be transformed into such a state, but for FPI chairman Habib Rizieq state typology is not important. In his view, the prophet Mohammad was more concerned with the formation of a Muslim society than an Islamic state. Thus, for him, as long as the state is administered in accordance with Islamic *shari'a,* there is no immediate need to question the religious legitimacy of such a state.[62]

It has been repeatedly claimed that these Islamic organizations use no violent measures in their attempts to realize their objectives. With the exception of FPI's radical opposition to the continuing practice of gambling, pornography, prostitution, and alcoholic consumption, and Lasykar Jihad's involvement in the conflict areas of Ambon and Maluku in particular, the general tone of the articulation of Islamic *shari'a* has been a peaceful one.[63] However, their adversaries tend to identify the whole movement as radical and/or hard-line and as a movement that may resort to violent acts. The psychological effects of the dreadful Bali bombing of October 2002 — allegedly masterminded by the Jama'ah Islamiyah leadership, working with the locals and assumed to have connection with the Al-Qaedah network — which took the lives of over 180 people and injured nearly 300 innocents, gave further impetus to such a stereotypical view.[64] In fact, because of its international flavour, which included the worldwide campaign against terrorism led by the United States, Great Britain, and Australia, such an event has brought about certain impacts not only on the *shari'a* movement, but also on political Islam in general. Though it may not be for a long time, the horrifying event has put political Islam in a very difficult and awkward position. Given the weak position of the Indonesian state, as long as international forces remain suspicious of political Islam, the likelihood is that the latter will turn inward, or at best moderate its rhetoric and objectives. The fact that shortly after the blast Lasykar Jihad voluntarily disbanded itself and FPI froze its activities are indications of the difficult position of political Islam.[65]

CONCLUSION: TOWARDS A PARTIAL ACCOMMODATION OF ISLAM

From what has been presented at length, it is difficult not to see the development of political Islam during the post-Soeharto period in the light of legalism and formalism. The intellectual transformation which occurred between the 1970s and 1990s seemed to have lost its significance when ideological, symbolic, and formal Islam gave the impression of dominating the new discourse on Indonesia's political Islam. The use of Islam as a party basis, the call for the implementation of Islamic *shari'a*, the attempt to insert the Jakarta Charter into the new Constitution, and opposition to Megawati's presidential candidacy in 1999, based on the religious argument that men are to lead (or be stronger than) women, are clear indicators of the rising tide of political Islamism.

In spite of this new development, one should not view it as a genuine phenomenon. In fact, the birth of forty-two Islamic parties, like other parties, has to been seen from the perspective of the shifting pendulum of Indonesia's political system, from authoritarian to democratic rule. This means that one should always question whether such new developments are genuine or permanent in nature. At a time when transition seems to be characterized by some degree of socio-economic and political fluidity, not to say breakdown, it is difficult to see things with certainty. The fact that only twenty Islamic parties met the electoral requirements in 1999, and only ten gained one or more seat, suggests that this new development is primarily due to the euphoric and myopic nature of the transition, rather than to a well thought-out and deliberated religious-political determination. When those who earlier opposed Megawati's presidential candidacy finally accepted her victory in her constitutional appointment to succeed

Abdurrahman Wahid to become the country's fifth president, this indicated that religious considerations are only temporarily and not permanently upheld. Should religious principles become a determining factor in politics, any leadership posts contested by Megawati or any female candidates for that matter should have been rejected.

A similar viewpoint can also be used to understand the fact that PPP, PBB, and PDU politicians, who fought for the insertion of the Jakarta Charter into the new Constitution during the process of amendment, eventually gave up their cause and did not block moves to stick to the original formulation of Article 29, which says that the state is based on one God. They might have accepted their constitutional defeats on a temporary basis. However, their choice not to have the case settled by way of voting can also cast doubt on their religious convictions in politics. Therefore, unlike the earlier Muslim politicians in the Constituent Assembly who tackled the issue by way of voting — though neither side of the spectrum received adequate support to win its cause — post-New Order Muslim politicians appear to have moderated themselves with regard to their efforts to articulate and aggregate Islamic interests.

What seems to be more certain is that the level and magnitude of support for ideological and symbolical Islam are relatively low and small. The majority of Muslims, as signified by the limited number of seats enjoyed by Islamic forces in the parliament and the rejection of the Jakarta Charter, remain moderate and aspire to a more viable and proper relationship between Islam and the state. This view is also shared by the two most important religious organizations in the country — Muhammadiyah and NU. In the light of Indonesia's political history, it is fair to say that in two democratic situations, a legalist and formalist political Islam was unequivocally defeated. Its fate and destiny, to say the least, was even bleaker in an authoritarian political setting.

This is not to suggest, however, that the majority of Muslims (politicians) oppose Islamic *shari'a*. Being Muslim, they accept the significance of *shari'a* and are obliged to implement Islamic teachings in all aspects of life. Yet they differ greatly with regard to how *shari'a* is to be understood, interpreted, and implemented. They do not believe that Islamic *shari'a* should be adopted in its entirety and serve as the positive law of the land. Instead, they share the idea that certain elements of Islamic *shari'a* can be formulated into legally binding law, such as on issues related to marriage and divorce, inheritance and endowment, *zakat* collection and distribution, the pilgrimage, and the like. The fact that many Muslims feel that the state's accommodation of Islamic law is still limited has not stopped them from struggling within the bounds of the existing system, laws, and regulations.

Having said this, it is safe to argue that partial accommodation seems to be a viable option for a more enduring relationship between Islam and the state. The commonly shared notion that Indonesia is neither a theocratic nor a secular state only suggests the importance of the obligatory nature of the state in accommodating the interests of Muslims. At the same time, realizing the heterogeneity of Indonesia's socio-religious origins, it is the task of all Muslims to articulate and express their interests in so far as they do not disrupt the construct of the country's nation state. For more than a half century, this country has been unable to conduct an uninterrupted dialogue concerning the proper role and position of religion in the state. In the 1940s and 1950s the effort was hampered by pressure of time and Soekarno's and the military's political manoeuvrings. Throughout the period of the New Order government, the debate was forbidden because of the deep-seated suspicions of the state regarding its disruptive potentials. Taking into consideration all the lessons we have learned in the last fifty years or so, it is time for the national elite — religious as well as political — to undertake such an important dialogue in order to reach an appropriate settlement.

Notes

1. Amien Rais, "Islam and Politics in Contemporary Indonesia", in *Post-Soeharto Indonesia: Renewal or Chaos?*, edited by Geoff Forrester (Singapore: Institute of Southeast Asian Studies, 1999), p. 201.

2. For a useful account of the crises, see Richard Mann, *Economic Crisis in Indonesia: The Full Story* (Singapore: Times Books, 1998). See also his *Plots and Schemes that Brought Down Soeharto* (Singapore: Gateway Books, 1998).

3. See "Rusuh di Medan, Padang, Yogya", *Gatra*, 16 May 1998, pp. 24–33; "Huru-Hara Jakarta", *Gatra*, 23 May 1998. See also relevant essays compiled in Geoff Forrester and R.J. May, eds., *The Fall of Soeharto* (Singapore: SelectBooks, 1999). In his article published in this book, Ikrar Nusa Bhakti notes that the Jakarta riot alone caused "more than 1,000 people, mostly looters, [to] die, trapped inside burning shopping malls. Official statistics show that at least 2,547 shops/houses, 40 malls, 1,819 stores, 383 office buildings, 535 banks, 24 restaurants, 15 markets, 12 hotels, 1,026 houses, 2 churches, 11 police stations, 1,119 cars, 821 motorcycles, and 9 gas stations were damaged or burned during the riots. Compared to previous riots in 1966 and 1974, the riots of 1998 can be regarded as the worst ever experienced in Indonesia." See his "Chronology of Events Leading to the Resignation of President Soeharto", in *The Fall of Soeharto*, p. 243.

4. In the afternoon of 18 May 1998 Harmoko, in his capacity as chairman of the People's Consultative Assembly/People's Representative Council, accompanied by his deputies, called for Soeharto's resignation. Two days later (20 May), fourteen ministers, including Akbar Tanjung, A.M. Hendropriyono, Ginandjar Kartasasmita, Giri Suseno Hadihardjono, Haryanto Dhanutirto, Justika S. Baharsjah, Kuntoro Mangkusubroto, Rachmadi Bambang Sumadhijo, Rahardi Ramelan, Subiakto Tjakrawerdaya, Sanyoto Sastrowardoyo, Sumahadi, Theo L. Sambuaga, and Tanri Abeng, resigned. For a description of Soeharto's final days, see "Reformasi Belum Selesai", *Gatra*, 30 May 1998, especially pp. 24–40. See also Ikrar Nusa Bhakti, "Chronology of Events Leading to the Resignation of President Soeharto", in *The Fall of Soeharto*, pp. 239–45.

5. For a good account of this period, see Geoff Forrester, ed., *Post-Soeharto Indonesia: Renewal or Chaos?*

6. The best treatment on this issue is still Guillermo O'Donnell and Philippe C. Schmitter, *Transitions from Authoritarian Rule: Tentative Conclusions about Uncertain Democracies* (Baltimore and London: Johns Hopkins University Press, 1986).

7. For a good grasp of this issue, see Michael R.J. Vatikiotis, *Indonesian Politics under Suharto: Order, Development, and Pressure for Change* (London and New York: Routledge, 1993); Adam Schwarz, *A Nation in Waiting: Indonesia in the 1990s* (St. Leonards: Allen & Unwin, 1994).

8. Not all of these parties registered with the Department of Justice. According to one report, only 141 parties registered. See *Partai-Partai Politik Indonesia: Ideologi, Strategi, dan Program* (Jakarta: Litbang *Kompas*, 1999), pp. xi-xii.

9. According to Arsekal Salim, who conducted primary research on this issue, those forty-two parties are: (1) Partai Ahlu Sunnah wal Jamaah, PAS; (2) Partai Aliansi Kebangkitan Muslim Sunni Indonesia, AKAMSI; (3) Partai Abul Yatama, PAY; (4) Partai Amanah Masyarakat Madani, PAMM; (5) Partai Amanat Nasional, PAN; (6) Partai Bhakti Muslim, PBM; (7) Partai Bulan Bintang, PBB; (8) Partai Cinta Damai, PCD; (9) Partai Demokrasi Islam Republik Indonesia, PADRI; (10) Partai Dinamika Umat, PDU; (11) Partai Dua Syahadat, PDS; (12) Partai Era Reformasi Tarbiyah Islamiyah, PERTI; (13) Partai Indonesia Baru, PIB; (14) Partai Islam Demokrat, PID; (15) Partai Islam Indonesia, PII; (16) Partai Islam Persatuan Indonesia, PIPI; (17) Partai Gerakan Insan Muttaqin Indonesia, GIMI; (18) Partai Ka'bah; (19) Partai Keadilan, PK; (20) Partai Kebangkitan Bangsa, PKB; (21) Partai Kebangkitan Kaum Ahlussunnah Wal Jamaah, PAKKAM; (22) Partai Kebangkitan Muslim Indonesia, KAMI: (23) Partai Kebangkitan Umat, PKU; (24) Partai Kesatuan Umat Indonesia, PKUI; (25) Partai Kesatuan Wahdatul Ummah, PKWU; (26) Partai Politik Islam Masyumi, PPIM; (27) Partai Majawangi; (28) Partai Masyumi Baru, PMB; (29) Partai Nahdlatul Ummah, PNU; (30) Partai Persatuan, PP; (31) Partai Persatuan Islam Indonesia, PPII; (32) Partai Persatuan Pembangunan, PPP; (33) Partai Persatuan Sabilillah, PPS; (34) Partai Pengamal Thareqat Indonesia, PPTI; (35) Partai Persatuan Tharikat Islam, PPTI; (36) Partai Politik Thareqat Islam, PPTI; (37) Partai Republik Islam, PRI; (38) Partai Solidaritas Uni Indonesia, Partai SUNI; (39)

Partai Syarikat Islam Indonesia, PSII 1905; (40) Partai Syarikat Islam Indonesia, PSII; (41) Partai Umat Islam, PUI; and (42) Partai Umat Muslimin Indonesia, PUMI. Out of this number, only thirty-five Islamic political parties met the requirements stipulated by the Department of Justice. Further, only twenty of them were eligible, through a verification process, to participate in the 7 June 1999 general elections. See Arsekal Salim, *Partai Islam dan Relasi Agama-Negara* (Jakarta: Pusat Penilitian IAIN Jakarta, 1999), pp. 7–12.

10. Fazlur Rahman, *Islam* (New York, Chicago, and San Francisco: Holt, Rinehart, and Winston, 1966), p. 241.

11. See a range of essays in Bahtiar Effendy, *(Re)politisasi Islam: Pernahkah Islam Berhenti Berpolitik?* (Bandung: Mizan, 2000).

12. For a background, see the discussion in chapter 2. For contemporary accounts, see the collection of essays in Musa Kazhim and Alfian Hamzah, eds., *5 Partai Islam dalam Timbangan: Analisis dan Prospek* (Jakarta: Pustaka Hidayah, 1999); Sahar L. Hassan, Kuat Sukardiyono, and Dadi M.H. Basri, eds., *Memilih Partai Islam: Visi, Misi, dan Persepsi* (Jakarta: Gema Insani Press, 1998).

13. Kuntowijoyo, "Enam Alasan untuk Tidak Mendirikan Parpol Islam", *Republika*, 18 July 1998.

14. See, for instance, M. Syafii Anwar, *Pemikiran dan Aksi Islam Indonesia: Sebuah Kajian Politik tentang Cendekiawan Muslim Orde Baru* (Jakarta: Paramadina, 1995).

15. One of the reasons why NU left Masyumi — an Islamic political party dominated by Muhammadiyah and other modernist elements of Indonesian Islam — was a political-bureaucratic rivalry between Muhammadiyah and NU over the Ministry of Religion. See Deliar Noer, *Partai Islam di Pentas Nasional 1945–1965* (Jakarta: Pustaka Utama Grafiti, 1987).

16. For a fuller account, see Clifford Geertz, *The Social History of an Indonesian Town* (Cambridge: MIT, 1965).

17. Kuntowijoyo, op. cit.

18. See relevant essays in Effendy, op. cit.

19. Rais, op. cit., p. 201.

20. See *Risalah Sidang Badan Penyelidik Usaha-Usaha Persiapan Kemerdekaan Indonesia (BPUPKI)* (Jakarta: Sekretariat Negara Republik Indonesia, 1995).

21. For a valuable account, see Noer, op. cit.; Ahmad Syafii Maarif, "Islam as the Basis of State: A Study of the Islamic Political Ideas as Reflected in the Constituent Assembly Debates in Indonesia" (Ph.D. dissertation, University of Chicago, 1983).

22. See, for instance, Allan Samson, "Islam and Politics in Indonesia" (Ph.D. dissertation, University of California, Berkeley, 1972); B.J. Boland, *The Struggle of Islam in Modern Indonesia* (The Hague: Martinus Nijhoff, 1971).

23. See, for instance, Nurcholish Madjid, "Integrasi Keislaman dalam Keindonesiaan untuk Menatap Masa Depan Bangsa" (Speech delivered at the opening of

Paramadina's Religious Study Club, Jakarta, 1986); Munawir Syadzali, "Wawasan Perjuangan Muslim Indonesia" (Paper presented at the HMI's forty-third commemoration, Yogyakarta, 4 February 1990).

24. See discussions in chapters 4, 5, and 6.

25. See, for instance, Deliar Noer, *Islam dan Pemikiran Politik: Bahasan Kitab Islam dan Tata Negara: Ajaran, Sejarah dan Pemikiran oleh H. Munawir Syadzali MA* (Jakarta: LIPPM, 1990).

26. See Bahtiar Effendy, "Fenomena Partai Islam", in *(Re)politisasi Islam: Pernahkah Islam Berhenti Berpolitik*, pp. 205–9.

27. Interview with former President B.J. Habibie in his Kakerbeck's residence, Germany, 2–4 July 2002. When asked for his view on the birth of numerous political parties, he said that it was a part of Indonesia's democratic experience. For a full description of his presidency, see Bilveer Singh, *Habibie and the Democratisation of Indonesia* (Sydney: Book House, 2001).

28. See Bahtiar Effendy, "(Re)politisasi Islam: Pernahkah Islam Berhenti Berpolitik?", in *(Re)politisasi Islam: Pernahkah Islam Berhenti Berpolitik*, pp. 195–99.

29. See *Republika*, 7 June 1998.

30. See "The Rising Tide of Indonesian Islam?", *Van Zorge Report on Indonesia* 2, no. 20 (30 November 2000): 4–21.

31. To cite a few examples, Partai Abul Yatama (Pancasila, 1945 Constitution, and the Qur'an and Hadits; Partai Cinta Damai (Pancasila); PAN (Pancasila); Partai Umat Muslimin Indonesia (Pancasila); Partai Indonesia Baru (Pancasila and 1945 Constitution); PKB (Pancasila); Partai Kebangkitan Umat (Pancasila); Partai Nahdlatul Ummah (Pancasila, Islam, and Ahl al-Sunnah wa al-Jama'ah); Partai Solidaritas Uni Indonesia (Pancasila); Partai Syarikat Islam Indonesia (Pancasila); and so forth.

32. In fact, such a manoeuvre was not supported by all members of PKB. Reportedly, there was a handful of party members who gave their votes to Megawati to become the fourth president.

33. Interview with Hajriyanto Y. Thohari in Jakarta, 28 August 2002.

34. Interview with Hajriyanto Y. Thohari in Jakarta, 28 August 2002.

35. See Bahtiar Effendy, "Antara Substansialisme dan Formalisme", *Panji Masyarakat*, no. 40, special ed. (2000).

36. See Lee Oey Hong, *Indonesia after the 1971 Elections* (London and Kuala Lumpur: Hull Monograph Series on Southeast Asia, no. 5, Oxford University Press, 1974); Afan Gaffar, *The Javanese Voters: A Case Study of Election under a Hegemonic Party System* (Yogyakarta: Gadjah Mada University Press, 1992); Leo Suryadinata, *Elections and Politics in Indonesia* (Singapore: Institute of Southeast Asian Studies, 2002).

37. For a full description of the elections, see Herbert Feith, *The Indonesian Elections of 1955* (Ithaca: Modern Indonesia Project, Southeast Asia Program,

Cornell University, 1957). See also Noer, *Partai Islam di Pentas Nasional 1945–1965*.

38. See Geertz, op. cit.; Robert Jay, *Religion and Politics in Rural Central Java* (New Haven: Southeast Asia Studies, Yale University, 1963).

39. Geertz, op. cit.

40. Suryadinata, op. cit., p. 32.

41. For a useful account of the decline of *aliran* politics, see Fachry Ali and Iqbal Abdurrauf Saimima, "Merosotnya Aliran dalam Partai Persatuan Pembangunan", in *Analisa Kekuatan Politik di Indonesia: Pilihan Artikel Prisma* (Jakarta: LP3ES, 1985), pp. 226–61.

42. Suryadinata, op. cit., p. 32.

43. See "Allocation of Seats to Political Parties for the People's Representative Assembly (DPR)" (International Foundation for Election Systems (IFES), 9 September 1999), p. vii. See also Kamaruddin, "Partisipasi Politik Islam di Indonesia: Studi tentang Aksi Partai Politik Islam pada Masa Reformasi (1998–99)" (Unpublished M.A. thesis, Graduate Studi Program, University of Indonesia, 2001), p. 223.

44. Suryadinata, op. cit., p. 106; Kamaruddin, op. cit., pp. 223–25.

45. See *Forum Keadilan*, no. 12 (27 June 1991).

46. For a range of essays on the defeat of political Islam, see Hamid Basyaib and Hamid Abidin, eds., *Mengapa Partai Islam Kalah?: Perjalanan Politik Islam dari Pra Pemilu sampai Pemilihan Presiden* (Jakarta: Alvabet, 1999).

47. See *Partai-Partai Politik Indonesia: Ideologi, Strategi, dan Program*; Salim, op. cit.; Kazhim and Hamzah, op. cit.; Hassan, Sukardiyono, and Basri, op. cit.

48. See "The Rising Tide of Indonesian Islam?", *Van Zorge Report on Indonesia* 2, no. 20 (30 November 2000): 4–18.

49. See, for instance, Akbar S. Ahmed and Hastings Donnan, eds., *Islam, Globalization and Postmodernity* (London and New York: Routledge, 1994); Bernard Lewis, *What Went Wrong?: The Clash Between Islam and Modernity in the Middle East* (London: Weidenfeld & Nicolson, 2002).

50. See "Penelitian Radikalisme Agama dan Perubahan Sosial di DKI Jakarta" (Jakarta: Pusat Budaya dan Bahasa (PBB) dan Pemda DKI Jakarta, 2000).

51. For a general account of this issue, see Peter W. Singer, *Time for Hard Choices: The Dilemmas Facing U.S. Policy Towards the Islamic World* (Brookings Project on U.S. Policy Towards the Islamic World, Analysis Paper no. 1, October 2002).

52. See "Penelitian Radikalisme Agama dan Perubahan Sosial di DKI Jakarta". See also "Indonesian Islam, TNI and Political Stability", *Van Zorge Report*, 3, no. 18 (19 October 2001), pp. 5–18; Khamami Zada, *Islam Radikal: Pergulatan Ormas-Ormas Islam Garis Keras di Indonesia* (Jakarta: Teraju, 2002).

53. These factors were used by the earlier proponents of Islam as the basis of state in their arguments in the 1940s and 1950s. See Maarif, op. cit.

54. See "Syariat Islam yang Bagaimana", *Panjimas*, 27 November-12 December 2002. See also Irfan S. Awwas, *Risalah Kongres Mujahidin I dan Penegakan Syari'ah Islam* (Yogyakarta: Wihdah Press, 2001).

55. Interview in Makassar, 12 October 2002.

56. Zada, op. cit., pp. 162–63.

57. Ibid., p. 165. For a full description of the conflict, see *Merajut Damai di Maluku: Telaah Konflik antar Umat 1999–2000* (Jakarta: Majelis Ulama Indonesia, 2000).

58. See "Keikhlasan Abdullah Dihukum Rajam", *Republika*, 10 May 2001.

59. See "Syariat Untuk Penangkal Korupsi", *Tempo*, 17 November 2002, pp. 98–99.

60. See "Syariat Islam yang Bagaimana", *Panjimas*, 27 November-12 December 2002.

61. Zada, op. cit., pp. 108–29.

62. Ibid., p. 114.

63. See an essay by Irfan S. Awwas, executive chairman of Majelis Mujahidin Indonesia (MMI), "Menegakkan Syariat Tanpa Teror", *Tempo*, 24 November 2002, p. 127.

64. See special reports on the Bali bomb blast in *Tempo*, 21–27 October and 18–24 November 2002; *Gatra*, 26 October and 23 November 2002.

65. See "Tiarapnya Kekuatan Politik Islam", *Panjimas*, 27 November–12 December 2002, p.18.

Bibliography

Books, Articles, and Government Documents

Abdullah, Taufik. "Pola Kepemimpinan Islam di Indonesia". In *Islam dan Masyarakat: Pantulan Sejarah Indonesia*. Jakarta: LP3ES, 1987.

——. "*Zakat* Collection and Distribution in Indonesia". In *The Islamic Voluntary Sector in Southeast Asia*, edited by Mohamed Ariff. Singapore: Institute of Southeast Asian Studies, 1991.

Abdurrahim, Imaduddin. *Kuliah Tauhid*. Bandung: Pustaka Salman, 1979.

Abdurrahman, Moeslim. "Wong Cilik dan Kebutuhan Teologi Transformative". In *Teologi Pembangunan: Paradigma Baru Pemikiran Islam*, edited by M. Masyhur Amin. Yogyakarta: LKPSM NU DIY, 1989.

Adnan, Abdul Basit. *Ada Apa di PPP*. Solo: Mayasari, 1982.

Ahmed, Akbar S. and Hastings Donnan, eds. *Islam, Globalization and Postmodernity*. London and New York: Routledge, 1994.

Alfian. *Muhammadiyah: The Political Behavior of a Muslim Modernist Organization under Dutch Colonialism*. Yogyakarta: Gadjah Mada University Press, 1989.

Ali, Fachry and Bahtiar Effendy. *Merambah Jalan Baru Islam: Rekonstruksi Pemikiran Islam Indonesia Masa Order Baru*. Bandung: Mizan, 1986.

Ali, Fachry and Iqbal Abdurrauf Saimima. "Merosotnya Aliran dalam Partai Persatuan Pembangunan". In *Analisa Kekuatan Politik di Indonesia: Pilihan Artikel Prisma*. Jakarta: LP3ES, 1985.

Ali, M. Daud. "Undang-Undang Peradilan Agama: Sistematik dan Garis-Garis Besar Isinya". *Media Dakwah*, April 1990.

Ali, Syed Ameer. *The Spirit of Islam: A History of the Evolution and Ideals of Islam*. London: Chatto & Windus, 1978.

"Allocation of Seats to Political Parties for the People's Representative Assembly (DPR)". International Foundation for Election Systems (IFES), 9 September 1999.

Amal, Ichlasul. *Regional and Central Government in Indonesian Politics: West Sumatra and South Sulawesi 1949-1979*. Yogyakarta: Gadjah Mada University Press, 1992.

Amin, Masyhur, ed. *Teologi Pembangunan: Paradigma Baru Pemikiran Islam*. Yogyakarta: LKPSM NU DIY, 1989.

Anderson, Benedict R.O'G. "Religion and Politics in Indonesia Since Independence". In *Religion and Social Ethos in Indonesia*. Clayton: Monash University, 1977.

——. "The Languages of Indonesian Politics". *Indonesia*, no. 1 (April 1966).

——. "Old State, New Society: Indonesia's New Order in Comparative Historical Perspective". *Journal of Asian Studies* 42, no. 3 (May 1983).

Anshari, Endang Saifuddin and Amien Rais, eds. *Pak Natsir 80 Tahun*. Vols. 1 and 2. Jakarta: Media Dakwah, 1988.

Anshari, Saifuddin. "Soal Dasar Negara Bagi Kelompok Islam Sudah Lama Selesai, Bagaimana Bagi Kelompok Lainnya?". Unpublished paper, no date.

——. *Kritik Atas Faham dan Gerakan "Pembaharuan" Drs. Nurcholish Madjid*. Bandung: Bulan Sabit, 1973.

——. *The Jakarta Charter 1945: The Struggle for an Islamic Constitution in Indonesia*. Kuala Lumpur: Muslim Youth Movement of Malaysia (ABIM), 1979.

——. "Negara Islam". Unpublished interview material with Leppenas, 4 September 1982.

——. "Pokok-Pokok Pikiran Tentang Asas Tunggal: Sebuah Kerangka Ikhtisar". Unpublished paper. Bandung, February 1983.

Anwar, Syafi'i. "Islam, Negara, dan Formasi Sosial dalam Order Baru: Menguak Dimensi Sosio-Historis Kelahiran dan Perkembangan ICMI". *Ulumul Qur'an* 3, no. 3, supplement (1992).

——. *Pemikiran dan Aksi Islam Indonesia: Sebuah Kajian Politik tentang Cendekiawan Muslim Orde Baru*. Jakarta: Paramadina, 1995.

Arkoun, Mohammed. "The Concept of Authority in Islamic Thought". In *Islam: State and Society*, edited by Klauss Ferdinand and Mehdi Mozaffari. London: Curzon Press, 1988.

Arnold, T.W. "The Spread of Islam in the Malay Archipelago". In *The Preaching of Islam: A History of the Propagation of the Muslim Faith*, edited by T.W. Arnold. New York: AMS Press, 1974.

Asad, Muhammad. *The Principles of State and Government in Islam*. Berkeley and Los Angeles: University of California Press, 1961.

Awwas, Irfan S. *Risalah Kongres Mijahidin I dan Penegakan Syari'ah Islam.* Yogyakarta: Wihdah Press, 2001.

——. "Menegakkan Syariat Tanpa Teror". *Tempo*, 24 November 2002.

Ayoob, Mohammed, ed. *The Politics of Islamic Reassertion.* London: Croom Helm, 1981.

Ayubi, Nazih. *Political Islam: Religion and Politics in the Arab World.* London and New York: Routledge, 1991.

Azhari, Muntaha and Abdul Mun'im Saleh, eds. *Islam Indonesia Menatap Masa Depan.* Jakarta: P3M, 1989.

Aziz, Abdul, Imam Tolkhah, and Soetarman, eds. *Gerakan Islam Kontemporer di Indonesia.* Jakarta: Pustaka Firdaus, 1989.

Aziz, M.A. *Japan's Colonialism and Indonesia.* The Hague: Martinus Nijhoff, 1955.

Bachtiar, Harsya W. "The Religion of Java: A Commentary". *Madjalah Ilmu-Ilmu Sastra Indonesia* 5 (1973).

Bakri, Hasbullah. "Lima Dalil Republik Indonesia Bisa Disebut Negara Islam Non-Konstitusional". *Panji Masyarakat*, no. 439 (1 August 1984).

Barton, Greg. "The International Context of the Emergence of Islamic Neo Modernism in Indonesia". In *Islam in the Indonesian Social Context*, edited by M.C. Ricklefs. Clayton: Annual Indonesian Lectures Series, no. 15, Monash University, 1991.

Basyaib, Hamid and Hamid Abidin, eds. *Mengapa Partai Islam Kalah?: Perjalanan Politik Islam dari Pra Pemilu sampai Pemilihan Presiden.* Jakarta: Alvabet, 1999.

Bellah, Robert N. *Beyond Belief: Essays on Religion in a Post-Traditionalist World.* Berkeley and Los Angeles: University of California Press, 1991.

——. *The Broken Covenant: American Civil Religion in Time of Trial.* Chicago and London: University of Chicago Press, 1992.

Bellah, Robert N., Richard Madsen, William Sulivan, Ann Swindler, and Steve Tipton, eds. *Habits of the Heart: Individualism and Commitment in American Life.* New York: Harper & Row, 1986.

Benda, Harry J. *The Crescent and the Rising Sun: Indonesian Islam under the Japanese Occupation 1942-1945.* The Hague and Bandung: W. van Hoeve Ltd., 1958.

——. "Continuity and Change in Indonesian Islam". *Asian and African Studies: Annual of the Israel Oriental Studies* 1 (1965).

Bhakti, Ikrar Nusa. "Chronology of Events Leading to the Resignation of President Soeharto". In *The Fall of Soeharto*, edited by Geoff Forrester and R.J. May. Singapore: SelectBooks, 1999.

Binder, Leonard. "Islamic Tradition and Politics: The Kijaji and the Alim". A commentary to Clifford Geertz's "The Javanese Kijaji: The Changing Role of a Cultural Broker", *Comparative Studies in Society and History* 2 (October 1959 - July 1960).

——. *Religion and Politics in Pakistan*. Berkeley and Los Angeles: University of California Press, 1963.

——. *The Ideological Revolution in the Middle East*. New York: Robert E. Krieger Publishing Company, 1979.

——. *Islamic Liberalism: A Critique of Developmental Ideologies*. Chicago and London: University of Chicago Press, 1988.

Boland, B.J. *The Struggle of Islam in Modern Indonesia*. The Hague: Martinus Nijhoff, 1971.

Bresnan, John. *Managing Indonesia: The Modern Political Economy*. New York: Columbia University Press, 1993.

Budiman, Arief. "The Emergence of Bureaucratic Capitalist State in Indonesia". In *Reflections on Development in Southeast Asia*, edited by Lim Teck Ghee. Singapore: Institute of Southeast Asian Studies, 1988.

——, ed. *State and Civil Society in Indonesia*. Clayton: Monash Papers on Southeast Asia, no. 22, Centre of Southeast Asian Studies, Monash University, 1990.

Bung Karno dan Islam: Kumpulan Pidato tentang Islam 1953-1966. Jakarta: Haji Masagung, 1990.

Burns, Peter. *Revelation and Revolution: Natsir and the Pancasila*. Townsville: Southeast Asian Monograph Series no. 9, Committee of Southeast Asian Studies, James Cook University of North Queensland, 1981.

Castles, Lance. *Religion, Politics, and Economic Behavior in Java: The Kudus Cigarette Industry*. New Haven: Cultural Report Series no. 15, Southeast Asia Studies, Yale University, 1967.

Chalid, Idham. *Islam dan Demokrasi Terpimpin*. Jakarta: Lembaga Penggali dan Penghimpun Sejarah Revolusi Indonesia, 1965.

——. *Mendajung Dalam Taufan*. Jakarta: Endang dan Api Islam, 1966.

Chatib, Fahmy. "Kaum Dhuafa, Ekonomi Pasar dan Muhammadiyah". *Panji Masyarakat*, 21-30 December 1990.

Cox, Harvey. *The Secular City: Secularization and Urbanization in Theological Perspective*. New York: Macmillan Company, 1966.

Crouch, Harold. *The Army and Politics in Indonesia*. Ithaca and London: Cornell University Press, 1978.

――. "Indonesia". In *The Politics of Islamic Reassertion*, edited by Mohammed Ayoob. London: Croom Helm, 1981.

Dahm, Bernhard. *Sukarno and the Struggle for Indonesian Independence*. Ithaca and London: Cornell University Press, 1969.

Dari Cicendo ke Meja Hijau: Imran Imam Jamaah. No author. Solo: C.V. Mayasari, 1982.

Dekmejian, R. Hrair. *Islam in Revolution: Fundamentalism in the Arab World*. Syracuse: Syracuse University Press, 1985.

Dijk, C. van. *Rebellion under the Banner of Islam: The Darul Islam in Indonesia*. The Hague: Martinus Nijhoff, 1981.

Dhofier, Zamakhsyari. "Santri-Abangan dalam Kehidupan Orang Jawa: Teropong dari Pesantren". *Prisma* 7, no. 5 (1978).

――. *Tradisi Pesantren: Studi Tentang Pandangan Hidup Kyai*. Jakarta: LP3ES, 1982.

Effendi, Djohan. "Persekusi Ataukah Persuasi". Unpublished paper. February 1986.

――. "Pluralisme Pemikiran dalam Islam". Unpublished paper. August 1987.

――. "Agama, Ideologi dan Politik dalam Negara Pancasila". In *Peranan Agama Agama dan Kepercayaan Terhadap Tuhan Yang Maha Esa dalam Negara Pancasila yang Membangun*, edited by T.B. Simatupang et al. Jakarta: BPK Gunung Mulia, 1987.

――. "Pluralisme Pemahaman dalam Perspektif Teologi Islam". In *Teologi Pembangunan: Paradigma Baru Pemikiran Islam*, edited by M. Masyhur Amin. Yogyakarta: LKPSM NU DIY, 1989.

Effendi, Djohan and Ismet Natsir, eds. *Pergolakan Pemikiran Islam: Catatan Harian Ahmad Wahib*. Jakarta: LP3ES, 1981.

Effendy, Bahtiar. "The 'Nine Stars' and Politics: A Study of the Nahdlatul Ulama's Acceptance of Asas Tunggal and Its Withdrawal from Politics". M.A. thesis, Ohio University, 1988.

——. "Islam dan Aktualisasi Politik PPP". *Panji Masyarakat*, 1–10 September 1991.

——. *(Re)politisasi Islam: Pernahkah Islam Berhenti Berpolitik?* Bandung: Mizan, 2000.

——. "Antara Substansialisme dan Formalisme". *Panji Masyarakat*, no. 40, special ed. (2000).

Eldridge, Philip. *NGOs in Indonesia: Popular Movement or Arm of Government*. Clayton: Working Paper no. 55, Centre of Southeast Asian Studies, Monash University, 1989.

——. "NGOs and the State in Indonesia". In *State and Civil Society in Indonesia*, edited by Arief Budiman. Clayton: Monash Papers on Southeast Asia no. 22, Centre of Southeast Asian Studies, Monash University, 1990.

Emmerson, Donald K. *Indonesia's Elite: Political Culture and Cultural Politics*. Ithaca and London: Cornell University Press, 1976.

——. "The Bureaucracy in Political Context: Weakness in Strength". In *Political Power and Communications in Indonesia*, edited by Karl Jackson and Lucian Pye. Berkeley: University of California Press, 1978.

——. "Islam in Modern Indonesia: Political Impasse, Cultural Opportunity". In *Change and the Muslim World*, edited by Philip H. Stoddard, David C. Cuthell, and Margaret W. Sullivan. Syracuse: Syracuse University Press, 1981.

——. "Islam and Regime in Indonesia: Who's Coopting Whom?". Paper delivered at the American Political Science Association annual meeting, 31 August 1989, in Atlanta, Georgia.

——. "Resurgence of Islam Is No Danger to Indonesia". *The Asian Wall Street Journal Weekly*, 11 October 1993.

Esposito, John L. *Islam and Politics*. Syracuse: Syracuse University Press, 1984.

——. *Islamic Revivalism*. Washington, D.C.: American Institute for Islamic Affairs, School of International Service, American University, 1985.

——. "Secular Bias and Islamic Revivalism". *The Chronicle of Higher Education*, 26 May 1993.

——, ed. *Voices of Resurgent Islam*. New York and Oxford: Oxford University Press, 1983.

Federspiel, Howard M. *Persatuan Islam: Islamic Reform in Twentieth Century Indonesia*. Ithaca: Modern Indonesia Project, Southeast Asia Program, Cornell University, 1970.

———. "The Military and Islam in Sukarno's Indonesia". *Pacific Affairs* 46, no. 3 (1973).

———. "Sukarno and His Muslim Apologists: A Study of Accommodation between Traditional Islam and an Ultranationalist Ideology". In *Essays on Islamic Civilization: Presented to Niyazi Berkes*, edited by Donald P. Little. Leiden: E.J. Brill, 1976.

———. *Muslim Intellectuals and National Development in Indonesia*. New York: Nova Science Publishers Inc., 1992.

Feith, Herbert. *The Indonesian Elections of 1955*. Ithaca: Modern Indonesia Project, Southeast Asia Program, Cornell University, 1957.

———. *The Decline of Constitutional Democracy in Indonesia*. Ithaca: Cornell University Press, 1962.

———. "Dynamics of Guided Democracy". In *Indonesia*, edited by Ruth McVey. New Haven: Southeast Asia Studies, Yale University, by arrangement with Human Relations Area Files Press, 1963.

———. "Democratization and the Indonesian Intellectuals: Some Perspective". Outline paper delivered at a conference on the State and Civil Society in Contemporary Indonesia, November 1988, at Monash University.

Feith, Herbert and Daniel S. Lev. "The End of Indonesian Rebellion". *Pacific Affairs* 36, no. 1 (Spring 1963).

Feith, Herbert and Lance Castles, eds. *Indonesian Political Thinking 1945-1965*. Ithaca and London: Cornell University Press, 1970.

———. *Pemikiran Politik Indonesia 1945-1965*. Jakarta: LP3ES, 1988.

Forrester, Geoff, ed. *Post-Soeharto Indonesia: Renewal or Chaos?* Singapore: Institute of Southeast Asian Studies, 1999.

Forrester, Geoff and R.J. May, eds. *The Fall of Soeharto*. Singapore: SelectBooks, 1999.

Gaffar, Afan. *The Javanese Voters: A Case Study of Election under a Hegemonic Party System*. Yogyakarta: Gadjah Mada University Press, 1992.

Geertz, Clifford. "The Social Context of Economic Change: An Indonesian Case Study". Mimeographed. Cambridge: Center for International Studies, MIT, 1956.

———. "The Javanese Village". In *Local, Ethnic, and National Loyalties in Village Indonesia*, edited by G. William Skinner. Ithaca: Cornell Modern Indonesia Project, Cornell University, 1959.

———. *The Social History of an Indonesian Town*. Cambridge: MIT, 1965.

———. *Islam Observed: Religious Development in Morocco and Indonesia*. New Haven and London: Yale University Press, 1968.

———. "From the Native's Point of View: On the Nature of Anthropological Understanding". *Bulletin of the Academy of Arts and Sciences* 28, no. 1 (1974).

———. *Religion of Java*. Chicago and London: University of Chicago Press, 1976.

Geertz, Hildred. "Indonesian Cultures and Communities". In *Indonesia*, edited by Ruth McVey. New Haven: Southeast Asia Studies, Yale University, by arrangement with Human Relations Area Files Press, 1963.

Gibb, H.A.R., ed. *Whither Islam?: A Survey of Modern Movements in the Moslem World*. London: Victor Gollancz Ltd., 1932.

Gibbons, Michael T. *Interpreting Politics*. New York: New York University Press, 1987.

Haar, B. ter. *Adat Law in Indonesia*, edited and translated by E.A. Hoebel and A.A. Schiller. New York: Institute of Pacific Relations, 1948.

Halide. "Potensi dan Permasalahan Usahawan Muslim". Paper delivered at the first meeting of Muslim intellectuals at the PKBI building, 26–28 December 1984, in Jakarta.

Halliday, Fred and Hamzah Alavi, eds. *State and Ideology in the Middle East and Pakistan*. New York: Monthly Review Press, 1988.

Harun, Lukman. *Muhammadiyah dan Asas Pancasila*. Jakarta: Pustaka Panjimas, 1986.

———. *Muhammadiyah dan Undang-Undang Pendidikan*. Jakarta: Pustaka Panjimas, 1990.

Harun, Saleh and Abdul Munir Mulkhan. *Latar Belakang Ummat Islam Menerima Pancasila Sebagai Asas Tunggal*. Yogyakarta: Aquarius, 1987.

Harvey, Barbara S. *Permesta: Half A Rebellion*. Ithaca: Southeast Asia Program, Cornell University, 1977.

Hasan, A. Rifa'i and Amrullah Achmad, eds. *Perspektif Islam dalam Pembangunan Bangsa*. Yogyakarta: PLP2M, 1987.

Hasan, A. Rifa'i and Sri Marhaeni. "Sejarah Forum Komunikasi Pembangunan Indonesia". Sekretariat Eksekutif FKPI, December 1986.

Hasballah, Jihad. "Intensifikasi Pelaksanaan Zakat di Indonesia". *Panji Masyarakat*, 1–10 August 1991.

Hasil-Hasil Ketetapan Kongres Himpunan Mahasiswa Islam ke-16. March 1986.

Hassan, Muhammad Kamal. *Muslim Intellectual Responses to "New Order" Modernization in Indonesia.* Kuala Lumpur: Dewan Bahasa dan Pustaka Kementrian Pelajaran Malaysia, 1982.

Hassan, Sahar, L., Kuat Sukardiyono, and Dadi M.H. Basri, eds. *Memilih Partai Islam: Visi, Misi, dan Persepsi.* Jakarta: Gema Insani Press, 1998.

Hatta, Mohammad. *Sekitar Proklamasi.* Jakarta: Tintamas, 1969.

Haykal, Muhammad Husayn. *The Life of Muhammad*, translated by Isma'il Ragi al-Faruqi. North American Publications, 1976.

Hefner, Robert W. "Islamizing Java?: Religion and Politics in Rural East Java". *Journal of Asian Studies* 46, no. 3 (August 1987).

——. "Islam Lebih Berkembang di Bidang Kebudayaan". *Pelita*, 15 September 1991.

——. "Islamizing Capitalism: On the Founding of Indonesia's First Islamic Bank". Paper presented at the conference on Intellectual Development in Indonesian Islam, 19-21 February 1993, at Arizona State University.

——. "Islam, State and Civil Society: I.C.M.I. and the Struggle for the Indonesian Middle Class". Paper delivered at the conference on Islam and the Social Construction of Identities: Comparative Perspectives on Southeast Asian Muslims, 4–6 August 1993, at the Center for Southeast Asian Studies, University of Hawaii.

Himpunan Ketetapan-Ketetapan MPR 1978. Jakarta: no publisher, 1978.

Hisham, Ibn. *The Life of Muhammad*, a translation of Ishaq's *Sirat al-Rasul Allah*, with introduction and notes by A. Guillaume. Lahore, Karachi, and Dacca: Oxford University Press, 1970.

Hodgson, Marshall G.S. *The Venture of Islam: Conscience and History in a World Civilization.* Vols. 1-3. Chicago: University of Chicago Press, 1974.

Hudson, Michael C. "Islam and Political Development". In *Islam and Development*, edited by John L. Esposito. Syracuse: Syracuse University Press, 1980.

Husein, Machnun. *Pendidikan Agama dalam Lintasan Sejarah*. Yogyakarta: Nur Cahaya, 1983.

'Imara, Muhammad. *Al-Islam wa al-Sultah al-Diniyah*. Cairo: Dar al-Thaqafa al-Jadida, 1979.

Iqbal, Muhammad. *The Reconstruction of Religious Thought in Islam*. Lahore: Muhammad Ashraf, 1962.

Irsyam, Machrus. *Ulama dan Partai Politik: Upaya Mengatasi Krisis*. Jakarta: Yayasan Perkhidmatan, 1984.

Jackson Karl D. *Traditional Authority, Islam, and Rebellion: A Study of Indonesian Political Behavior*. Berkeley, Los Angeles, and London: University of California Press, 1980.

Jay, Robert. "Santri and Abangan: Religious Schism in Rural Central Java". Ph.D. dissertation, Harvard University, 1957.

———. *Religion and Politics in Rural Central Java*. New Haven: Southeast Asia Studies, Yale University, 1963.

———. "History and Personal Experience: Religious and Political Conflict in Java". In *Religion and Change in Contemporary Asia*, edited by Robert F. Spencer. Minneapolis: University of Minnesota Press, 1971.

Jaylani, Ahmad Timur. "The Sarekat Islam Movement: Its Contribution to Indonesian Nationalism". M.A. thesis, McGill University, 1959.

Jenkins, David. *Suharto and His Generals: Indonesian Military Politics 1975–1983*. Ithaca: Monograph Series, Publication no. 64, Cornell Modern Indonesia Project, Southeast Asia Program, Cornell University, 1984.

Johns, A.H. "An Islamic System or Islamic Values?: Nucleus of a Debate in Contemporary Indonesia". In *Islam and the Political Economy of Meaning: Comparative Studies of Muslim Discourse*, edited by William Roff. London and Sydney: Croom Helm, 1987.

Kafrawi, H. *Pembaharuan Sistem Pendidikan Pondok Pesantren*. Jakarta: Cemara Indah, 1978.

Kahin, Audrey, ed. *Regional Dynamics of the Indonesian Revolution: Unity from Diversity*. Honolulu: Hawaii University Press, 1985.

Kahin, George Mc.T. *Nationalism and Revolution in Indonesia*. Ithaca: Cornell University Press, 1952.

Kamaruddin. "Partisipasi Politik Islam di Indonesia: Studi tentang Aksi Partai Politik Islam pada Masa Reformasi (1998–99)". Unpublished M.A. thesis, Graduate Studi Program, University of Indonesia, 2001.

Karim, M. Rusli. *Dinamika Islam di Indonesia: Suatu Tinjauan Sosial Politik.* Yogyakarta: PT Hanindita, 1985.

Kazhim, Musa and Alfian Hamzah, eds. *5 Partai Islam dalam Timbangan: Analisis dan Prospek.* Jakarta: Pustaka Hidayah, 1999.

Keddie, Nikki R. "The Revolt of Islam and Its Roots". In *Comparative Political Dynamics: Global Research Perspective*, edited by Dankwart A. Rustow and Kenneth Paul Erickson. New York: Harper Collins Publishers, 1991.

Khan, Qamaruddin. *Political Concepts in the Qur'an.* Lahore: Islamic Book Foundation, 1982.

——. *The Political Thought of Ibn Taymiyah.* Lahore: Islamic Book Foundation, 1983.

Kroef, Justus M. van der. *Indonesia after Sukarno.* Vancouver: University of British Columbia Press, 1971.

Kumpulan Fatwa Majelis Ulama Indonesia. Jakarta: Pustaka Panjimas, 1984.

Kuntowijoyo. "Serat Cebolek dan Mitos Pembangkangan Islam: Melacak Asal-Usul Ketegangan Antara Islam dan Birokrasi". *Paradigma Islam: Interpretasi Untuk Aksi.* Bandung: Mizan, 1991.

——. "Kiblat Baru Politik Kaum Santri". *Pesan*, no. 1 (1992).

——. "Enam Alasan untuk Tidak Mendirikan Parpol Islam". *Republika*, 18 July 1998.

Laswell, Harold D. *Politics: Who Gets What, When, How.* New York: McGraw Hill, 1936.

Lee Oey Hong. ed. *Indonesia after the 1971 Elections.* London and Kuala Lumpur: Hull Monograph Series on Southeast Asia, no. 5, Oxford University Press, 1974.

Legge, John D. *Central Authority and Regional Autonomy in Indonesia.* Ithaca: Cornell University Press, 1961.

——. *Intellectuals and Nationalism in Indonesia: A Study of the Following Recruited by Sutan Syahrir in Occupation Jakarta.* Ithaca: Monograph Series, Cornell Modern Indonesia Project, Cornell University, 1988.

Lev, Daniel S. *The Transition to Guided Democracy: Indonesian Politics 1957-1959.* Ithaca: Modern Indonesia Project, Southeast Asia Program, Cornell University, 1966.

——. *Islamic Courts in Indonesia: A Study of the Political Bases of Legal Institutions*. Berkeley, Los Angeles, and London: University of California Press, 1972.

Lewis, Bernard. *The Political Language of Islam*. Chicago: University of Chicago Press, 1988.

——. *What Went Wrong?: The Clash between Islam and Modernity in the Middle East*. London: Weidenfeld & Nicolson, 2002.

Liddle, R. William. *Ethnicity, Party, and National Integration: An Indonesian Case Study*. New Haven: Yale University Press, 1970.

——. "Evolution from above: National Development and Local Leadership in Indonesia". *Journal of Asian Studies*, no. 32 (February 1973).

——. "Modernizing Indonesian Politics". In *Political Participation in Modern Indonesia*, edited by R. William Liddle. New Haven: Southeast Asia Studies, Yale University, 1973.

——. *Cultural and Class Politics in New Order Indonesia*. Singapore: Institute of Southeast Asian Studies, 1977.

——. "Soeharto's Indonesia: Personal Rule and Political Institutions". *Pacific Affairs* 58, no. 1 (Spring 1985).

——. "Indonesia in 1987: The New Order at the Height of Its Power". *Asian Survey* 28, no. 2 (1988).

——. "Indonesia's Democratic Past and Future". *Comparative Politics*, no. 24 (July 1992).

——. "Indonesia's Threefold Crisis". *Journal of Democracy* 3, no. 4 (October 1992).

——. "RMS". *Tempo*, 10 April 1993.

——. "*Media Dakwah* Scripturalism: One Form of Islamic Political Thought and Action in New Order Indonesia". Paper delivered at a conference on Intellectual Development in Indonesian Islam, 20–21 February 1993, at Arizona State University.

——. "Politics 1992-1993: Sixth-term Adjustments in the Ruling Formula". In *Indonesia Assessment 1993*, edited by Chris Manning and Joan Hardjono. Canberra: Australian National University, 1993.

——. "Improvising Political Cultural Change: Three Indonesian Cases". In *Indonesian Political Culture: Asking the Right Questions*, edited by James and Barbara-Martin Schiller. Athens: Center for Southeast Asian Studies, Ohio University, 1997.

Lijphart, Arend. *The Politics of Accommodation: Pluralism and Democracy in the Netherlands*. Berkeley and Los Angeles: University of California Press, 1968.

——. *Democracy in Plural Societies: A Comparative Exploration*. New Haven and London: Yale University Press, 1977.

Lyon, Margo L. "The Hindu Revival in Java: Politics and Religious Identity". In *Indonesia: The Making of a Culture*, edited by James Fox. Canberra: Research School of Pacific Studies, Australian National University, 1980.

Maarif, Ahmad Syafii. "Islamic Politics under Guided Democracy in Indonesia, 1959–1965". M.A. thesis, Ohio University, 1980.

——. "Islam as the Basis of State: A Study of the Islamic Political Ideas as Reflected in the Constituent Assembly Debates in Indonesia". Ph.D. dissertation, University of Chicago, 1983.

——. "Islam, Politik dan Demokrasi di Indonesia". In *Aspirasi Umat Islam Indonesia*, edited by Bosco Carvallo and Dasrizal. Jakarta: Leppenas, 1983.

——. *Islam dan Masalah Kenegaraan: Studi Tentang Percaturan dalam Konstituante*. Jakarta: LP3ES, 1985.

——. "Kedudukan Negara dalam Perspektif Doktrin Islam". Paper presented at a conference on the concept of the state in Islam, 18 October 1987, at Universitas Islam Indonesia (UII), Yogyakarta.

——. *Islam dan Politik di Indonesia Pada Masa Demokrasi Terpimpin (1959–1965)*. Yogyakarta: IAIN Sunan Kalijaga Press, 1988.

——. "Gejala Kemandegan Muhammadiyah dalam Pembaharuan Pemikiran Islam di Indonesia: Mitos Atau Realitas". Discussion paper, November 1985.

Madjid, Nurcholish. *Modernisasi Adalah Rasionalisasi Bukan Westernisasi*. Bandung: Mimbar Demokrasi, 1968.

——. "Keharusan Pembaharuan Pemikiran Islam dan Masalah Integrasi Ummat". Nurcholish Madjid et al., *Pembaharuan Pemikiran Islam*. Jakarta: Islamic Research Centre, 1970.

——. "Islam in Indonesia: Challenges and Opportunities". In *Islam in the Contemporary World*, edited by Cyriac K. Pullapilly. Notre Dame: Cross Roads Books, 1980.

——. "Cita-Cita Politik Kita". In *Aspirasi Umat Islam Indonesia*, edited by Bosco Carvallo and Dasrizal. Jakarta: Leppenas, 1983.

——. "Khilafah dan Perkembangannya". *Nuansa*, December 1984.

——. "Suatu Tatapan Islam Terhadap Masa Depan Politik Indonesia". *Prisma,* extra ed., 1984.

——. "The Issue of Modernization among Muslims in Indonesia: From a Participant's Point of View". In *Readings on Islam in Southeast Asia*, edited by Ahmad Ibrahim, Sharon Siddique, and Yasmin Hussain. Singapore: Institute of Southeast Asian Studies, 1985.

——. "Sekitar Usaha Membangkitkan Etos Intelektualisme Islam di Indonesia". In *70 Tahun Prof. Dr. H.M. Rasjidi*, edited by Endang Basri Ananda. Jakarta: Pelita, 1985.

——. "Integrasi Keislaman dalam Keindonesiaan untuk Menatap Masa Depan Bangsa". Speech delivered in 1986 at the opening of the Paramadina Religious Study Club, Jakarta.

——. *Islam Kemoderenan dan Keindonesiaan*. Bandung: Mizan, 1987.

——. "Demokrasi dan Demokratisasi di Indonesia". *Media Indonesia*, 7–12 August 1989.

——. "Demokrasi Sebagai Cara dan Proses". *Media Indonesia*, 8 August 1989.

——. "Agama dan Negara dalam Islam: Sebuah Telaah atas Fiqh Siyasi Sunni". Paper delivered in 1991 at Paramadina Religious Study Club, Jakarta.

——. "Masalah Tradisi dan Inovasi Keislaman dalam Bidang Pemikiran serta Tantangan dan Harapannya di Indonesia". Paper delivered at the Istiqlal Festival, 21–24 October 1991, in Jakarta.

——. "Islam dan Birokrasi". *Tempo*, 28 December 1991.

——. *Islam Doktrin dan Peradaban: Sebuah Telaah Kritis Tentang Masalah Keimanan, Kemanusiaan, dan Keindonesiaan*. Jakarta: Yayasan Wakaf Paramadina, 1992.

——. "Oposisi". *Tempo*, 26 December 1992.

Mahasin, Aswab. "NGOs show strength in nation's socio-political development". *The Jakarta Post*, 12 August 1988.

——. "The Santri Middle Class: An Insider's View". In *The Politics of Middle Class Indonesia*, edited by Richard Tanter and Kenneth Young. Clayton: Monash Papers on Southeast Asia no. 19, Centre of Southeast Asian Studies, Monash University, 1990.

——. "Islam 'Politik' ". *Tempo*, 2 November 1991.

Mann, Richard. *Economic Crisis in Indonesia: The Full Story*. Singapore: Times Books, 1998.

——. *Plots and Schemes that Brought Down Soeharto*. Singapore: Gateway Books, 1998.

Martosukarto, Bachrun. "Negara Versi Abdurrahman Wahid Versus Pancasila". *Media Dakwah*, October 1993.

al-Maududi, Abu A'la. *The Islamic Law and Constitution*, translated and edited by Khurshid Ahmed. Lahore: Islamic Publications, 1977.

May, Darlene R. "Al-Mawardi's Al-Ahkam as-Sultaniyyah: A Partial Translation with Introduction and Annotations". Ph.D. dissertation, Indiana University, 1981.

McVey, Ruth. "Faith as the Outsider: Islam in Indonesian Politics". In *Islam in the Political Process*, edited by James P. Piscatori. Cambridge: Cambridge University Press, 1983.

Mehden, Fred R. von der. "Islam and the Rise of Nationalism in Indonesia". Ph.D. dissertation, University of California Berkeley, 1957.

Merajut Damai di Maluku: Telaah Konflik antar Umat 1999–2000. Jakarta: Mejelis Ulama Indonesia, 2000.

Mestenhauser, Josef A. "Ideologies in Conflict in Indonesia, 1945-1955". Ph.D. dissertation, University of Minnesota, 1960.

Migdal, Joel S. *Strong Societies and Weak States: State-Society Relations and State Capabilities in the Third World*. Princeton: Princeton University Press, 1988.

Mintaredja, H.M.S. *Renungan Pembaharuan Pemikiran Masyarakat Islam dan Politik di Indonesia*. Jakarta: Penerbit Permata, 1971.

Moertopo, Ali. *Dasar-Dasar Pemikiran Tentang Akselerasi Modernisasi Pembangunan 25 Tahun*. Centre for Strategic and International Studies. Jakarta: Yayasan Proklamasi, 1973.

Morris, Eric Eugene. "Islam and Politics in Aceh: A Study of Center-Periphery Relations in Indonesia". Ph.D. dissertation, Cornell University, 1983.

Mortimer, Edward. *Faith and Power: The Politics of Islam*. London: Faber and Faber, 1982.

Mortimer, Rex. *Indonesian Communism Under Sukarno: Ideology and Politics 1959-1965*. Ithaca: Cornell University Press, 1974.

Mudatsir, Arief. "Dari Situbondo Menuju NU Baru: Sebuah Catatan Awal". *Prisma*, extra ed., 1984.

Mudzhar, M. Atho. "Fatwas of the Council of Indonesian Ulama: A Study of Islamic Legal Thought in Indonesia, 1975-1988". Ph.D. dissertation, University of California Los Angeles, 1990.

Musa, Muhammad Yusuf. *Nizam al-Hukm fi al-Islam*. Cairo: Dar al-Kitab al-Arabi, 1963.

Nakamura, Mitsuo. "The Radical Traditionalism of the Nahdlatul Ulama in Indonesia: A Personal Account of the 26th National Congress, June 1979, Semarang". *Southeast Asian Studies* 19, no. 12 (September 1981).

——. *The Crescent Arises Over the Banyan Tree: A Study of the Muhammadiyah Movement in a Central Javanese Town*. Yogyakarta: Gadjah Mada University Press, 1983.

Nasr, Seyyed Hossein. *Muhammad: Man of Allah*. London: Muhammadi Trust, 1982.

Nasution, Adnan Buyung. *The Aspiration for Constitutional Government in Indonesia: A Socio-legal Study of the Indonesian Konstituante 1956–1959*. Jakarta: Pustaka Sinar Harapan, 1992.

Nasution, Harun. "The Islamic State in Indonesia: The Rise of the Ideology, the Movement for Its Creation and the Theory of the Masyumi". M.A. thesis, McGill University, 1965.

——. "The Place of Reason in Abduh's Theology: Its Impact on His Theological System and Views". Ph.D. dissertation, McGill University, 1968.

——. "Islam dan Sistem Pemerintahan dalam Perkembangan Sejarah". *Nuansa*, December 1984.

——. *Islam Ditinjau dari Berbagai Aspeknya*. 2 vols. Jakarta: UI Press, 1984.

Natsir, Mohammad. *Some Observations Concerning the Role of Islam in National and International Affairs*. Ithaca: Southeast Asia Program, Department of Far Eastern Studies, Cornell University, 1954.

——. "Bertetangankah Pancasila dengan Al-Qur'an". *Hikmah*, 29 May 1954.

——. *Islam Sebagai Dasar Negara*. Bandung: Pimpinan Fraksi Masyumi dalam Konstituante, 1957.

——. *Capita Selecta*. Jakarta: Bulan Bintang, 1973.

——. "Sekali Lagi: Kerukunan Hidup Umat Beragama di Indonesia". *Islam dan Kristen di Indonesia*. Jakarta: Media Dakwah, 1978.

Niel, Robert Van. *The Emergence of the Modern Indonesian Elite*. The Hague: W. van Hoeve Ltd., 1960.

Nieuwenhuijze, C.A.O. Van. *Aspects of Islam in Post-Colonial Indonesia*. The Hague and Bandung: W. van Hoeve Ltd., 1958.

——. "The Indonesian State and 'Deconfessionalized' Muslim Concepts". *Aspects of Islam in Post-Colonial Indonesia*. The Hague and Bandung: W. van Hoeve Ltd., 1958.

——. "The Dar ul-Islam Movement in Western Java Till 1949". *Aspects of Islam in Post-Colonial Indonesia*. The Hague and Bandung: W. van Hoeve Ltd., 1958.

——. "Islam and National Self-Realization in Indonesia". *Cross-Cultural Studies*. The Hague: Monton and Co., 1963.

Nishihara, Masashi. *Golkar and the Indonesian Elections of 1971*. Ithaca: Monograph Series, Modern Indonesia Project, Cornell University, 1972.

Noer, Deliar. *The Modernist Muslim Movement in Indonesia 1900-1942*. Oxford, New York, and Jakarta: Oxford University Press, 1978.

——. *Administration of Islam in Indonesia*. Ithaca: Modern Indonesia Project, Cornell University, 1978.

——. *Administrasi Islam di Indonesia*. Jakarta: Rajawali, 1982.

——. "Contemporary Political Dimension of Islam". In *Islam in Southeast Asia*, edited by M.B. Hooker. Leiden: E.J. Brill, 1983.

——. *Ideologi, Politik dan Pembangunan*. Jakarta: Yayasan Perkhidmatan, 1983.

——. *Islam, Pancasila dan Asas Tunggal*. Jakarta: Yayasan Perkhidmatan, 1984.

——. *Partai Islam di Pentas Nasional 1945-1965*. Jakarta: Pustaka Utama Grafiti, 1987.

——. "Islam dan Politik: Mayoritas atau Minoritas". *Prisma* 17, no. 5 (1988).

——. *Islam dan Pemikiran Politik: Bahasan Kitab Islam dan Tata Negara: Ajaran, Sejarah dan Pemikiran oleh H. Munawir Syadzali MA*. Jakarta: LIPPM, 1990.

O'Donnell, Guillermo and Philippe C. Schmitter. *Transitions from Authoritarian Rule: Tentative Conclusions about Uncertain Democracies.* Baltimore and London: Johns Hopkins University Press, 1986.

O'Donnell, Guillermo, Philippe C. Schmitter, and Laurence Whitehead, eds. *Transitions from Authoritarian Rule: Latin America.* Baltimore and London: Johns Hopkins University Press, 1986.

Oepen, Manfred and Wolfgang Karcher, eds. *The Impact of Pesantren in Education and Community Development in Indonesia.* Jakarta: P3M, 1988.

Osman, Fathi. "Parameters of the Islamic State". *Arabia: The Islamic World Review*, no. 17 (January 1983).

Parsons, Talcott, Edward Shils, Kaspar D. Naegelle, and Jesse R. Pitts, eds. *Theories of Society: Foundations of Modern Sociological Theory.* New York: Free Press of Glencoe, 1961.

Partai-Partai Politik Indonesia: Ideologi, Strategi, dan Program. Jakarta: Litbang *Kompas*, 1999.

Peacock, James L. *Rites of Modernization: Symbolic and Social Aspects of Indonesian Proletarian Drama.* Chicago: University of Chicago Press, 1968.

Pedoman Zakat. Jakarta: Direktorat Jendral Bimas Islam dan Urusan Haji, Departemen Agama, 1984.

Penelitian Radikalisme Agama dan Perubahan Sosial di DKI Jakarta. Jakarta: Pusat Budaya dan Bahasa (PBB) dan Pemda DKI Jakarta, 2000.

Percakapan Cendekiawan Tentang Pembaharuan Pemikiran Islam di Indonesia. Bandung: Mizan, 1991.

Permono, Syechul Hadi. "Pendayagunaan Sumber Dana Umat Islam". *Panji Masyarakat*, 1-10 May 1991.

Perwiranegara, Alamsyah Ratu. *Islam dan Pembangunan Politik di Indonesia.* Jakarta: Haji Masagung, 1987.

Pickthall, Marmaduke. *The Glorious Koran.* Bilingual edition with English translation, introduction, and notes. Albany: State University of New York Press, 1976.

Pigeaud, Theodore G. Th. *Islamic States in Java 1500-1700.* The Hague: Martinus Nijhoff, 1976.

Piscatori, James P., ed. *Islam in the Political Process.* Cambridge: Cambridge University Press, 1983.

——. *Islam in a World of Nation States*. Cambridge: Cambridge University Press, 1986.

Poerbakawatja, Soegarda. *Pendidikan dalam Alam Indonesia Merdeka*. Jakarta, 1970.

Prasodjo, Sudjoko et al. *Profil Pesantren: Laporan Hasil Penelitian Pesantren Al-Falak dan Delapan Pesantren Lain di Bogor*. Jakarta: LP3ES, 1974.

Pratiknya, Ahmad Watik, ed. *Pesan Perjuangan Seorang Bapak: Percakapan Antar Generasi*. Jakarta: Dewan Dakwah Islamiyah Indonesia, 1989.

Prawiranegara, Sjafruddin. *Ekonomi dan Keuangan, Makna Ekonomi Islam: Kumpulan Karangan Terpilih 2*. Jakarta: Haji Masagung, 1986.

Radi, Umaidi. *Strategi PPP 1973-1982: Suatu Studi Tentang Kekuatan Politik Islam Tingkat Nasional*. Jakarta: Integrita Press, 1984.

Rahardjo, M. Dawam. "Pluriformitas dalam Perkembangan Islam di Indonesia dan Kebangkitan Agama-Agama". Unpublished paper, no date.

——. "LSM dan Program-Program Pengembangan Masyarakat". Unpublished paper, no date.

——. "Metode Pelibatan Partisipasi Masyarakat dalam Pembangunan Pedesaan". Unpublished paper, no date.

——. "Lembaga Keulamaan". No publisher, no date.

——. "Tujuan Perjuangan Politik Ummat Islam di Indonesia". *Panji Masyarakat*, no. 85 (August 1971).

——. "Kyai, Pesantren dan Desa". *Prisma*, no. 4 (August 1973).

——. "Dunia Pesantren dalam Peta Pembaharuan". In *Pesantren dan Pembaharuan*, edited by M. Dawam Rahardjo. Jakarta: LP3ES, 1974.

——. "Gambaran Pemuda Santri: Penglihatan dari Jendela Pesantren di Pabelan". In *Pemuda dan Perubahan Sosial*, edited by Taufik Abdullah. Jakarta: LP3ES, 1974.

——. "Mencari Konsep Zakat Dalam Alam Pembangunan". *Panji Masyarakat*, 21–30 July 1981.

——. *Esei-Esei Ekonomi Politik*. Jakarta: LP3ES, 1983.

——. "Umat Islam dan Pembaharuan Teologi". In *Aspirasi Umat Islam Indonesia*, edited by Bosco Carvallo and Dasrizal. Jakarta: Leppenas, 1983.

——. "Menilai Sejarah Ummat Islam dari Sudut Al-Qur'an". *Panji Masyarakat*, nos. 441 and 442 (27 August and 1 September 1984).

——. *Insan Kamil: Konsepsi Manusia Menurut Islam*. Jakarta: Pustaka Grafitipers, 1985.

——. *Perspektif Deklarasi Makkah: Menuju Ekonomi Islam*. Bandung: Mizan, 1987.

——. "Critical Islamic View of the State". *Mizan* 3, no. 2 (1990).

——. "Eklusivisme Kelompok dan Perekonomian Nasional". *Media Indonesia*, 20 August 1990.

——. "Demokrasi Ekonomi, Revolusi Manajerial dan Peranan Perguruan Tinggi Islam". *Media Dakwah*, October 1990.

——. "LSM dalam sistem politik Indonesia". *Berita Buana*, 19 and 20 February 1991.

——. "Basis Sosial Pemikiran Islam di Indonesia Sejak Orde Baru". *Prisma*, no. 3 (March 1991).

——. "Mandito". *Tempo*, 6 July 1991.

——. "Bank Muamalat". *Tempo*, 2 November 1991.

——. "Kenangan Reflektif Atas Mohammad Natsir (1908-1993)". *Ulumul Qur'an* 4, no. 1 (1993).

Rahman, Fazlur. *Islam*. New York, Chicago, and San Francisco: Holt, Rinehart, and Winston, 1966.

——. "Roots of Islamic Neo-Fundamentalism". In *Change and the Muslim World*, edited by Philip H. Stoddard, David C. Cuthell, and Margaret W. Sullivan. Syracuse: Syracuse University Press, 1981.

——. *Islam and Modernity: Transformation of an Intellectual Tradition*. Chicago and London: University of Chicago Press, 1982.

Rais, M. Amien. "Islam dan Demokrasi". In *Aspirasi Umat Islam Indonesia*, edited by Bosco Carvallo and Dasrizal. Jakarta: Leppenas, 1983.

——, ed. *Islam di Indonesia: Suatu Ikhtiar Mengaca Diri*. Jakarta: C.V. Rajawali, 1986.

——. *Cakrawala Islam: Antara Cita dan Fakta*. Bandung: Mizan, 1987.

——. "Islam and Politics in Contemporary Indonesia". In *Post-Soeharto Indonesia: Renewal or Chaos?*, edited by Geoff Forrester. Singapore: Institute of Southeast Asian Studies, 1999.

Rais, M. Lukman Fathullah, Muhammad Syah Agusdin, and Nasmay Lofita Anas, eds. *Mohammad Natsir Pemandu Ummat*. Jakarta: Bulan Bintang, 1989.

Rasjidi, H.M. *Koreksi Terhadap Drs. Nurcholish Madjid tentang Sekularisasi*. Jakarta: Bulan Bintang, 1972.

——. *Koreksi Terhadap Dr. Harun Nasution Tentang Islam Ditinjau Dari Berbagai Aspeknya*. Jakarta: Bulan Bintang, 1977.

al-Raziq, Ali ibn Abd. *Al-Islam wa Ushul al-Hukm*. Beirut: Dar Maktabah al-Hayah, 1966.

Reeve, David. *Golkar of Indonesia: An Alternative to the Party System*. Singapore: Oxford University Press, 1985.

Refleksi Pembaharuan Pemikiran Islam: 70 Tahun Harun Nasution. Jakarta: Lembaga Studi Agama dan Filsafat, 1989.

Rekomendasi dan Pedoman Pelaksanaan Zakat. Jakarta: Bazis, 1978.

Risalah Sidang Badan Penyelidik Usaha-Usaha Persiapan Kemerdekaan Indonesia (BPUPKI). Jakarta: Sekretariat Negara Republik Indonesia, 1995.

Rose, Mavis. *Indonesia Free: A Political Biography of Mohammad Hatta*. Ithaca: Cornell Modern Indonesia Project, Southeast Asia Program, Cornell University, 1987.

Rosenthal, Erwin I.J. *Political Thought in Medieval Islam: An Introductory Outline*. Cambridge: Cambridge University Press, 1958.

——. *Islam in the Modern National State*. Cambridge: Cambridge University Press, 1965.

Saidi, Ridwan. *Islam: Pembangunan Politik dan Politik Pembangunan*. Jakarta: Pustaka Panjimas, 1983.

——. *Islam dan Moralitas Pembangunan*. Jakarta: Pustaka Panjimas, 1984.

——. "Cendekiawan Muslim dan Struktur Politik". *Kompas*, 8 December 1990.

——. "Undang-Undang Untuk Siapa?". *Risalah*, June 1991.

——. "Hijaunya Hijau". *Pelita*, 19 October 1992.

Salim, Arsekal. *Partai Islam dan Relasi Agama-Negara*. Jakarta: Pusat Penilitian IAIN Jakarta, 1999.

Samson, Allan. "Islam in Indonesian Politics". *Asian Survey* 8, no. 12 (December 1968).

———. "Islam and Politics in Indonesia". Ph.D. dissertation, University of California, 1972.

———. "Religious Belief and Political Action in Indonesian Islamic Modernism". In *Political Participation in Modern Indonesia*, edited by R. William Liddle. New Haven: Southeast Asia Studies, Yale University, 1973.

———. "Conceptions of Politics, Power, and Ideology in Contemporary Indonesian Islam". In *Political Power and Communications in Indonesia*, edited by Karl D. Jackson and Lucian W. Pye. Berkeley, Los Angeles, and London: University of California Press, 1978.

———. "Indonesian Islam since the New Order". In *Readings on Islam in Southeast Asia*, edited by Ahmad Ibrahim, Sharon Siddique, and Yasmin Hussain. Singapore: Institute of Southeast Asian Studies, 1985.

Sasono, Adi. "Islam dan Sosialisme Religius". In *Aspirasi Umat Islam Indonesia*, edited by Bosco Carvallo and Dasrizal. Jakarta: Leppenas, 1983.

———. "Peta Permasalahan Sosial Umat Islam dan Pokok-Pokok Pemikiran Usaha Pengembangannya: Beberapa Catatan". Paper delivered at the BKS PTIS third annual meeting, 28-30 May 1984, in Jakarta.

———. "Moral Agama dan Masalah Kemiskinan". Unpublished discussion paper, 21 April 1985.

———. "Usaha Pengembangan Emansipasi Sosial: Beberapa Catatan". In *Perspektif Islam dalam Pembangunan Bangsa*, edited by A. Rifa'i Hassan and Amrullah Achmad. Yogyakarta: PLP2M, 1986.

———. "Keadilan Sosial Tema Abadi". In *Islam Indonesia Menatap Masa Depan*, edited by Muntaha Azhari and Abdul Mun'im Saleh. Jakarta: P3M, 1989.

Sasono, Adi and Achmad Rofi'ie. *People's Economy*. Jakarta: Southeast Asian Forum for Development Alternatives, 1988.

Sasono, Adi and Sritua Arif. *Indonesia: Ketergantungan dan Keterbelakangan*. Jakarta: Lembaga Studi Pembangunan, 1981.

———. *Indonesia: Dependency and Underdevelopment*. Kuala Lumpur: Meta, 1981.

Schwarz, Adam. *A Nation in Waiting: Indonesia in the 1990s*. St. Leonards: Allen & Unwin, 1994.

Sikap Majelis Ulama dan Pemimpin-Pemimpin Islam Indonesia Terhadap Aliran Kepercayaan. No author, no publisher, no date.

Singer, Peter W. *Time for Hard Choices: The Dilemmas Facing U.S. Policy Towards the Islamic World.* Brookings Project on U.S. Policy Towards the Islamic World, Analysis Paper no. 1, October 2002.

Singh, Bilveer. *Habibie and the Democratisation of Indonesia.* Sydney: Book House, 2001.

Sjamsuddin, Nazaruddin. *The Republican Revolt: A Study of the Acehnese Rebellion.* Singapore: Institute of Southeast Asian Studies, 1985.

Smith, Donald Eugene, ed. *Religion, Politics, and Social Change in the Third World.* New York: Free Press, 1971.

——. *Religion and Political Modernization.* New Haven and London: Yale University Press, 1974.

Soeharto. *Agama dalam Pembangunan Nasional: Himpunan Sambutan Presiden Soeharto.* Jakarta: Pustaka Biru, 1981.

——. *Amanat Kenegaraan IV 1982-1985.* Jakarta: Inti Idayu Press, 1985.

Soekarno. *Surat-Surat Islam dari Endeh.* Bandung: Persatuan Islam, 1936.

——. "Negara Nasional dan Cita-Cita Islam". Lecture delivered at the University of Indonesia, 7 May 1953.

——. *The Birth of Pancasila: An Outline of the Five Principles of the Indonesian State.* Jakarta: Ministry of Information, 1958.

——. *Dibawah Bendera Revolusi*, vol. 1. Jakarta: Panitia Penerbitan Dibawah Bendera Revolusi, 1964.

——. *Nationalism, Islam and Marxism.* Translated by Karel H. Warouw and Peter D. Weldon, with an introduction by Ruth McVey. Ithaca: Modern Indonesia Project, Southeast Asia Program, Cornell University, 1984.

Steenbrink, Karl A. *Pesantren, Madrasah, Sekolah: Pendidikan Islam dalam Kurun Modern.* Jakarta: LP3ES, 1986.

Suminto, H.A. *Politik Islam Hindia Belanda.* Jakarta: LP3ES, 1982.

Sundhaussen, Ulf. "Regime Crisis in Indonesia: Facts, Fiction, Predictions". *Asian Survey* 21, no. 8 (August 1981).

Sunny, Ismail. "Peraturan Perundangan Mengenai Pendidikan Agama". *Panji Masyarakat*, 21–31 October 1991.

Surur, Taha Abd al-Baqi. *Dawla al-Qur'an*. Cairo: Daru al-Nadha Misr, 1972.

Suryadinata, Leo. *Military Ascendancy and Political Culture: A Study of Indonesia's Golkar*. Athens: Monograph in International Studies, Southeast Asia Series, no. 85, Ohio University, 1989.

——. *Elections and Politics in Indonesia*. Singapore: Institute of Southeast Asian Studies, 2002.

Suseno, Franz Magnis. "Seputar Rencana UU Peradilan Agama". *Kompas*, 16 June 1989.

Sutter, John O. *Indonesianisasi: Politics in a Changing Economy 1940–1955*. Ithaca: Southeast Asia Program, Cornell University, 1959.

Syadzali, Munawir. "Negara Pancasila Bukan Negara Agama dan Bukan Negara Sekuler". Unpublished paper, no date.

——. *Islam dan Tata Negara: Ajaran, Sejarah dan Pemikiran*. Jakarta: UI Press, 1990.

——. "Indonesia's Muslim Parties and Their Political Concepts". M.A. thesis, Georgetown University, 1959.

——. "Reaktualisasi Ajaran Islam". In *Polemik Reaktualisasi Ajaran Islam*, edited by Iqbal Abdurrauf Saimima. Jakarta: Pustaka Panjimas, 1988.

——. "Dinamika dan Vitalitas Hukum Islam". *Panji Masyarakat*, no. 459 (21 February 1985).

——. "Shari'a: A Dynamic Legal System". Paper presented at a conference on Shari'a and Codification, December 1985, in Colombo, Sri Lanka.

——. "Gejala Krisis Integritas Ilmiah di Kalangan Ilmuwan Islam". *Pelita*, 24 and 25 July 1987.

——. "Wawasan Perjuangan Muslim Indonesia". Paper delivered at the HMI's forty-third commemoration, 4 February 1990, in Yogyakarta.

——. "Agama Sebagai Landasan Spiritual, Etik dan Moral Pembangunan". Keynote address delivered at the Manggala Training Forum, 12 June 1990, in Bogor.

Syamsuddin, M. Din, ed. *Muhammadiyah Kini dan Esok*. Jakarta: Pustaka Panjimas, 1990.

Syamsuddin, M. Sirajuddin. "Religion and Politics in Islam: The Case of Muhammadiyah in Indonesia's New Order". Ph.D. dissertation, University of California Los Angeles, 1991.

——, ed. *Muhammadiyah Kini dan Esok*. Jakarta: Pustaka Panjimas, 1990.

Tamara, M. Nasir. *Indonesia in the Wake of Islam: 1965–1985*. Kuala Lumpur: Institute of Strategic and International Studies, 1986.

——. "Sejarah Politik Islam Order Baru". *Prisma*, no. 5 (1988).

Tanja, Victor. "Himpunan Mahasiswa Islam: Its History and Its Place among Muslim Reformist Movement in Indonesia". Ph.D. dissertation, Hartford Seminary Foundation, 1979.

——. *Himpunan Mahasiswa Islam: Sejarah dan Kedudukannya di Tengah Gerakan Muslim Pembaharu di Indonesia*. Jakarta: Sinar Harapan, 1982.

Tanter, Richard and Kenneth Young, eds. *The Politics of Middle Class Indonesia*. Clayton: Monash Papers on Southeast Asia no. 19, Centre of Southeast Asian Studies, Monash University, 1990.

Tebba, Sudirman. "Islam di Indonesia: Dari Minoritas Politik Menuju Mayoritas Budaya". *Jurnal Ilmu Politik*, no. 4 (1989).

Tentang Dasar Negara Republik Indonesia dalam Konstituante. Vols. 1–3. Bandung, 1958.

Thalib, M. and Haris Fajar, eds. *Pembaharuan Faham Islam di Indonesia: Dialog Bung Karno–A. Hassan*. Yogyakarta: Sumber Ilmu, 1985.

Tjokroaminoto. *Islam dan Sosialisme*. Jakarta: Bulan Bintang, 1950.

Vatikiotis, Michael R.J. *Indonesian Politics under Suharto: Order, Development, and Pressure for Change*. London and New York: Routledge, 1993.

Vatikiotis, P.J. *Islam and the State*. London, New York, and Sydney: Croom Helm, 1987.

Vlekke, Bernard H.M. *Nusantara: A History of Indonesia*. The Hague and Bandung: W. van Hoeve Ltd., 1959.

Wahid, Aburrahman. *Muslim di Tengah Pergumulan*. Jakarta: Leppenas, 1981.

——. "Islam: Punyakah Konsep Kenegaraan?". *Tempo*, 26 March 1983.

——. "Islam, the State, and Development in Indonesia". In *Ethical Dilemmas of Development in Asia*, edited by Godfrey Gunatilleke, Neelan Tiruchelvam, and Radhika Coomaraswamy. Lexington: Lexington Books, 1983.

——. "Massa Islam dalam Kehidupan Bernegara dan Berbangsa". *Prisma*, extra ed. 1984.

——. "Merumuskan Hubungan Ideologi Nasional dan Agama". *Aula*, May 1985.

——. "Islam dan Masyarakat Bangsa". *Pelita*, 6 June 1986.

——. "The Nahdlatul Ulama and Islam in Present Day Indonesia". In *Islam and Society in Southeast Asia*, edited by Taufik Abdullah and Sharon Siddique. Singapore: Institute of Southeast Asian Studies, 1986.

——. "NU dan Politik". *Kompas*, 24 June 1987.

——. "Masih Relevankah Teori Kenegaraan Islam: Tinjauan Kontemporer Atas Prinsip-Prinsip Rekonstruksinya". Discussion paper on Islamic Concept of the State, 7 February 1988, at Universitas Islam Indonesia (UII), Yogyakarta.

——. "Pribumisasi Islam". In *Islam Indonesia Menatap Masa Depan*, edited by Muntaha Azhari and Abdul Mun'im Saleh. Jakarta: P3M, 1989.

——. "Islam, Ideologi dan Etos Kerja di Indonesia". Discussion paper presented in 1990 at Paramadina Religious Study Club.

——. "Salahkah Jika Dipribumikan?". *Tempo*, 16 July 1991.

——. "Peranan Ummat dalam Berbagai Pendekatan". *Universalisme Islam dan Kosmopolitanisme Peradaban Islam*. Limited edition, no publisher, 1991.

Ward, Kenneth E. *The Foundation of the Partai Muslimin Indonesia*. Ithaca: Modern Indonesia Project, Southeast Asia Program, Cornell University, 1970.

——. *The 1971 Election in Indonesia: An East Java Case Study*. Clayton: Monash Papers on Southeast Asia, no. 2, Centre of Southeast Asian Studies, Monash University, 1974.

Watt, W. Montgomery. *Muhammad at Medina*. Oxford: Clarendon Press, 1956.

——. *Islamic Political Thought*. Edinburgh: Edinburgh University Press, 1960.

Weber, Max. *The Protestant Ethic and the Spirit of Capitalism*, translated by Talcott Parsons. London: George Allen and Unwin Ltd., 1985.

Wertheim, W.F. "Islam before and after the Election". In *Indonesia after the 1971 Elections*, edited by Lee Oey Hong. London and Kuala Lumpur: Hull Monograph Series on Southeast Asia, no. 5, Oxford University Press, 1974.

———. "Indonesian Moslems under Sukarno and Suharto: Majority with Minority Mentality". In *Studies on Indonesian Islam*. Townsville: Occasional Paper no. 19, Centre for Southeast Asian Studies, James Cook University of North Queensland, 1986.

Woodward, Mark R. *Islam in Java: Normative Piety and Mysticism in the Sultanate of Yogyakarta*. Tucson: University of Arizona Press, 1989.

Yamin, Muhammad. *Naskah Persiapan Undang-Undang Dasar 1945*. Vols. 1 and 2. Jakarta: Yayasan Prapanca, 1959.

Zada, Khamami. *Islam Radikal: Pergulatan Ormas-Ormas Islam Garis Keras di Indonesia*. Jakarta: Teraju, 2002.

Zaman, M. Raquibuz, ed. *Some Aspects of the Economics of Zakah*. Plainfield: American Trust Publication, 1979.

Zuhri, Saifuddin et al. *PPP, NU dan MI: Gejolak Wadah Politik Islam*. Jakarta: Integrita Press, 1984.

Newspapers and Magazines

Amanah

Aula

Detik

Editor

Far Eastern Economic Review

Forum Keadilan

Gatra

Kompas

Matra

Media Dakwah

Media Indonesia

Panji Masyarakat

Panjimas

Pelita

Prospek

Republika

Suara Pembaharuan

Tempo

Interviews

M. Imaduddin Abdurrahim

Ichlasul Amal

Fuad Amsyari

Endang Saifuddin Anshari

Djohan Effendi

Yusuf Amir Feisal

B.J. Habibie

Lukman Harun

Aswar Hassan

Kuntowijoyo

Nurcholish Madjid

Aswab Mahasin

Hartono Mardjono

Yahya Muhaimin

Deliar Noer

A. Watik Pratiknya

M. Dawam Rahardjo

M. Amien Rais

Jalaluddin Rakhmat

Ridwan Saidi

Adi Sasono

Sulastomo

Munawir Syadzali

Victor Tanja

Hajriyanto Y. Thohari

Abdurrahman Wahid

Index

About the Author

Born in a small town, Ambarawa, Central Java, in 1958, **Bahtiar Effendy** was a student of an Islamic boarding school – Pesantren Pabelan. While a student at Pesantren Pabelan, he received an American Field Service (AFS) scholarship and attended Columbia Falls High School (1976–77) in Montana. He received his BA degree from the State Institute of Islamic Studies (IAIN), Jakarta, in 1983 and his Doctorandus degree from the same institute in 1985. From 1986 to 1988 he was a student at the Southeast Asia Studies Program, Ohio University, Athens, OH. From there, he went to the Ohio State University, enrolled at the Department of Political Science, and received his doctorate degree in 1994. Currently, he is a lecturer at the Islamic State University (UIN), Jakarta, and the University of Indonesia. In addition to his teaching career, he is also a Deputy Director at the Institute for the Study and Advancement of Business Ethics (LSPEU Indonesia).